INTRODUCTION TO PHYSICAL EDUCATION, EXERCISE SCIENCE, AND SPORT

TENTH EDITION

Angela Lumpkin, B.S.E., M.A., M.B.A., Ph.D.
Texas Tech University

Mc
Graw
Hill
Education

INTRODUCTION TO PHYSICAL EDUCATION, EXERCISE SCIENCE, AND SPORT,
TENTH EDITION

Published by McGraw-Hill Education, 2 Penn Plaza, New York, NY 10121. Copyright © 2017 by
McGraw-Hill Education. All rights reserved. Printed in the United States of America. Previous editions
© 2014, 2011, and 2008. No part of this publication may be reproduced or distributed in any form
or by any means, or stored in a database or retrieval system, without the prior written consent of
McGraw-Hill Education, including, but not limited to, in any network or other electronic storage or
transmission, or broadcast for distance learning.

Some ancillaries, including electronic and print components, may not be available to customers outside
the United States.

This book is printed on acid-free paper.

2 3 4 5 6 7 8 9 LCR 21 20 19 18 17

ISBN 978-1-259-82398-5
MHID 1-259-82398-9

Chief Product Officer, SVP, Products & Markets:
  G. Scott Virkler
Vice President, General Manager, Products &
  Markets: Michael Ryan
Brand Manager: Penina Braffman
Product Developer: Anthony McHugh
Marketing Manager: Meredith Leo
Director, Content Design & Delivery: Terri Schiesl
Content Project Manager: Mary Jane Lampe
Buyer: Susan K. Culbertson

Cover Designer: Egzon Shaqiri
Cover Image: Mother and young daughter
  exercising in the park, Portland, Oregon, USA:
  © Radius Images/Alamy. People lifting weights
  in gym: ©Erik Isakson/Blend Images, LLC.
  Caucasian woman exercising in swimming
  pool: ©Terry Vine/Blend Images LLC.
Compositor: SPi Global
Typeface: 10/12 URWPalladioTOT
Printer: LSC Communications

All credits appearing on page or at the end of the book are considered to be an extension of the
copyright page.

Library of Congress Cataloging-in-Publication Data

Names: Lumpkin, Angela, author.
Title: Introduction to physical education exercise science, and sport /
  Angela Lumpkin, B.S.E., M.A., M.B.A., Ph.D., Texas Tech University.
Description: New York : McGraw-Hill, inc., [2017]
Identifiers: LCCN 2016012991 | ISBN 9781259823985 (alk. paper)
Subjects: LCSH: Physical education and training. | Sports.
Classification: LCC GV341 .L85 2016 | DDC 796.07--dc23 LC record available at
https://lccn.loc.gov/2016012991

www.mhhe.com

Brief Contents

Contents

UNIT TWO

HISTORY AND DEVELOPMENT OF PHYSICAL EDUCATION, EXERCISE SCIENCE, AND SPORT

UNIT THREE

IMPORTANCE OF PHYSICAL EDUCATION, EXERCISE SCIENCE, AND SPORT FOR EVERYONE

Preface

Introduction to Physical Education, Exercise Science, and Sport provides students with an exciting opportunity to discover the diversity of physical education, exercise science, and sport and the wealth of careers available in these fields. Students are introduced to the heritage, current programs, and future potential of the field they are considering. This book introduces students to these multifaceted fields and involves them in examining potential careers in physical education, exercise science, and sports.

The intent of this book is to broaden students' understanding of how the philosophies and programs in physical education, exercise science, and sports evolved as well as to present the current status of these fields. Inherent within the changing nature of physical education, exercise science, and sports is a need to examine how Title IX of the 1972 Education Amendments, the inclusion into classrooms of physically and mentally challenged students, the increased emphasis on physical activity and fitness for all ages, past programs in the United States and in Europe, and various philosophies and ethical perspectives have affected and will continue to influence professionals in these fields.

No longer are physical education, exercise science, and sport programs just for schools or colleges, although teaching in these settings is certainly an important endeavor. By learning about careers in leisure services, athletic training, corporate fitness, sport management, fitness club instruction and management, recreation for all ages and abilities, coaching, cardiac rehabilitation, and a variety of other activity-related pursuits, students will gain a clearer perspective of the future role physical education, exercise science, and sports will play in American society. Individuals who accept the challenges and opportunities of these careers will help women, ethnic minorities, senior citizens, individuals in lower socioeconomic classes, individuals with special needs, students, and others benefit from living active, fit lives. Practical suggestions are provided to help students choose and prepare for careers. To enhance this process, the importance of physical education, exercise science, and sports as expanding and diverse fields of service, enjoyment, and employment is emphasized throughout the book.

UPDATES TO THIS EDITION

The tenth edition provides the latest information about the exercise and sport sciences, physical activity, and fitness. Each chapter has been updated and includes some of the latest research to stimulate students' critical thinking and continued study. Review questions, boxed material, student activities, key points, and Web connections have been revised and updated. Other specific additions by chapter include the following:

Chapter 1   Physical Education, Exercise Science, and Sport—Dynamic Fields

- Revised text as needed for clarity
- Checked and updated all links in text and Web Connections
- Updated statistics about obesity

Chapter 2   Exercise and Sport Sciences

- Revised text as needed for clarity
- Checked and updated all links in text and Web Connections

Chapter 3   Professions of Physical Education, Exercise Science, and Sport

- Revised text as needed for clarity
- Replaced all references to AAHPERD (and NASPE) and replaced with information about SHAPE America
- Revised certification information about athletic training
- Checked and updated all links in text and Web Connections

Chapter 4   Philosophy of Physical Education, Exercise Science, and Sport

- Revised text as needed for clarity
- Checked and updated all links in text and Web Connections

Chapter 5   Career Options

- Revised text as needed for clarity
- Checked and updated all links in text and Web Connections

Chapter 6   Preparation for a Career

- Revised text as needed for clarity
- Checked and updated all links in text and Web Connections
- Updated and added information about certifications
- New career perspective of Director of recreational sports

Chapter 7   Early Heritage in Sports and Gymnastics

- Checked and updated all links in text and Web Connections

Chapter 8   Early American Physical Education and Sport

- Added new career perspective of supervisor of cardiac and pulmonary rehabilitation

Chapter 9   Twentieth and Twenty-First Century Physical Education, Exercise Science, and Sport

- Revised text as needed for clarity
- Checked and updated all links in text and Web Connections
- Added new career perspective of an owner of fitness and sport centers

Chapter 10   Opportunities and Challenges in Physical Education and Exercise Science

- Revised text as needed for clarity
- Checked and updated all links in text and Web Connections

Chapter 11   Issues in Sports

- Updated Table 11-1 with the latest data and Table 11-2 with data about the number of athletes by gender and divisional level
- Checked and updated all links in text and Web Connections
- Added new career perspective of an intercollegiate athletic conference commissioner

Chapter 12   Leadership for Active Living

- Added figure depicting the two dimensions of leadership

CONTENT DESIGN

Written in a conversational and personal style, *Introduction to Physical Education, Exercise Science, and Sport* is designed for students enrolled in their first course related to exercise science, sport management, physical education, athletic training, or related majors.

An overview of the field is stressed rather than an in-depth examination of the disciplinary areas. The relevant topics discussed include practical suggestions for choosing and obtaining a job in the chosen career; current issues affecting job selection; girls and women in sport; ethnic minorities in physical education and sport; the standards and accountability movement; teacher, coach, athletic trainer, and exercise specialist certifications; educational values of sports; and the importance of physical activity for all.

The book's three units are self-contained and may be read in any order, although each is important to a full understanding of these fields. Unit One provides foundational information in the first four chapters before focusing on careers. In Chapter 1, numerous terms, including physical education, exercise science, and sport, are defined to help describe these dynamic fields. The cognitive, affective, and psychomotor development objectives of physical education, exercise science, and sport indicate how these can contribute to improvements in quality of life for all. Chapter 2 provides an in-depth look at the exercise and sport sciences, such as exercise physiology, athletic training, and sport management. An explanation of several undergraduate majors organizations in the field adds to the discussion about preparation programs for school and non-school careers in Chapter 3. The five traditional philosophies and a discussion of ethics are presented in Chapter 4 and provide reference points for the development of a personal philosophy.

A career emphasis is integrated throughout and given special attention in Chapters 5 and 6. Chapter 5 describes more than 80 careers in education, exercise science, recreation, fitness, sports, and athletics. Students learn about job responsibilities, prerequisite education and preparation, and potential availability of positions. Chapter 6 provides practical ideas for preparing for careers, with an emphasis on the importance of internships, volunteer experiences, and obtaining certifications. Recommendations for writing a résumé, developing a portfolio, and seeking a job are provided.

Unit Two covers the history and development of physical education, exercise science, and sport from early cultures through today. Athletics in Athens and Sparta, European gymnastics programs, and sports and games in Great Britain are emphasized in Chapter 7 because of their influence on programs in the United States. In Chapter 8, early American physical education, exercise science, and sport are traced from early sporting diversions through formalized gymnastics programs of the late 1800s. Chapter 9 completes the chronology of evolving programs that are diverse in philosophy, clientele, and activity. In addition to the historical information, Chapter 9 provides up-to-date information about recreation programs for all, competitive sports for both genders, and the impact of federation legislation on school and public physical activity programs.

Unit Three describes issues and trends in physical education, exercise science, and sport. Chapter 10 examines the value of physical activity for everyone; exercise science program developments; curricular features of elementary, middle, and secondary school physical education; challenges facing physical educators; standards and accountability; and career burnout. The beneficial outcomes and associated issues of sports for girls and women, ethnic minorities, senior citizens, individuals with special needs, youth, school students, college athletes, and Olympic athletes are addressed in Chapter 11. The final chapter emphasizes leadership, name changes, future challenges, and physical activity for life.

SUCCESSFUL FEATURES

Learning Outcomes

Each chapter begins with expectations by emphasizing what students should know and be able to understand and apply. These statements help students focus on what they should be learning from each chapter.

Introductions

The first paragraphs in each chapter briefly set the stage for and preview the content. They help students gain further perspectives on the relevance of the most salient points.

Illustrations

More than 136 photographs help students see the diversity of physical education, exercise science, and sport and potential careers in these fields. The photographs also reemphasize the popularity of sports and activities for all and help reinforce important concepts. Several line figures also help explicate the content.

Boxed Material

Throughout the text, specially highlighted information is designed to enhance students' understanding and provide additional insights into the profession. The insights contained in these boxes expand on and add significantly to the information provided in the text.

Web Connections

Each chapter provides students with annotations about content that can enhance learning at the sites of the URLs provided.

Summaries

A summary paragraph at the conclusion of each chapter emphasizes the primary areas of importance, and refocuses students on achieving the learning outcomes. These summaries help students recall and remember the key points in each chapter.

Career Perspectives

A unique feature of this book is the integration of biographical sketches of sport, exercise science, and physical education professionals in several diverse careers. The featured individuals list their job responsibilities, hours, course work, and degrees, discuss experiences needed for their careers, describe satisfying aspects of their careers and job potential, and offer suggestions for students.

Review Questions

To enhance retention of each chapter's content, students are encouraged to answer the review questions. Rather than seeking rote memorization of facts, these questions stress understanding key concepts.

Key Points

Points of emphasis help students focus on what is most important to learn. These short statements help student emphasize remembering key "take-home" points.

Student Activities

The student activities encourage students to think about and use the chapter content in greater depth and to extract practical ideas for career application. These activities also encourage active participation in the learning process.

Glossary

A comprehensive glossary of important terms reinforces students' understanding of the terminology used in the book and in physical education, exercise science, and sports.

▪ connect

The tenth edition of *Introduction to Physical Education, Exercise Science, and Sport* is now available online with Connect, McGraw-Hill Education's integrated assignment and assessment platform. Connect also offers SmartBook for the new edition, which is the first adaptive reading experience proven to improve grades and help students study more effectively. All of the title's Web site content is also available on Connect, including a full course Instructor's Manual, Test Bank, and PowerPoint presentations.

connect®

Required=Results

McGraw-Hill Connect®
Learn Without Limits

Connect is a teaching and learning platform that is proven to deliver better results for students and instructors.

Connect empowers students by continually adapting to deliver precisely what they need, when they need it and how they need it, so your class time is more engaging and effective.

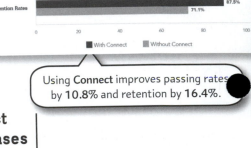

Course outcomes improve with Connect.

	With Connect	Without Connect
Exam Scores	80.4%	74.7%
Pass Rates	83.7%	72.9%
Attendance Rates	92.5%	74.5%
Retention Rates	87.5%	71.1%

Using **Connect** improves passing rates by **10.8%** and retention by **16.4%**.

88% of instructors who use **Connect** require it; instructor satisfaction **increases** by 38% when **Connect** is required.

Analytics—
Connect Insight®

Connect helps students achieve better grades

	A	B	C	D	F
With Connect	36%	29.5%	22%	4.3%	8.2%
Without Connect	22.2%	22.3%	25.6%	9.8%	20%

Based on McGraw-Hill Education Connect Effectiveness Study 2013

Connect Insight is Connect's new one-of-a-kind visual analytics dashboard—now available for both instructors and students—that provides at-a-glance information regarding student performance, which is immediately actionable. By presenting assignment, assessment, and topical performance results together with a time metric that is easily visible for aggregate or individual results, Connect Insight gives the user the ability to take a just-in-time approach to teaching and learning, which was never before available. Connect Insight presents data that empowers students and helps instructors improve class performance in a way that is efficient and effective.

Students can view their results for any **Connect** course.

Mobile—

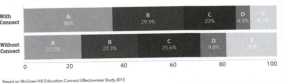

Connect's new, intuitive mobile interface gives students and instructors flexible and convenient, anytime–anywhere access to all components of the Connect platform.

Adaptive

THE FIRST AND ONLY **ADAPTIVE READING EXPERIENCE** DESIGNED TO TRANSFORM THE WAY STUDENTS READ

More students earn **A's** and **B's** when they use McGraw-Hill Education **Adaptive** products.

SmartBook®

Proven to help students improve grades and study more efficiently, SmartBook contains the same content within the print book, but actively tailors that content to the needs of the individual. SmartBook's adaptive technology provides precise, personalized instruction on what the student should do next, guiding the student to master and remember key concepts, targeting gaps in knowledge and offering customized feedback, driving the student toward comprehension and retention of the subject matter. Available on smartphones and tablets, SmartBook puts learning at the student's fingertips—anywhere, anytime.

Over **4 billion questions** have been answered making McGraw-Hill Education products more intelligent, reliable, & precise.

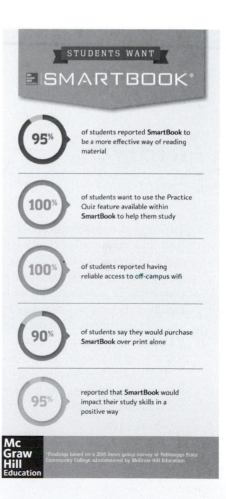

STUDENTS WANT

SMARTBOOK®

95% of students reported **SmartBook** to be a more effective way of reading material

100% of students want to use the Practice Quiz feature available within **SmartBook** to help them study

100% of students reported having reliable access to off-campus wifi

90% of students say they would purchase **SmartBook** over print alone

95% reported that **SmartBook** would impact their study skills in a positive way

Mc Graw Hill Education

*Findings based on a 2015 focus group survey at Pellissippi State Community College administered by McGraw-Hill Education

ACKNOWLEDGMENTS

I would like to express my deepest appreciation to my parents, Janice and Carol Lumpkin, who instilled in me a love for learning, provided me with many educational opportunities through personal sacrifice, and have continually encouraged all of my endeavors. I dedicate this book to them with my love.

I also appreciate the help given to me by the reviewers, who have provided valuable suggestions for this revision:

Mike Bamman,
Huntingdon College

Regan Dodd,
Missouri Western State University

Miriam J. Evans,
South Carolina State University

Mary Freeland,
Indiana University East

Molly Jacques,
Folsom Lake College

Park Lockwood,
Washburn University

Starla McCollum,
Georgia Southern University

Marie Cantwell Norton,
Montgomery County Community College

Dr. Jill D. Owen,
Eastern Illinois University

Angela Lumpkin

Vitalsource

This text is available as an eTextbook from VitalSource, a new way for faculty to find and review eTextbooks. It's also a great option for students who are interested in accessing their course materials digitally and saving money. VitalSource offers thousands of the most commonly adopted textbooks across hundreds of courses from a wide variety of higher education publishers. It is the only place for faculty to review and compare the full text of a textbook online, providing immediate access without the environmental impact of requesting a print exam copy. At VitalSource, students can save up to 50% off the cost of a print book, reduce their impact on the environment, and gain access to powerful Web tools for learning including full text search, notes and highlighting, and e-mail tools for sharing notes between classmates. For further details, contact your sales representative or go to www.vitalsource.com.

PRINCIPLES AND SCOPE OF PHYSICAL EDUCATION, EXERCISE SCIENCE, AND SPORT

© Royalty-Free/Corbis

CHAPTER

1

PHYSICAL EDUCATION, EXERCISE SCIENCE, AND SPORT–DYNAMIC FIELDS

LEARNING OUTCOMES

- Students will be able to explain the dynamic fields of physical education, exercise science, and sport and the ways professionals in each of these fields can directly impact the quality of life for individuals they serve.
- Students will be able to describe how to develop the five components of health-related physical fitness and the importance of each.
- Students will articulate the importance of the federal government's initiatives, such as the 2008 Physical Activity Guidelines and Healthy People 2020, in helping citizens live healthier lives.
- Students will explore the parameters of cognitive development, affective development, and psychomotor development and identify ways they can contribute to these as physical educators, exercise scientists, and sport professionals.

Children love to move because it is fun. Adults choose to engage in physical activities because they find them enjoyable. With increased leisure time, people of all ages are seeking instructional, recreational, competitive, and entertaining physical activity and sport programs. This interest promises a dynamic future for professionals who want to contribute to the well-being and quality of life of others. The millions who enroll in a variety of aerobic activity classes, join fitness clubs, bowl in leagues, hike, camp, swim, jog, climb, sail, walk, skate, and engage in many other physical pursuits already have determined that these activities are fun. Many also value the mental, social, and physical development resulting from their regular participation. Others enjoy being entertained by watching highly skilled individuals compete.

Although many people value maintaining physically active and fit lifestyles, others are not yet convinced to get moving. Motivating this latter group is the challenge awaiting you when you begin your career. Historically, the term physical

Aerobic activities develop cardiorespiratory endurance, an important component of physical fitness.
© Ryan McVay/Getty Images RF

educator has been used to encompass professionals in various careers who teach fitness and sport skills. This descriptor identifies individuals who are committed to using physical activities to develop the whole person.

To help you meet the challenge to contribute to the wellness of others, this text introduces you to current concepts and objectives in the dynamic fields of physical education, exercise science, and sport and their rich heritage. Past physical education programs provide the foundation for today's ever-expanding programs in the United States, shaping the way we structure and describe these fields. Understanding the definition and objectives of physical education today and in the past will help you conceptualize the breadth and depth of these fields. Understanding affective, cognitive, and psychomotor domains of learning will ensure you know what physical education, exercise science, and sport programs seek to accomplish.

THE DYNAMIC FIELDS OF HUMAN MOVEMENT

The human body is like a machine because it will no longer function efficiently or effectively if used only minimally. For example, a broken arm placed in a cast for several weeks will noticeably atrophy as its muscular strength and endurance and flexibility diminish. The human body is designed to move, and its potential for future movement is predicated upon past movement. The functioning of the cardiovascular, musculoskeletal, metabolic, endocrine, and immune systems is enhanced through movement.

Because of their natural predisposition to move, humans learn to walk, catch, throw, and kick as they model their movements after what they see; at the same time, moving contributes to growth and development. Watching children hop, skip, and jump with exuberance reinforces the idea that moving is intrinsically rewarding.

Adults of all ages who choose to engage in activities that require moderate to vigorous movement usually do so because they personally reap physical, emotional, mental, or social benefits. That is, there are inevitable positive outcomes accruing to those who prioritize keeping their bodies moving (an analogy would be a well-oiled machine). Human movement, in its many types, variations, and settings, also appeals to individuals' tendencies or desires to share active experiences that are socially rewarding. This may entail joining a health club to work out with friends, joining a recreational softball team, or playing golf with associates from work.

Choosing to work in a field that can help people engage in enjoyable activities has a built-in advantage, because it is easier to get people to engage and persist in activities that are fun. This book provides a comprehensive examination of the dynamic fields that help facilitate human movement. It will introduce numerous terms to help you gain a greater appreciation of the various aspects of human move-ment as well as the breadth and depth of these dynamic fields. Learning and under-standing the terminology of human movement will help you prepare for a career in one of these professions.

Physical education, exercise science, and sport are allied fields that share a common heritage and have grown more distinctive with the knowledge explosion and through disciplinary specialization. They relate to, but are not synonymous with, exercise, play, games, leisure, recreation, and athletics. Defining each of these terms can help clarify the distinctions and similarities. **Exercise** involves physical movement that increases the rate of energy expenditure and is engaged in for the purpose of getting fit. **Play** refers to amusements engaged in freely for fun with less formality in rules. **Games** can describe playful activities, rule-governed contests, and athletic competitions. Examples include hopscotch during recess, a recreation league softball game, or a professional sport competition. Similarly, **recreation** refreshes or renews one's strength and spirit after work; it is a diversion that occurs during leisure hours. **Athletics** are highly organized and structured competitions among skilled athletes. Interscholastic sports, intercollegiate athletics, and profes-sional sports are examples.

Sports are physical activities governed by formal or informal rules that involve competition against an opponent or oneself and are engaged in for fun or reward. Examples of sports are basketball, golf, and tennis. Sports may be played both for exercise and as a game. Sport participants may use their leisure time to play games recreationally. Some describe bridge and chess games as sports, while others claim that rock climbing, fly fishing, and sky-diving are sports. When the rules govern-ing the skill levels required of participants and significance placed on the outcome are rigidly structured, sport becomes athletics. Usually sport refers to a contest in which the outcome is viewed as important by the players, who will emerge as either winners or losers.

To encompass the various outcomes experienced by all people in diverse pro-grams, **physical education** is defined as a process through which an individual

Walking is a moderate activity that can be enjoyed throughout life.
© Comstock Images RF

obtains optimal physical, mental, and social skills and fitness through physical activity. In recent years, many colleges have chosen to rename their departments, using terms such as kinesiology, exercise science, human movement, and sport. **Kinesiology,** which many prefer as a more scientific descriptor than physical education, is the study of human movement. **Exercise science** describes the scientific analysis of the human body in motion. This broad term encompasses content from exercise physiology, biomechanics, kinesiology, anatomy, physiology, motor behavior, and some aspects of sports medicine. Exercise science researchers explore how to maximize the potential of human movement through physiological, biomechanical, and psychological studies. Practitioners apply these findings to improve the quality of life for all who incorporate physical activity into their lives. Thus, the term exercise science rather than physical education may more broadly define what people know and do relative to human movement. **Sport** is a broad term that encompasses the application of components of the social sciences of history, management, philosophy, psychology, and sociology in a sporting context. Sport includes the examination of how each of these disciplines impacts participants and observers and helps shape their attitudes, beliefs, and behaviors.

QUALITY OF LIFE

What does quality of life mean? Is it happiness, wellness, health, fitness, or fun? Maybe it refers to enjoyable use of leisure time, relief from stress, safety from harm, or absence of disease. In today's world quality of life, although defined individually, increasingly means a long and healthy life. Inherent therein is the concept that a feeling of well-being or some level of fitness enhances life. Maybe it is an outgrowth of Americans' search for the fountain of youth, but fitness, or at least the appearance of fitness, appears to be valued.

Cycling is an example of a popular aerobic activity.
© David Buffington/Blend Images RF

This commitment to fitness is not a fad; it has become an integral part of life for many. Executives may choose where to take a job based on the availability of exercise programs, or employers may hire only healthy and fit employees. Families often plan vacations and leisure time around various recreational and sport activities. Thousands of people sign up for marathons, 10-kilometer road races, and fun runs. Walking has become popular for people of all ages. Sporting goods and sport clothing sales continue to gross millions of dollars. Sport facilities, such as health clubs, aerobics centers, tennis courts, swimming pools, and golf courses, are increasingly attracting people who take their health and sports seriously.

The contributions of physical education, exercise science, and sport to quality of life can be enhanced by encouraging participation in team sports and individual sports. Schools, recreation departments, and independent organizations offer league competitions in baseball, basketball, football, soccer, softball, and volleyball. Within these settings, team members potentially can learn and demonstrate teamwork, cooperation, communication skills, and the ability to lead and follow. Team camaraderie may lead to lifelong friendships and the willingness to place the team's benefit above individual goals. Although some of these sports can become lifelong pursuits, many individuals discontinue participation because their teams lack sufficient players or because of the physical demands of the sport.

Individual sports are often called lifetime sports because of the greater likelihood of continued participation throughout life. Most of these sports can be engaged in by an individual either alone or with only one other person. Bowling, fishing, golf, hiking, jogging, swimming, tennis, walking, and weight lifting are among the most popular of these sports and activities. They can be engaged in recreationally or competitively through leagues, tournaments, and organized events. Individual sports, like team sports, can teach fair play, self-confidence, and how to win and lose graciously, as well as specific sport skills.

Individuals of all ages are seeking to achieve the healthy benefits of physical activity.
© Keith Thomas Productions/Brand X Pictures/PictureQuest RF

Typically, interscholastic athletic teams and city or business recreational leagues attract skilled participants or those at least moderately comfortable with their skills. Those lacking skills, however, are often relegated to spectator roles or easy chairs in front of their televisions, video games, or computers. More instructional programs and beginning-level leagues and teams are needed for individuals of all ages. Often though, there is an overlap between the lower skilled and the economically disadvantaged. Because of their cost, golf, swimming, and tennis, for example, have often been categorized as upper-class sports. To bridge this gap, tax-supported recreation departments need to provide opportunities for these and other activities for all individuals.

Senior citizens, a growing percentage of the U.S. population, also have recreational needs. For example, exercise has been found to reduce osteoporosis (a breakdown of calcium in the bones), especially for women in their post-menopausal years. Senior citizens need activities matched with their capabilities. On the other end of the spectrum, children have many needs for physical activity that remain unfulfilled. Daily physical education from kindergarten through grade 12 would greatly enhance children's movement skills and fitness capacities, if all school students were provided this instruction. Nonschool sport programs also can provide opportunities for physical activity and play. Increased fun-filled opportunities for physical activities will contribute to the development of healthy lifestyles for everyone. You, as a coach, recreation leader, personal trainer, or teacher, hold the key to unlocking the doors of opportunity to the physical, psychological, and social benefits of physical activity.

IMPORTANCE OF PHYSICAL ACTIVITY

Making physical activity a priority in one's daily schedule is relatively easy, even for the person who is really busy. Among the tips for becoming more active are taking 10-minute fitness breaks at work, school, or home; choosing to walk or cycle to work, school, or the store; walking up stairs instead of taking the elevator or escalator; parking the car farther away from a destination and walking (rather than seeking the closest possible spot); and exercising by using hand weights while watching television or a movie, riding a stationary bicycle, or performing stretching exercises. The key point is to choose a fun and rewarding physical activity and one that will continue to be enjoyable.

Significant health benefits can be obtained by adults including a moderate amount of physical activity in weekly routines (e.g., 30 minutes of brisk walking, 15 minutes of running, or 45 minutes of playing volleyball on most, if not all, days of the week). Regular physical activity improves health by reducing the risk of premature death, dying from heart disease, developing type 2 diabetes, developing high blood pressure, or developing colon cancer. Daily, moderate physical activity helps reduce blood pressure in people who already have high blood pressure, reduces feelings of depression and anxiety, helps control weight, helps older adults become stronger and better able to move without falling, and promotes psychological well-being.

However, many people have a plethora of excuses or rationalizations for why they are not physically active. At the top of most lists is "I don't have time." Rather than rationalizing that it is impossible or inconvenient to find time for exercise, most people should be able to look at the 1,440 minutes in each day and allocate at least 20 minutes to exercise. Many people claim they need to spend more time with family or friends, so setting aside time for personal exercise would be too selfish or neglectful. Alternatively, exercising with a group of family members or friends allows all to benefit. On a very personal level, some people find physical activity boring, do not like to sweat so much that a shower is required, or they have had a bad experience with sports or exercise in the past. A moderate and enjoyable activity, such as gardening or walking, could address each of these excuses, especially when a friend joins in the activity. Individuals who are worried about existing or anticipated injuries, aches, and pains should check with their physicians, who can prescribe the appropriate types of exercises and the slow, progressive initiation of exercise programs. Few people are too old to start or learn how to be physically active in ways that will benefit them not only physically but also emotionally, mentally, and socially. The motivation comes from within each person, so everyone is encouraged to set a goal to get moving. The reward will be an increased feeling of well-being.

A few other tips for exercise programs include starting slowly at an easy pace and then increasing time or distance gradually as muscles warm up; listening to the body—monitoring the level of fatigue, heart rate, and any physical discomfort; being aware of any signs of breathlessness, muscle soreness, and overexertion; wearing comfortable and appropriate clothing and shoes for the activity; finishing by stretching the muscles used; and drinking water before, during, and after exercise.

Developing and maintaining fitness can be fun.
© Royalty-Free/Corbis

In 1996, the first-ever Surgeon General's report on *Physical Activity and Health* emphasized that Americans could substantially improve their health and the quality of their lives by participating in regular physical activity. Despite the *Healthy People 2000* goals, the patterns and trends in physical activity reported in the Surgeon General's report indicated little progress and even some decreases in activity levels. A few of these low participation levels included the following:

- Approximately 15% of adults and about 50% of individuals 12 to 21 years old in this country engaged in vigorous physical activity at least 3 times a week for at least 20 minutes.
- Approximately 22% of adults in this country engaged in sustained physical activity at least 5 times a week for at least 30 minutes.
- About 25% of adults and 25% of individuals 12 to 21 years old in this country engaged in no physical activity.
- Daily attendance in high school physical education classes between 1991 and 1995 declined from approximately 42% to 25%.

These data verified the significant challenge facing this nation and confirmed a national concern for the physical welfare of most citizens.

Healthy People 2010, published by the federal government in 2000, continued to report disturbing statistics (as did *Healthy People 2000,* published in 1990) about the poor status of Americans' overall health. Millions of citizens were overweight and inactive and suffering the consequences of unhealthy lifestyles. National efforts to address the health of all citizens continue with *Healthy People 2020.* Box 1.1 describes its goals, the determinants of health, leading health indicators, and physical activity objectives.

BOX 1.1   HEALTHY PEOPLE 2020

Healthy People 2020 is based on the accomplishments of four previous Healthy People initiatives:

- 1979 Surgeon General's Report, Healthy People: The Surgeon General's Report on Health Promotion and Disease Prevention
- Healthy People 1990: Promoting Health/Preventing Disease: Objectives for the Nation
- Healthy People 2000: National Health Promotion and Disease Prevention Objectives
- Healthy People 2010: Objectives for Improving Health

Healthy People 2020 continues this tradition with the launch on December 2, 2010, of its ambitious, yet achievable, 10-year agenda for improving the nation's health.

The **vision** of Healthy People 2020 is a society in which all people live long, healthy lives.

The **mission** of Healthy People 2020 strives to:

- Identify nationwide health improvement priorities.
- Increase public awareness and understanding of the determinants of health, disease, and disability and the opportunities for progress.
- Provide measurable objectives and goals that are applicable at the national, state, and local levels.
- Engage multiple sectors to take actions to strengthen policies and improve practices that are driven by the best available evidence and knowledge.
- Identify critical research, evaluation, and data collection needs.

The **overarching goals** of Healthy People 2020 are:

- Attain high-quality, longer lives free of preventable disease, disability, injury, and premature death.
- Achieve health equity, eliminate disparities, and improve the health of all groups.
- Create social and physical environments that promote good health for all.
- Promote quality of life, healthy development, and healthy behaviors across all life stages.

Determinants of Health

What makes some people healthy and others unhealthy?

How can we create a society in which everyone has a chance to live a long, healthy life?

Healthy People 2020 is exploring these questions by:

- Developing objectives that address the relationship between health status and biology, individual behavior, health services, social factors, and policies.
- Emphasizing an ecological approach to disease prevention and health promotion. An ecological approach focuses on both individual-level and population-level determinants of health and interventions.

Leading Health Indicators

The leading health indicators are composed of 26 indicators organized under 12 topics.

- Access to Health Services
  - Persons with medical insurance
  - Persons with a usual primary care provider
- Clinical Preventive Services
  - Adults who receive a colorectal cancer screening based on the most recent guidelines

(continued)

BOX 1.1   HEALTHY PEOPLE 2020 (continued)

- Adults with hypertension whose blood pressure is under control
- Adult diabetic population with an A1c value greater than 9%
- Children aged 19 to 35 months who receive the recommended doses of DTaP, polio, MMR, Hib, hepatitis B, varicella, and PCV vaccines
- Environmental Quality
  - Air Quality Index exceeding 100
  - Children aged 3 to 11 years exposed to secondhand smoke
- Injury and Violence
  - Fatal injuries
  - Homicides
- Maternal, Infant, and Child Health
  - Infant deaths
  - Preterm births
- Mental Health
  - Suicides
  - Adolescents who experience major depressive episodes
- Nutrition, Physical Activity, and Obesity
  - Adults who meet current federal physical activity guidelines for aerobic physical activity and muscle-strengthening activity
  - Adults who are obese
  - Children and adolescents who are considered obese
  - Total vegetable intake for persons aged 2 years and older
- Oral Health
  - Persons aged 2 years and older who used the oral health system in past 12 months
- Reproductive and Sexual Health
  - Sexually active females aged 15 to 44 years who received reproductive health services in the past 12 months
  - Persons living with HIV who know their serostatus
- Social Determinants
  - Students who graduate with a regular diploma 4 years after starting 9th grade
- Substance Abuse
  - Adolescents using alcohol or any illicit drugs during the past 30 days
  - Adults engaging in binge drinking during the past 30 days
- Tobacco
  - Adults who are current cigarette smokers
  - Adolescents who smoked cigarettes in the past 30 days

Physical Activity Objectives

PA–1: Reduce the proportion of adults who engage in no leisure-time physical activity.

PA–2: Increase the proportion of adults who meet current federal physical activity guidelines for aerobic physical activity and for muscle-strengthening activity.

PA–3: Increase the proportion of adolescents who meet current federal physical activity guidelines for aerobic physical activity and for muscle-strengthening activity.

(continued)

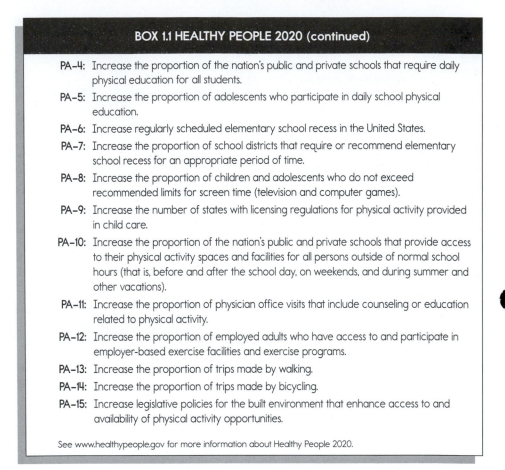

BOX 1.1 HEALTHY PEOPLE 2020 (continued)

PA-4: Increase the proportion of the nation's public and private schools that require daily physical education for all students.

PA-5: Increase the proportion of adolescents who participate in daily school physical education.

PA-6: Increase regularly scheduled elementary school recess in the United States.

PA-7: Increase the proportion of school districts that require or recommend elementary school recess for an appropriate period of time.

PA-8: Increase the proportion of children and adolescents who do not exceed recommended limits for screen time (television and computer games).

PA-9: Increase the number of states with licensing regulations for physical activity provided in child care.

PA-10: Increase the proportion of the nation's public and private schools that provide access to their physical activity spaces and facilities for all persons outside of normal school hours (that is, before and after the school day, on weekends, and during summer and other vacations).

PA-11: Increase the proportion of physician office visits that include counseling or education related to physical activity.

PA-12: Increase the proportion of employed adults who have access to and participate in employer-based exercise facilities and exercise programs.

PA-13: Increase the proportion of trips made by walking.

PA-14: Increase the proportion of trips made by bicycling.

PA-15: Increase legislative policies for the built environment that enhance access to and availability of physical activity opportunities.

See www.healthypeople.gov for more information about Healthy People 2020.

OBESITY

A major problem in the United States is the increasing prevalence of obesity. According to the Centers for Disease Control and Prevention (CDC), obesity is defined as having a very high amount of body fat in relation to lean body mass, or Body Mass Index (BMI) of 30 or higher. BMI is the measure of an adult's weight in relation to his or her height. The CDC reports that in 2010, the number of states with an obesity prevalence of 30% or more had increased to 12 (Alabama; Arkansas; Kentucky; Louisiana; Michigan; Mississippi; Missouri; Oklahoma; South Carolina; Tennessee; Texas; West Virginia). No state had a prevalence of obesity less than 20%. (Go to www.cdc.gov/obesity/data/prevalence-maps.html for an animated map that shows trends in increased obesity in the United States between 1985 and 2010.) In 2011–2012, 34.9% of all adults 20 years and older in the United States were obese. The CDC also reported 16.9% of children and adolescents (2–19 years) are obese, which is triple the rate of one generation ago. Obesity has significant implications for health because it increases the risk of diseases and health problems like coronary heart disease, type 2 diabetes, endometrial, breast, and colon cancers, high blood pressure, high cholesterol, stroke, liver and gallbladder disease, sleep apnea and respiratory problems, osteoarthritis (a degeneration of cartilage and its underlying bone within a joint), and gynecological problems like abnormal menses and infertility.

Hypokinetic disease refers to those diseases and health problems associated with physical inactivity and a sedentary lifestyle. Coronary heart disease, high blood pressure, stress, ulcers, obesity, and low back pain often afflict individuals who fail to engage in regular exercise. When school, work, family, and use of leisure time place few physical demands on our bodies, degenerative diseases may develop. Health education and physical activity can help alter or deter the disease process.

In 1992, the American Heart Association identified physical inactivity (along with high blood pressure and high cholesterol) as a primary risk factor for coronary heart disease. Millions need to realize that participating in regular physical activity and exercise is essential to good health. Physical activity has numerous beneficial physiological effects on the cardiovascular and musculoskeletal systems, but it also benefits the metabolic, endocrine, and immune systems. Maintaining normal muscular strength, joint structure, and joint function occurs only when activity is sustained. Thus, the health benefits can be enjoyed only if physical activity becomes a regular part of a person's life.

Seeking to engage people in physical activity, in 2008 the U.S. Department of Health and Human Services established the *Physical Activity Guidelines for Americans.* A summary of these research-based guidelines and their importance is provided in the Research View. The guidelines also can be found at health.gov/paguidelines/guidelines.

⊘ RESEARCH VIEW

2008 Physical Activity Guidelines for Americans Summary

The *2008 Physical Activity Guidelines for Americans* describes the major research findings on the health benefits of physical activity:

- Regular physical activity reduces the risk of many adverse health outcomes.

- Some physical activity is better than none.

- For most health outcomes, additional benefits occur as the amount of physical activity increases through higher intensity, greater frequency, and/or longer duration.

- Most health benefits occur with at least 150 minutes (2 hours and 30 minutes) each week of moderate intensity physical activity, such as brisk walking. Additional benefits occur with more physical activity.

(continued)

- Both aerobic (endurance) and muscle-strengthening (resistance) physical activity are beneficial.
- Health benefits occur for children and adolescents, young and middle-aged adults, older adults, and those in every studied racial and ethnic group.
- The health benefits of physical activity occur for people with disabilities.
- The benefits of physical activity far outweigh the possibility of adverse outcomes.

Key Guidelines for Children and Adolescents

- Children and adolescents should participate in 60 minutes of physical activity daily.

  - Aerobic: Most of the 60 or more minutes a day should be either moderate- or vigorous-intensity aerobic physical activity and should include vigorous-intensity physical activity at least 3 days each week.
  - Muscle-strengthening: As part of their 60 or more minutes of daily physical activity, children and adolescents should include muscle-strengthening physical activity on at least 3 days each week.
  - Bone-strengthening: As part of their 60 or more minutes of daily physical activity, children and adolescents should include bone-strengthening physical activity on at least 3 days each week.

- It is important to encourage young people to participate in physical activities that are appropriate for their ages, are enjoyable, and offer variety.

Key Guidelines for Adults

- All adults should avoid inactivity. Some physical activity is better than none, and adults who participate in any amount of physical activity gain some health benefits.
- For substantial health benefits, adults should participate in at least 150 minutes (2 hours and 30 minutes) each week of moderate-intensity, or 75 minutes (1 hour and 15 minutes) each week of vigorous-intensity, aerobic physical activity, or an equivalent combination of moderate- and vigorous-intensity aerobic activity. Aerobic activity should be performed in episodes of at least 10 minutes and, preferably, it should be spread throughout the week.
- For additional and more extensive health benefits, adults should increase their aerobic physical activity to 300 minutes (5 hours) per week of moderate-intensity, or 150 minutes a week of vigorous-intensity, aerobic physical activity, or an equivalent combination of moderate- and vigorous-intensity activity. Additional health benefits are gained by engaging in physical activity beyond this amount.

(continued)

- Adults should also do muscle-strengthening activities that are moderate- or high-intensity and involve all major muscle groups on 2 or more days per week, since these activities provide additional health benefits.

Key Guidelines for Older Adults

The key guidelines for adults also apply to older adults. In addition, the following guidelines are just for older adults:

- When older adults cannot do 150 minutes of moderate-intensity aerobic activity per week because of chronic conditions, they should be as physically active as their abilities and conditions allow.
- Older adults should do exercises that maintain or improve balance if they are at risk of falling.
- Older adults should determine their level of effort for physical activity relative to their levels of fitness.
- Older adults with chronic conditions should understand whether and how their conditions affect their abilities to do regular physical activity safely.

Key Guidelines for Safe Physical Activity

To do physical activity safely and reduce the risk of injuries and other adverse events, people should:

- Understand the risks, and yet be confident that physical activity is safe for almost everyone.
- Choose to participate in types of physical activities that are appropriate for their current fitness levels and health goals, because some activities are safer than others.
- Increase physical activity gradually over time whenever more activity is necessary to meet guidelines or health goals. Inactive people should "start low and go slow" by gradually increasing how often and how long activities are done.
- Protect yourself by using appropriate sports equipment, looking for safe environments, following rules and policies, and making sensible choices about when, where, and how to be active.
- Be under the care of a health care provider if you have chronic conditions or symptoms. People with chronic conditions and symptoms should consult their health care providers about the types and amounts of activity appropriate for them.

Key Guidelines for Adults with Disabilities

- Adults with disabilities, who are able to, should get at least 150 minutes per week of moderate-intensity, or 75 minutes per week of vigorous-intensity, aerobic activity, or an equivalent combination of moderate and

(continued)

vigorous-intensity aerobic activity. Aerobic activity should be performed in episodes of at least 10 minutes and, preferably, should be spread throughout the week.

- Adults with disabilities, who are able to, also should participate in muscle-strengthening activities of moderate- or high-intensity that involve all major muscle groups on 2 or more days a week, as these activities provide additional health benefits.

- When adults with disabilities are not able to meet the guidelines, they should engage in regular physical activity according to their abilities and should avoid inactivity.

- Adults with disabilities should consult their health care providers about the amounts and types of physical activity appropriate for their abilities.

Key Messages for People with Chronic Medical Conditions

- Adults with chronic conditions obtain health benefits from regular physical activity.

- When adults with chronic conditions do activity according to their abilities, physical activity is safe.

- Adults with chronic conditions should be under the care of a health care provider. People with chronic conditions and symptoms should consult their health care providers about the types and amounts of activity appropriate for them.

PURPOSE

What exactly do physical education, exercise science, and sport programs seek to accomplish? A purpose is a stated intention, aim, or goal that provides the answer to the question "why." Used interchangeably, these terms describe desirable long-range achievements that will occur only after many hours of effort and incremental progress. Working to make the dean's list this semester, earning an athletic grant-in-aid based on performance as a walk-on athlete, getting invited into an academic honor society, and saving money from a part-time job to purchase a car are all examples of setting and accomplishing goals. Whether you call it an aim, a goal, or a purpose, each is achieved by meeting several objectives, such as spending long hours studying or perfecting athletic skills. The **purpose** of physical education, exercise science, and sport programs is to optimize quality of life by encouraging people to make long-term commitments to enjoyable physical activity and sport experiences that will meet their varied needs in a changing world. Secondarily, people who make this commitment will find themselves better prepared to meet other goals because they will have successfully made attitudinal and behavioral changes.

Physical activity, physical fitness, health, and wellness are components essential to the achievement of the purpose of physical education, exercise science, and

Jogging contributes to health-related fitness.
© Royalty-Free/Corbis

sport. **Physical activity** is broadly defined as large muscle movements that may include participation in games, sports, work, daily activities of life, and exercise. **Physical fitness** is the body's capacity to adapt and respond favorably to physical effort. The physically fit person can move efficiently and effectively in meeting physical demands. Physical fitness includes the five components of **health-related fitness,** which is the level of positive well-being associated with enhanced functioning of the heart, muscles, and joints to improve the healthfulness of life. Physical fitness also includes six components of **skill-related fitness,** which entails achieving levels of ability to perform physical movements that are efficient and effective. (See the Research View for a description of these 11 components of fitness, 10 principles of training, and several guidelines for flexibility and resistance training.) The physically fit person, who is better able to handle the daily demands of work and enjoy recreational activities during leisure time, is healthier and better able to resist hypokinetic diseases or conditions. **Health,** often defined as the absence of illness or disease, is a positive state of physiological function that includes physical fitness and the five dimensions of wellness. **Wellness,** which is very personal and individualized, includes the emotional, mental, physical, social, and spiritual factors that lead to an overall state of well-being, quality of life, and ability to contribute to society.

⌕ RESEARCH VIEW

Fundamentals of Physical Fitness

Components of Health-Related Physical Fitness

- Cardiorespiratory endurance—the ability of the lungs, heart, and blood vessels to deliver adequate amounts of oxygen to the cells to meet the demands of prolonged physical activity
- Muscular strength—the ability to exert maximum force against resistance
- Muscular endurance—the ability of a muscle to exert submaximal force repeatedly over a period of time
- Flexibility—the ability of a joint to move freely through its full range of motion
- Body composition—percentage of body fat or lean body mass

Components of Skill-Related Physical Fitness

- Agility—ability to change directions rapidly and accurately
- Balance—ability to maintain equilibrium while stationary or moving
- Coordination—ability to perform motor tasks smoothly and accurately
- Power—ability to exert force rapidly through a combination of strength and speed
- Reaction time—ability to respond or react quickly to a stimulus
- Speed—ability to quickly perform a movement

FITT Principles

- Frequency—how often a person should train
- Intensity—how hard a person should exercise
- Time—how long, or the duration, a person should exercise
- Type—kind, or mode, of exercise performed

Principles of Training (PROVIRRRBS)

- Progression—increasing gradually the stress on the muscles so the body can adapt
- Regularity—number of times exercising per week
- Overload—placing increasing amounts of stress on the body to cause adaptations that improve fitness
- Variety—changing equipment, exercises, and activities to avoid boredom, reduce risk of overuse injuries, and increase motivation or adherence

(continued)

- Individualism—knowing personal capabilities and limitations to be able to maintain strength and work on weaknesses
- Realism—setting achievable training plans and goals to help maintain an exercise program
- Recovery—ensuring optimal amount of rest and sleep to allow for rebuilding tissues and replenishing stored energy
- Reversibility—loss of fitness improvements when physical demands on the body are not maintained
- Balance—focusing on all of the health-related components of physical fitness, the push and pull movements of each joint, and both upper body and lower body fitness
- Specificity—training exact areas of muscles, energy systems, and ranges of motion to improve fitness

Guidelines for Flexibility and Resistance Training

Flexibility

- Warm up muscles, such as by walking
- Stretch after moderate or vigorous physical activity
- Stretch slowly and under control, with no bouncing, to the point of tension but not pain
- Relax and breathe freely while stretching
- Focus on the major muscle groups like calves, hips, lower back, neck, shoulders, and thighs
- Hold stretches comfortably for 15 to 30 seconds and repeat each stretch 3 to 5 times
- Stretch every day, but at least a minimum of 3 times per week

Benefits of Stretching to Develop and Maintain Flexibility

- Increases flexibility for exercise and other daily activities
- Improves range of motion of joints
- Enhances circulation of the blood and healing of muscular injuries
- Relieves stress and relaxes muscles

Resistance Training

- Select 8 to 10 exercises, such as abdominal crunch, chest press, shoulder press, leg press, leg curls, triceps extension, and biceps curls that develop the major muscle groups
- Execute each set of each exercise between 8 and 15 repetitions to the point of volitional fatigue (working to the point of exhaustion is what

(continued)

causes changes in muscle fibers leading to increased muscular strength and endurance during the recuperation time between workouts)

- Complete all exercises at least 2 days per week and preferably 3 days per week
- Perform exercises in a controlled manner using proper form and technique including movements through the full range of motion
- Maintain a normal breathing pattern throughout each exercise
- Exercise with a partner, who can provide feedback, assistance, and motivation

Benefits of Resistance Training
- Increases muscular strength
- Enhances muscle fiber adaptation and hypertrophy (increase in the size of the muscle)
- Increases bone mineral density and offsets osteoporosis
- Decreases the percentage of body fat and increases fat-free mass
- Enhances functioning of the cardiovascular system

OBJECTIVES OR OUTCOMES OF PHYSICAL EDUCATION, EXERCISE SCIENCE, AND SPORT PROGRAMS

The objectives of physical education, exercise science, and sport programs are often stated more specifically than the purpose because they consist of particular learning outcomes. Professional colleagues and the general public often learn about a program's worth through an examination of its objectives and their fulfillment.

Flexibility is one of the health-related components of physical fitness.
© McGraw-Hill Education/Ken Karp, photographer

Cognitive Development

Cognitive development focuses on the acquisition, comprehension, analysis, synthesis, application, and evaluation of knowledge. Increased cognitive involvement usually leads to better execution of a skill and a better understanding of the activity. In meeting cognitive objectives, teachers and exercise leaders in all settings need to explain not only how but especially why the body's movements result in certain outcomes. For example, they can explain why hand position, release technique, and follow-through are critical to the success of throwing a ball. They can emphasize learning rules, strategies, skills, safety principles, and proper etiquette. Playing any sport requires at least some knowledge of the rules. Physical activity has been shown to enhance cognitive development and academic performance.

Affective Development

Affective development emphasizes the formation of attitudes, appreciations, and values; this domain contains both social and emotional dimensions. In the social realm, both individual and group needs are met while positive characteristics are developed. Learning self-confidence, courtesy, fair play, sportsmanship, and cooperation benefits all students. In team sports, decision-making abilities, communication skills, and affiliation needs are enhanced, as long as winning is not overemphasized. Individuals' values and attitudes toward involvement in physical activity are solidified, as are appreciations for participation and performance when the achievement of realistic personal goals is paramount. On the emotional side, self-discipline, fun, learning how to win and lose, tension release, self-control, and self-expression are enhanced through the give-and-take of challenging oneself and competing with and against others.

Psychomotor Development

Movement undergirds all physical education, exercise science, and sport programs that seek to achieve the objectives of **psychomotor development,** which is an educational outcome that emphasizes the learning of fundamental movements, motor skills, and sports skills. Although any person can learn fundamental movement skills, children learn more easily because they do not have to break habitual inefficient motor patterns. Also, if the basic locomotor, manipulative, and perceptual-motor skills are learned early in life, they provide the foundation for lifelong enjoyment of physical activity. Box 1.2 provides examples of cognitive, affective, and psychomotor objectives.

Movement concepts include body awareness; spatial awareness, including space, direction, level, and pathways; qualities of movement such as time, force, and flow; and relationships with objects and with people. Walking, running, jumping, leaping, and sliding are some of the basic locomotor movements; conversely, stretching, twisting, pushing, lifting, and swinging are nonlocomotor movements. Manipulative skills, involving propelling or absorbing force from an object, include throwing, catching, striking, and kicking.

Developing and improving fundamental movement skills and game or sport skills are important objectives, since sport, aquatic, and dance skills begin with

BOX 1.2   EDUCATIONAL OBJECTIVES WHOSE ACHIEVEMENT IS ENHANCED THROUGH PHYSICAL EDUCATION, EXERCISE SCIENCE, AND SPORT PROGRAMS

Mental (Cognitive)
- Improve academic performance
- Increase interest in learning
- Improve judgment
- Promote self-discipline
- Encourage setting health-related goals and achieving these goals
- Prevent or ameliorate feelings of depression

Social-Emotional (Affective)
- Improve self-confidence, self-discipline, and self-control
- Strengthen peer relationships
- Reduce the likelihood of experiencing depression
- Promote healthier lifestyles

Physical (Psychomotor)
- Reduce risk of coronary heart disease, type 2 diabetes, obesity, high blood pressure, and colon cancer
- Improve muscular strength and endurance, flexibility, and cardiorespiratory endurance
- Regulate weight and improve body composition
- Strengthen bones
- Develop fundamental movement and sport skills
- Promote overall health and fitness

Tennis is a lifetime activity that can be enjoyed with family and friends.
© JUPITERIMAGES/Creatas/Alamy RF

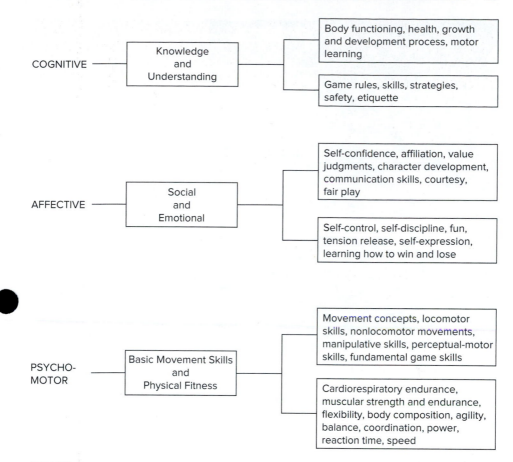

FIGURE 1.1

Objectives of physical education, exercise science, and sport.

learning basic and efficient movement patterns. Children explore their bodies' capabilities as they learn to walk, run, or jump independently, in conjunction with others, or while using a piece of equipment. Similar principles can apply as individuals experiment with solving other movement challenges. Manipulative skills are developed by moving your body relative to hoops, ropes, balls, rackets, bats, and other implements. Perceptual-motor skills, such as the eye-hand coordination needed to strike a ball with a racket or the reaction time needed to judge how quickly a partner's thrown ball will arrive, also are fundamental skills. Once these abilities are mastered developmentally and independently, skills such as catching, throwing, and batting can be incorporated into playing lead-up games and sports.

Figure 1.1 summarizes the objectives of physical education, exercise science, and sport. It is essential to recognize that these objectives interrelate rather than exist in isolation. For example, while learning to hit a tennis ball, people not only enhance their eye-hand coordination but also learn proper body position for a level swing and cooperation with those with whom they take turns tossing a ball.

Rafting can contribute to cognitive, affective, and psychomotor benefits.
Courtesy Terry Dash

Physical activity enhances quality of life beginning in the early years.
© Christopher Futcher/Getty Images RF

Box 1.3 provides several examples of how the objectives of physical education and sport are achieved and interrelated. It also should be emphasized that the breadth of the outcomes sought through physical education, exercise science, and sport programs makes it challenging to maintain a focused field of study.

SUMMARY

Physical education, exercise science, and sport programs seek to improve the quality of life and the physical well-being of participants. People of all ages enjoy playing games, engaging in recreational activities, and exercising to maintain good health. Competitive, rule-bound sports provide opportunities to test one's skills against opponents. Through these programs, the all-around development of the individual

BOX 1.3   EXAMPLES OF PHYSICAL EDUCATION, EXERCISE SCIENCE, AND SPORT OBJECTIVES

Cognitive Development

- The participant will explain the principles for playing zone defense in basketball.
- The participant will analyze the technique for executing a tennis serve.
- The participant, using the entire stroke (whole teaching method), will synthesize the principles of learning the crawl stroke in swimming.
- The participant will apply knowledge of cardiovascular system functioning in establishing a personal fitness program.
- The participant will evaluate another person's weight-lifting technique and provide corrective feedback.

Affective Development

- The participant will express appreciation for the excellence of an opponent's performance.
- The participant will enjoy playing hard and doing his or her best, regardless of the outcome of the game or event.
- The participant will cooperate and take turns with others.
- The participant will demonstrate fair play in unsupervised and non-officiated sports and activities.
- The participant will value the rights of others and regulations governing the situation.

Psychomotor Development

- The participant will improve eye-hand coordination by regularly practicing racquetball forehand and backhand shots. (motor skill development)
- The participant will explore ways to manipulate a ball without using the hands. (motor skill development)
- The participant will demonstrate the proper technique for executing a volleyball spike. (motor skill development)
- The participant will execute four exercises designed to improve flexibility of the shoulders. (physical fitness)
- The participant will develop and implement a daily program of at least 30 minutes of aerobic activity. (physical fitness)
- The participant will engage in a weight-lifting program at least 3 times a week. (physical fitness)

is enhanced during activity. The purpose of these programs is to optimize quality of life through enjoyable physical activity and sport experiences. Educational objectives through cognitive, affective, and psychomotor (physical fitness and motor skill) development are sought and achieved. A significant challenge facing you as a physical education, exercise science, and sport professional is to help others participate in regular physical activity so they can enjoy the associated health benefits. Complete the lifestyle survey in Box 1.4 to see what your personal status is. You also might want to take advantage of resources like those for Student Fitness Assessments in (Box 1.5).

BOX 1.4   LIFESTYLE SURVEY

Do you make healthy choices and behave in ways that contribute to living a physically fit life? Do you daily act in ways that positively contribute to each of the five dimensions of wellness? Complete this short survey by answering yes or no and see whether this is the case. If not, what changes should you make to help you enact these healthy behaviors?

Yes	No	
		1. I engage in vigorous physical activity that elevates my heart rate for at least 30 minutes at least 3 days a week.
		2. I engage in exercises to increase my muscular strength and endurance at least 3 times a week.
		3. I engage in stretching exercises to increase my flexibility at least 3 times a week.
		4. I eat a balanced diet based on the appropriate number of servings based on the guidelines of ChooseMyPlate each day.
		5. I eat the same number of calories that I expend so that I maintain a healthy weight.
		6. I am able to identify and appropriately deal with the stress in my daily life.
		7. I take time out each day to relax and relieve the tension that I experience.
		8. I get an adequate amount of sleep each day.
		9. I do not smoke or use smokeless tobacco products.
		10. I do not abuse alcohol.
		11. I do not use performance-enhancing drugs.
		12. I do not use drugs other than those prescribed by a physician.
		13. I follow the directions of athletic trainers and physicians in recovering from injuries.
		14. I avoid behaviors that will lead to the transmission of sexually transmitted diseases.
		15. I spend time with family and friends in socially enjoyable situations.
		16. I set aside quiet time for myself whenever it is needed.
		17. I have an identified value system that I live by each day.
		18. I am a good friend to other people and enjoy the friendship of others.
		19. I am committed to using my intellectual abilities to learn and develop.
		20. I have set career goals that I am working to achieve.

BOX 1.5   FITNESS ASSESSMENTS

Check out these resources to help determine how fit you are.

1. Go to www.active.com/fitness/calculators/heartrate to calculate your target heart rate.
2. Go to www.healthchecksystems.com/heart.asp to calculate your exercise or training heart rate zone.
3. Go to www.choosemyplate.gov/ to determine a healthy nutritional plan just for you.
4. Go to http://www.nhlbi.nih.gov/health/educational/wecan/healthy-weight-basics/body-mass-index.htm to calculate your BMI.
5. Go to www.adultfitnesstest.org to take the President's Challenge Adult Fitness Test.

CAREER PERSPECTIVE

KATHIE DAVIS

Co-Founder and Executive Director
IDEA Health and Fitness Association
San Diego, California

EDUCATION

B.S., physical education, San Diego State University

Courtesy Kathie Davis

JOB RESPONSIBILITIES AND HOURS

Kathie and her husband oversee the operations of the IDEA Health and Fitness Association, which provides information and educational products, services, and opportunities to 62,000 fitness professionals in over 80 countries. In her leadership role, she ensures that all external communications are consistent with company values and acts as the IDEA spokesperson to the media. She oversees three annual conventions, three publications, a website, IDEA's awards processes and ceremonies, and all advisory committees. She helps ensure that the 43 staff members are productive and enjoy rewarding experiences while serving in their various roles. In addition to a 9 A.M. to 5 P.M. workday at the office on Monday through Friday, Kathie keeps current through reading industry publications at home. She also completes other job-related functions, such as responding to e-mail messages, in the evening hours. During the three conventions, her days start early and end late due to the intensity of these special events.

SPECIALIZED COURSE WORK, DEGREES, AND EXPERIENCES NEEDED FOR THIS CAREER

An undergraduate degree in physical education helped prepare Kathie to establish her company. While no certifications or advanced degrees are required in her role, she has found that basic nutrition courses and public speaking courses and experiences have been especially helpful to her. She also benefited from the anatomy, kinesiology, and adult fitness courses she completed. As an entrepreneur, she has continuously expanded her knowledge, skills, and abilities through the years as she managed the operations of her company. Her husband oversees many of the business aspects of the organization, including marketing, advertising, exhibiting, hiring, and strategic planning.

SATISFYING ASPECTS

Ever since Kathie and her husband started IDEA Health and Fitness Association in 1982, the most satisfying aspect of her career has been helping fitness professionals grow to their full potential. To reemphasize this point, she and Peter are committed to this premise: "that by fostering professionalism in the health and fitness industry, we could help millions of people around the world live healthier, happier lives." Kathie enjoys what she does so much that there is nothing she dislikes about her professional position.

JOB POTENTIAL

As an owner and executive director, there are no opportunities for advancement, but none are desired. Broadly within the health and fitness industry, though, interested individuals can become personal trainers, work with special populations, such as senior citizens, cardiac rehabilitation patients, or people with special needs, or work in public or private clubs. Like Kathie, you could choose to start your own business to help others get and maintain fit lifestyles.

SUGGESTIONS FOR STUDENTS

If you would like a career working in, managing, or owning a health or fitness organization, an undergraduate degree in the field of physical education or exercise science is a must.

Kathie also recommends considering a double major in business or a minor in business because what you would learn in these courses would greatly supplement your knowledge about the human body and how it functions optimally. A master's degree in the field of health and fitness also would be beneficial. Kathie strongly encourages you to join a professional association in the health and fitness area. What you learn through reading professional publications and attending conferences will give you an advantage when entering the workplace.

IDEA offers a comprehensive Career Guide on its website (http://www.ideafit.com /fitness-career) for individuals in all stages of their fitness or exercise-related careers. This online platform is free and provides students with expert advice on fitness and exercise-related careers, educational programs, certification guidance, and practical career enhancing tools. Users can access industry statistics on compensation and benefits by job title/ specialty area and by region of the United States and also learn how to establish and build a personal and professional brand in the fitness industry.

KEY POINTS

Physical education	Educational process of developing physically, mentally, socially, and emotionally.
Sports	Competitive physical activities governed by rules.
Exercise science	Application of science to the study of the body in motion.
Quality of life	Physical activity is for everyone because it is essential to health and well-being.
Health benefits of participating in physical activity	Children and adolescents: Improved cardiorespiratory and muscular fitness; improved bone health; improved cardiovascular and metabolic functioning; favorable body composition. Adults: Lower risk of coronary heart disease, stroke, high blood pressure, type 2 diabetes, colon cancer, and breast cancer; prevention of weight gain; improved cardiorespiratory and muscular fitness; prevention of falls; reduced depression.
Surgeon General's report on *Physical Activity and Health*	Americans could significantly improve their health and the quality of their lives by participating in regular physical activity.
Obesity	Adults: 34.9% are obese. Children and adolescents: 16.9% are obese (have high BMI).

Healthy People 2020	Continued the national efforts to help people live longer, healthy lives with an emphasis on regular participation in physical activities and an ecological approach to disease prevention and health promotion.
2008 Physical Activity Guidelines for Americans	Regular physical activity reduces the risk of many adverse health outcomes, with additional benefits occurring as the amount of physical activity increases through higher intensity, greater frequency, and/or longer duration.
Components of health-related physical fitness	Cardiorespiratory endurance; muscular strength; muscular endurance; flexibility; body composition.
FITT principles	Frequency; intensity; time; type.
Benefits of flexibility	Increases flexibility for exercise and other daily activities; improves range of motion of joints; enhances circulation of the blood and healing of muscular injuries; relieves stress and relaxes muscles.
Benefits of resistance training	Increase muscular strength; enhances muscle fiber adaptation and hypertrophy (increase in the size of the muscle); increases bone mineral density and offsets osteoporosis; decreases the percentage of body fat and increases fat-free mass; enhances functioning of the cardiovascular system.
Basic movement skills	Locomotor skills like running and jumping; non-locomotor skills like twisting and balancing; manipulative skills like swinging a racket or a bat; perceptual-motor skills like heading a soccer ball or catching a fly ball.

REVIEW QUESTIONS

1. What are the two overarching goals of *Healthy People 2020* and two examples of the physical activity objectives?

2. What are the five components of health-related physical fitness and what does each include?

3. What are six components of skill-related physical fitness and what does each include?

4. How does each of the principles of training impact the development of physical fitness?

5. What types of knowledge are important within the cognitive domain of physical education, exercise science, and sport?

6. How are the social and emotional outcomes of the affective objective achieved in physical education, exercise science, and sport programs?

7. What are locomotor skills, non locomotor movements, manipulative skills, and perceptual-motor skills?

STUDENT ACTIVITIES

1. Interview three individuals of different ages (for example, below 18, mid-30s, and over 60) to determine what role physical activity plays in their lives.

2. Ask at least two friends who are not majors in your field what they think physical education, exercise science, and sport are.

3. Write a one- or two-page description of how you would incorporate three movement concepts or skills into a youth soccer or tennis program.

4. Write a one-page summary of how the three domains of physical education, exercise science, and sport objectives have influenced your life and career choice.

5. Investigate the physical fitness status of youth with special emphasis on the risk of obesity. Write a one-page description of this health crisis.

REFERENCES

Healthy people 2020. (2010). Washington, DC: U.S. Government.

Physical activity and health, a report of the Surgeon General. (1996). Washington, DC: Department of Health and Human Services.

2008 Physical activity guidelines for Americans. Washington, DC: U.S. Government.

 **WEB CONNECTIONS**

1. www.healthypeople.gov
   This site includes extensive information about the *Healthy People 2020* initiative, including links to state health plans and a wealth of information about health topics.

2. www.cdc.gov/
   The Centers for Disease Control and Prevention provide a plethora of information and data about healthy living and health-related topics.

3. www.nih.gov/
   The National Institutes of Health provide health information on topics from A to Z, MedlinePlus (a health database maintained by the National Library of Medicine), and a wealth of other health-related resources.

4. www.fitness.gov/
   Visit this site of the President's Council on Fitness, Sports and Nutrition to learn more about its activities to coordinate and promote opportunities in physical activity, fitness, sports, and nutrition for all Americans, as well as to find links to the physical activity guidelines and dietary guidelines.

5. www.cdc.gov/nccdphp/sgr/
   Read the text of the Surgeon General's report on *Physical Activity and Health*.

6. www.healthfinder.gov/
   This handy reference site of the U.S. Department of Health and Human Services provides an encyclopedia of over 1,600 health topics, free interactive personal health tools, health news, and much more.

7. www.projectfitamerica.org/
   Project Fit America provides funding to schools for developing exemplary fitness education programs for students in grades K–12. Nearly 1,000 schools have benefited from donations from hospitals and health care organizations to get youth engaged in cardiovascular health and fitness.

8. www.ncppa.org/
   The National Coalition for Promoting Physical Activity is a collaborative partnership of national organizations that seeks to engage all Americans in more physically active lives through coordinated educational campaigns, including facts sheets and policy development.

2

EXERCISE AND SPORT SCIENCES

LEARNING OUTCOMES

- Students will be able to describe the four characteristics of an academic discipline.
- Students will be able to explain how the 10 exercise and sport sciences borrow from the content knowledge, research methods, and scientific foundations of traditional fields of study.
- Students will be able to describe the fundamentals and basic research interests of researchers in the ten exercise and sport sciences.
- Students will be able to articulate how art, music, and literature can relate to the exercise and sport sciences.

A critical issue in the fields of physical education, exercise science, and sport is whether they can be considered academic fields of study. A major question debated has been whether exercise physiology, athletic training, motor development, motor learning, sport biomechanics, sport history, sport management, sport philosophy, sport and exercise psychology, and sport sociology possess a theoretical body of knowledge that merits scholarly study. In this chapter, each of these exercise and sport sciences will be described with an emphasis on their theoretical and scholarly content.

WHAT IS AN ACADEMIC DISCIPLINE?

An **academic discipline** is a formal body of knowledge discovered, developed, and disseminated through scholarly research and inquiry. The components of an academic discipline include:

- A body of knowledge
- A conceptual framework
- Scholarly procedures and methods of inquiry
- Combination of the process of discovery and end result

If physical education, exercise science, and sport merit the distinction of being called academic disciplines, these four criteria must be met.

A body of knowledge refers to a specific area of study yielding answers to important questions. Researchers have discovered and continue to share information of value with other researchers and practitioners. Examples of their contributions include studies about the effects of drugs on physical performance, importance of feedback to learning, role of sports in developing cultures, and the physiological, psychological, historical, or sociological impact of physical activity on people.

Similarly, research studies in an academic discipline must be guided by a conceptual framework. Hypotheses and experimental designs, strict controls, absence of bias, accurate reporting of findings, and interpretive analyses should characterize the process of discovering new knowledge. This process requires stringent adherence to protocols to give credibility to the results (see the Research View Research Methods for descriptions of these and other terms).

⌕ RESEARCH VIEW

Research Methods

Research questions   are the specific inquiries researchers conducting experiments or investigations seek to answer.

Hypothesis   is a tentative assumption or statement established to test its empirical consequences through experiments or interventions.

Experimental design   is the process through which researchers develop experiments or data collection methods to ensure that the data collected will answer the research questions.

Experiment   is the imposing of a treatment or intervention on a group of subjects and observing the responses.

Controls   are subjects who receive no treatment or intervention.

Experimental bias   favors certain outcomes over others in the absence of controls.

Randomization   occurs when subjects are assigned randomly to experimental groups to create homogeneous treatment groups and eliminate potential biases.

Placebo effect   prevents subjects from perceiving a positive outcome even though they receive no treatment.

Double-blind   studies prevent experimental bias and the placebo effect by ensuring that neither the researcher nor the subjects know what treatment is being received by whom.

Replication   is the repetition of an experiment on another or larger group of subjects.

Validity   is the degree to which a study accurately assesses what the researcher is measuring.

(continued)

External validity   is the extent to which the results can be applied or generalized more broadly.

Internal validity   describes inferences regarding cause-and-effect or causal relationships.

Reliability   is the accuracy of the measuring instrument or procedure.

Sampling   is a statistical procedure for selecting units from a population of interest to measure in a research project, so the results can be generalized or applied to this population.

Data analysis   is the process of examining and transforming data in order to summarize a situation, highlight useful information, discover relationships, and suggest conclusions.

Observational studies   collection and analysis of data without making any changes or using any interventions.

Primary sources   are first-hand testimonies, direct evidence, or original materials or information about a topic being investigated.

Secondary sources   are after-the-fact accounts, interpretations, or summarizations of primary sources.

Steps of the Scientific Method

1. Ask a question or state a problem that is measurable.

2. Conduct background research and gather information to learn from the work of others what is already known and what might be the best way to answer the stated question.

3. Formulate a hypothesis, which is an educated guess of what you think will happen.

4. Perform an experiment to test the hypothesis.

5. Collect, analyze, and display the data from the experiment to determine if the hypothesis is true or false, possibly using statistical software, charts, and graphs.

6. Draw conclusions based on the results of the experiment, which may lead to a new hypothesis or replication of the study in a different way to confirm the results.

7. Communicate the results to others.

A **research study** typically includes an introduction; a review of the literature to explain and analyze previous, related research; methods that describe how the data were collected and analyzed; results; and discussion and conclusions.

Types of Research

- Quantitative research, which is often used in the physical and natural sciences such as chemistry and physiology, relies on a hypothesis that can be proved or disproved based on mathematical or statistical means using the manipulation or one or more variables with an experimental group.

- Qualitative research, which is often used in the social sciences such as psychology and sociology, is a flexible approach that seeks information about human behavior and what governs this behavior. Data or information gathered cannot be analyzed mathematically but can be used to draw conclusions about the individuals studied.

- Mixed methods research uses a combination of qualitative and quantitative approaches in the research process and collects, analyzes, and reports quantitative and qualitative data to better understand and answer research questions.

Research Designs

- Experimental research deals with the manipulation of independent variables to generate data and draw statistical conclusions.

- Quasi-experimental research use pre-existing or naturally formed groups so there is an absence of random assignment. Because of the possibility of confounding variables, conclusions about causal relationships may not be possible.

- Descriptive research depicts characteristics of people that already exist rather than measuring the effect of a variable, such as through case studies, interviews, and ethnographic observations.

- Opinion-based research, such as through the use of questionnaires or surveys, collects data from a sample group of people to determine their preferences.

Scholarly procedures and methods of inquiry are built on a conceptual framework. For example, the sport historian, whenever possible, uses primary, rather than only secondary, sources in examining significant events. Motor development specialists evaluate the role of genetics and the environment in assessing readiness to learn. The exercise physiologist controls extraneous variables when analyzing the effect of a treatment, such as consuming a different diet or taking a specific drug, on a training regimen.

In seeking knowledge, the process of discovery and the end result are equally important. How the researcher collects data influences the findings; therefore, accuracy in reporting and interpretation is vital. Also, replication studies should consistently verify the results.

Other characteristics of an academic discipline include a substantial history and tradition, a broad scope that is unique in comparison with other fields, and a specific language. Thus, to qualify as an academic discipline, a field of study must contribute to the body of knowledge by using a conceptual framework, scholarly procedures and methods of inquiry, theoretical processes of discovery, and analyses of the end results.

THE SCIENTIFIC FOUNDATIONS OF THE EXERCISE AND SPORT SCIENCES

Kinesiology is broadly defined as the study of human movement. This term is used commonly in higher education to describe academic departments that take an interdisciplinary approach to studying physical activity and human movement and their consequences, such as through exercise physiology, sport psychology, biomechanics, and motor learning.

Numerous academic fields of study contribute principles and methods of scientific inquiry used by researchers in kinesiology. One cornerstone is biology, the study of life and life processes. On these biological facts and information are built anatomy, physiology, chemistry, and physics. Anatomy and physiology are the studies of the structure and function, respectively, of the human body. Chemistry is the study of the composition, properties, and reactions of matter. The specialization of biochemistry focuses on biological substances and processes, such as how the body's cells use food to obtain energy through respiration. The study of physics examines interactions between matter and energy, including various types of motion and forces. These and other sciences rely on applied mathematical concepts and computations.

History, philosophy (including sport ethics), psychology, and sociology are often called social sciences because they seek knowledge in more experiential ways and involve people. Table 2-1 shows relationships between these disciplines and those specific to sport. Figure 2.1 shows the association of the exercise and sport sciences with the natural, physical, and social sciences.

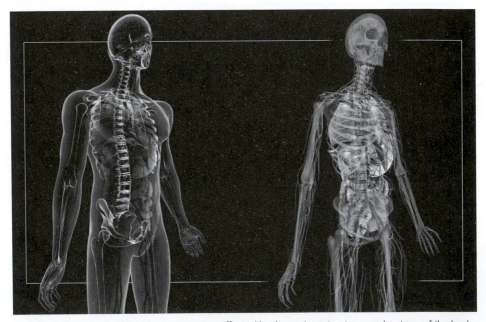

Kinesiology is the study of human movement as affected by the various structures and systems of the body.
© MedicalRF.com/Getty Images

TABLE 2-1		
RELATIONSHIPS AMONG DISCIPLINES		
Influencing Discipline	*Exercise and Sport Science*	*Shared Research Interests with*
Anatomy Biology Chemistry Physiology	Exercise physiology	Motor learning Sport biomechanics Athletic training Sport and exercise psychology
Anatomy Physical therapy Physiology Psychology	Athletic training	Exercise physiology Sport biomechanics Sport and exercise psychology
Biology Physiology Psychology	Motor development	Exercise physiology Motor learning Sport biomechanics
Anatomy Physiology Psychology	Motor learning	Exercise physiology Motor development Sport biomechanics
Mathematics Physics	Sport biomechanics	Exercise physiology Motor learning Athletic training
History Philosophy Sociology	Sport history	Sport philosophy Sport sociology
Accounting Ethics Finance Law Management Marketing	Sport management	Sport philosophy Sport sociology
History Philosophy	Sport philosophy	Sport history Sport sociology
Physiology Psychology Sociology	Sport and exercise psychology	Exercise physiology Athletic training Sport sociology
History Philosophy Sociology	Sport sociology	Athletic training Sport history Sport philosophy Sport and exercise psychology

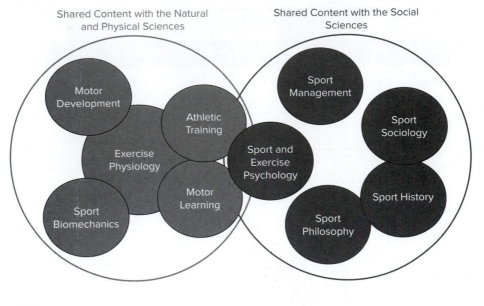

FIGURE 2.1

Interrelationships among the Exercise and Sport Sciences.

SUB-DISCIPLINES IN THE EXERCISE AND SPORT SCIENCES

Exercise physiology is the study of the body's response to physical activity and stress. This disciplinary field includes the analysis and improvement of fitness and health, guidance of active individuals as they adapt to exercise programs, and the prescription of exercise for rehabilitation from diseases and disabilities.

As described in Chapter 8, George Fitz helped establish the first exercise physiology laboratory at Harvard University over a century ago through which he advocated using research to substantiate or refute physical activity claims. Exercise physiology, which became the cornerstone of early collegiate physical education programs, grew in stature after the establishment of the American College of Sports Medicine in 1954. This organization brought together (or rejoined—see Chapter 8) the medical and scientific communities in the shared quest to investigate all aspects of the impact of physical activity on the body.

The study of exercise physiology is built on an understanding of the anatomical and physiological bases for human movement, including the 208 bones in the human skeleton; joint structure, which includes cartilage, ligaments, and muscular attachments; muscular system; nervous system; and circulatory and respiratory systems. More than 400 muscles, through a system of levers in conjunction with the skeletal system, provide the physiological key and guide to human movement. This potential for motion is released through the initiation of the nervous system and the biochemical reactions that supply muscles with energy.

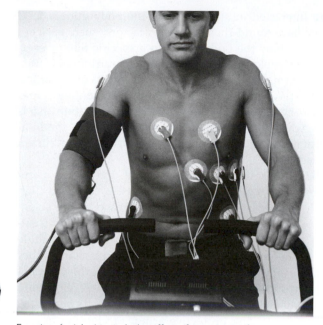

Exercise physiologists study the effect of exercise on the functioning of the cardiovascular system.
© Digital Vision/PunchStock RF

Exercise physiologists measure the metabolic responses of the body to exercise and training through various endurance, flexibility, and strength programs. Some researchers examine changes in the cardiovascular system, stroke volume, pulse rate, blood composition, and other physiological parameters. Other researchers study how the body utilizes carbohydrates, fats, and proteins during exercise; the effects of diet, smoking, and temperature on performance; and differences between trained and untrained individuals based on variables such as sleep, diet, or gender.

Because of their expertise in understanding bodily functions under the stress of muscular activity, exercise physiologists are often consulted about or given responsibility for prescribing and monitoring exercise programs for cardiac patients. Specialists in cardiac rehabilitation monitor exercise paradigms for individuals who have experienced cardiovascular trauma or prescribe preventive programs for people demonstrating coronary disease risk factors. Biomechanists and exercise physiologists often work together to design the most appropriate training programs for elite athletes, such as those at the United States Olympic Training Center in Colorado Springs.

Researchers in exercise physiology often prescribe workouts on treadmills to monitor oxygen uptake and expired carbon dioxide, take heart rate and function measurements, and analyze the chemical activities of the body. Exercise physiologists also conduct research projects with athletic trainers concerning the prevention and rehabilitation of injuries and with physicians in the areas of muscle biopsies and blood lactate analyses.

Exercise physiologists are interested in studying how the body utilizes food relative to energy output. They have found that numerous factors, such as sleep, drugs, work, and stress, influence how the body reacts to a specific diet or exercise paradigm. Biochemical and physiological tests isolate those nutritional factors that most dramatically affect performance. Studies include the effects of marathon training on nutritional needs, the risks or benefits of vitamin supplementation, and the effects of caffeine on various heart parameters. Nutritional information also is vital for the athlete in training who needs to maintain a specific weight, the individual with a disabling condition who is minimally active, and the senior citizen whose metabolic rate has slowed.

Clinical exercise physiology uses exercise and physical activity, in clinical and pathological situations, to provide functional benefits to clients at high risk for or living with chronic diseases. Specialists in this area promote scientific inquiry and the application of research findings to the prevention and treatment of chronic diseases and specific medical conditions. Those served include patients with cardiovascular, pulmonary, metabolic, neuromuscular, and other diseases. Environmental exercise physiology focuses on examining how factors such as climate and altitude may impact the abilities of humans to develop their fitness levels. For example, the military benefits from knowing how its personnel deal with carrying weapons while wearing protective armor or clothing in arid countries; or the military may need to know how to ensure that its personnel maintain adequate hydration when engaged in extended military engagements. Exercise epidemiology studies the public health benefits of physical activity. Since researchers in this branch of medicine deal with the study and control of diseases, the exercise epidemiologist determines how individuals of different demographic groups may improve their quality of life, and possibly length of life, through regular participation in physical activity. For example, research on the effects of asthma on respiration has helped exercise physiologists develop specialized conditioning programs for athletes who have exercise-induced asthma (see the Research View Exercise Physiology).

Sport nutrition is an emerging field of study and interest as professionals discover and disseminate information about the science of applied nutrition. The *Dietary Guidelines for Americans, 2010* provide sound nutritional information and advice for everyone, children through senior citizens, and serve as the basis for federal food and nutrition education programs. Physical inactivity and poor diet are major contributing factors to health problems like cardiovascular disease and obesity. Some dietary plans by focusing on weight control and calorie counting, fail to emphasize balance, moderation, and variety in food choices. Everyone, including athletes and those who are physically active, should eat a healthy balance of nutritious foods. Sometimes, problems like eating disorders can result from an overemphasis on calories leading to an inadequate intake of nutrients, especially calcium and iron for females.

Some exercise physiologists concentrate their research on sport nutrition because of its impact on athletic performance. One way that athletes differ is in their need for carbohydrates, the body's most efficient energy source. While protein

RESEARCH VIEW

Exercise Physiology

In studying how the body functions during muscular activity, exercise physiologists may conduct research to answer these questions:

- What are the metabolic responses of nonfit adult bodies during endurance training?

- What is the most effective method for developing and maintaining muscular strength for female athletes?

- How do various diets or nutritional supplements affect the performances of elite athletes?

- What types of fitness programs are appropriate for senior citizens?

- How do individuals with high levels of cardiorespiratory fitness differ in their stroke volume, blood lactates, perceived exertion, and pain tolerance from those who engage in no cardiorespiratory fitness training?

- What kinds of fitness routines should an exercise physiologist prescribe for participants in a cardiac rehabilitation program?

- What should be the optimal frequency, intensity, and duration for an off-season conditioning program for athletes on a baseball team?

- What effect does ethnicity have on athletic performances such as sprints in track or rebounding in basketball?

- What is the current physical fitness status of school-age children?

---

helps build muscle mass, a balanced diet meets the body's needs without protein supplementation. Similarly, there is no research that shows that performance is enhanced by taking vitamin or mineral supplements. Sport nutritionists can provide guidance to athletes and other active people on these and other topics, such as when to eat relative to competition and hydration issues.

Athletic training is the study and application of the prevention, analysis, treatment, and rehabilitation of sport injuries. The term sports medicine includes athletic trainers, physicians (who may be general practitioners), orthopedic surgeons, or other specialists. Physicians often are responsible for clearing athletes for practice and competition as well as attending to the needs of athletes in events in which the risks of injury are high. Athletic trainers are involved with athletes almost daily. They help design conditioning programs appropriate to specific sports during the preseason, postseason, and off-season; they tape, preventively as well as protectively, athletes before activity; and they are responsible for assessing injuries at the time they occur, providing immediate and appropriate first aid,

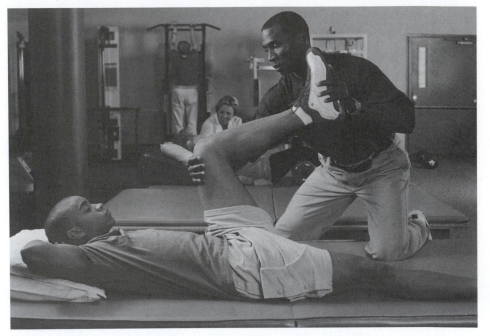

Athletic trainers can help athletes increase their range of motion following an injury.
© Royalty-Free/Corbis

and supervising the rehabilitation process, which may include recommendations from a physician.

Extensive knowledge of the anatomy and physiology of the body and skill in applying this knowledge to injury situations are essential for athletic trainers. Sometimes they need to be able to console injured athletes and keep them from trying to return to competitions or practices too quickly. At other times, athletic trainers need to encourage athletes to work more diligently during their rehabilitation (see the Research View Athletic Training).

Athletic trainers are expected to use various treatments, such as ultrasound, whirlpool, ice massage, or heat. These professionals constantly help athletes play despite minor injuries by using various treatments or taping techniques.

The National Athletic Trainers' Association (NATA) seeks to enhance the quality of health care for athletes and those engaged in physical activity and also advances the profession of athletic training through education and research in the prevention, evaluation, management, and rehabilitation of injuries. NATA was founded in 1950 and has grown to more than 30,000 members. NATA publishes the *Journal of Athletic Training,* a scientific journal published 6 times a year, and the *Athletic Training Education Journal*, a quarterly publication that combines theory and practice in the field. The Commission on Accreditation of Athletic Training Education is responsible for the accreditation of 360 professional (entry-level) athletic training programs.

Motor development encompasses the maturation and changes in motor behavior throughout life and the factors that affect them. Researchers in this field

⌕ RESEARCH VIEW

Athletic Training

The athletic trainer studies the prevention, evaluation, management, and rehabilitation of injuries through seeking answers to questions like these:

- What type of flexibility training will help reduce injuries in football?
- Why do more female athletes suffer from anterior cruciate ligament damage than do male athletes?
- What should athletes who seldom play during competitions do to maintain their cardiorespiratory conditioning?
- What is the optimal type of weight training for youth below age 12?
- What is the optimal rehabilitation program for a soccer athlete recovering from a hamstring strain?
- What is the proper protocol for assessing if an athlete has experienced a concussion and monitoring an athlete's full recovery from it?
- How can an athletic trainer help a gymnast who suffers from an eating disorder?
- What is the best treatment for ankle sprains?
- What is the athletic trainer's role in the nutrition of athletes?

---

examine factors that influence the performance of motor skills, including developmental differences that occur over time. Movement competencies are influenced by contributions from genetics as well as the environment. Throughout life, individuals continually progress from unskilled movements to the demonstration of more complex motor skills with accommodations made for age and any physical limitations. Motor development includes the process and results of motor behavior as well as the factors that affect it.

Motor development historically has been closely aligned with developmental psychology, such as through studies that examined behavioral sequences and the maturational process. Motor development includes the relationships between physical performance and growth and maturity and the positive influence of physical growth and development on motor performance. Educational psychology studies in perceptual-motor development concluded that improved motor skills lead to an enhancement of academic performance, and cognitive development positively affects skill acquisition over time. These findings were especially important because data from studies in this area have been used to justify school physical education programs for children. Researchers have found that dynamic systems, more than cognitive processes, account for enhanced motor performance (see the Research View Motor Development).

Much of the research in motor development is associated with children as they learn fundamental motor skills. However, adults also can learn new

🔍 RESEARCH VIEW

Motor Development

Specialists in motor development investigate questions such as these:

- When are children developmentally ready for weight training and cardiorespiratory training programs?
- What are the hereditary and environmental factors that most significantly influence obesity in children?
- How and why do weight training and cardiorespiratory training programs combat decreases in strength and endurance associated with advancing age?
- What are the characteristics of children who are developmentally ready for competitive sports?
- What are the developmental stages for learning fundamental movement skills?
- How does socioeconomic status, which affects nutritional health, affect the development of motor skills?
- How does a person's developmental level limit his or her ability to learn or improve performance of a motor skill?
- What factors determine the relationship between cognitive development and motor development in learning a complex motor skill?
- How does gender affect developmental readiness in motor development?

perceptual-motor skills. Longitudinal studies are especially beneficial in determining the varied factors that determine what, how, and why motor performance progresses. Interdisciplinary research, such as with exercise physiologists or motor learning specialists, not only strengthens present understanding but also paves the way for improved motor behavior.

Motor behavior is a broad term that encompasses motor control, motor learning, and motor development. Motor control is the study of the integration and maturation of muscular, skeletal, and neurological functions in executing movements. **Motor learning** is the study of the internal processes associated with movement or repetitive actions that result in changes in response or performance. Research in solving industrial problems (such as safe and efficient movements in the workplace) and military needs (such as pilot selection and training) laid the foundation for the emergence of the field of motor learning. Motor learning specialists have expanded their research and published scholarly manuscripts in journals such as the *Journal of Motor Behavior*. They complete studies dealing with the following:

- Closed-loop theory—how feedback following slow and discrete movements can be used to improve subsequent motor performances

Motor development researchers examine the process and sequence of learning movement skills.
Courtesy Judy Young

- Open-loop theory—how motor patterns, such as striking skills, can be generalized to a variety of sports or settings, with or without limited feedback
- Dynamic systems theory—how degrees of freedom in joints and muscles, along with neural control, can lead to enhanced motor performance
- Types of practice—the appropriateness and effectiveness of massed or distributed, blocked or random, mental or physical, and full- or reduced-speed practice sessions
- Cognitive processes in learning motor skills—how knowledge of results and knowledge of performance can affect subsequent motor patterns
- Transfer of learning—how motor skills learned in one setting can be generalized to another sport

Motor learning knowledge, such as various types of feedback, can enhance an archer's performance.
© Digital Vision/PunchStock RF

- Types of feedback—how intrinsic, extrinsic, terminal, concurrent, visual, verbal, constant, and interval feedback can influence motor performance
- Special needs—how individuals with special needs, including senior citizens, can regain and maintain their balance, coordination, reaction time, fundamental movement skills, and fitness levels

Motor program theory states that many movements or actions are performed with no explicit conscious control. In this open-loop control system, an individual identifies a stimulus, selects a response, initiates a motor program, and executes the movement. This motor program works efficiently in executing rapid serial skills that do not require feedback.

The fields of motor control and motor learning grew out of the area of psychology dealing with human performance and behavior. Whereas motor control focuses on the neurophysiological factors of how and why people move as they do, motor learning integrates the cognitive processing of information with motor skill acquisition (see the Research View Motor Learning).

The objective of these researchers is to understand and enhance human movement. In motor control, it is essential to investigate the neuromuscular pathways to improve the learning of motor skills. In motor learning, it is essential to build on this information and add knowledge of feedback and optimal practice methods. Motor control and learning researchers may use imaging or manipulation to help children with special needs learn new motor patterns. They may use verbal and kinesthetic cues to help young athletes learn complex motor skills such as heading a soccer ball.

RESEARCH VIEW

Motor Learning

Specialists in motor learning examine the variables that lead to improved performance of motor skills by responding to questions such as these:

- How and why do people's muscles respond differently to similar stimuli?
- How do massed and distributed types of practice affect motor performance?
- How do neurological responses to cues affect motor performance?
- What type of feedback should be provided to enhance motor skill acquisition and with what frequency?
- What type of practice, mental or physical, is optimal for improving a skill such as putting a golf ball or shooting a basketball free throw, and why?
- What is the relationship among a student's learning style, information-processing system, and ability to improve a motor skill?
- How do varying cognitive abilities affect the enhancement of motor skills?
- What is the interrelationship between information processing and skill acquisition?
- How does a person's reaction time influence the enhancement of motor skills?
- How does the aging process affect motor learning?

Sport biomechanics is the study of the anatomical and physiological effects of natural laws and internal and external forces acting on the human body during movement. Biomechanists study the musculoskeletal system, the principles of mechanics, and activity analyses. They examine the force of muscular contractions; flexion, extension, pronation, and supination of the muscles during activity; the composition of muscle fibers; equilibrium, center of gravity, and base of support; transfer of momentum; and projection of the body or an object. Their findings have contributed to improved athletic performance and have been used to prevent injuries, which is of special interest to physical therapists and athletic trainers. For example, through biomechanical analysis, minor flaws in throwing technique for the discus or stride length for sprinting can be identified and corrected to increase distance or reduce time. Scientific answers can be provided to questions such as What kind of shoe support is needed for individuals participating regularly in aerobics? What type of weight training is appropriate for judo or volleyball players? What type of exercise program is best for increasing joint flexibility of senior citizens?

Biomechanists explain movement in relation to acceleration, energy, mass, power, torque, and velocity. They rely on mechanical principles such as force

Pole vaulters can benefit from biomechanical analysis of their technique to enhance the height they can jump.
© Digital Vision/Getty Images RF

application and absorption, leverage, and stability. Use of cinematography (motion picture photography) has become common among coaches and teachers for the analysis of performance. Electromyography is the measurement of electrical discharges from a muscle to study the action potential and sequence of muscular activity. An analysis of the position and movements of joints is possible with electrogoniometry. Biomechanists also measure muscular forces using a force platform, determine speeds or frequencies using a stroboscope, and record movements and electrical responses (such as heart rate) using a telemeter. Computer-assisted analyses have helped isolate components of physical and movement skills that can be corrected or changed to improve efficiency.

Interest in the science of applying mechanics to human movement can be traced to the early 1900s, when the focus was on understanding anatomy and physiology. Notable curricular and research emphases during the following decades included body dynamics, efficiency of work, cinematic studies of sport skills, mechanical analysis of human performance, electromyography, and neurophysiology. Several scholars have conducted kinesiological studies grounded in the scientific foundation of physical education and sport that provided the basis for the development of this field. The founding of the International Society of Biomechanics and the publication of the *Journal of Biomechanics* were leading forces in the emergence of biomechanics as a specialty (see the Research View Sport Biomechanics).

Sport history is the descriptive and analytical examination of significant people, events, organizations, and trends that shaped the past. Sport historians investigate

RESEARCH VIEW

Sport Biomechanics

The sport biomechanist investigates questions such as these:

- What are the optimal design and composition of the pole used in pole vaulting?
- How can a sport biomechanist use computer-enhanced images to analyze and improve the performance of sport skills?
- What biomechanical factors contribute to muscular and joint injuries in baseball pitchers?
- How can fundamental movement skills such as running, jumping, and throwing be taught most effectively and efficiently?
- What mechanical principles are most important for reducing injuries and increasing the attainment of strength goals in weight-training programs?
- How does weight transfer affect force and aerodynamics in striking motions?
- Biomechanically, why did the crawl stroke and the Fosbury flop revolutionize swimming and the high jump, respectively?
- What are the most effective approaches for increasing an athlete's vertical jump?
- How and why does stride length differ between a sprinter and a distance runner?
- What biomechanical factors contribute to an effective tennis serve?

the past seeking to explain how, what, when, where, and why things occurred. Descriptive history explores events, individuals' contributions, and pivotal happenings using primary sources, such as archeological artifacts, original writings, and eyewitness accounts. Such first-hand information is judged to be reliable and accurate, especially when confirmed by other primary sources. When no original information is available, secondary sources must be used to document history. History reported in secondary sources, however, must be verified meticulously to ensure accuracy. The narrative approach is often used in descriptive history to chronicle events, individual lives, and developments.

Vital to an understanding of why events happened as they did is the more difficult interpretive or analytical work of historians. Such analyses attempt to explain the significance of events within their historical and social contexts. Sport historians record biographies, examine organizations and their activities, describe trends and movements, and analyze how and why societal events occurred as they did.

A clear understanding of modern sports depends on an examination of the significant events and practices of the past. Changes in this country that have

Sport historians examine how and why sporting events, such as the 1932 Los Angeles Olympic Games, have impacted the popularity of sports.
Library of Congress, Prints and Photographs Division [pan 6a28494]

influenced the emergence and predominance of sport include colonialism, the expanding frontier, rural life, the industrialized age, military involvement, the information age, and technological advances. Seminal works that laid the foundation for the emergence of the field of sport history include Foster Dulles's *Americans Learn to Play* (1940), John Betts's *America's Sporting Heritage, 1850–1950* (1974), and Robert Boyle's *Sport—Mirror of American Life* (1963). Led by physical educators, the North American Society for Sport History was established to legitimize the rising academic interest in this field. Through its *Journal of Sport History,* this organization, which includes individuals from a diverse group of disciplines, serves as the central forum for the promotion of sport history (see the Research View Sport History).

🔍 RESEARCH VIEW

Sport History

The sport historian may examine questions such as these:

- What was the significance of Greek athletes competing in the nude?
- When African Americans were excluded for decades from Major League Baseball, what developed and what role did they serve?
- Why were women initially excluded, then gradually included, in the modern Olympic Games?
- What role did the Industrial Revolution play in the growth and development of organized sport?
- What factors contributed to the establishment of the National Football League? How and why did its relationship with college football evolve as it did?
- How have sports played a role in the Americanization of various immigrant groups in this country?
- How and why was basketball spread internationally?
- How did upper-class sport affect the popularity of commercialized sport in this country?
- What role has gambling played in sports?
- Why do many consider the National Collegiate Athletic Association the most powerful amateur sport organization in the United States?

Sport management is the study of the theoretical and applied aspects of leading, planning, organizing, staffing, funding, and conducting sporting events. It includes accounting and budgeting, marketing, financing, the law, personnel, facilities, and organizational operations. This field encompasses the spectator sport and fitness industries, sporting goods sales, and recreational and sport programs in schools and colleges (see the Research View Sport Management).

Professionals working in the management of sport and leisure programs in the 1980s recognized the need to study and develop a specialized body of knowledge. The North American Society for Sport Management (NASSM) was established to promote, stimulate, and encourage research, scholarly writing, and professional development in sport management. This cross-disciplinary field encompasses management, leadership, and organizational behavior in sport, sport ethics, sport marketing, sport finance, sport economics, sport business in the social context, sport law, and sport governance. NASSM's *Journal of Sport Management* and *Sport Management Education Journal* provide venues for the publication of theoretical and

⬤ 🔍 RESEARCH VIEW

Sport Management

Academics and practitioners in sport management are interested in learning the answers to questions such as these:

- What amenities and experiences are important for increasing attendance at sporting events at the high school, college, and professional levels?
- How can private health and fitness clubs attract and retain members?
- What recreational and leisure-time activities are of most interest to individuals of all ages?
- How can professional sport teams in smaller metropolitan areas financially compete within Major League Baseball given the disproportionate revenues in comparison to teams in larger metropolitan areas?
- What economic factors are involved in joining a major college athletic conference? How does such a change affect the college's revenue- and non-revenue-producing sports?
- What are the legal liabilities for a professional sport team when fans are injured or cause injury to other fans?
- What leadership and management characteristics or traits are most important for the success of sport managers?
- What are the costs and benefits of awarding naming rights to a stadium or an arena?
- Why is market research important in sports?
- What responsibility does an athletic director have for the ethical conduct of interscholastic or intercollegiate athletes?

Sport managers are responsible for ensuring that fans enjoy all aspects of sporting events.
© Royalty-Free/Corbis

applied aspects of management related to sport, exercise, and recreation in a variety of settings, such as professional sports, intercollegiate athletics, interscholastic sports, health and fitness clubs, and recreational sport leagues.

Broadly defined, the sport industry involves sport products and services, all of which need sport managers. Career options exist in professional sports, intercollegiate athletics, interscholastic sports, recreation programs, the leisure and travel industry, private and public health and fitness clubs, and sporting goods businesses.

Sport managers must be competent in a number of areas to succeed in their careers. Demonstrating communication skills, facility and event management abilities, sport marketing skills, financial management skills, and personnel management abilities is imperative.

Sport philosophy is the study of the beliefs and values of humans as displayed within sport and an analysis of their meaning and significance. That is, sport philosophers examine the beautiful and ugly and the good and bad in sport as well as seek to understand how and why people play and engage in sport. Every person has a philosophy, although it may be unstated. One's philosophy is revealed through thought patterns, aspirations, and behaviors. Sport philosophers analyze concepts, make normative statements that guide practical activity, and speculate or extrapolate beyond the limits of scientific knowledge. Sport philosophers examine how physical education contributes to both educational objectives and social values by explaining the nature, importance, and reason for play and physical activity. Meeting people's needs, relating physical activity to human performance of all kinds, and enhancing the quality of life for others are roles of sport philosophy outside the schools. The establishment of the Philosophical Society for the Study of Sport and the publication of the *Journal of the Philosophy of Sport* helped establish the identity of this field (see the Research View Sport Philosophy).

RESEARCH VIEW

Sport Philosophy

The sport philosopher seeks truth and understanding by investigating questions such as these:

- What is the meaning of competition to an athlete?
- Why do sport fans develop strong allegiances to an athletic team?
- How and why do sports lose their elements of fun for many competitors?
- If sportsmanship is considered integral to sport, why do so many unsportsmanlike actions occur?
- Does participation in sport lead to the development of moral values? If so, how does this occur?
- Why is "taking out an opponent" considered ethical by some athletes?
- What is beautiful about sport?
- What is the role of play in life?
- Why is sport of such paramount interest to millions in this country?

Most individuals in physical education and sport use philosophy to analyze real-world issues. For example, what are the moral values depicted in films like *Chariots of Fire* or *Hoosiers?* Why do problems such as gambling, unscrupulous sport agents, and a lack of sportsmanship plague intercollegiate athletic programs today? Why do many athletes, even at the high school level, use performance-enhancing drugs? What lesson is learned by youth soccer players when the congratulatory hand-slap at the end of the game is eliminated because members of one team spit on their hands and then slapped their opponents' hands? Sport philosophy seeks to understand why such actions occur and what values they reflect.

Sport and exercise psychology is the study of human behavior in sports, including an understanding of the mental processes that interact with motor skill performance. Theories and laws of learning, the importance of reinforcement, and the linking of perceptual abilities with motor performance contribute to this body of knowledge. Sport and exercise psychologists utilize this information when studying topics such as achievement motivation, arousal, attribution, and personality development. Achievement motivation research examines how individuals perceive themselves and their accomplishments. Excitement and relaxation (as well as tension reduction) are among the parameters of arousal studies. The study of causal attribution weighs the importance placed on ability, effort, luck, and task difficulty relative to contest outcome. Aggression, competitiveness, anxiety, independence, extroversion, and self-confidence are among the personality traits researched. Sport and exercise psychologists also examine the

Restraining the progress of an opponent during a game is an example of trying to gain an unfair advantage in sports.
© altrendo images/Getty Images RF

influence of group dynamics, exercise addiction, and enhanced body image on people who are physically active.

The mental aspect of sports has intrigued researchers for years. Some have stated that at the elite level of sport, where all athletes are highly skilled, the outcome of the contest is overwhelmingly dependent on mental preparation and cognitive execution. Early researchers who stated there were psychological benefits from participating in sport and physical activity laid the foundation for the emergence of this field of study. The founding of the North American Society for the Psychology of Sport and Physical Activity in 1967 and the Association for Applied Sport Psychology in 1985, and their publications, the *Journal of Sport and Exercise Psychology* and *Journal of Motor Learning and Development* and the *Journal of Applied Sport Psychology, Journal of Sport Psychology in Action,* and *Case Studies in Sport and Exercise Psychology,* respectively, strengthened the development of this discipline.

Applied sport psychology focuses on understanding psychological theories and techniques to help athletes improve their performances. This area has grown in popularity as coaches and athletes seek competitive advantages. Specific strategies assist athletes in managing stress, concentrating more effectively, and maintaining confidence. Sport psychologists help athletes achieve their physical potential by improving their mental state (see the Research View Sport and Exercise Psychology).

RESEARCH VIEW

Sport and Exercise Psychology

The sport and exercise psychologist studies how to enhance motor performance through an examination of and interventions in areas such as these:

- How does an athlete's self-efficacy (how one feels about one's self and abilities) affect performance?
- Why is managing stress essential to success in sport?
- What role does mental imaging play in the execution of motor skills?
- How does participation in physical activity affect performance in cognitive tasks?
- What is the relationship between the body's psychological and physiological responses within sports?
- How does attribution influence the way an athlete deals with winning and losing?
- What is the difference in the arousal states of football linemen and elite golfers, and how can appropriate levels of arousal be shaped?
- How might the traditional pep talk given by a coach prior to a competition affect individual athletes differently?
- What are the most effective techniques for relaxation training?
- Why are sport psychologists increasingly being hired by individual athletes and teams?

Sport psychologists can help athletics deal with poor performances by visualizing how they will improve the mental and physical aspects of how they will play in the future.

© Brand X Pictures/PunchStock RF

The clinical interventions used by sport psychologists include relaxation training, biofeedback, breath control, desensitization, and mental imaging. These interventions help athletes cope with the pressures of competition.

Exercise psychologists advocate for the benefit that physical activity and physical fitness have on mental health and overall well-being. For example, exercise psychologists may work with individuals who are battling depression, which is an overall and persistent feeling of being dejected. Exercise psychologists use a variety of cognitive and behavioral therapies to help individuals deal with their depression through exercise, and especially cardiorespiratory exercise.

Sport sociology is the study of the social relationships of gender, race, ethnicity, class, and culture in the context of sport, and the social behavior of individuals, groups, organizations, institutions, and societies in sporting contexts. Sport sociologists examine social relationships in sports relative to equity, power, the media, politics, economics, and religion, as well as investigate issues of social inequality, social mobility, and social justice. They also analyze how sports shape society and society shapes sports. This discipline examines the role of sports in society by seeking to determine why people play and how participation in various physical activities influences them. The sport sociologist examines play, games, sports, recreational activities, and leisure-time pursuits in analyzing the expected outcomes of fun, relaxation, self-expression, wish fulfillment, and social interaction. The dynamics of socialization may reveal examples of racial and gender integration, exclusion, affiliation, competition, cooperation, conflict, rivalry, teamwork, and fair play.

Sport sociologists investigate sport as a game and as an institution. They examine the concepts of social mobility, class and gender stratification, status, racial and ethnic discrimination, team dynamics, social consciousness, and social values. Understanding the sociology of sport requires dealing with the relationship between sports and social institutions.

Gender issues, such as how females at early age may be encouraged to cheer for boys rather than participate in sports themselves, are studied by sport psychologists.
© SW Productions/Brand X Pictures/Getty Images RF

Sports are woven into the daily and seasonal fabric of American society. The social significance of sporting pastimes emerged from the British emphasis on sports in private boarding schools for boys in the mid-1800s. Schoolmasters and fathers came to believe that manly virtues learned through playing sports would prepare upper-class youth for their anticipated leadership roles in business, politics, and the military. This emphasis on character development through sports was adopted by organized sports in this country and has influenced attitudes toward sports at all levels.

Publications such as the *International Review of Sport Sociology* and the *Sociology of Sport Journal,* as well as the establishment of the North American Society for the Sociology of Sport, marked the emergence and acceptance of sport sociology as a distinct discipline. While a positivist, empirical-analytical paradigm that focused on describing and analyzing the social order of sport continues, sport sociology has moved to an interpretive research model. Scholars of this genre examine sport cultures from a variety of theoretical and methodological perspectives with an emphasis on interpretation. Today many sport sociologists take a critical inquiry approach that not only analyzes and interprets social dynamics but makes suggestions for transforming social structures (see the Research View Sport Sociology).

⌕ RESEARCH VIEW

Sport Sociology

The sport sociologist addresses questions such as these:

- What sociological factors may have contributed to a mother purchasing a death contract on a girl who beat out her daughter for a spot on a high school cheerleading squad?
- Why did a sophomore quarterback in high school commit suicide after leading his team to the state football championship?
- What are the sociological factors that have contributed to the current funding levels of girls' and women's athletic teams?
- Why are relatively few African Americans hired to coach professional and college sport teams?
- How are males and females socialized differently in and through sport?
- Why do over half of all children drop out of organized sports by age 12?
- Why are athletes permitted to act in violent ways during sporting events when these same acts would be illegal if they occurred outside of sport?
- Why has television been allowed to dictate rule changes and starting times for sporting events?
- How do socioeconomic factors affect individuals' participation in physical activity and sport?
- Does sport reflect society, or does society reflect what occurs in sport?

Box 2.1 is provided to help students more fully understand the interrelationships among the exercise and sport sciences. As shown in the Research Views, each of the exercise and sport sciences can make important contributions in the discovery of knowledge. Take the Exercise and Sport Sciences Quiz in Box 2.2 to review the key areas of emphasis for each of the exercise and sport sciences. All of the exercise and sport sciences contribute to the greater whole. Rather than being mutually exclusive, they interact with one another.

BOX 2.1   INTERRELATIONSHIPS AMONG THE EXERCISE AND SPORT SCIENCES

Content drawn mostly from the natural and physical sciences
- Athletic training
- Exercise physiology
- Motor development
- Motor learning
- Sport biomechanics

Content drawn mostly from the social sciences
- Sport history
- Sport management
- Sport philosophy
- Sport and exercise psychology
- Sport sociology

What do the Exercise and Sport Sciences emphasize the most in relative priority order?
- Athletic training—application; education; research
- Exercise physiology—research; education; application
- Motor development—education; application; research
- Motor learning—research; education; application
- Sport biomechanics—research; application; education
- Sport history—research; education; application
- Sport management—education; application; research
- Sport philosophy—research; application; education
- Sport and exercise psychology—research; education; application
- Sport sociology—research; education; application

What is the difference between motor development and motor learning?
- Motor development focuses on the development of fundamental movement patterns at any age, including factors such as genetic or environmental limitations. Running, jumping, throwing, and kicking are examples of motor development skills.
- Motor learning emphasizes making advances in motor skills through repetition and practice. Motor learning involves enhanced learning and skill enhancement such as through transfer of throwing skills from one sport to another and using feedback to change performance.

(continued)

BOX 2.1   INTERRELATIONSHIPS AMONG THE EXERCISE AND SPORT SCIENCES (continued)

How are motor learning and sport and exercise psychology related?

- Motor learning emphasizes motor skill enhancement using a variety of practice approaches, repetition, and knowledge of results. Motor learning focuses on bodily movements.
- Sport and exercise psychology emphasizes mental skill development, such as how the mind relates to positive and negative reinforcement and how the mind responds to motivation, arousal, and stress. Sport and exercise psychology focuses on how the mind impacts or influences how or why the body performs skillfully.

How are sport history and sport sociology intertwined?

- Sport history describes and analyzes the past with an emphasis on who, what, when, where, why, and how. It interrelates with sport sociology whenever interpretations are made about past occurrences within the societal sporting context.
- Sport sociology seeks to understand social behaviors and interpersonal relationships as impacted by class, culture, ethnicity, gender, and race in the context of sport. It interrelates with sport history through gaining an understanding of the role that sport serves in people's lives and identities.

BOX 2.2   EXERCISE AND SPORT SCIENCES QUIZ

Individual Exercise and Sport Sciences

1. Which of the exercise and sport sciences includes the study of oxygen utilization during cardiorespiratory exercise and metabolic responses to exercise and training?
2. Which of the exercise and sport sciences includes descriptions and analyses of past performances of athletes?
3. Which of the exercise and sport sciences includes the study of how people learn skills, especially through practice and feedback?
4. Which of the exercise and sport sciences includes the study of the social relationships of gender, race, ethnicity, class, and culture in the context of sport?
5. Which of the exercise and sport sciences includes analysis of the impact of motion, force, and energy on sport performance?
6. Which of the exercise and sport sciences includes analysis of the developmental patterns associated with movement and skill performance?
7. Which of the exercise and sport sciences includes extensive knowledge of the body to help athletes stay injury free and return to competition safely?
8. Which of the exercise and sport sciences includes the study of why people act as they do based on their values?
9. Which of the exercise and sport sciences includes the study of the theoretical and applied aspects of leading, planning, organizing, staffing, funding, and conducting sporting events?

(continued)

BOX 2.2   EXERCISE AND SPORT SCIENCES QUIZ (continued)

10. Which of the exercise and sport sciences includes the study of various mental coping strategies to enhance sport performances?

Exercise and Sport Sciences Working Collaboratively

11. In which two or three of the exercise and sport sciences would professionals be interested in, and possibly conduct research studies about, the development of muscular strength and endurance following injury or surgery?

12. In which two or three of the exercise and sport sciences would professionals be interested in, and possibly conduct research studies about, how acceleration or force affects the learning and enhancement of motor skills?

13. In which two or three of the exercise and sport sciences would professionals be interested in, and possibly conduct research studies about, how race and gender have historically resulted in limited competitive opportunities in sports?

14. In which two or three of the exercise and sport sciences would professionals be interested in, and possibly conduct research studies about, how developmental readiness for strength and endurance training might help combat depression?

15. In which two or three of the exercise and sport sciences would professionals be involved when a director of athletics is confronted with the issue of non-compliance with academic standards by athletes?

16. In which two or three of the exercise and sport sciences would professionals be interested in dealing with an individual athlete's performance and the interactions among team members with different ethnicities?

17. In which two or three of the exercise and sport sciences would professionals be interested in, and possibly conduct research studies about, how skills in a lifetime sport are developed and participation in this sport maintained by formerly sedentary and overweight individuals?

18. In which two or three of the exercise and sport sciences would professionals be interested in designing a rehabilitation program that would enable an athlete to increase his or her ability to exert greater force and velocity when swinging a bat?

19. In which two or three of the exercise and sport sciences would professionals be interested in and possibly conduct research studies that examine gambling scandals in intercollegiate athletics?

20. In which two or three of the exercise and sport sciences would professionals be interested in, and possibly conduct research studies about, how various training regiments would enhance the performances of professional athletes in order to increase tickets sales and revenues?

Although the **humanities** are not a part of the exercise and sport sciences, they have made a significant contribution to sports. The humanities, which encompass the areas of art, literature, and music, are noteworthy from both historical and practical perspectives. Archaeological discoveries from early civilizations verify the significance attached to physical activity for survival, group affiliation, religious worship, and enjoyment. From Myron's *Discobolus* during the Greek zenith to R. Tait McKenzie's *The Joy of Effort* (which received the King's Medal in the Fine Arts Competition at the 1912 Stockholm Olympic Games) to a wall fresco of the first women's Olympic marathon champion Joan Benoit, art has vividly shown the beauty of human movement.

Homer's *Iliad* and *Odyssey* verify the importance of athletics in Greek times. Biographies of sport heroes and heroines abound. Sport historians and sociologists from an analytical perspective and journalists from a popular vantage point have been prolific in describing and praising sport teams, champions, and major events.

Music provides the rhythm for movement experiences for all ages. The Greeks exercised to the music of the lyre, and music became a vital component of German school gymnastics in the 1800s. Children in elementary physical education frequently experiment with and explore movement to the accompaniment of their favorite songs. In the 1980s, the addition of music to exercise routines helped popularize aerobics. Weight-training workouts and daily jogs often include music. Art, literature, and music can enhance the focus on the development of a fit body, the socializing nature of sport, and the free experimentation of movement, thereby facilitating the application of the body of knowledge comprising the exercise and sport sciences.

R. Tait McKenzie's *The Joy of Effort.*

Reprinted with permission from the University of Tennessee Press. From A.J. Kozar, R. Tait McKenzie, *The Sculptor of Athletes,* 1975, The University of Tennessee Press

SUMMARY

An academic discipline includes a body of knowledge, a conceptual framework, and scholarly procedures and methods of inquiry. Based on the heritage of physical education as a teaching profession, the exercise and sport sciences have drawn from and contributed to the knowledge base in multiple academic disciplines. Integral to the emergence and acceptance of the exercise and sport sciences as recognized academic disciplines are the extensive scholarly and scientific research studies that have informed the academic community as well as the general public about the importance of physical activity. The exercise and sport sciences have improved the human movement experiences of individuals of all ages and skill levels. Research findings have helped prevent health-related disabilities as well as assisted in the rehabilitation of individuals who have suffered from medical maladies. Despite critics who claim that these fields have no unique bodies of knowledge, scholars in the exercise and sport sciences have made significant contributions to a broader understanding of the historical, sociological, psychological, and physiological roles of exercise and sport in the lives of everyone.

CAREER PERSPECTIVE

RENÉ REVIS SHINGLES

Professor/Program Director
Central Michigan University
Mount Pleasant, Michigan

EDUCATION

B.A., health and physical education, University of North
Carolina at Chapel Hill
M.S., physical education: athletic training/sports medicine,
Illinois State University
Ph.D., psychosocial aspects of sport and physical activity,
Michigan State University

Courtesy of Central Michigan
University

JOB RESPONSIBILITIES AND HOURS

As a university professor and certified athletic trainer, Dr. Shingles teaches and directs an
athletic training curriculum accredited by the Commission on Accreditation of Athletic
Training Education. Courses taught include Cultural Considerations in Athletic Training,
Professional Development, and Athletic Training Internship. As the program director, she
also coordinates all aspects of the athletic training education program including the budget,
curriculum development, program assessments, and maintenance of accreditation standards; Dr. Shingles evaluates and supervises the front office staff, student staff, and faculty,
keeps records, and writes reports. Her typical work hours are 8:00 A.M. to 6:00 P.M. Some
evening and weekend hours also are required for class preparation, student evaluations,
and clinical supervision.

SPECIALIZED COURSE WORK, DEGREES, AND WORK EXPERIENCES NEEDED FOR THIS CAREER

Certification by the Board of Certification, Inc. and experience as a volunteer, intern, or
employed athletic trainer are essential prerequisites to teaching in this area. Licensure or
registration as an athletic trainer is required in some states. Dr. Shingles states that all athletic
training courses, sport sciences classes such as exercise physiology, and courses in instructional methodology have been beneficial in her current position. A master's degree is the minimal academic credential for a college position, although a doctoral degree in athletic training,
sports medicine, or a related area is the standard for a tenure-track position.

SATISFYING ASPECTS

Dr. Shingles enjoys sharing her experiences and developing relationships with students
who want to become athletic trainers. She finds it rewarding to work with and mentor
future professionals.

JOB POTENTIAL

Dr. Shingles holds a tenured position that carries the opportunity to advance from assistant
to associate to full professor. Depending on experience and academic degrees held, assistant professors at her university get starting salaries of about $42,500. Research, scholarly
publications, and teaching proficiency are required for promotion in rank and achievement of tenure. Salary increases and additional responsibilities are usually associated with
advancement.

SUGGESTIONS FOR STUDENTS

Obtaining a terminal (doctoral) degree is essential for teachers to advance in higher education. Dr. Shingles advises students to get involved in professional organizations (such as the National Athletic Trainers' Association) and to appreciate and cultivate relationships with mentors.

KEY POINTS

Academic discipline	Discovery of knowledge through a scholarly process of inquiry.
Research methods and scientific method	The discovery of knowledge must follow a rigorous process including research questions, experiments, data collection and analysis, reporting of results, and discussion of findings.
Exercise physiology	Scientific examination of how the body responds to physical movement, often using experimental treatments.
Athletic training	Prevention, analysis, treatment, and rehabilitation of sport injuries.
Motor development	Learning of motor patterns by individuals of all ages.
Motor learning	Changes in motor skill performance based on refinement in muscular, skeletal, and neurological function.
Sport biomechanics	Application of natural laws and forces to movement.
Sport history	Describing, analyzing, and learning from the past.
Sport management	Application of business principles and operations to sports.
Sport philosophy	Finding and applying beliefs and values in sports.
Sport and exercise psychology	Integration of mental processes with motor skill performances.
Sport sociology	Interactions among diverse social groups with society.
Humanities	Art, music, and literature enjoy numerous synergies and relationships with the exercise and sport sciences.

REVIEW QUESTIONS

1. What are the four characteristics of an academic discipline?
2. What is exercise physiology, and how has it become the leading disciplinary foundation of the exercise and sport sciences?
3. What are the differences between motor development and motor learning?
4. Describe the various content areas that constitute sport management.
5. Describe the scope of responsibilities for an athletic trainer.

6. What role could a sport psychologist serve with a professional athlete?
7. Explain two examples of how multiple exercise or sport sciences share research and application topics, questions, or issues.

STUDENT ACTIVITIES

1. Select any two of the 10 exercise and sport sciences and describe their contributions to sport.
2. Volunteer to help a faculty member or graduate student conduct a research project in one of the exercise and sport sciences.
3. Read a research article that contributes to the body of knowledge in any of the exercise and sport sciences. Summarize the major points of this article, the scholarly procedures and methods of inquiry used, and the end result of this study.
4. Invite specialists in any two of the exercise and sport sciences to your majors club to present overviews of each field of study and how these interrelate with the others.
5. Divide the exercise and sport sciences into the following groups:
   - Motor learning, motor development, and sport and exercise psychology
   - Exercise physiology, biomechanics, and athletic training
   - Sport history, sport philosophy, sport sociology, and sport management

   Conduct a class debate about the relative significance of the contributions of each of these groups.
6. Interview one of your professors who works in one of the exercise and sport sciences. Describe the type of research conducted by this person.

WEB CONNECTIONS

1. http://www.asep.org

   At this site learn more about how members of the American Society of Exercise Physiologists expand knowledge about the physiological mechanisms underlying physical activity. They provide analysis, improvement, and maintenance of health and fitness and study rehabilitation of heart disease and other chronic diseases and disabilities.

2. www.nassm.org/

   Visit this site to learn more about the North American Society for Sport Management, which has the purpose of promoting the study, research, and scholarship of the theoretical and applied aspects of sport management.

3. www.nata.org/

   This site for the National Athletic Trainers' Association provides a wealth of information for certified athletic trainers and links to the Board of Certification that certifies and recertifies athletic trainers.

4. http://naspspa.com/

   Learn more about the multidisciplinary North American Society for the Psychology of Sport and Physical Activity and its work to improve the quality of the scientific study of humans engaged in sport and physical activity and teaching and research in sport psychology, motor development, and motor learning.

5. www.gssiweb.org.en

   The Gatorade Sports Science Institute seeks to help athletes optimize their health and performance through education and research in nutrition and hydration.

6. www.acsm.org/

   The American College of Sports Medicine is comprised of physicians, academics, researchers, and students in sports medicine, exercise science, and health and fitness professions who conduct and disseminate research to help people live healthy lifestyles.

7. www.asbweb.org/

   The American Society of Biomechanics fosters an interdisciplinary exchange of information and ideas about the biological sciences, exercise and sport sciences, health sciences, ergonomics and human factors, and engineering and applied science.

8. www.asmi.org/

   The American Sports Medicine Institute seeks to improve the understanding, prevention, and treatment of sports-related injuries through research, technology-based education, and dissemination of information.

3

PROFESSIONS OF PHYSICAL EDUCATION, EXERCISE SCIENCE, AND SPORT

LEARNING OUTCOMES

- Students will be able to describe the characteristics of a profession and apply how these relate to individuals working in careers in physical education, exercise science, and sports.
- Students will be able to explain the meaning of pedagogy and how it applies in a variety of settings.
- Students will be able to expound on the scope of responsibilities, career options, and advantages and disadvantages of careers in physical education, athletic training, coaching, fitness, sport management, exercise science, and physical therapy following completion of majors or undergraduate programs of study in these areas.
- Students will be able to explain the programs, products, and services of several specialized professional organizations.

Physical education has long been recognized as a part of the teaching profession, evidenced by its affiliation with the National Education Association beginning in 1937. Teaching today has broadened significantly to include the use of effective instructional strategies in a variety of setting and with individuals of all ages. Today SHAPE America (Society of Health and Physical Educators) focuses its programs and services on school and college programs in physical education and health education. Additionally, this chapter describes several professional organizations so you can become interested in joining one of these as you begin your professional journey.

WHAT IS A PROFESSION?

While physical education has historically been classified as a profession, today numerous other fields of study and employment have earned this classification.

A **profession** is a specialized occupation that requires mastery of knowledge and the meeting of standards demonstrating competence. The characteristics of a profession include:

- A complex, systematic body of theoretical knowledge
- Individuals who have attained extensive knowledge and experience through a formal educational process
- Standards and competencies for entry into the profession, often through a certification process
- Mechanisms and opportunities for growth and development within the field to ensure adherence to established standards, competencies, and practices
- A socially valuable service that has received societal recognition and status
- Governance by a code of ethics to protect those served

Physical educators and exercise and sport scientists must have at least a bachelor's degree and frequently have advanced study and training in an extensive body of knowledge that takes considerable time and effort to learn. Individuals in these fields share research findings and new ideas while serving people throughout society.

Physical education teachers encourage children to have fun while challenging themselves with various movement experiences.
© McGraw-Hill Education/Lars Niki, photographer

While the preceding paragraph describes a profession, Chapter 2 presented the exercise and sport sciences as academic disciplines. Are these contradictory or complementary perspectives? Physical education, exercise science, and sport include the 10 specialized disciplines described in the previous chapter, any of which can be a career emphasis. As individuals study one of these disciplines in depth, they often take on a specialized identity like an exercise physiologist or a sport manager, even though their areas of work are based on physical activity or sport. Historically, physical education has been one of the professions focused on teaching. It has retained the characteristics of a profession even though it has expanded into teaching in numerous nonschool settings and into nonteaching, activity-related careers. Thus, physical education, exercise science, and sport have broadened to encompass aspects of both an academic discipline and a profession.

PEDAGOGY

Pedagogy is the art and science of teaching; the study of theories and application of teaching methods. The pedagogist (or teacher) must provide an effective learning environment that focuses on opportunities to master knowledge, skills, and attitudes. Each student or participant should spend most practice time "on task" rather than being subjected to management or organizational distractions such as waiting for a turn to use equipment. Each individual needs to be sequentially challenged by the movement experience or sport skill to achieve success while being motivated to pursue additional learning (see the Research View Pedagogy).

Qualified teachers are needed in numerous settings, such as exercise classes.
© ColorBlind Images/Blend Images RF

⌕ RESEARCH VIEW

Pedagogy

Teachers, in their continuing efforts to enhance pedagogical practices, seek answers to questions like these:

- What instructional strategies should be used to meet the various learning styles and multiple intelligences of students with a diversity of skills and abilities?
- How much class time in schools should be devoted to providing instruction, allowing for practice, giving feedback, dealing with discipline problems, managing equipment distribution, and checking attendance?
- At each developmental level, what is the appropriate amount of activity in physical education needed for school-age students?
- What adjustments, if any, should be made to provide the optimal learning environment for learners of all ages?
- How do the genders of teachers and students affect the number and quality of interactions?
- How can students and clients become engaged in developing personalized fitness programs?
- What role should students have in the selection and implementation of their physical education curriculum?
- What type of grouping, homogeneous or heterogeneous (or both), should be used to increase student learning in all types of instructional settings?
- How can a middle school physical educator design and implement a program that focuses on skill development and fun?
- What is the most effective method of giving feedback to students learning fundamental movement skills, new motor skills, and advanced sport skills?
- How can an accurate and effective assessment process be developed and implemented?
- Why and how should a personal trainer adapt strength training programs for adolescents, unfit adults, or senior citizens in a cardiac rehabilitation program?

A key objective for effective pedagogical practice is to use class or practice time optimally. Each teacher must plan extensively to ensure that equipment is readily accessible, handouts explaining the day's lesson are prepared for distribution, and instructional learning cues appropriate for students with heterogeneous abilities and ages are ready for use. The good teacher also is prepared to handle management tasks (such as calling roll and passing out equipment) and discipline problems with minimal loss of instructional and practice time. Each day's lesson should be sequentially structured to provide maximal opportunities to practice each new skill.

Another essential criterion of exemplary teaching focuses on helping students or participants achieve success and challenge themselves to higher levels of skill development. Specific, corrective feedback and positive reinforcing comments about proper execution of a skill or movement must be provided by the teacher. Only when each participant, within his or her individual limitations, enjoys learning will that person want to learn even more. A feeling of success is the key to enjoyment.

The primary reason people choose a career in teaching is the pleasure and reinforcement they receive when their students learn, enjoy the learning process, and continue to participate and develop their skills. Teaching is personally, more than financially, rewarding. This feeling of success occurs when teachers plan and implement innovative curricula, commit to the improvement of student-to-student and teacher-to-student interactions, assess students' performance to ensure learning is occurring, and continually evaluate their work and make enhancements.

Pedagogical researchers seek to improve the instructional process through observation, analysis, and evaluation. By examining the amount of academic learning, direct instruction, and management time, one can determine how teachers' and students' or clients' behaviors influence learning. Research studies also look at teachers' expectations for students, the classroom learning climate, and the type and amount of feedback—all critical to student learning.

UNDERGRADUATE MAJORS

Assuming you are considering a career in physical education, exercise science, or sport, this section of the chapter introduces you to a variety of options or majors offered by many colleges. This discussion will stimulate your interest in Chapter 5, which describes many careers related to physical education and sport, and Chapter 6, which explains many specific programs and certifications.

Professional preparation programs in physical education traditionally have been oriented toward teacher education, although today most colleges offer a variety of majors, such as exercise science, sport management, and athletic training. As the demand for physical education teachers decreased, beginning in the late 1970s, colleges and faculty revised their curricula to include the increasingly popular sport- and fitness-related majors. The expansion in the fields of fitness, leisure, recreation, athletics, and sports has resulted in diverse career opportunities for students majoring in these areas.

Teaching

Teacher certification following graduation from an accredited, degree-granting institution is the goal of graduates choosing a career in teaching. Teacher preparation courses may be taken throughout the undergraduate years or concentrated in just 2 years following the completion of general education courses taken at a community college or four-year institution. Certifications for physical education may include those for prekindergarten (P) through grade 6, grades 5 through 8, grades 7 through 12, P through grade 12, health education, and dance.

The Council for the Accreditation of Educator Preparation (CAEP) is the sole accrediting body for educator preparation providers like colleges that prepare teachers.

Teachers help individuals of all ages and in various settings learn new skills.
© PhotoDisc/Getty Images RF

To ensure quality and competence of teachers, CAEP bases its accreditation process on five standards including content and pedagogical knowledge and clinical practice. CAEP recognizes and works with specialized professional organizations, like SHAPE America for physical education and health education, to establish specific professional content standards. These standards, containing all the attitudes, knowledge, and skills required of a physical education teacher, have been subdivided into three elements: academic, professional, and pedagogical. Aquatics, dance, exercise, games, sports, and other leisure pursuits are components of the unique academic content of physical education. Motor development, sport management, motor learning, sport philosophy, sport biomechanics, exercise physiology, sport history, sport and exercise psychology, sport sociology, and athletic training, as discussed in Chapter 2, provide the intellectual and theoretical bases for studies in physical education. The professional aspect of the undergraduate program develops an awareness of and commitment to the various educational, research, and service activities of physical education. These include studies of curriculum models, organizational structures, diagnostic and assessment procedures, and problem-solving techniques. Knowledge about teaching and learning physical skills constitutes the pedagogical element. Abilities to plan lessons, implement instruction, and evaluate learning are observed in a supervised student teaching experience. (See Box 3.1 for guiding principles regarding what new teachers should know and be able to do.)

Because education is delegated to the states, there is no national curriculum for any school subject, including physical education. There is some guidance, however, about what constitutes a competent and highly qualified teacher. The National Board for Professional Teaching Standards (NBPTS) has established five core

BOX 3.1   CORE TEACHING STANDARDS

Many teacher preparation programs are based on the Core Teaching Standards developed by the Council of Chief State School Officers' Interstate Teacher Assessment and Support Consortium.

The Learner and Learning

Standard #1: Learner Development. The teacher understands how learners grow and develop, recognizing that patterns of learning and development vary individually within and across the cognitive, linguistic, social, emotional, and physical areas, and designs and implements developmentally appropriate and challenging learning experiences.

Standard #2: Learning Differences. The teacher uses understanding of individual differences and diverse cultures and communities to ensure inclusive learning environments that enable each learner to meet high standards.

Standard #3: Learning Environments. The teacher works with others to create environments that support individual and collaborative learning, and that encourage positive social interaction, active engagement in learning, and self motivation.

Content

Standard #4: Content Knowledge. The teacher understands the central concepts, tools of inquiry, and structures of the discipline(s) he or she teaches and creates learning experiences that make the discipline accessible and meaningful for learners to assure mastery of the content.

Standard #5: Application of Content. The teacher understands how to connect concepts and use differing perspectives to engage learners in critical thinking, creativity, and collaborative problem solving related to authentic local and global issues.

Instructional Practice

Standard #6: Assessment. The teacher understands and uses multiple methods of assessment to engage learners in their own growth, to monitor learner progress, and to guide the teacher's and learner's decision making.

Standard #7: Planning for Instruction. The teacher plans instruction that supports every student in meeting rigorous learning goals by drawing upon knowledge of content areas, curriculum, cross-disciplinary skills, and pedagogy, as well as knowledge of learners and the community context.

Standard #8: Instructional Strategies. The teacher understands and uses a variety of instructional strategies to encourage learners to develop deep understanding of content areas and their connections, and to build skills to apply knowledge in meaningful ways.

Professional Responsibility

Standard #9: Professional Learning and Ethical Practice. The teacher engages in ongoing professional learning and uses evidence to continually evaluate his/her practice, particularly the effects of his/her choices and actions on others (learners, families, other professionals, and the community), and adapts practice to meet the needs of each learner.

Standard #10: Leadership and Collaboration. The teacher seeks appropriate leadership roles and opportunities to take responsibility for student learning, to collaborate with learners, families, colleagues, other school professionals, and community members to ensure learner growth, and to advance the profession.

*The Interstate New Teacher Assessment and Support Consortium (InTASC) model core teaching standards were developed by the Council of Chief State School Officers and member states. Copies may be downloaded from the Council's website at http://www.ccsso.org/Documents/2011/InTASC_Model_Core_Teaching_Standards_2011.pdf.

propositions that characterize those teachers who possess the knowledge, skills, and abilities of the best teachers. These teachers are committed to students and their learning, know their subjects and how to teach them to students, manage and monitor student learning, think systematically about their teaching and learning from their experiences, and are members of learning communities (see www.nbpts .org for more information). Physical education is one of the subject areas in which the NBPTS recognizes teachers with board certification.

Physical education teacher education programs prepare teachers in pedagogical and content knowledge, offer an array of practical field experiences, and help ensure professional behaviors. The pedagogical and content knowledge base for future physical education teachers includes the ability to teach developmentally appropriate physical activities to children in kindergarten through grade 12. The curricular components they learn are aligned with the psychomotor, cognitive, and affective domains in the National Standards for Physical Education (see www.shapeamerica .org/standards/pe/). Physical education teachers learn how to assess student learning, demonstrate professional and ethical behaviors, and engage in ongoing reflection and professional development.

The faculty at each institution offering a physical education program leading to teacher certification or licensure determines the content for the curriculum. After completion of general education requirements, students typically complete courses such as team and individual sports and activities, physical conditioning, history and foundations of physical education, adapted physical education, exercise physiology, biomechanics, motor learning, motor development, kindergarten through grade 12 in-school teaching experiences, and measurement and assessment. The culminating experience in each program is student teaching or an internship in a school.

Several majors while not the only ones available, illustrate the variety of alternative career choices in physical education and sport. Chapter 5, "Career Options," will assist in your career choice and career development process.

Athletic Training

Many students opt to major in athletic training because they have experienced injuries and were helped by athletic trainers in their struggles to recover and return to their sports. Athletic trainers must have a comprehensive understanding of the structure and function of the human body since this specialty deals with the prevention, treatment, and rehabilitation of sport injuries. When injuries occur, athletic trainers must have the knowledge and analytical ability to conduct onsite assessments of the severity of injuries. If injuries are minor, athletic trainers are the primary caregivers of first aid and the administration of ice, whirlpool, ultrasound, or other treatments. Under a physician's supervision, athletic trainers rehabilitate athletes suffering from more serious conditions, such as concussions, loss of mobility due to a broken bone or surgery. Athletic trainers are responsible, along with physicians if injuries are severe, for clearing athletes for participation; they must withstand pressure from players and coaches to return athletes to play prematurely and risk causing more permanent damage to the recovering areas. In addition, athletic trainers often counsel athletes to help them deal with injuries and rehabilitation, setbacks, and residual limitations.

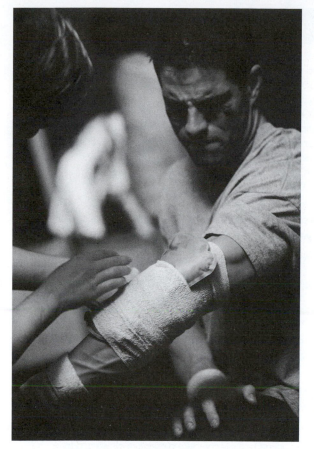

Careers in athletic training are available in schools, colleges, professional leagues, and clinical settings.
© 1998 EyeWire, Inc./Getty Images RF

In coordination with sport coaches and strength and conditioning coaches, athletic trainers help develop conditioning programs to optimally prepare athletes for competition. For example, athletic trainers may work with strength and conditioning coaches to ensure athletes have achieved appropriate muscular strength and endurance and flexibility in injured areas before returning to competitions and practices. Athletics trainers may collaborate with dietitians who plan meals for athletes and sport psychologists who guide athletes in dealing with the mental challenges that ensue when recovering from injuries. Athletic trainers must be cognizant of the harmful effects of performance-enhancing drugs and help ensure athletes do not take pills or injections that will harm them.

Almost all states regulate the practice of athletic training, although the requirements vary from state to state. Students should contact the state regulatory agency to learn about specific requirements. Almost all colleges, professional teams, and sports medicine clinics stipulate that applicants for athletic trainer positions must hold certifications from the National Athletic Trainers' Association Board of Certification for employment (see Box 3.2 for more information). In addition, licensed athletic trainers also must comply with state regulatory requirements to legally engage in athletic training practice.

BOX 3.2   CERTIFICATION IN ATHLETIC TRAINING

An athletic trainer, who is educated and experienced in the management of health care problems associated with physical activity, works with physicians and other health care personnel as an integral member of the health care team in secondary schools, colleges, professional sport programs, sports medicine clinics, and other health care settings.

The Board of Certification (BOC) for the athletic trainer upholds the standards for the profession by providing a certification program for entry-level athletic trainers and recertification standards for certified athletic trainers. A candidate must satisfy the basic requirements, successfully complete an entry-level athletic training program accredited by the Commission on Accreditation of Athletic Training Education (CAATE), and pass the Board of Certification exam.

Basic Requirements
- Complete an entry-level athletic training education program accredited by CAATE.
- Pass the BOC certification exam.

Curriculum Requirements
Students must demonstrate educational competencies and clinical proficiencies in these content areas:

- Evidence-based practice
- Prevention and health promotion
- Clinical examination and diagnosis
- Acute care of injury and illness
- Therapeutic interventions
- Psychosocial strategies and referral
- Health care administration
- Professional development and responsibility

Associated with these competencies, students typically complete a minimum of two academic years of clinical experience in athletic training rooms, athletic practices, and competitive events at various levels under the direct supervision of certified athletic trainers. These clinical experiences must include exposure to upper extremity, lower extremity, equipment-intensive, general medical experiences of both genders, and opportunities for observation of and involvement in the first aid and emergency care of a variety of acute athletic injuries and illnesses. Students should be aware that state-level licensure regulations for high school athletic trainers vary, so you are encouraged to investigate if this career appeals to you.

Certification Exam
Students must successfully complete the certification examination developed to assess knowledge on the five domains of athletic training:

- Injury/Illness Prevention and Wellness Protection
- Clinical Evaluation and Diagnosis
- Immediate and Emergency Care
- Treatment and Rehabilitation
- Organizational and Professional Health and Well-Being

See www.bocatc.org and caate.net for additional information.

In schools, athletic trainers can expect to teach at least a partial load of classes (if they hold a teaching certification) because the athletic trainer position is seldom full time. However, it is difficult to meet certification requirements for athletic training and for teaching in less than 5 (and maybe more) years due to the strict course work and clinical hours each program requires. Salaries are determined by the local school district's salary schedule and are based on years of experience and educational degrees. Additional stipends for extracurricular work are possible.

Depending on the size of the institution and the number of personnel, collegiate athletic trainers may be full- or part-time. They may teach in an accredited athletic training program or in some other field. They may serve one team (such as football) or be responsible for all the intercollegiate athletic teams. It should be emphasized that athletic trainers in schools and colleges work in the evening hours and on weekends when practices and competitions often are held.

Another popular career choice for athletic trainers is a clinical setting. These jobs may be affiliated with a hospital (with a rehabilitative focus) or in a private clinic that serves the public. Individuals helped by athletic trainers may have suffered sport-related injuries or need assistance in returning to activity after inactivity or some non-sport-related injuries.

Coaching

Coaches shape and mold the sport experiences of athletes. Coaches can help develop the skills and knowledge of individuals who, in almost all cases, have chosen to participate and who are eager to learn and compete. Largely, coaches will determine what kind of learning will occur for their athletes and specifically whether they will develop skills, fitness, and a love of the game, internalize the potential values that can be learned and reinforced through sport, or drop out because of negative experiences.

The influential position that a coach holds, however, carries with it a huge responsibility to ensure athletes enjoy and benefit from their sporting experiences. Coaches must be knowledgeable about the skills, rules, and strategies of their sports, but they also should provide physically, mentally, emotionally, socially, and morally appropriate and healthy environments for their athletes. They should emphasize effort, skill development, and fun and provide positive reinforcement for these. They should model and insist on sportsmanship and civility to opponents, officials, and teammates.

Coaching is a popular major for undergraduates who want to continue their involvement with sports. Interscholastic and youth programs need individuals who want to coach young athletes. The demand for coaches of school teams exceeds the supply because of increased numbers of girls' teams, the hiring of fewer new physical education teachers, and the resignation of tenured physical educators from coaching but not from teaching. The millions of children competing on youth sport teams deserve coaches who know how to teach fundamental skills while making sports fun.

Few individuals only coach in the schools; the dual role of teacher-coach characterizes most. Typically the teacher-coach is paid according to a state or district salary

Many physical education teachers also coach.
© Creatas/PunchStock RF

scale, along with an additional stipend for coaching. These amounts and salaries vary widely. According to the National Coaches Report (2008), 84% of states have some type of coaching education requirement for interscholastic coaches, although these requirements vary widely. For example, these requirements may apply only to head varsity coaches, paid coaches, first-time coaches, or coaches who are not teachers in the schools. Coaching curricula in colleges typically include courses in first aid, care and prevention of athletic injuries, anatomy, physiology, exercise physiology, coaching theory, coaching techniques in specific sports, motor development, sport management, and sport psychology. Students interested in becoming coaches of school teams should check with their state's licensing agencies or local school districts to learn the requirements they must fulfill.

Almost all youth league coaches, however, are volunteers. Regardless of the type of employment of these volunteers, they need a basic knowledge in first aid, coaching concepts, motor development, and the exercise and sport sciences. Although a few independent programs offer educational opportunities and certifications for these coaches, most volunteers demonstrate minimal competence.

Fitness

A fitness major prepares students to enter a myriad of careers in this growing field. One appealing feature is the opportunity to help others attain and maintain healthy lifestyles. Another is the pleasure of associating with people who value fitness. Although fitness specialists avoid most of the discipline problems and management minutiae in schools, they typically work during their clients' leisure hours.

Regardless of the setting, the fitness specialist must have a strong scientific background, such as in biomechanics and exercise physiology, especially if activity programs are being designed and prescribed. Knowledge of business and management is essential for career advancement and helps in getting an entry-level position. Fitness specialists typically find jobs in corporate, industrial, and community fitness settings, health, fitness, and sports clubs, or recreation departments. However, there also are job opportunities on cruise ships, at resorts, or as personal trainers.

While eating a balanced, nutritious diet in combination with participating in regular physical activity lead to a healthier life, poor eating habits and inactivity contribute to related health problems, such as obesity, type 2 diabetes, high blood pressure, and heart disease. Nutritional workshops, such as those offered by professionals in health clubs and recreation departments, include recommendations about food selection (with an emphasis on fruits and vegetables), food preparation (broiled rather than fried foods; seasoning with spices rather than fats), smaller serving sizes, and healthy snacks (such as low-fat yogurt or baby carrots), as well as tips about losing weight.

Teachers of aerobic activities include dancing, walking, jogging, swimming, and cycling in their programs to help participants increase their cardiorespiratory endurance. In classes, individually, or with the assistance of personal trainers, adults of all ages are encouraged to lift weights, use resistance bands, and do push-ups or abdominal crunches to increase muscular strength and endurance, reduce injury risk, and maintain strong bones. Organizations like the Aerobics and Fitness Association of America, American Council on Exercise, and IDEA Fitness and Health Association prepare teachers for work in fitness clubs.

Personal trainers working in private clubs and public agencies offer a wealth of advice about increasing one's physical activity. They are personally committed to and model being physically fit, and they share their enthusiasm with others to help them enhance the quality of their lives. Personal trainers must be knowledgeable about how to properly educate others to develop their bodies. Many adults who decide to lose weight, increase cardiorespiratory endurance, develop muscular strength and endurance, improve flexibility, or rehabilitate after an injury or disease may choose to work with personal trainers. The greatest challenge facing the personal trainer is not designing a safe and effective program—although this is important—rather, it is motivating individuals to adhere to physical activity programs so that regular physical activity becomes a part of their lifestyles. Only then will the personal trainer have been successful. Students interested in becoming a personal trainer, aerobics instructor, or fitness specialist, working in the area of cardiac rehabilitation, or using their knowledge and experiences in the health and fitness industry frequently must become certified as will be discussed in Chapter 6.

Sport Management

The burgeoning sport industry attracts graduates who seek to apply business and management knowledge to sport settings. The best academic preparation encompasses the triad of management foundations, sport applications, and an internship and volunteer experiences within the field. It is imperative students understand that careers in this area are "bottom line," or profit oriented. Therefore, courses in accounting, economics, finance, and marketing are important. Built on these should be applications courses such as sport law, facility and event management, sport ethics, and personnel management. The culminating experience that links this knowledge and application is the internship. Students considering careers in sport management are encouraged to join the North American Society for Sport Management and join with professionals in promoting and advancing this field.

A love of sport, along with a desire to pursue some type of career in the world of sports, has propelled many students to think about this major. Given the increasing number of commercial sporting events, many opportunities are available. For example, hundreds of people are required to plan, organize, and implement a professional football game in which a few dozen athletes compete. The sport manager, in addition to producing entertaining sporting events, organizes physical activity programs, such as road races and sport competitions for individuals of all ages and ability levels. Sport managers have the advantage of working in a field that serves individuals eager to have fun, be entertained, interact socially with friends and family, and release the stress of other aspects of their lives. In most cases, though, sport managers work while others are enjoying their leisure hours. This negative is compensated for by the pleasure of being around sports and staying engaged in something they really enjoy.

Sport managers use their talents in a plethora of careers. Within recreational services, young professionals serve as instructors and program coordinators for individuals of all ages in adventure activities, arts and crafts, camps, fitness, sports, and other leisure pursuits. As a recreation specialist, you can coach, officiate, teach, or supervise community-based programs as well as operate facilities such as lakeside recreation centers, parks, pools, sport complexes, and recreation centers. Educationally focused programs in colleges require sport managers who are responsible for compliance with rules, facility and event management, fund-raising, game-day operations, publicity, sports information, and ticket sales. Professional sports from auto racing to beach volleyball are in the entertainment business, so sport managers are focused on providing enjoyable experiences for spectators. Advertising, marketing, and selling tickets are obvious requirements for filling seats, while customer services include managing all aspects of concessions, health and safety, merchandise sales, and parking. Within the sports themselves, managers and other personnel are responsible for planning, accounting, financing, human resources, scouting, community relations, player development, travel, and much more.

Exercise Science

Academic preparation of the exercise science student focuses on the sciences. Usually courses are completed in biology, anatomy, physiology, chemistry, exercise physiology, biomechanics, and possibly biochemistry. Also beneficial is the development of strong statistical and computer technology skills, along with a background in nutrition. This strong scientific foundation also helps prepare a student to pursue advanced degrees for a college professorship.

On the practical side, exercise prescription skills are necessary to qualify for many positions, such as those in corporate fitness programs, clinics, or cardiac rehabilitation centers. Gaining invaluable experiences through an internship or part-time employment helps in obtaining a position in these settings. Salaries are determined by the degree held, work setting, and level of experience.

Exercise scientists in clinical settings are committed to helping people of all ages learn more about the importance of physical activity to their health and well-being. While most individuals can and should begin and maintain a regular exercise program, often under the direction of an exercise scientist, some people may require a doctor's permission and possibly even an exercise prescription program if a cardiac, pulmonary, or metabolic condition exists. Exercise scientists in laboratory settings are dedicated to the analysis of human movement, determination of the effectiveness of various exercise programs, and integration of scientific research into educational and practical applications of exercise.

Students interested in this option are encouraged to join a professional organization. For example, the American College of Sports Medicine (ACSM) has an online student section at http://www.acsm.org/membership/who-should-join/students. ACSM offers a reduced student membership with multiple benefits, including its publications.

Physical Therapy

Physical therapy is the treatment of physical injury or dysfunction using therapeutic exercises and modalities with the goal of restoring normal function. Physical therapists examine individuals with physical impairments or limitations so they can help prevent, diagnose, and treat movement dysfunctions. Through designing and implementing therapeutic interventions, physical therapists help enhance the health and functional abilities of clients to improve their quality of life.

Physical therapists must complete a strong scientific curriculum including courses in anatomy, physiology, neuroscience, organic chemistry, biochemistry, microbiology, genetics, and molecular biology. Shadowing or volunteer experiences and internships working with people with different disabling conditions are required for learning and applying therapeutic knowledge and skills. A strong scientific foundation and experiences in a physical therapy setting are a prerequisite to gaining admission into a graduate program in physical therapy, completing extensive clinical experiences, and passing a licensing exam.

Physical therapists may choose to work in a variety of settings. Many hospitals provide physical therapy services to patients who are recovering from injuries and medical conditions. Physical therapy clinics work with clients based on prescriptions of physicians to help rehabilitate clients from an injury, accident, chronic condition, or acute health problem. Physical therapists may choose to work in specialties like orthopedics (dealing with the musculoskeletal system), geriatrics (working with older adults), cardiovascular and pulmonary (dealing with heart and lung functioning), and pediatrics (working with infants, children, and adolescents).

Physical therapists focus on helping
individuals rehabilitate from injuries.
© Keith Brofsky/PhotoDisc/Getty
Images RF

Physical educators are increasingly sharing their expertise with and borrowing from the various therapeutic fields. The value of exercise in preventing osteoporosis and other degenerative diseases carries broad implications for recreational activities for senior citizens. Physical therapists and athletic trainers are seeking the best programs for injury rehabilitation. Exercise physiologists are working with physicians in the prescription of exercises for individuals who have suffered heart attacks. Recreational therapists and adapted physical educators together may provide appropriate activities for employees and schoolchildren with special needs. In each of these cases, the medium of exercise is involved and, through consultation, the best activities are prescribed.

Health Education

Health educators teach behaviors that help promote the five components of wellness—mental, physical, emotional, social, and spiritual—to individuals of all ages. Health educators are responsible for developing programs and materials that encourage people to make healthy decisions about all aspects of their lives. Duties and responsibilities of professionals in this field may include determining the needs of the people they serve, developing and implementing programs and services to teach health topics, connecting people with needed and appropriate health services and information, and advocating for improved health policies, services, and resources.

Health educators may provide individual health screenings, such as checking blood pressure, refer people to health resources, such as support groups and home health agencies, and teach classes on a variety of health topics in health care facilities. In schools, health educators teach classes and work with teachers, administrators, and nurses to help monitor the health and well-being of students. Collegiate health services develop and deliver programs to educate young adults about lifestyle choices, such as how they may use alcohol and drugs. Opportunities to become peer health educators are available on many college campuses. In public and community health departments, health educators educate people through classes and written materials and advocate for policies, such as about proper nutrition, vaccinations, dealing with health conditions such as diabetes, and coping with the limitations of aging. In private businesses, health educators create and lead programs for employees, such as weight management, smoking cessation, and stress management.

Recreation

Recreation specialists develop and lead leisure activities for individuals of all ages and ability levels. They direct activities ranging from arts and crafts to sports in camps, parks, playgrounds, recreation centers, and senior centers. Professionals in this field may plan and organize individual and group activities, teach the skills and rules of activities, games, and sports, ensure the safety of all participants, modify activities that meet the needs of all participants, and manage facilities, equipment, and events. Responsibilities fulfilled by recreation specialists vary widely depending on the size, scope, location of programs and each person's expertise and experience.

Camp counselors are needed in residential and day camps to teach skills and lead youth in activities such as archery, boating, camping, hiking, horseback riding, and swimming. Camp directors oversee the entire camp including planning and managing all camp activities and programs. In publically funded programs, recreation leaders organize and direct daily operations from scheduling and maintaining facilities, distributing and managing equipment, and scheduling and overseeing leagues, competitions, practice sessions, and individual workout opportunities. They also may teach classes in traditional sports like tennis and swimming and nontraditional activities like skateboarding and windsurfing. Directors of parks and recreation programs are responsible for the financial and personnel management of city and community parks, playgrounds, swimming pools, and other recreational facilities.

SPECIALIZED PROFESSIONAL ORGANIZATIONS

There are numerous professional organizations that students may consider joining. Becoming a professional is a process of learning about and gaining competence in a career of interest to you. Professional organizations provide the impetus for you to get started by publishing professional journals for you to read and offering professional conferences and workshops that you can attend and where you can begin to network with other professionals. What a great way to launch into a profession.

SHAPE America

SHAPE America has served its members for over a century. In 1937, as a department of the National Education Association, the former American Physical Education Association became the American Association for Health and Physical Education. (It became an alliance in 1974.) Recreation was added to its title in 1938; dance was added in 1979. In 2014, it became SHAPE America.

SHAPE America is an educational organization designed to facilitate and promote the purposes and activities of physical and health educators. Its mission is the promotion of physical education, physical activity, and health education in schools, institutions of higher education, and the community and to provide members with professional development opportunities that increase knowledge, improve skills, and encourage sound professional practices.

Services SHAPE America provides include holding an annual national convention; publishing standards and other information pertinent to its fields of interest; providing professional development opportunities; positively influencing public opinion and legislation; and providing consultant services. For more information about SHAPE America call 1-800-213-7193 or visit www.shapeamerica.org.

Periodicals published by the Alliance include the *Journal of Physical Education, Recreation and Dance,* which includes articles of a broad and practical nature, *Research Quarterly for Exercise and Sport,* which reports research findings, *American Journal of Health Education* offering health promotion articles, and *Strategies: A Journal for Physical and Sport Educators* offering practical ideas and information.

Students are invited to attend SHAPE America's annual convention, participate on committees and councils, and read its journals and other publications. Since the future of physical education and health education depends on students who join the profession and take an active role, it is essential that these opportunities remain beneficial and interesting. Involvement often begins at the college level where there are clubs for majors in physical education and health education. Through collegiate experiences, students develop leadership abilities, learn more about their fields of study from professors and guest lecturers, and have fun with friends. Often members of these clubs participate in service learning activities by providing after-school fitness programs for at-risk kids, conducting events for Special Olympics, or assisting with fund-raising events for the American Heart Association or American Cancer Society. These service activities not only give back to the community but also strengthen and expand students' knowledge and skills.

Nonconvention workshops, clinics, and seminars provide SHAPE America members with the latest research findings, innovative activities, and teaching approaches, as well as opportunities for personal enrichment and growth. Affiliated state associations give professionals the opportunity to learn different coaching techniques, acquire new skills, and interact and exchange information with

All students should have opportunities to participate in daily, quality physical education classes.
© McGraw-Hill Education/Lars Niki, photographer

other members at their annual conventions. Students, especially you, should take advantage of state conventions. Not only will you learn from these experiences, but you may also make and build networks contacts with individuals who later could hire you or help you get a job.

American College of Sports Medicine

ACSM, the world's largest multidisciplinary sports medicine and exercise science organization, was founded in 1954 to promote and integrate scientific research, education, and practical applications of sports medicine and exercise science. Its primary focus is advancing health through science, medicine, and education. Among its objectives are advancing scientific research dealing with the effects of physical activities on health and well-being, such as in the areas of injury prevention, exercise and heart rate response, exercise and aging, and exercise and cardiovascular disease risk factors; encouraging cooperation and professional exchange among physicians, scientists, and educators; and initiating, promoting, and applying research in sports medicine and exercise science.

Another vital component of its mission is to facilitate public awareness and education about the positive aspects of physical activity for people of all ages. For example, through its position statements, which include evidence-based research, ACSM generates interest, awareness, and knowledge among the general public to help motivate people to engage in physical activities.

ACSM offers full-time undergraduates studying in a field related to exercise science or sports medicine the opportunity to join at a cost half that charged to professional members. Benefits of membership include subscriptions to its scientific journal, *Medicine & Science in Sports & Exercise,* the review of current research topics in *Exercise & Sport Sciences Reviews,* and *Current Sports Medicine Reports;* discounted registration for any ACSM certification exam; and discounted registration on ACSM meetings. Another, less costly, option offered by ACSM is membership in its Alliance of Health and Fitness Professionals, which includes among its benefits ACSM's *Health & Fitness Journal* and discounted registration for ACSM's Health & Fitness Summit and Exposition. This annual summit seeks to bridge the gap between the science of sports medicine and practice of fitness professionals.

National Athletic Trainers' Association

The need to establish professional standards and disseminate information led to the establishment in 1950 of the National Athletic Trainers' Association (NATA). The NATA works with the American Academy of Family Physicians, American Academy of Pediatrics, American Orthopaedic Society for Sports Medicine, and Commission on Accreditation of Athletic Training Education to establish, maintain, and promote appropriate standards of quality for educational programs in this field. Athletic trainers cooperate with medical personnel, athletic personnel, individuals involved in physical activity, and parents and guardians in the development and coordination of responsive athletic health care delivery systems. Among the services provided by athletic trainers are injury prevention, risk management, assessment and evaluation, therapeutic modalities, nutritional aspects of injury and illness, psychosocial intervention and referral, and acute care of injury and illness. Athletic trainers provide these services in clinics, offices, and industrial settings working with other health care professionals.

NATA members receive the *Journal of Athletic Training, Athletic Training Education Journal,* online job listings and a résumé bank, discounted registration fees at the NATA annual meeting and district meetings, and many other benefits. Students can take advantage of these benefits at a reduced cost.

American Society of Exercise Physiologists

The American Society of Exercise Physiologists (ASEP), founded in 1997, has established academic standards that are used to verify the quality of academic programs students complete in preparing for this field. Members, who are scholars and practitioners in the fields of fitness, health promotion, rehabilitation, and sports training, enhance discussion and collaboration among exercise physiologists. Through its Exercise Physiologist Certified program, ASEP ensures the public that the academic preparation and skills of exercise physiology candidates have been verified. ASEP publishes the *Journal of Exercise Physiology* online with research-based articles, *Professionalization of Exercise Physiology*, online with information for the professional development of exercise physiologists, and the *Journal of Professional Exercise Physiology*, a peer-reviewed online journal. Networking with professionals helps to promote the role of exercise physiology in the health care system and fosters improvements in research and practice. ASEP hosts an annual conference for the sharing of the latest exercise physiology data, techniques, and theories.

The exercise and sport sciences are listed in Box 3.3 along with the leading professional organizations (and their websites) and journals. Most of these organizations offer student membership at reduced costs so that you can get involved early and join leading professionals in expanding your knowledge in a career of interest to you.

National Strength and Conditioning Association

The National Strength and Conditioning Association (NSCA), founded in 1978, is an international educational association that disseminates research-based knowledge about strength and conditioning and its practical application to improve

Maintaining muscular strength and endurance is important throughout life.

© Royalty-Free/Corbis

BOX 3.3   PROFESSIONAL ORGANIZATION IN THE EXERCISE AND SPORT SCIENCES

Exercise and Sport Sciences	Organizations	Websites	Journals
Athletic training	National Athletic Trainers' Association	www.nata.org/	Journal of Athletic Training; Athletic Training Education Journal
Exercise physiology	American College of Sports Medicine	www.acsm.org	Medicine & Science in Sports & Exercise; Exercise & Sport Sciences Reviews; Current Sports Medicine Reports; ACSM's Health and Fitness Journal
	American Society of Exercise Physiologists	http://www.asep.org	Journal of Exercise Physiology; Professionalization of Exercise Physiology; Journal of Professional Exercise Physiology
Motor control	International Society of Motor Control	www.i-s-m-c.org/	Motor Control
Sport biomechanics	American Society of Biomechanics	www.asbweb.org/	Journal of Biomechanics; Clinical Biomechanics
Sport history	North American Society for Sport History	www.nassh.org/	Journal of Sport History
Sport management	North American Society for Sport Management	www.nassm.com/	Journal of Sport Management; Sport Management Education Journal
Sport philosophy	International Association for the Philosophy of Sport	iasp.net	Journal of the Philosophy of Sport
Sport and exercise psychology	North American Society for the Psychology of Sport and Physical Activity	http://naspspa.com/	Journal of Sport and Exercise Psychology; Journal of Motor Learning and Development
	Association for Applied Sport Psychology	www.appliedsportpsych.org/	Journal of Applied Sport Psychology; Journal of Sport Psychology in Action; Case Studies in Sport and Exercise Psychology
Sport sociology	North American Society for the Sociology of Sport	www.nasss.org/	Sociology of Sport Journal

athletic performance, help prevent injuries, and develop fitness. Its diverse membership includes teachers, personal trainers, collegiate strength and conditioning coaches, physical therapists, sports medicine physicians, and sport science researchers. NSCA members seek practical applications for new research findings in the strength and conditioning field and help foster the development of strength training and conditioning as a discipline and profession. It publishes *The Journal of Strength and Conditioning Research, Strength and Conditioning Journal, NSCA Coach, Personal Training Quarterly* (see www.nsca.com/publications/ for more information).

American School Health Association

Since 1927, the American School Health Association has been committed to safeguarding the health of school-age children. It is a multidisciplinary organization of administrators, counselors, health educators, physical educators, psychologists, school health coordinators, school nurses, school physicians, and social workers. It promotes coordinated school health programs that include health instruction, health services, and healthful living practices in schools. It publishes the *Journal of School Health* (see www.ashaweb.org/).

National Recreation and Park Association

The National Recreation and Park Association (NRPA) promotes public awareness of the importance of the park systems that provide opportunities for people to lead healthy, active lives. Its members are dedicated to improving the human condition through improved park, recreation, and leisure opportunities as well as by addressing environmental concerns. NRPA facilitates the work of communities that provide facilities, services, and programs to help meet the emotional, social, and physical needs of individuals of all ages. The *Journal of Leisure Research, Parks and Recreation, Schole,* and *Therapeutic Recreation Journal* are NRPA journals (see www.nrpa.org/member-benefits/#education for more information).

National Intramural-Recreational Sports Association

The National Intramural-Recreational Sports Association (NIRSA) was begun in 1950 to provide an opportunity for college intramural directors to meet annually to exchange ideas and information. It has grown into the leading resource for professional and student development and education in collegiate recreational sports, including intramural sports, sport clubs, recreational facilities, fitness programming, outdoor recreation, wellness programs, informal recreation, and aquatic programs. Its *Recreational Sports Journal* provides empirical, theoretical, and applied research for professionals in this field (see www.nirsa.org for more information).

The value and importance of joining and participating in a professional organization are multifaceted. First, membership entitles each person to receive journals, newsletters, directories, and other materials to help keep the practitioner up to date on the latest techniques, research, methodology, and applications. Second, many of these organizations sponsor conferences and workshops, which provide additional opportunities to stay current through timely updates and to inter-act with and learn from colleagues in similar careers. Third, organizational affiliation may lead to service on committees and leadership opportunities where members can contribute to the promotion of standards and share expertise with others. Fourth, job announcements in newsletters and placement centers at conferences may lead to career advancement. Thus, professional involvement enlivens your career.

The basic objectives of all professional groups are to exchange information, to learn, and to serve. To enhance your knowledge about and commitment to your chosen career, you should seek opportunities through these organizations to grow professionally. By exchanging program ideas and instructional and motivational techniques, members can improve their abilities to serve others and learn how to communicate their goals and activities to colleagues and to the general public. Shar-ing of experiences and research generates many ideas for further study. Therefore, as a young professional, you are encouraged to join your college's clubs for students in certain majors, state and national professional and disciplinary associations. You are encouraged to join at least one that matches your interest and begin to read its publications.

SUMMARY

This chapter focuses on being a professional rather than on joining a profession. Physical education, exercise science, and sport are characterized by extensive train-ing in a disciplinary body of knowledge and service; communication among col-leagues is essential for personal growth and development.

Undergraduate majors include athletic training, coaching, fitness, sport man-agement, exercise science, physical therapy, and teaching. Various career options await graduates with specialized knowledge and skills in one of these fields.

The services provided by SHAPE America will enhance development of each component of the profession. Numerous other professional associations provide opportunities for collaboration and individual career development. Journals and conferences are two of the most important services provided by these organiza-tions. Become involved while you are a student. Participate in conferences, attend workshops, and read publications of professional organizations to prepare for your chosen career.

As a young professional, you can make a significant contribution to the quality of life of those you serve as a teacher, researcher, or program leader. You have the opportunity to become a role model by planning and implementing effective pro-grams that meet the activity needs of diverse groups. Rather than reacting, you can become proactive by promoting the values of physical education, exercise science, and sport and implementing exemplary programs.

CAREER PERSPECTIVE

Courtesy Shirley Ann Holt/Hale

SHIRLEY ANN HOLT/HALE

Elementary Physical Education Specialist (Retired)

EDUCATION

A.B., elementary education, Berea College, Berea, Kentucky
M.Ed., physical education, Eastern Kentucky University, Richmond, Kentucky
Ph.D., early childhood education, Peabody College of Vanderbilt University, Nashville, Tennessee

JOB RESPONSIBILITIES AND HOURS

Shirley taught 38 years at Linden Elementary School in Oak Ridge, Tennessee. During those years of teaching elementary physical education, classes ranged from a high of 13 per day to 11 classes per day. Shirley's teaching career began with 875 students in grades K–6 and dropped to 500+ students when the school was reconfigured for kindergarten through grade 4. Her normal work hours were 7:30 A.M. to 4:00 P.M. These hours included conducting before-school jogging and jump rope clubs and supervising students during after-school bus duty. The work required by the school system beyond the normal school day was limited to an occasional request to attend city council or school board meetings. However, to be prepared for classes, as a veteran teacher Shirley spent another two hours at night writing lesson plans and doing professional reading. The salary range for teachers in her school system is from $32,000 for beginning teachers to over $65,000, depending on years of experience and advanced degrees.

SPECIALIZED COURSE WORK, DEGREES, AND EXPERIENCES NEEDED FOR THIS CAREER

An undergraduate degree in elementary education, with minors in physical education and music, coupled with the student labor program at Berea, provided Shirley with a rich combination of "competency in the many movement forms of dance, gymnastics, and games/sports" and a focus on teaching children. That focus on the teaching of children in physical education has been central to Shirley's teaching, writing, and consulting endeavors throughout her career. It has also served her extremely well in communicating with classroom teachers and integrating various curricula within elementary school classes. Also valuable were her experiences in field placements and student teaching in schools, as well as the opportunity to serve as a teaching assistant in the physical education department. Thus, Shirley graduated with teaching experiences in primary, middle school, and secondary physical education, as well as in college-level classes. As a public school teacher, she must hold state certification in physical education, which her academic degrees prepared her to obtain.

SATISFYING ASPECTS

To Shirley, teaching children has been satisfaction beyond measure. She has experienced daily "highs" from teaching children as well as treasured the joys of seeing a number of her students succeeding in their chosen careers in physical activity and health; the adoption of healthy, active lifestyles; and, most importantly, watching them grow into confident, contributing citizens of the community and nation.

JOB POTENTIAL

Salary increases come from advancement steps on the index, advanced degrees, and state incentives for merit pay. Certification by the National Board for Professional Teaching Standards provides financial incentive in many states. Opportunities for responsibility are always available; they are, however, added to the normal workload with no reduction in teaching duties. Promotion, if desired, can come through leaving the teaching of students and moving into administration.

SUGGESTIONS FOR STUDENTS

When named National Teacher of the Year several years ago, Shirley stated, "I consider the teaching of children the greatest career one can choose and the ability to do so the greatest gift one can be given." Shirley emphasizes that there are a few requirements for success in this career: an absolute love of physical education/activity, a joy in being with children, an abundance of energy, the ability to laugh at oneself and to laugh often, and knowing "Monday is my favorite day of the week!"

Footnote: May all your days of teaching physical education be as blessed!

KEY POINTS

Profession	Application of knowledge, competencies, and experiences, lifelong learning, service to others, and adherence to a code of ethics are essential for professionals.
Pedagogy	The focus of teaching should be on student learning.
Athletic training	An athletic trainer identifies injuries and helps athletes recover from sport injuries in schools, colleges, and clinical and professional settings.
Coaching	From volunteering to the top competitive levels, coaches help athletes learn sport skills, strategies, fitness, and values.
Fitness	Fitness specialists, such as personal trainers, use their knowledge to help clients enjoy the benefits of regular physical activity.
Sport management	A wealth of opportunities awaits the person who understands how to apply business concepts to sports for entertainment and participation.
Exercise science	The application of scientific principles to physical activities helps expand knowledge about and benefits for participants.
Teaching	Teachers are guided by standards for themselves and their students about what each should know and be able to do.

Specialized professional organizations   Joining a professional organization in an area of interest provides benefits, such as journals, conventions, professional development opportunities, policy or position statements, advocacy, certifications, and networking opportunities.

REVIEW QUESTIONS

1. What are the six characteristics of a profession?
2. What is pedagogy and how does it apply to teachers inside and outside of schools?
3. Select any two of the undergraduate majors and briefly describe the knowledge and abilities required of a graduate from each of these.
4. How does SHAPE America serve its members?
5. What are the purposes of the American College of Sports Medicine?
6. What is the purpose of the National Strength and Conditioning Association?
7. What is required for certification as an athletic trainer?

STUDENT ACTIVITIES

1. Join a professional organization and begin reading its journal. (Be sure and check for a discounted student membership rate.)
2. Investigate the website of one physical education, exercise science, or sport organization that interests you to learn more about its services and the benefits of membership.
3. Read one article from a professional journal published by a professional organization related to a career in which you are interested. Describe the key points in this article.
4. Write a one-page statement defending the importance of being a professional.
5. Attend at least one professional workshop or clinic during this semester or term.
6. In small groups, prepare a five-minute defense for the importance and advantages of joining a professional organization.
7. Interview one person in any two of the undergraduate majors to gain more information about careers in this field. Write a one-page report comparing these or share this information in a two-minute class presentation.
8. Select one of the professional organizations and give a two-minute presentation about its unique programs and services.
9. Read one position paper of a professional organization or article in a professional journal and write a one-page report about it.

10.   The American College of Sports Medicine in 2007 working with the American Medical Association launched the Exercise Is Medicine initiative. The purpose of this global program is to make everyone aware of the scientifically proven benefits of physical activity. Health care providers are urged to assess every patient's level of physical activity at every clinic visit, determine if the patient is meeting physical activity guidelines, and provide counseling to patients about how to meet these guidelines including through referrals to community resources. Exercise Is Medicine on Campus calls for colleges to engage in the promotion of physical activity as an essential component of health. Working with classmates, research and learn more about this program (see http://www.exerciseismedicine.org/support_page.php?p=17). Develop a 1–2 page proposal to present to your institution's student organization to gain its support for conducting an Exercise Is Medicine on Campus annual event and earn national recognition for your work.

REFERENCES

Council of Chief State School Officers. (2011, April). Interstate Teacher Assessment and Support Consortium (InTASC) Model Core Teaching Standards: A Resource for State Dialogue. Washington, DC: Author.

National coaches report. (2008). Reston, VA. National Association for Sport and Physical Education.

 # WEB CONNECTIONS

1. www.ashaweb.org/
   Learn more about the American School Health Association and its programs and services for promoting the health of the nation's youth.

2. www.shapeamerica.org
   SHAPE America provides programs and services for school and college physical and health educators.

3. www.pecentral.org
   This PE Central site contains a plethora of information to assist teachers in helping children become physically active and healthy for a lifetime. The treasure lode of resources for teachers available from this site is invaluable for curricular and instructional enhancement.

4. http://www.pheamerica.org/
   This site provides a wealth of information for promoting active and healthy lifestyles, with an emphasis on physical education programs in schools.

5. www.hscoaches.org/
   The National High School Athletic Coaches Association provides professional development opportunities and other services to high school coaches and athletic directors.

6. www.pesoftware.com
   This on-line newsletter for K–12 physical educators helps them use technology in physical education.

7. www.nbpts.org/
   The National Board for Professional Teaching Standards is committed to better teaching, learning, and schools. National Board Certified Teachers have met rigorous standards through intensive study, expert evaluation, self-assessment, and peer review.

8. www.apta.org/
   Learn more about the American Physical Therapy Association, which fosters advancements in physical therapy practice, research, and education.

4

PHILOSOPHY OF PHYSICAL EDUCATION, EXERCISE SCIENCE, AND SPORT

LEARNING OUTCOMES

- Students will be able to explain the meaning and importance of philosophy.
- Students will be able to distinguish among the traditional philosophies of idealism, realism, naturalism, pragmatism, and existentialism.
- Students will be able to describe the role of ethics and morally reasoned decision-making in their careers.
- Students will be able to articulate their personal philosophies as they relate to their anticipated careers.

It is important for people to think about what they believe is important and valued. When this occurs, their lives will more likely display positive traits, and their actions may indicate that they are law-abiding citizens, loving family members, and athletes who play fair. In order to understand philosophy more easily, it is helpful to think about or reflect on what you believe and why you believe it. Consider the meaning and significance of words such as commitment, honesty, loyalty, respect, and sportsmanship, because these will inevitably influence actions. People's understanding of how to deal with other people, handle challenging situations, and resolve ethical dilemmas will determine how they treat others, react appropriately under difficult circumstances, and reason morally in order to do the right thing. Each individual's philosophy, even if never written or stated, is lived out and reflected on a daily basis.

The pursuit of truth, wisdom, and knowledge is as pervasive today as it was during the development of diverse philosophies in the past. This chapter examines the importance of philosophy, focusing on five of the traditional philosophies, with emphasis on how these philosophies have influenced physical education, exercise science, and sport programs. Ethics is discussed more fully because of its importance across all programs. Based on the knowledge gained from this study, you are encouraged to develop a personal philosophy of physical education, exercise science, and sport.

WHY STUDY PHILOSOPHY?

Philosophy can be defined as the love, study, or pursuit of wisdom, knowledge, and truth. It includes an exploration of what we know, how we know it, and why it is important that we know it as well as the study of the processes governing thought, conduct, and reality. Philosophy encompasses a developmental process and the resultant factors, theories, and values. Philosophy is an attempt to understand the meaning of life by analyzing and synthesizing why people believe or act as they do; simply having a purpose and objectives, as discussed in Chapter 1, is not sufficient. You must know what your values are and be able to articulate their importance to others.

Kretchmar (2005) suggests that philosophy can be divided into areas of study based on the questions asked. Metaphysics is concerned with the nature of things, or how actions or events are related to one another. This philosophical study describes the qualities or characteristics of physical as well as nonphysical things. Metaphysical philosophers might answer questions, such as "What is the nature of sport?" or "What is the role of creativity in sport or play?" Axiology deals with the value of things and discovering whether actions, things, or circumstances are good and virtuous. In seeking truth, the axiologist attempts to answer the question of how people should act in certain situations. Questions that relate to axiology include "What should be the value of competitive sports?" or "Is intentionally harming an opponent right?"

Epistemology is the branch of philosophy that examines what people know and how and why they hold certain beliefs, or an examination of the specifics of understanding. The epistemologist might ask, "Will having been a successful athlete make

Through yoga, some individuals seek to enhance their overall physical and mental well-being.
© Rob Melnychuk/Getty Images RF

a person a successful coach?" or "Does a former professional athlete necessarily have the instructional abilities to teach sport skills effectively?" Aesthetics is the philosophical area that focuses on the artistic, sensual, or beautiful aspects of movement. A person who values aesthetics is pleased more by the beauty of the human body in motion than by the outcome of the contest or athletes' skills. Questions a person stressing aesthetics might ask include "What is the beauty of the figure skater or hurdler?" or "What is the rhythm of the gymnast's movements during a floor exercise routine?" Ethics refers to the study of moral values or the doing of good toward others or oneself. The ethical person believes that it would be morally wrong to violate the rules of the game in order to win. Ethical questions might include "When, if ever, is it fair for an athlete to take performance-enhancing drugs?" or "When, if ever, is it morally wrong for a coach to do whatever it takes to win?"

What is the worth of physical education to a school child? What is the value of learning a lifetime sport? What constitutes a healthy lifestyle? What is the role of play? These are just a few of the questions that your philosophy can help answer.

Developing a personal philosophy can improve your teaching effectiveness, influence your behavior, provide direction in program development, contribute to society's awareness of the value of physical activity, and encourage a feeling of commonality among co-workers. How, you might ask, could a personal philosophy help accomplish all of these? When you determine what goals you want your students or those with whom you work to attain, it will influence what you include in your program and how you proceed. For example, if you value the development of physical fitness, you will emphasize content and activities that can contribute to improving the fitness levels of those with whom you work. Conversely, if you prioritize the development of movement and sport skills, you will focus on instructing and having learners practice these skills. Another example of how a personal philosophy influences what is accomplished would be to consider whether you will emphasize fair play as a coach. If you believe in playing by the rules and living ethically, you can serve as a positive role model for your students, athletes, and co-workers. (See the Research View Developing a Personal Code of Conduct . . . to help you in developing your personal philosophy.)

⌕ RESEARCH VIEW

Developing a Personal Code of Conduct as a Physical Education, Exercise Science, and Sport Professional

What is the responsibility of the physical education, exercise science, or sport professional to each of the following?

- Responsibilities relative to moral values
- Professional knowledge and expertise
- Program content relative to standards
- Delivery of instruction and dissemination of information

(continued)

- Treatment of individuals from various socioeconomic backgrounds, ages, genders, ethnicities, or ability levels
- Utilization of equipment and other resources
- Personal health and well-being

The United Nations Educational, Scientific and Cultural Organization's Code of Sports Ethics emphasizes fair play as integral to sport activities, policy, management, and levels of involvement. Fair play and sportsmanship provide the ethical framework to combat commercialized and monetized pressures to win. From a young age and throughout life, sport participants are expected to embrace fair play as they enjoy movement, physical activity, and sports. Playing within the rules and the spirit of the rules discourages and helps eliminate cheating, gamesmanship, doping, violence, harassment, and exploitation. Fair play enriches sport, society, and friendship among nations.

A Coach's Code of Conduct can be found at http://www.shapeamerica.org /advocacy/positionstatements/sports/loader.cfm?csModule=security/getfile& pageid=4628. This document stresses that coaches must know and demonstrate expertise in coaching competencies, such as safety and injury prevention, physical conditioning, growth and development, teaching and communication, and learning, and sports skills and tactics. This code emphasizes proper conduct of coaches who serve as role models for fair play, integrity, sportsmanship, and professionalism as well as focus on their athletes' development of skills and fitness in safe environments.

The Code of Ethics of the American Society of Exercise Physiologists (see www .asep.org/index.php/organization/code-ethics/) offers guidance for professional conduct by individuals who apply exercise physiology to health, fitness, exercise, and preventive and rehabilitative services. Its 10 statements hold members responsible for nondiscriminatory treatment of all individuals, professional competence, adherence to legal, scientific, ethical, and other professional standards, confidentiality about the health and safety of clients, and prevention of conflicts of interest.

The ethical creed of the North American Society for Sport Management (see www.nassm.com/InfoAbout/NASSM/Creed) includes principles of professional conduct and obligations and responsibilities to others. This ethical creed guides sport managers to act in ways that meet the highest standards of professional integrity as they serve others, employing agencies, the profession, and society.

The Code of Ethics for the American Physical Therapist Association available at http://www.apta.org/uploadedFiles/APTAorg/About_Us/Policies/HOD /Ethics/CodeofEthics.pdf emphasizes maintaining and promoting ethical practice in the best interest of the client. Included among its 8 principles are respecting the rights and dignity of all individuals including through the provision of compassionate care, exercising sound professional judgments, demonstrating integrity in all relationships, fulfilling all legal and professional obligations, promoting behaviors and practices to benefit clients, and helping meet the health needs of all people.

The discussion of the traditional philosophies that follows will challenge your thinking as you decide what you value and how to formulate your personal philosophy. By articulating what you believe in and what is important, you are laying the foundation for your personal philosophy.

FIVE TRADITIONAL PHILOSOPHIES

Idealism, realism, naturalism, pragmatism, and existentialism provide the foundation for educational philosophy, including that of physical education, exercise science, and sport. A brief overview of the basic tenets of each philosophy and their application is provided.

Idealism

Idealism centers on the mind as critical to understanding, since only through reasoning and mental processes can truth emerge. Never-changing ideals, not things, constitute the ultimate reality. Idealists since the Greek philosopher Plato have stressed that only the reflective and intuitive individual can arrive at truth.

Ideals, virtues, and truths are universal and remain the same regardless of how individual interpretations vary. As people develop and exercise their free will, they make choices through their intellectual powers. These decisions, whether right or wrong, do not alter the values important to the idealist. The development of the total person is the objective of idealism as applied to physical education, exercise science, and sport. The individual is important and should be nurtured through an emphasis on the mind and its thought processes.

Relative to physical education, exercise science, and sport, the idealist expects students, athletes, and others engaged in physical activities to learn how and why any skill or movement is important and how it is executed. The idealist stresses that while there is one correct way to perform an overhead shot in tennis or to putt a golf ball, it is important that the participant understand why this is the proper technique.

The mental side of sports, such as learning from mistakes made in a game, is valued by the idealist.
© Royalty-Free/Corbis

The teacher or exercise leader will model how to execute a specific movement and, through questions and answers, ensure that the participant conceptualizes how to execute the skill.

Realism

As a revolt against some of the tenets of idealism, the Greek philosopher Aristotle and today's advocates of **realism** state that scientific laws, rather than perceived truths, are in control. The scientific method provides the realist with the process for acquiring and applying truth (i.e., the knowledge that originates in the physical world but emerges through experimentation). Scientific investigation examines the material things of the world when seeking truth.

The role of education, according to the realist, is to train the student to discover and interpret the real things in life (i.e., things that can be shown by the scientific method) to ensure the individual's adjustment in the real world. Since the emphasis is on the whole individual, physical activity—including the traditional objectives of psychomotor development, intellectual ability, and social and emotional development—makes a vital contribution.

Relative to physical education, exercise science, and sport, the realist does not assume that physical fitness is developed just because this is a curricular or programmatic focus. Rather, the realist administers fitness tests to verify that an increase in fitness, such as cardiorespiratory endurance or flexibility, has occurred. The realist presents factual information, such as how to execute a forearm pass in volleyball, uses a variety of drills so that all students can progress sequentially in learning how to do this skill, and administers an objective test to assess skill development.

Skiers adhere to the philosophy of realism when they recognize that scientific laws influence how they deal with the demands of varying slopes and conditions.
© Bruno Herdt/Getty Images RF

Naturalism

The naturalist believes in things that exist within the physical realm of nature, which is itself the source of value. Since **naturalism** emphasizes the individual over society, education should focus on meeting each student's needs.

Stressing "everything according to nature," the eighteenth-century philosopher Jean-Jacques Rousseau echoed the oldest known philosophy of the Western world (dating back to some pre-Socratic Greek philosophers). Rousseau advocated that education must use the physical world as the classroom and by example teachers should guide students through inductive reasoning to draw their own conclusions. The laws of nature dictate to the teacher and student the logical pattern of growth, development, and learning. Rousseau encouraged education of the mind and body simultaneously. Physical well-being should then enhance a readiness to learn mental, moral, and social skills.

Relative to physical education, exercise science, and sport, the naturalist prefers to use nature as the teacher, such as learning about preserving the environment while backpacking and learning about marine biology while scuba diving. The naturalist encourages students to explore how to execute a locomotor movement like jumping or to discover through trial and error the most effective technique for catching a ball. Through problem solving, individuals progress at their own rates to learn how to do forward rolls or hit balls tossed to them. The naturalist in

A natural setting provides an excellent learning environment for developing social, intellectual, and physical skills.
Courtesy Aram Attarian

The pragmatist has found that having a personal trainer will help him become fit and persist in his fitness program.
© McGraw-Hill Education/Gary He, photographer

physical education uses the principles of movement education and individualized instruction.

Pragmatism

Pragmatism states that experiences, not ideals, provide the key to seeking truth. Ultimate reality must be experienced and is not absolute. Circumstances and situations constantly vary from person to person; thus, pragmatism is characterized as dynamic and ever changing.

The overall objective of a pragmatic education is the development of social efficiency in students, according to the most famous American pragmatist, John Dewey. That is, students need to have opportunities to experience solving problems of life and to learn how to become better functioning members of society.

Relative to physical education, exercise science, and sport, the pragmatist loves to play sports and experience physical activities, especially with others. Pragmatists enjoy developing their social skills through sports and other activities because these interpersonal skills can help them in other situations in life. Self-pacing and self-evaluation activities, such as developing and implementing a personal weight-training program, lead to achieving the pragmatic goal of improved health and fitness.

Existentialism

According to **existentialism,** individual experiences determine reality. Emerging in the 1900s as a reaction against societal conformity, this philosophy subjugated everything to the individual as long as acceptance of responsibility for oneself was recognized. Leaders of existential thought include Jean-Paul Sartre and Karl Jaspers. For the existentialist, reality is composed of human experiences and is determined by the choices made. One's experiences and free choices result in truth and are

The existentialist teaches acceptance of individual responsibility, such as self-motivation in designing and implementing a personal fitness program.
© Ronnie Kaufman/Blend Images RF

uniquely personal. No values are imposed by society; instead, each person is free to think and to act as personal desires dictate.

Relative to physical education, exercise science, and sport, the existentialist emphasizes individuality, so the curriculum or program will focus on individual activities. The existentialist allows students to make choices, such as choosing to go snowboarding, skydiving, or participate in other self-challenging or adventure activities, so they can enjoy their experiences individually. The existentialist gives the individual tremendous self-responsibility for learning, such as through self-paced instruction and contract grading. Box 4.1 provides an overview of the

BOX 4.1   DIFFERENCES AMONG THE FIVE TRADITIONAL PHILOSOPHIES

	Idealism	Realism	Naturalism	Pragmatism	Existentialism
Time period	Historical	Historical	Historical	Contemporary	Contemporary
Reality	Never-changing ideas	Physical objects	Laws of nature	Ever changing and dynamic	Subjective choices
Truth and values	Absolute and universal	Scientifically proven	Exist within the realm of nature	Individual experiences	Uniquely personal

(continued)

**BOX 4.1   DIFFERENCES AMONG
THE FIVE TRADITIONAL PHILOSOPHIES (continued)**

	Idealism	Realism	Naturalism	Pragmatism	Existentialism
Focus	Mind	Body	Self-discovery	Experience	Freedom
Subject matter or curricular emphasis	The mind	The physical world	Nature	Social experiences	Personal choice
Character development	Imitating examples of heroes	Training in rules of conduct	Readiness to learn morally	Making group decisions relative to consequences	Individual responsibility for decisions and preferences
Non-sport example	Physical therapists demonstrating empathy for all clients regardless of their attitudes or limitations	Exercise physiologists providing evidence of the effectiveness of a muscular strength development program	During recess, children developing a new game using playground equipment	Members of a fitness club getting the manager to start an aquatics program for individuals with arthritis who regularly encourage each other to exercise	An individual choosing to engage in a regular physical activity program and eat more healthy foods to help lose weight
Sport example	Athletic director explaining to his staff that complying with a sport organization's rules is required	Based on limitations in range of motion, an athletic trainer not allowing an athlete with a possible concussion to return to a practice session	A coach working with an athlete in experimenting with different take-off angles when practicing the high jump	Strength coach implementing a training program with a college sport team and using team members to help motivate each other's work effort	Intercollegiate athletic administrator deciding to go back to college to earn an advanced degree to improve opportunities for career advancement

differences among the five traditional philosophies. Box 4.2 provides an opportunity to assess your understanding of each of these philosophies.

As a way to review the five traditional philosophies, however, it is helpful to consider a few examples of how individuals in physical education, exercise science, and sport use these philosophies in their work.

BOX 4.2   PHILOSOPHY QUIZ

Fill in the blanks with one of the following: *existentialist, idealist, naturalist, pragmatist,* or *realist.*

1. The _____ advocates that students must indicate their readiness to attempt to learn a cartwheel.
2. The _____ models or provides demonstrations of exactly how to serve a volleyball.
3. The _____ encourages students to use their reasoning powers to decide how to align defensive players to stop an opposing team that fast breaks in basketball.
4. Since a curriculum based on this philosophy focuses on the individual, the _____ focuses on teaching acceptance of self-responsibility.
5. The _____ emphasizes learning team sports in which social skills are developed.
6. A physical education and sport researcher is sometimes called a/an _____ because she or he utilizes the scientific method of inquiry.
7. To the _____ free choices determine reality and truth, such as in setting up an exercise program she or he prefers.
8. The _____ advocates that reality is more mental than physical, such as perfecting shooting technique for free throws through mental practice.
9. Since to the _____ experience, especially as a member of a group, is critical for learning, students are encouraged to experiment with their own techniques in executing bodily movements.
10. The _____ uses natural settings as learning laboratories during leisure hours.

Idealism

- Since reasoning and mental processes are important in understanding truth, physical therapists use idealism in working with clients to help them set realistic goals, persist in their movement experiences, and realize that only by dealing with temporary discomfort can they recover as fully as possible.
- The idealist and the sport psychologist understand that reality is more mental than physical, so helping elite athletes manage the mental side of putting a golf ball or kicking a field goal is vitally important.

Realism

- The exercise physiologist uses the scientific method in investigating the effects of performance-enhancing drugs to understand their positive and negative effects on the body.
- Prior to recommending an exercise program, a personal trainer will assess the capabilities of the client and, as would a realist, continue to use measurements to determine progress made in achieving personal fitness goals.

Naturalism

- Lakes, mountains, and other outdoor settings provide a wealth of opportunities where recreation specialists who believe in naturalism use natural settings as learning laboratories during their leisure hours.
- Physical education teachers agree with the philosophy of naturalism and a readiness to learn as they instruct students in movement activities that are developmentally appropriate.

Pragmatism

- Athletic directors are pragmatic in understanding that they must generate increased revenues from ticket sales, broadcasting rights fees, corporate sponsorships, and private donations to adequately finance their sport teams.
- Directors of recreational facilities realize that participants are practical and pragmatic about the use of their leisure time. They seek to enjoy pleasurable, convenient activities with friends, such as playing on a softball team or using walking trails.

Existentialism

- While health educators stress the importance of making nutritious selections of foods and physical educators emphasize engaging in daily physical activities, each individual has the free will to make choices in life with the full realization of the consequences of choices on health and well-being.
- While an athletic trainer can inform an athlete about the rehabilitation program to be completed, athletes must accept the personal responsibility and demonstrate the self-discipline to complete the exercises and adhere faithfully to the rehabilitation program so they can return to competition.

ETHICS

Ethics is the study of moral values or the doing of good toward others or oneself. It is also the study of the principles of human duty and the study of all moral qualities that distinguish an individual relative to others. Morals pertain to an individual's motives, intentions, and actions as being right or wrong, virtuous or vicious, or good or bad, while values are anything having relative worth. Principles are the universal rules of conduct that identify what kinds of actions, intentions, and motives are valued. Moral values are the relative worth that is placed on virtuous behaviors. Examples of moral values include justice, honesty, responsibility, and beneficence.

   Moral reasoning is the systematic process of evaluating personal values and developing a consistent and an impartial set of moral principles by which to live. The moral reasoning process consists of three steps used to determine the right thing to do in a particular situation. The first step is moral knowing, which is the cognitive phase of learning about moral issues and how to resolve them. The second

Ethical dilemmas are often associated with whether behaviors are within the spirit of the rules.

© Karl Weatherly/Getty Images RF

step is moral valuing, as people decide the basis of what they believe about themselves, society, and others. The third step is moral acting, which is the critical final step of behaving based on what is known and valued.

Ethical theories have been posited to try to understand how individuals resolve ethical questions. **Teleological** theories focus on the end results or consequences of processes or actions. The most prominent of teleological theories is **Utilitarianism,** as advanced by John Stuart Mill. Utilitarianism advocates that decisions should be made based on the greatest good to the greatest number. For example, if a teacher is pressured to give an athlete a passing grade, even when it was unearned, so the athlete can maintain his eligibility to compete, it might be argued that this benefits the team, school, and community more than it disadvantages other students who were not given passing grades without earning them. Since the benefit of the group or society as a whole is the goal for the utilitarian, actions are judged to ensure that the good outcomes outweigh the bad. Another example of teleological theories occurs when an intercollegiate coach violates a recruiting rule without getting caught and penalized, and the athlete who was recruited helps the team win a conference championship. Because the end result or consequence was positive, the coach is more likely to continue violating recruiting rules. Professional sports provide another example. Many athletes have taken performance-enhancing drugs that led to better than natural achievements in their sports, but in the absence of penalties or negative repercussions, they continued to take these drugs to gain competitive advantages. That is, the consequences of their actions reinforced their immoral behaviors.

Immanuel Kant helped formulate the theory of moral obligation or duty known as **deontology.** According to this ethical theory, people have the duty to conform to absolute rules of moral behavior, which are characterized by universality and respect for the individual. Since **Kantian or non-consequential** theories state that actions must conform to absolute rules of moral behavior, there is an inherent rightness, or a **categorical imperative,** apart from all consequences. For example, if the soccer player who last touched the ball that went out-of-bounds conforms to the absolute rules of moral behavior, this player will admit knocking the ball out. Another example of deontological theories occurs when high school and college athletes refuse to allow other people to complete their written assignments because this is academic fraud or cheating. Non-consequential theory states that when athletic directors voluntarily report violations of conference rules, even though they know games will have to be forfeited, they make the morally right decision. Kant's categorical imperative states that moral duties are prescriptive and independent of consequences. Box 4.3 provides examples of how this moral imperative can apply to sports.

In applying the moral reasoning process and possibly using one of these ethical theories, answer the questions associated with each situation.

- A high school defensive tackle sharpens the edges of the fasteners that hold his chin straps to his helmet. After he plays a few downs, several of the opposing players have been cut and are bleeding. Is this action ethical? Is suspending this player from the team and school ethical?

- An elementary school student in a physical education class records that she walked one mile each day to help her team win the special field trip to the zoo, even though she did not do all of this exercise. Is this action ethical? Is suspending this student from school ethical?

- An athletic trainer gives a track athlete amphetamines to help boost his energy level. Is this action ethical? Is this athletic trainer violating the National Athletic Trainers' Association Code of Ethics (see Box 4.5 on page 113–114)?

- A high school athlete cheats on a test to maintain his or her eligibility to play on a school team. Is this action ethical? Does it make any difference if other students (non-athletes) in the class cheated on the same test?

BOX 4.3 MORAL IMPERATIVES IN SPORT

- Fair play means playing within the letter and spirit of the rules.
- Seeking to win within the letter and spirit of the rules is acceptable, while winning "at all costs" is unacceptable.
- An opponent should be treated with respect and exactly as everyone would wish to be treated.
- Games are to be played as mutual quests for excellence where intimidation is inappropriate.
- Retribution for a violent or unfair action by an opponent or an official is never acceptable.

- An exercise scientist inaccurately reports data from a research study in an article published in a journal. Is this action ethical? What action, if any, should be taken?

These scenarios deal with making moral decisions—that is, what is good or bad, right or wrong—and principles of conduct. From the time of the ancient Greeks until today, educators have been held responsible for the nurturance and enhancement of ethical behavior. Character development, for example, has traditionally been a vital concern of professionals. Drawing from the fields of religion, philosophy, and psychology, moral values serve as the foundation of a way of life: People are expected to conduct themselves in accordance with certain principles of conduct.

The essential foundation of ethical decision-making and philosophical analysis is integrity, which is defined as adherence to ethical principles and soundness of moral character. Integrity requires intellectual honesty and open-mindedness so that when people are presented with convincing evidence, they are willing and able to challenge assumptions and imagine and explore alternatives to resolve this dilemma based on moral principles. Practically applied, integrity means that you consistently respect others, accept responsibility for your actions, treat others with fairness, demonstrate trustworthiness in all decisions and actions, and are honest.

Arête is the aggregate of qualities such as values and virtues that comprise good character. To the Greeks (see Chapter 7), arête meant virtue or achieving your highest potential, including athletically through bravery and strength. Applied to competitive sports, this means striving for excellence by playing hard and to best of one's ability and playing fair by respecting the dignity of others including opponents, officials, and teammates. Thus, how a victory is achieved is much more praiseworthy than is the victory itself.

The concept of arête is aligned with the idea of moral goods, which include things like friendship, happiness, health, and justice. Virtues or qualities of character are considered internal goods of excellence, while external goods of effectiveness describe what people do, such as building positive relationships with co-workers and clients. How might internal goods and external goods relate to motivation in sports? Are athletes motivated to participate in sports intrinsically or extrinsically? Are athletes motivated to excel in sports intrinsically or extrinsically?

Sports hold the potential to help athletes, participants, and spectators achieve qualities of character such as respect, responsibility, fairness, and justice, but only if these are taught, modeled, and consistently reinforced. Whenever values and virtues are not emphasized properly or sufficiently, research has shown the following: (1) The moral reasoning of interscholastic athletes is less consistent, impartial, and reflective than is that of non-athletes; (2) Team sport athletes show lower levels of moral reasoning than do individual sport athletes; (3) Males have lower levels of moral reasoning than do females; and (4) The longer athletes participate in sport, the lower their moral reasoning.

How to teach ethical standards most effectively has been a dilemma for a long time. Since fair play is not an inherent characteristic of physical activities, why and how does it occur? When play, games, sports, and other physical pursuits are engaged in for their inherent pleasure, ethical problems seldom emerge. When the outcome becomes so highly significant that some or all participants employ whatever means possible to achieve success, questionable behavior is often chosen to the detriment of values.

Sport participants often face ethical choices such as whether to acknowledge touching the net during a volleyball match.
© Royalty-Free/Corbis

A person's moral values do not preclude seeking to perform to the best of his or her ability. But doing so at the risk of impinging on what is good, one's obligation to others, or principles of ethical conduct violates these values.

The consequences of unethical decisions may seem minimal or limited in impact only to the person making the choice. Too often, though, significant negative repercussions occur when individuals fail to act in morally responsible ways. A few examples in physical education, exercise, and sport settings illustrate how unethical behaviors can have harmful consequences:

- A sport manager at an intercollegiate sporting event ignores the rowdy and obscene behaviors of an intoxicated fan until a fight breaks out in the stands, leaving several individuals hospitalized, including a child who loses an eye from a thrown object and a man who experienced a heart attack.

- An exercise scientist prescribes an exercise program not approved by the client's physician, resulting in the death of the client.

- A volleyball coach emphasizes to his players that winning while looking feminine is most important. To meet weight requirements, one of his volleyball athletes severely curtails her food intake and develops an eating disorder.

- A physical educator allows her students to tease and harass other students who are less skillful. A lawsuit is filed by the parent of one of the children who has special needs and has been bullied repeatedly.

- An individual alleges that he has a Health Fitness Instructor Certification from the American College of Sports Medicine to get hired by a local fitness club, even though this claim is untrue. Several patrons of the club drop their membership due to injuries sustained in programs led by this unqualified person.

As these incidents show, unethical actions can have serious and long-lasting consequences for others.

Can ethical decision-making be taught and modeled by physical educators, exercise scientists, and sport leaders? Yes, professionals have the duty to teach and to uphold moral and ethical principles that are basic to society. Among these principles are sensitivity to individual needs and differences, responsibility for personal conduct, concern for others, and demonstration of integrity and fair play. Teachers and leaders in all settings should exemplify ethical behavior and treat everyone fairly so that others are positively influenced. Professionals must constantly be aware that their actions will teach character more loudly than their statements.

The 25 questions in Box 4.4 challenge you to make ethical choices. These can be discussed in class or with others. Each question could lead to several alternative responses, or you may believe there is only one response. Your answer is a direct reflection of the ethical values that are uniquely yours. You also should realize that your attitudes toward and reactions to these and similar situations will influence those with whom you work in a physical education, exercise science, or sport career. Box 4.5 illustrates how the National Athletic Trainers' Association emphasizes the importance of ethical conduct through its code of professional practices.

BOX 4.4   ETHICAL CHOICES IN SPORTS

1. Should children be cut when trying out for a youth sport team?
2. Should every child play in every contest in youth sport programs?
3. Should every child get an opportunity to play all positions in youth sport programs?
4. Should sport competitions be open to individuals of both sexes playing together?
5. Should extrinsic awards (such as trophies, plaques, or money) be given to sport champions?
6. Should a coach have the right to require that an athlete (at any age) compete in only one sport (i.e., specialize)?
7. Should an athlete be required to pass all school subjects to earn the right to play on an interscholastic team?
8. Should males and females receive similar treatment in school and college sports?
9. Should an athlete ever be allowed or required to play when injured?
10. Should a coach ever have the right to verbally or physically abuse an athlete?
11. Should athletes be allowed to befriend their opponents before or after competitions?
12. Should a coach be allowed to verbally abuse officials?
13. Should an athlete be allowed to use drugs (such as amphetamines or anabolic steroids) to enhance performance?
14. Should a coach teach athletes how to circumvent sports rules to gain competitive advantages?

(continued)

BOX 4.4   ETHICAL CHOICES IN SPORTS (continued)

15. Should high school or college alumni or donors be allowed to influence the hiring and firing of coaches?

16. Should alumni be allowed to give money or tangible gifts to prospective college athletes during their recruitment?

17. Should college coaches who violate recruiting regulations be banned from coaching?

18. Who should make the decision about whether an athlete who has suffered a concussion, and who should decide when a concussed athlete can return to competition?

19. Should fans be protected from the misbehavior of other fans?

20. Should all college students be required to pay fees to finance athletic teams?

21. Should a television broadcaster be allowed to dictate the date and time of a college or professional competition?

22. Should fans have to pay to view major sporting events on television?

23. Should strikes (refusal to compete) for more benefits or rights by professional athletes be allowed? How about lockouts by owners?

24. Should gambling on sports be legalized?

25. Should athletes be suspended from playing for violating federal or state laws during the season?

BOX 4.5   NATA CODE OF ETHICS

PREAMBLE

The National Athletic Trainers' Association Code of Ethics states the principles of ethical behavior that should be followed in the practice of athletic training. It is intended to establish and maintain high standards and professionalism for the athletic training profession.

    The principles do not cover every situation encountered by the practicing athletic trainer, but are representative of the spirit with which athletic trainers should make decisions. The principles are written generally; the circumstances of a situation will determine the interpretation and application of a given principle and of the Code as a whole. When a conflict exists between the Code and the law, the law prevails.

PRINCIPLE 1:

Members shall respect the rights, welfare and dignity of all.

1.1   Members shall not discriminate against any legally protected class.

1.2   Members shall be committed to providing competent care.

1.3   Members shall preserve the confidentiality of privileged information and shall not release such information to a third party not involved in the patient's care without a release unless required by law.

(continued)

BOX 4.5   NATA CODE OF ETHICS (continued)

PRINCIPLE 2:

Members shall comply with the laws and regulations governing the practice of athletic training.

2.1   Members shall comply with applicable local, state, and federal laws and institutional guidelines.

2.2   Members shall be familiar with and abide by all National Athletic Trainers' Association standards, rules and regulations.

2.3   Members shall report illegal or unethical practices related to athletic training to the appropriate person or authority.

2.4   Members shall avoid substance abuse and, when necessary, seek rehabilitation for chemical dependency.

PRINCIPLE 3:

Members shall maintain and promote high standards in their provision of services.

3.1   Members shall not misrepresent, either directly or indirectly, their skills, training, professional credentials, identity or services.

3.2   Members shall provide only those services for which they are qualified through education or experience and which are allowed by their practice acts and other pertinent regulation.

3.3   Members shall provide services, make referrals, and seek compensation only for those services that are necessary.

3.4   Members shall recognize the need for continuing education and participate in educational activities that enhance their skills and knowledge.

3.5   Members shall educate those whom they supervise in the practice of athletic training about the Code of Ethics and stress the importance of adherence.

3.6   Members who are researchers or educators should maintain and promote ethical conduct in research and educational activities.

PRINCIPLE 4:

Members shall not engage in conduct that could be construed as a conflict of interest or that reflects negatively on the profession.

4.1   Members should conduct themselves personally and professionally in a manner that does not compromise their professional responsibilities or the practice of athletic training.

4.2   National Athletic Trainers' Association current or past volunteer leaders shall not use the NATA logo in the endorsement of products or services or exploit their affiliation with the NATA in a manner that reflects badly upon the profession.

4.3   Members shall not place financial gain above the patient's welfare and shall not participate in any arrangement that exploits the patient.

4.4   Members shall not, through direct or indirect means, use information obtained in the course of the practice of athletic training to try to influence the score or outcome of an athletic event, or attempt to induce financial gain through gambling.

4.5   Members shall not provide or publish information, photographs, or any other communications related to athletic training that negatively reflects the profession.

For each of the following situations, what action would you take, if any, to address the ethical dilemma?

The Situation	Questions	Possible Responses	Morally Right Actions
1. During a basketball game, two players attempt to control a loose ball, but it goes out of bounds. An official awards the ball to your team.	A. Why (or why not) would you tell the official you were the last player to touch the ball?	A-1 Everyone knows it is the official's, not a player's, responsibility to make the call. A-2 If your team gains an advantage, great.	A-1 A player honestly acknowledges knocking the ball out of bounds. A-2 Gaining an advantage because of an official's error is unfair.
	B. Why (or why not) would you change your answer if this was a game without officials?	B-1 Yes, a player should admit knocking the ball out-of-bounds so the game can keep going.	B-1 A player should be honest and acknowledge knocking the ball out of bounds. B-2 The presence or absence of officials does not make an action right or wrong.
2. Sporting goods companies offer you gifts, such as free golf clubs or clothing items, if you make sure your high school purchases team equipment or uniforms from these companies.	A. Why (or why not) should you accept these personal gifts?	A-1 These are perks that coaches deserve, especially since most coaches are paid so little compared to the time they dedicate to their teams. A-2 Every coach gets gifts like these, so it must be okay.	A-1 Because of the real or perceived conflict of interest (i.e., you make purchase decisions because of the gifts you receive), you are honor-bound not to accept these gifts. A-2 While others may accept gifts, this does not justify their actions and make them right.
3. As an employee in a corporate fitness center, you learn that other employees are claiming mythical expenses in order to pay for golf greens fees and tickets to sporting events.	A. Why (or why not) should you report the actions of other employees? B. Why should you (or shouldn't you) claim mythical expenses so you can purchase personal items on your expense account?	A-1 Since everyone is doing it, it is acceptable for you to do this as well. A-2 Since salaries are so low, these extra benefits are justified in keeping employees happy. A-3 Nobody is really being hurt, since the company is doing well financially.	A-1 The actions of these employees should be reported because they are being dishonest. A-2 Falsifying one's expense account is lying and shows a lack of integrity.
4. As an exercise physiology graduate student, you believe that your advisor is making up data that show the results he is seeking, rather than reporting what he actually found during the experiment.	A. Why (or why not) should you talk with your advisor about your concerns?	A-1 Because this study will help your advisor get promoted and earn a higher salary, you should keep quiet. A-2 As a student, you should not question the actions of your advisor. A-3 It is okay because nobody is really being harmed.	A-1 Difficult though it may be, you are morally obligated to talk with your advisor to clarify what is actually occurring and to prevent its continuation if there has been an intentional fabrication of data. A-2 If you have evidence that your advisor fabricated or falsified data, you are morally obligated to report him or her through the proper institutional process.

5. You, as a sportswriter for a local newspaper, have obtained factual evidence that an outstanding 14-year-old basketball player just transferred to a public magnet (specialized) school and was induced by financial benefits to transfer.

A. Why (or why not) do you write this story?

A-1 High school players receive financial benefits all the time, so this is no big deal.

A-2 Since nobody else seems to know this and this player can potentially help a local school win a state championship, more good is accomplished by keeping this story quiet.

A-1 If payments to high school athletes are not permitted by state regulations, the morally right action is to draw attention to this violation of the rules so that the school does not receive an unfair advantage.

---

6. A defensive back is beaten by the opposing wide receiver, resulting in a big play for the offense. On a subsequent play, the defensive back "takes out" his opponent with vicious blind side hit to the knees, even though he is not involved with action near the ball.

A. Why (or why not) is this hit ethical?

A-1 It is an acceptable tackle because a defensive back's job is to intimidate the opposing wide receiver to make him tentative and less likely to catch a pass.

A-2 As long as a play is not penalized by the official, it is permissible to hit an opponent in any way to gain an advantage.

A-1 Since the objective is to win, but not "at any cost," hits with the intention of causing injury are irresponsible, disrespectful, and unfair.

A-2 While it is extremely difficult to judge intent to harm, coaches should teach and reward playing fairly and exhibiting good sportsmanship, not winning at all costs.

---

7. In his first at-bat after his grand-slam home run, Mike is prepared for a brush-back pitch. He is not ready for the inside fast ball aimed straight at his head. He attempts to bail out of the batter's box but is hit by a pitch on the arm. A brawl breaks out between the two teams after the pitcher and batter trade punches.

A. Why is the brush-back pitch seemingly an acceptable form of gamesmanship in baseball?

A-1 The culture of baseball accepts a brush-back pitch to prevent batters from crowding the plate and gaining an advantage over pitchers.

A-2 The pitcher is told by his coach to hit the batter to try to intimidate him into making an out.

A-1 The purpose of baseball is to play within the rules, which do not include throwing at a batter.

A-2 Coaches should teach their pitchers not to throw balls at opposing players but rather to use their physical abilities to strike them out. If pitchers persisting in throwing balls at opposing players, coaches must take them out of games and not let them pitch.

B. Why are teammates expected to join in the fray?

B-1 The culture of baseball expects teammates to "stand up" for each other.

B-1 Fighting in baseball is a violation of the rules.

B-2 Coaches can eliminate fighting in baseball through properly educating their players and penalizing any players who continue to fight.

---

8. Your high school girls' basketball team will play in the state championship game the next day. Everyone in the school and small town is excited. Unfortunately, you just realized that Jody, your 24-points-per-game star, is 20 years old and has been all season, thus making her ineligible for high school sports.

A. Will you report this rule violation or decide to keep quiet and play the game?

A-1 The greatest amount of good for Jody, the team, school, and town is to keep quiet, since nobody will ever find out.

A-2 It is right to play Jody, because this increases the possibility that she will earn a scholarship to play basketball in college.

A-1 The morally right thing to do is to immediately report the rule violation to the high school athletic association, the school principal, and the athletic director.

A-2 The coach should explain to the team that even though the mistake was not made intentionally, the team gained an unfair advantage all season, so all games must be forfeited. This disqualifies the team from playing in the championship game.

DEVELOPING A PERSONAL PHILOSOPHY OF PHYSICAL EDUCATION, EXERCISE SCIENCE, AND SPORT

Everyone who plans a career in physical education, exercise science, and sports needs to develop a personal philosophy as a guide to future actions. For example, if fair play is essential to your philosophy, you will stress this in your own behavior, your instruction of others, and the programs you lead. The development of a personal philosophy causes you to think logically and analytically and to explain the worth and value of what you do and how you serve others. This developmental process will enhance your professional growth. Too frequently, professionals fail to develop definite personal philosophies, resulting in a loss of career direction and purpose. Therefore, it is important that you formulate principles, guidelines, and directions for your career. If you do not know where you are going, it is unlikely you will end up where you want to be (wherever that is!). Box 4.6 provides some tips for what could be included in a personal philosophy.

Many educators and philosophers have adopted an eclectic approach rather than accepting all aspects of a traditional philosophy. **Eclecticism** is a combination of theories and doctrines from several philosophies into a consistent and compatible set of beliefs. For example, you may believe that the teacher should model correct skill performance as the idealist would, yet encourage problem solving as the pragmatist and naturalist advocate. You may design your program to focus on individualized learning (naturalism) that allows for individuality (existentialism), yet also emphasizes developing social skills valued by pragmatists. You may choose to evaluate your students using subjective (idealist) and quantitative (realist) measures. Based on your experiences and established values, an eclectic philosophy may emerge as the foundation for your personal philosophy. Again, the key is to realize the importance of examining what you believe, why you believe it, and what your values mean (see Box 4.7, "Sample of a Teaching Philosophy"). Another example of a personal philosophy illustrates how a personal trainer lives out professional values (see Box 4.8).

Before developing your personal philosophy (and to show how your attitudes, beliefs, and values influence your moral reasoning process), read the following situations and give your responses. A composite of your opinions should help you better understand your values and how they provide the foundation for your personal philosophy.

BOX 4.6   TIPS FOR WRITING A PERSONAL PHILOSOPHY

- Discuss your personal values (i.e., those qualities or characteristics that describe who you are, what you believe in, and what you do)
- Explain a specific example of how your values have resulted in principle-based decisions that are reflective of your personal philosophy of life
- Describe your professional goals and aspirations

(continued)

BOX 4.6   TIPS FOR WRITING A PERSONAL PHILOSOPHY (continued)

- Identify a current activity that illustrates how you are working toward the accomplishment of your goals in a way congruent with your values
- Give an illustration of how your values will interface with the type of professional actions you believe are important in your chosen career

BOX 4.7   SAMPLE OF A TEACHING PHILOSOPHY

Student learning is my focus. My goal for this student-centered approach is to facilitate a creative and engaging journey with students to attain a deeper understanding and application of course content. Four questions guide my preparation for and leadership in this quest. First, what do my students know? Second, what do my students want to know? Third, what can I do to help my students attain their goals? Fourth, how can I facilitate the learning process?

What do my students know? Given the inevitable heterogeneity of students, it is challenging, but important, to determine what knowledge, skills, and attitudes students bring to my classes. By learning every student's name, including in large classes, and engaging everyone in class discussions, I seek to establish a comfortable class culture for the intellectual exchange of a diversity of ideas and perspectives. I am dedicated to helping students connect course content to their existing knowledge and personal experiences as they construct and apply new knowledge. Throughout each of my classes, I ask introductory, content specific, application-based questions, and check for understanding to challenge students to think critically and use what they are learning in addressing real world issues.

What do my students want to know? It is important to understand what motivates my students. If students perceive that information presented and discussed is relevant personally and professionally in their careers and lives, they are more eager to learn. If more actively engaged, they will learn more and enjoy the experience of learning. Maybe most significantly, students want an enthusiastic, caring, and competent teacher who knows them by name, respects and trusts them, and helps them along their educational journey. Demonstrating that I care and am competent in helping students achieve their individual goals is integral to my commitment to the teaching and learning process.

What can I do to help my students attain their goals? I teach to help students gain knowledge and learn applications as I encourage them to ask questions to stimulate their interest and engagement. Each class is organized to ensure clear, sequential presentations, using a variety of instructional strategies and approaches. I encourage dialogue in whole-class and small-group formats to facilitate critical thinking by involving every student. I challenge students to think critically, reflect on what they are learning and how it is relevant to them, and collaborate with each other in the learning process.

How can I facilitate the learning process? In every class I demonstrate my personal enthusiasm for the content, thereby helping students realize the importance of, excitement for, and continual nature of learning. By engaging students through questions, one-on-one and group interactions, instructional technology resources, and practical application scenarios, my goal is to guide students in appreciating the diversity of knowledge and experiences that the multiple perspectives of their classmates provide. Since repetition helps facilitate learning, I use a variety of formative and summative assessments, such as minute papers, opinion polls, quizzes, review questions, reports, and group blogs, to ensure that students are monitoring their learning and demonstrating that they are progressing in the achievement of learning outcomes. Feedback from students enables me to reflect upon and continually improve my instructional approaches as well as to help ensure the relevancy, meaningfulness, and application of student learning.

(continued)

BOX 4.7   SAMPLE OF A TEACHING PHILOSOPHY (continued)

My teaching is enriched by my personal commitment to lifelong learning. I am dedicated to and excited by opportunities to expand my knowledge and expertise through the numerous books, research articles, and other professional works that I read and utilize to ensure course content is current, engaging, and relevant.

Teaching, to me, is an ethical profession, so I seek always to model integrity and civility in class sessions, one-on-one interactions, and informal conversations as I model moral values, such as respect for and fairness toward everyone. I have an awesome responsibility and opportunity to impact lives and play a small role in shaping students' futures. I try to organize and manage the best possible learning environments and foster student-centered class cultures. I believe students respond positively to high standards and learn optimally through intellectually challenging experiences, so these characterize my classes. As a lifelong learner, I want students to see the importance of reflection and have a willingness to consider perspectives that challenge prior thinking. I care deeply about helping my students learn as I am rewarded by seeing them achieve their goals.

BOX 4.8   SAMPLE PHILOSOPHY OF A PERSONAL TRAINER

I believe that every person should have the knowledge and skills to lead a healthy life. As a personal trainer, this belief is founded upon the values instilled in me by my parents, coaches, teachers, and other significant individuals in my life. These values are integrity, based on being honest in all my interactions with others; respect for the importance and uniqueness of each individual; equity in treating each person fairly, kindly, and with compassion; and responsibility in fulfilling all duties assigned and commitments made.

My values shape who I am and how I act, which can be verified by the network of friends I developed throughout my years in college. I earned a reputation of playing fair while playing on intramural teams as well as a contributing team member while doing excellent work on group projects. Although others have encouraged me to lie or cheat in games and classes, I have demonstrated my integrity by being true to my values.

My short-term goal is to become certified and work in a fitness club as a personal trainer. After working for a few years and completing a master's degree in business administration, I plan to pursue my long-term goal of establishing and operating a personal training company that provides personal training to professional football players. As a personal trainer, I am dedicated to helping each of my clients learn how to exercise regularly, eat nutritious foods, and practice healthy behaviors. The specific strategies that I will use to achieve these goals include the following:

- Individualized instruction in exercise programs—Teach and guide through fundamental and advanced techniques and activities for the development of cardiorespiratory endurance, muscular strength and endurance, and flexibility

- Nutritional counseling—Guide clients in the selection, preparation, and consumption of nutritious foods that will lead to the maintenance of good health

- Motivation and positive reinforcement—Help clients develop the intrinsic motivation to enjoy healthy behaviors by providing positive comments about their effort, commitment, responsible actions, and persistence, as well as their progress in achieving nutritional and fitness goals

(continued)

BOX 4.8   SAMPLE PHILOSOPHY OF A PERSONAL TRAINER (continued)

- Safety—Ensure that clients complete each exercise, activity, and lifestyle change in a safe environment with appropriate supervision
- Specificity of training—Direct prescribed exercises and programs in congruence with personal goals, physical limitations, and physicians' directions
- Injury or disease rehabilitation—Assist clients in regaining levels of mobility and fitness commensurate with individual circumstances and within guidelines provided by physicians
- Education—Provide information and resources to help clients incorporate healthy behaviors into all aspects of their lives

To illustrate my commitment to these strategies, I am currently working as a student personal trainer for other students at the Recreation Center on campus. I have received exemplary evaluations from my supervisor because I have demonstrated my values in the way I work with clients. I am planning to complete the internship for my sport management major in a nationally-franchised fitness club and continue to live by these values.

I am confident that my values of integrity, respect, fairness, and responsibility will serve me well as a personal trainer. These are important in maintaining positive personal trainer—client relationships; they will be essential in gaining and retaining the confidence of professional athletes, whose careers and success depend on the physical training and overall well-being that I can help ensure.

SUMMARY

The pursuit of knowledge, wisdom, and truth occurs throughout life. The idealist focuses on the mind using reasoning and reflection to understand never-changing ideals and truth. The realist relies on scientific laws and investigations to reveal the truth. The naturalist believes that truth exists in the physical realm and can be learned in and through nature. The pragmatist states that truth must be experienced, is ever-changing, and is contextually based within society. The existentialist argues that each individual is personally responsible for determining truth through experiences and free choice. As you progress in your education and enter your career, your philosophy will change or evolve. You may borrow concepts from idealism, realism, naturalism, pragmatism, or existentialism, or you may adopt an eclectic approach borrowing from more than one of these traditional philosophies. Ethics is the study of moral values and the principles of human duty. Throughout your career and life, you will face numerous ethical decisions. To help you make morally reasoned decisions, having a philosophy based on your personal values is essential. Your personal philosophy describes who you are and believe in as a person as well as your commitment to living true to your values while working in your career.

CAREER PERSPECTIVE

SHARON KAY STOLL, PH.D.
Professor and Director, Center for ETHICS*
University of Idaho
Moscow, Idaho

EDUCATION

B.S. Ed., Physical Education, College of the Ozarks
M.Ed., Physical Education, Kent State University
Ph.D., History and Philosophy of Sport, Kent State
University

Courtesy Sharon Kay Stoll

JOB RESPONSIBILITIES AND HOURS

Sharon directs the Center for ETHICS* at the University of Idaho, which offers study, inter-vention, outreach, consultation, and leadership in developing and advancing the theory, knowledge, and understanding of character education, including moral and ethical reasoning, development, and application. She teaches undergraduate and graduate classes in sport phi-losophy and sport ethics, and advises master's and doctoral students in sport ethics study. At the center, professionals model ethical conduct; perform global research on competitive ethics, moral reasoning, and character development; develop and provide teaching methodologies and curricula supporting the practical application of moral reasoning in competitive communities; sponsor conferences through which participants utilize practical application of moral reasoning to confront problematic ethical reasoning and action; provide professional training programs to help decision makers navigate current ethical issues or trends; nurture a commitment to ethics, moral reasoning, and character development within competitive communities; and serve aca-demic, professional, and public agencies in developing competitive moral excellence.

SPECIALIZED COURSE WORK, DEGREES, AND WORK EXPERIENCE NEEDED FOR THIS CAREER

An advanced degree in pedagogy and sport ethics is necessary for this career, as well as the good fortune to work in such an environment.

SATISFYING ASPECTS

Sharon believes that she has the greatest job in the world. She works with young, intelligent people every day. She travels around the world helping others meet their needs and teaches eth-ics and moral reasoning. Her teaching, research, and service focus on moral reasoning. She is currently working or has worked with the United States Military Academy, United States Naval Academy, United States Air Force Academy, Atlanta Braves, all levels of football teams from university level to high school, the American Bar Association, NCAA, and World Anti-Doping Agency as well as numerous colleges, high schools, and communities that aim to teach some aspect of ethics through their competitive programs. Her work includes assistance provided to 55 national and international high schools through the Winning with Character foundation.

JOB POTENTIAL

Jobs in this field are available but not abundant. There is an emerging career in professional sport and Division I sport called the character coach. Most organizations have ethics as a required element, but most need help in teaching their own ethical perspectives. There is also the need for good sport ethics teachers and professors. During your graduate work, make sure you are employable and take classes in many different fields, such as sport psychology and exercise physiology.

SUGGESTIONS FOR STUDENTS

First and most important, know yourself. What does it mean to be ethical? Take classes in ethics with physical education professors and undertake further study of ethics and moral development at your university. This field demands your ability to be an active and consummate reader, with reading including theoretical works to current, common media writings. After graduation, attend an institution that offers an advanced degree in sport ethics or sport philosophy. Make contacts with individuals who work in the field of sport ethics and develop a research profile that will support employment with agencies and businesses.

KEY POINTS

Philosophy	The study of wisdom and knowledge.
Code of conduct	Professionals are guided by codes of ethical behavior in their careers.
Idealism	Using the mind and reasoning to understand what is true.
Realism	Seeking the truth through scientific investigation.
Naturalism	Nature, or everything according to nature, is the source of truth.
Pragmatism	Since truth is dynamic and changing, truth must be experienced as each person becomes a better-functioning member of society.
Existentialism	Personal experiences along with personal responsibility determine truth.
Eclecticism	Borrowing from various philosophies in developing a personal philosophy.
Ethics	The study of moral values and doing good toward others and oneself.
Moral reasoning process	Evaluating personal values and determining a personal set of moral principles by which to live; includes moral knowing, valuing, and acting.
Utilitarianism theory	Greatest good for the greatest number is what is right.
Non-consequential theory	Absolute rules about what is right should govern human behavior.
Moral imperatives in sport	Fair play, playing by the spirit of the rules, and treating others with respect, while avoiding intimidation and violent actions.

REVIEW QUESTIONS

1. What does philosophy mean?
2. How do idealists and realists seek truth?
3. How would a naturalist, pragmatist, and existentialist emphasize attaining individual goals?
4. What is the moral reasoning process?
5. How can a physical educator, exercise scientist, or sport leader teach ethics?
6. Why is having a personal philosophy of physical education, exercise science, and sport important?
7. What is an eclectic philosophy?

STUDENT ACTIVITIES

1. Select one of the five traditional philosophies discussed in this chapter and write a two-page paper explaining how it applies to your experiences as a student.
2. Select one of the five traditional philosophies discussed in this chapter and write a two-page paper explaining how it would apply to your career as a physical education teacher, exercise scientist, or sport manager.
3. In groups of 4–6 students, discuss multiple responses to the questions in Box 4.4. Based on the discussion, what would be best response from the group? Reconvene as a class and have each group report its response with a rationale for the group's decision.
4. Respond to each of the 8 situations listed on pages 115–116 and be prepared to discuss them in class. Be ready to justify your opinions.
5. Write your personal philosophy of physical education, exercise science, or sport.
6. A philosophical controversy dealing with aesthetics is whether activities like cheerleading, figure skating, and the equestrian events of dressage or showjumping are sports. Divide the class in two groups, with one advocating that these activities are sports and the other arguing that these activities are not sports. Questions that might guide the discussion or debate could be: Who determined the criteria for judging or scoring in these activities? What defines what is beautiful or aesthetically pleasing? What were the qualifications of the individuals who established the judging or scoring criteria or decide that some action is or is not beautiful?

REFERENCE

Kretchmar, R. S. (2005). *Practical philosophy of sport and physical activity* (2nd ed.). Champaign, IL: Human Kinetics.

WEB CONNECTIONS

1. www.webpages.uidaho.edu/center_for_ethics/
   This site of the Center for ETHICS* at the University of Idaho offers educational programs, consultation, and leadership in the theory, knowledge, and understanding of character education, ethical reasoning, moral development, and ethical leadership.

2. http://sportsmanship.org/
   The National Sportsmanship Foundation develops educational programs, conducts research, and convenes groups focused on sportsmanship and youth sports.

3. http://www.sportsparenting.org/
   The Center for Sports Parenting provides guidance and information to parents, coaches, and others to help them work with young athletes as they deal with the psychological and physical challenges in sports.

4. www.positivecoach.org/
   By helping organizational leaders, coaches, and parents ensure a positive playing environment, the Positive Coaching Alliance advocates for the development of life skills by young athletes that will serve them well beyond the playing field or court.

5. www.championsofcharacter.org/
   The National Association of Intercollegiate Athletics' Champions of Character program is designed to instill an understanding of the values of integrity, respect, responsibility, sportsmanship, and servant leadership in sport. This site provides practical tools for student-athletes, coaches, and parents to use in modeling exemplary character traits.

6. https://charactercounts.org/
   CHARACTER COUNTS! has been used by schools, communities, and non-profit organizations to teach the six pillars of character—trustworthiness, respect, responsibility, fairness, caring, and citizenship. This site provides information about materials and services used to support this program.

7. http://cces.ca/
   The Canadian Centre for Ethics in Sport promotes fair and ethical sport to athletes, coaches, sport organizations, governments, and the general public.

(continued)

8. http://portal.unesco.org/education/en/ev.php-URL_ID=2223&URL_
   DO=DO_TOPIC&URL_SECTION=201.html
   The United Nations Educational, Scientific and Cultural Organization
   (UNESCO) stresses one theme of learning to live together and
   emphasizes the importance of fair play as integral to all sports activities
   as "the winning way." UNESCO's Code of Sports Ethics defines fair play
   and describes the responsibilities of governments, sport organizations,
   and individuals.

5

CAREER OPTIONS

LEARNING OUTCOMES

- Students will be able to identify personal preferences through the completion of self-assessment inventories related to their aspirational careers.
- Students will be able to describe the responsibilities, clientele served, and pros and cons of possible careers that include teaching.
- Students will be able to explain the responsibilities, clientele served, and pros and cons of possible careers in fields related to the exercise sciences.
- Students will be able to differentiate among the responsibilities, clientele served, and pros and cons of possible careers involving sports.

Career choices today involve more complex decisions than ever before because of the obsolescence of some jobs, burgeoning technology, demographic shifts in population, and economic necessity. People seldom continue in their initial career choices; they change jobs several times during their working years, and especially as they begin and advance in their careers.

The preceding chapters described the broad spectrum of physical education, exercise science, and sport, laying the foundation for the career options presented in this chapter. You should now be prepared to assess objectively your future career. Your initial career choice is not necessarily a lifetime commitment, because it often may be reevaluated. As you read this chapter and assess your interests, abilities, and goals, remember that you are choosing a career pathway, not necessarily a single job.

Before embarking on this process, identify your attitudes and expectations. Your attitude toward a career greatly influences whether you will be successful and happy. A major factor is your self-concept: How do you evaluate your abilities? Are you willing to listen to the advice of teachers, coaches, parents, and others? Can you objectively assess your personal strengths and weaknesses? Are you people oriented? Are you motivated to do your best?

Before considering available careers, analyze the relative importance of some personal and job-related factors. Two self-assessment inventories are provided in Boxes 5.1 and 5.2. Your responses to these inventories will help you determine which a physical education, exercise science, or sport career best meets your needs and aspirations.

BOX 5.1   FACTORS INFLUENCING CAREER CHOICES

Using the scale below, indicate how much you value each of the following in relation to your potential career choice:

5	4	3	2	1
Most highly valued	Strong influencing factor	Average consideration	Weak influencing factor	Not valued at all

____ A.   Family, friends, and significant others work in this career

____ B.   A specific role model in this career whom you want to emulate

____ C.   Being knowledgeable about aspects of this career

____ D.   Being interested in this career

____ E.   Mental challenge expected from this career

____ F.   Opportunity to be creative in this career

____ G.   Opportunity to work with people and interact with them socially in this career

____ H.   Desire to serve others through this career

____ I.   Ease of entrance into this career

____ J.   Anticipated sense of accomplishment in this career

____ K.   Opportunity to be responsible for other people and their performances in this career

____ L.   Anticipated power associated with this career

____ M.   Opportunity to work independently in this career

____ N.   Anticipated variety in the work in this career

____ O.   Anticipated feeling of competence from this career

____ P.   Monetary and other benefits from this career

____ Q.   Time compatibility (work hours versus leisure time) in this career

____ R.   Job security in this career

____ S.   Job location of this career

____ T.   Prestige associated with working in this career

____ U.   Mutual trust and respect among those with whom you would work in this career

____ V.   Shared values with whom you would work in this career

List any other factors that would influence your career choice.

____ W.

____ X.

____ Y.

____ Z.

From items A through V as well as any factors you added in W through Z, select the five that you think are most important to you in your career choice and write them below (in descending order of importance).

1. _____

2. _____

3. _____

4. _____

5. _____

BOX 5.2   LIFESTYLE PREFERENCE ASSESSMENT

Read each of these questions and give the answer that best describes your opinion of their importance.
   Beginning with a few specifics:

1. Where would you prefer to live (state, region, or nation)?
2. Do you prefer to work for yourself or someone else?
3. Do you prefer a work setting with few or numerous coworkers?
4. What age groups would you prefer to interact with daily?
5. Do you prefer an outdoor or indoor work setting?
6. Do you prefer primarily active or sedentary work?
7. How much travel (if any) would you want as a regular part of your work?
8. What days of the week would you prefer to work?
9. What hours of the day would you prefer to work?
10. What salary would you want in your first position? In 5 years? In 10 years?
11. How much annual vacation time would you want initially? After 10 years?
12. What fringe benefits (such as insurance, retirement, special perks) would you want as an essential part of your compensation?
13. How important to you are opportunities for career advancement?
14. What other job characteristics do you think would be important to your job satisfaction? What would your preferences be?
15. Would you prefer to plan out your career path or keep your options open? Why?
16. Would you prefer a work environment that is unlikely to have conflict among employees, or is conflict something you think you can handle? Why?
17. Would you prefer a career in which you were continually challenged to take on new and different responsibilities or one in which you are able to continue to do mostly the same duties on a regular basis? Why?
18. Would you prefer to have your work space in the middle of the action, close by your friends, in a quiet, enclosed office, or in another arrangement? Why?
19. Would you prefer a job in which you are expected to make numerous decisions each day? Why?
20. Would you prefer a job in which you are responsible for the performance of others? Why?
21. Would you prefer a job in which you were expected to gain new knowledge, abilities, and skills in order to be successful? Why?
22. Would you prefer a job in which you are eager to go to work each day or any job that paid you a high salary so you could spend your free time doing what you really enjoyed? Why?
23. Would you prefer a job in which on a daily basis you had time to maintain your physical fitness? Why?
24. Would you prefer to work in a job that is mentally stimulating? Why?
25. Would you prefer to work for an employer who is located close to where you want to live?
26. Would you prefer to work in a job that provides you flexibility in your schedule so you can take care of family matters, if needed?
27. Would you prefer to work for an employer who rewards performance, longevity, or both? Why?
28. Would you prefer to work for an employer who shares your moral values? Why?

FACTORS INFLUENCING CAREER CHOICES

Family influences regarding a career choice can be positive, negative, or both. Parents may overtly or subtly persuade you to pursue a specific career. Some parents have discouraged their children from majoring in physical education because they view it as frivolous, nonacademic, or not prestigious enough. On the other hand, parents may encourage their children to pursue a career in sports because the parents enjoyed rewarding experiences in sports. Regardless of the situation, remember that your family will not be going to work for you each day or fulfilling the responsibilities of your chosen career. Although parents, siblings, and significant others can express their opinions and share their experiences, they should not choose your career (and major in college).

Whether consciously or not, many people select a career because they respect and admire someone who is in a particular position, a role model whom they wish to emulate. This may be a parent, sibling, coach, teacher, or friend who has demonstrated enjoyment of and dedication to a career that you wish to emulate. One cautionary note: You may not be able to find the same type of position or may not possess the same abilities. Remember, you need to develop your own career pathway niche rather than try to mimic another person's.

The skills, knowledge, abilities, and experiences that you bring to your career will influence whether you are successful. This is not to imply that all career preparation precedes employment; certainly considerable learning occurs while you are on the job. Your confidence in accepting an initial position is based on two factors, only one of which is prior formal preparation. Always remember the importance of the second factor: gaining experiences, including voluntary or internship experiences, that may enhance your chances of career change or advancement.

An important criterion for continuation in a job is the level of personal fulfillment and satisfaction. If you dread going to work, hate the day-to-day routine, and think the negative aspects far outweigh the positive gains, it is probably time for a change. It is not disastrous to sacrifice job security and financial benefits to start a career that enhances self-worth and pleasure. One way to make a career change less traumatic is to prepare yourself for a broad physical education, exercise science, and sport career pathway that can offer you numerous alternatives or options.

Some people prefer a solitary setting; others need to interact frequently with people. If you are people oriented, you need to identify the ages of those with whom you find the greatest enjoyment and seek a career that includes these opportunities. It is also important to identify which aspects of working with people you enjoy most. Do you prefer to work with large groups, small groups, or one-on-one? Do you prefer frequent or periodic interactions? Can you make decisions with others or concerning others?

Sometimes interaction with people is so highly valued that your personal needs become secondary to those of others. Altruism, which regards the good of others as the desired result of moral action, is the selfless giving to other people out of a genuine concern without expecting anything in return. Teachers in various settings focus on helping their students develop healthy lifestyles, often by spending personal time to provide individualized instruction or help.

Coaches teach sport skills to young athletes as well as teach them values and life skills.
© BananaStock/Alamy RF

Career opportunities in physical education, exercise science, and sport are expanding. Your expertise is needed because many people desire to use their leisure time engaged in a variety of sports and physical activities. However, your ideal job in the exact location you wish and with the dreamed-for salary may not be available. After realizing that jobs are available for educated individuals who actively seek them, you must be willing to accept the probability of starting in a low-paying, entry-level position. As a young professional, you should expect to work hard, volunteer for extra duties, learn new ideas, gain experiences, and accept less desirable responsibilities as a test of commitment to your field. If you do so successfully, you will advance.

You must weigh the importance you place on monetary and other financial benefits as you choose a career. Your responses on the Lifestyle Preference Assessment indicate the importance of the salary, overall compensation package, and vacation time you have and how these relate to other aspects of your life, such as family, status, location, and travel. The importance salary has for you also is shown in the hours and days you prefer to work. Money, however, is only one type of remuneration. Other benefits, including health insurance, retirement benefits, an expense account, travel, club memberships, and prestige, may offset a lower salary. Only you can decide the importance of money and other benefits, but you must do so honestly, since frequently these are pivotal factors in career selection.

A 5-day, 8-to-5 workweek is unlikely in many physical education, exercise science, and sport careers. Your career choice could result in working any number of hours a week, nights, holidays, and weekends, and anywhere from 9 to 12 months a year. Only you can weigh your personal preferences versus each job's characteristics. Begrudging time spent working often results in negative feelings toward that task. How important are the amount and scheduling of leisure time for you? How do work hours relate to monetary benefits in importance?

Job security varies dramatically in physical education, exercise science, and sport careers. Competent fulfillment of job responsibilities in some careers results in retention of positions based on merit; most careers in educational institutions require earning tenure for job security. Some careers carry no guarantee of future employment other than the demand for your services. Associated with the concept of job security is the potential for advancement. Relocation is often necessary for advancement because the position you qualify for or seek may not be available in the same city or with the same employer. Challenge and stimulation are important to many people for continuation in a career, as are recognition for a job well done and increased monetary benefits.

As you consider career options, review and weigh all these factors. Take advantage of your institution's career services office, which can assist you in evaluating various career options. To help decide what career path to take, you might consider interviewing someone who works in your area of interest. Possible questions include the following:

1. What academic degrees, certifications, or licenses are required for your job?

2. What college courses or professional experiences have been most useful in fulfilling your job responsibilities?

3. What are your primary job responsibilities?

4. What specialized experiences were required as a prerequisite to being qualified for your position?

5. What are your normal work hours?

6. What is the salary range for individuals in positions similar to yours?

7. What are the opportunities for advancement (salary, responsibility, and promotion) in your career?

8. What are the most satisfying aspects of your career?

9. What are the least enjoyable aspects of your career?

10. What suggestions and advice would you give to students considering a career like yours?

Only after evaluating the most influential considerations and your own personal preferences can you objectively select a career pathway. Regardless of your choice, the key to personal satisfaction in your career is your commitment and motivation.

Box 5.3 provides a broad overview of career opportunities. The rest of this chapter describes these broad categories and some of the options, presenting educational requirements, job availability, and advantages and disadvantages.

BOX 5.3   EXAMPLES OF CAREER OPPORTUNITIES AND EDUCATIONAL REQUIREMENTS

Teaching

- Adapted physical education

- Elementary, middle, and secondary schools
- City recreation program, sport club, or sport camp
- College

- Specialized settings like a dance studio or the armed services

Educational Requirements

- Bachelor's degree in adapted physical education or equivalent and state certification or licensure
- Bachelor's degree in physical education and state certification or licensure
- Expertise in teaching physical activities and sports
- Master's degree in physical education or equivalent in smaller institutions; doctoral degree in one of the exercise or sport sciences or pedagogy in larger institutions
- Expertise in teaching dance, physical activities, or sports; fitness leader or equivalent certification preferred

Fitness

- Cardiac rehabilitation

- Corporate fitness programs and sports leagues

- Dietitian or nutritionist

- Health and fitness club classes such as in aerobics and Pilates
- Personal training

- Protective services (police and fire)

- Specialized settings like a cruise ship or resort

Educational Requirements

- Master's degree in exercise physiology or equivalent field
- Expertise in teaching physical activities or sports; minimum of a bachelor's degree in exercise science if prescribing exercise programs
- Bachelor's degree in dietetics, foods and nutrition, or related field; most states require licensure
- Expertise in each class area

- Expertise in cardiorespiratory and endurance training; personal trainer certification preferred
- Bachelor's degree in exercise science; master's degree in exercise physiology preferred
- Expertise in developing and maintaining physical fitness of clients

Sport Management

- Accounting and finance

- Athletic administration

Educational Requirements

- Bachelor's degree in accounting or finance; master's degree preferred
- Bachelor's degree in any field; master's degree preferred

(continued)

BOX 5.3   EXAMPLES OF CAREER OPPORTUNITIES AND EDUCATIONAL REQUIREMENTS (continued)

• Event management	• Bachelor's degree, preferably in sport management; master's degree for advancement
• Facility management	• Bachelor's degree, preferably in sport management; master's degree for advancement
• Marketing and promotions	• Bachelor's degree, preferably in marketing or business; master's degree for advancement
• Media relations	• Bachelor's degree, preferably in journalism or communication
• Public relations	• Bachelor's degree, preferably in journalism or communication
• Sports clothing and equipment sales	• Bachelor's degree, preferably in business
• Ticket sales	• Bachelor's degree, preferably in sport management; master's degree for advancement

Sport Communication	*Educational Requirements*
• Broadcasting	• Bachelor's degree, preferably in communication
• Journalism	• Bachelor's degree, preferably in journalism
• Photography	• Expertise as a photographer

Recreation	*Educational Requirements*
• Aquatics programs and facilities	• Bachelor's degree in recreation or equivalent; aquatics certifications
• Campus recreation (college)	• Master's degree in recreation or equivalent
• Public recreation programs	• Bachelor's degree in recreation or equivalent
• Senior citizens center	• Expertise in leading exercise programs for senior citizens
• Therapeutic recreation	• Bachelor's degree in therapeutic recreation

TEACHING

Schools and Colleges

Employment for college graduates majoring in physical education has traditionally been in public and private schools. Teaching remains a viable choice for beginning and lifelong careers. Teachers' salaries are determined by each state's salary schedule and local school district supplements. Additional stipends for extra responsibilities, like coaching, are likely possible. Base salaries for beginning teachers with baccalaureate degrees will be at least $25,000, with larger, urban school systems paying over $50,000 and some offering signing bonuses due to teacher shortages. To find jobs, graduates may have to move to smaller communities, urban settings, or different states. In the last situation, a reciprocal agreement may exist between the licensing state and the new state, or additional course work may be required before full licensure is granted.

The Praxis Series contains assessments used by many states in awarding teacher certification or licensure. Praxis Core Academic Skills for Educators, which measures basic skills in reading, writing, and mathematics, is used to evaluate students prior to entry into teacher education programs. Praxis Subject Assessments, which measures knowledge of the content that K–12 teachers will teach, as well as general and subject-specific teaching skills and knowledge, is used as a criterion for professional licensing decisions by states.

Junior high and senior high physical educators in their first years sometimes teach classes outside their licensure fields. Preparing to teach in a second subject area through taking courses and obtaining a license in a second teaching field will enhance the likelihood of securing a position. Willingness to accept these teaching assignments may lead to full-time physical education positions in subsequent years. Physical educators, although perhaps not prepared to teach or interested in teaching health, frequently are assigned classes in this area. Some schools hire licensed health educators and others have health consultants, but because of budget constraints many health classes are taught by physical educators in middle or secondary schools. Physical education teachers work a minimum of 7 hours at school, which usually includes one planning period and at least five classes. In addition, each teacher is expected to plan classes; grade papers; monitor the halls, lunchroom, and buses; and complete administrative reports. Some teachers face discipline problems, apathetic students, student drug abuse, inadequate facilities and equipment, lack of administrative and community support, and bullying and other misbehaviors of students. On the other hand, professional involvement and educational enrichment are encouraged by supportive administrators. Low salaries deter some good candidates from choosing teaching careers, while opportunities to positively influence students' lives, retirement and health benefits, summer vacations, and job security are attractive job characteristics.

Adapted physical education specialists are hired most frequently by large systems and state departments of education so that many schools may share the expertise of one individual. This specialist helps classroom teachers and physical educators meet the needs of students with special needs or limitations who have been included in regular classes, or they may individualize instruction for students. Educational background and experience emphasizing adapted physical education is important for this career. Hours and salaries correspond with those of other teachers.

In some states, elementary school physical educators are in demand; in others, jobs are scarce. Their responsibilities vary from teaching daily classes for children at one school to conducting ten 30-minute classes at a different school each day of the week. The intrinsic satisfaction of helping children learn and develop is the reward these teachers cite most often. The benefits of positively influencing children's attitudes toward movement skills and encouraging healthy lifestyles outweigh problems like inadequate facilities and equipment and limited administrative support.

Children need guidance in learning fundamental movement skills.
© images 100 Ltd RF

PE Central (www.pecentral.org/) is an outstanding resource for health and physical education teachers, as well as for parents and students. This site provides a wealth of information about developmentally appropriate physical education instruction for children and youth. A primary strength is the provision of hundreds of lesson ideas to help teachers motivate their students to engage and persist in sport development and physical fitness activities. Additional resources include assessments, bulletin board ideas, instructional best practices, physical activity adaptations, video suggestions, research in action strategies, and links to other helpful websites.

Teaching physical education in community colleges or in four-year colleges requires education beyond a bachelor's degree. In smaller institutions, faculty with master's degrees are expected to teach pre-major or major courses. Most institutions also require sports and activity instructors to hold at least master's degrees. Since university activity instructors and small college teachers spend most of their time teaching rather than conducting research, job security or tenure is based primarily on teaching and service rather than on scholarly productivity. (These same teachers are often expected to advise students and to serve on departmental and university committees.) Beginning salaries range widely according to location and status of the institution, with benefits including health insurance, retirement programs, and summer vacations. In their activity and theory classes, these teachers enjoy helping adult students learn healthy lifestyles and relish the generalist approach to teaching physical education 3 to 6 hours per day and 4 or 5 days a week.

In larger institutions, exercise and sport scientists in specialties such as biomechanics, exercise physiology, and sport and exercise psychology teach undergraduate and graduate courses in addition to conducting research. Research productivity, teaching effectiveness, and professional service are required for tenure, which is granted in 5 to 7 years. For university professors, conducting research, writing articles for professional journals, and giving scholarly presentations are prerequisites for job security. Lack of time for research and class preparation is cited frequently as a problem by university teachers. Although their hours are somewhat flexible, committee meetings, student advising, and other departmental responsibilities besides teaching, research, and service often extend the workweek well beyond 40 hours.

Other Instructional Settings

Opportunities abound for those who want to teach fitness and sports skills outside a school environment. Dance studios provide instruction in aerobic, jazz, ballet, tap, and modern dance for children and adults. Individuals with dance majors or specialized dance course work teach various dance forms to customers for fees (ranging from $10 per hour for group lessons to $100 per hour for private lessons) at these studios. Classes may be scheduled throughout the day and evening as well as on weekends.

Private clubs focus on individual sports, such as tennis, swimming, or martial arts and need instructors for individual and group lessons. Other clubs, which usually have membership fees, may cater to several sports, such as country clubs that offer swimming, golf, and tennis. Vacation resorts are increasingly providing sport instruction for their guests. Health clubs usually offer fitness programs in aerobic conditioning and weight training; instructional programs in rock climbing or racquetball; and sometimes classes in stress management and weight control. Because of the extensive variety in clubs, salaries depend on location, clientele, instructional expertise, and assigned responsibilities. Salaries for instructors may start at $10 an hour and increase as responsibilities grow.

Sport camps have become booming businesses. Both children and adults attend these highly successful ventures in the summer or on weekends and holidays. Sport camps provide excellent opportunities for gaining teaching experience and making valuable contacts that may lead to permanent positions. For school teachers looking for summer employment, opportunities abound in sport camps. Expertise in teaching one or more activities is important for employment, as is a desire to work with various age and skill levels. Responsibilities, such as those of an instructor or program director, determine salaries, which may vary widely. Day camp instructors may earn $25 to $100 per day, while residence camp instructors can expect salaries at about twice this level.

Concomitant with increasing life spans in the United States is the critical need for professionals trained to provide recreational and leisure activities for senior citizens. In 2012, according to federal statistics over 13% of the U.S. population, or over one in eight, was 65 years old or older. The number of Americans aged 45–64 who will reach 65 over the next two decades increased by 33% between 2000 and 2012. Federal programs, as well as private agencies, increasingly provide physical activity programs in retirement homes, elder care centers, and senior citizens' residential complexes. Given these facts, the job potential for individuals trained to prescribe and to direct activities for this clientele will expand rapidly in the years ahead.

Golf instruction is popular in schools and colleges as well as in private and public clubs.
© PhotoLink/PhotoDisc/Getty Images RF

Opportunities to teach and lead sport and fitness programs in the military abound because fitness training is highly valued by the various branches of the armed services. Instructional assignments in physical fitness programs are available to enlistees. Civilians instruct at the service academies, on military installations, and at special training facilities. Programs for the military vary widely, from basic conditioning drills for men and women to broad-based fitness and sport opportunities for career personnel to family-oriented recreational offerings. Highly competitive leagues in a variety of sports are commonplace on most military bases, since skilled, fit servicemen and servicewomen are valued. As an employee of the federal government, your pay would depend on classification; benefits are excellent.

FITNESS, EXERCISE, AND SPORT SCIENCES

Many large corporations provide fitness centers for their executives. Concerns about work efficiency and loss of time and money from absenteeism have resulted in the addition of facilities to provide daily aerobic, strength, and flexibility workouts for employees. The directors of corporate fitness centers are usually individuals trained in one of the exercise sciences with a bachelor's degree. However, because of the attractiveness of these jobs and the in-depth knowledge needed, holders of master's degrees are often hired. Minimally, each individual should hold a certification as a group exercise instructor, if not a higher certification such as Clinical Exercise Specialist (awarded by the American College of Sports Medicine). Directors of corporate fitness centers are responsible for designing individually prescribed programs that include exercise sessions, nutritional changes, stress management strategies, and other recommended lifestyle alterations. Close monitoring is required because for many people, these programs expect participants to dramatically change their inactive habits. Since lack of **exercise adherence,** which means development and maintenance of a physical activity program that results in physical fitness, is the primary reason goals are not achieved, exercise scientists and leaders, along with their instructional staffs, strive to constantly help motivate participants to adhere to their personal programs. In addition, personnel and program management skills are critical in these corporate settings. Working with people in a non-structured setting appeals to many professionals in spite of the hours, which are frequently scheduled during workers' leisure time.

Many corporations have chosen to outsource their fitness programs. In this arrangement, the business provides the equipped facility, but the daily administration and staff are provided by an outside supplier. This management firm hires fitness specialists to teach classes and to instruct one-on-one. Instructors can expect starting salaries of around $20,000, with significant variance depending on the location, number of clients served, and experience. Often corporate and commercial fitness centers also contract with sports medicine clinics so that employees and members can receive treatment and rehabilitation services as needed.

Related to corporate fitness is the need for professionals to design and implement training programs for workers in the protective services (public safety officers). Exercise scientists are being hired to test the fitness levels of these workers and prescribe exercise programs to meet employees' individual needs and prepare them to meet the demands of their jobs. Observing positive lifestyle changes is rewarding to those who choose this career.

The fitness emphasis pervading the United States has led to a proliferation of public facilities and programs promoting lifestyle changes for various groups. Directors and program coordinators organize and implement fitness programs, sport teams, and various social activities. Job security is good; however, few advancement opportunities exist unless the management skills learned are transferred to a related career. The minimal wages earned in many part-time positions in public recreation are offset by the invaluable experiences gained.

Sport nutrition has become a popular career specialty because of the competitiveness of athletes at all levels. With increased pressure to perform at the highest level possible, athletes realize their success depends on good nutrition. That is, eating the right foods ensures the required energy stores, enhances physical fitness, optimizes nerve-muscle reflexes, and helps maintain desired weight. Proper nutrition may be the most important aspect of game preparation.

Sport nutritionists work with athletes to make sure that their nutritional needs are met. They help athletes get the proper balance of proteins, carbohydrates, fats, vitamins, minerals, and water. Carbohydrates are eaten to build up glycogen stores several days before competition to help ensure that this key energy source is available to the muscles. Rather than failing to eat or eating improperly, eating the right foods on a daily basis helps prevent fatigue or lack of energy late in the game. The pregame meal is planned by a sport nutritionist to add to the existing energy stores and help avoid hunger or gastrointestinal upset during intense competition. By eating a variety of nutritious foods daily, athletes do not need supplements and will not succumb to problems associated with deficiencies in nutrients.

Proper hydration is essential, as all sport nutritionists know; they are responsible for ensuring that athletes drink plenty of fluids, which may include fluids with electrolytes added. Water is essential for blood circulation with its nutrients and energy, as well as for sweating as a mechanism to prevent overheating. Dehydration may lead to heat stroke and even death.

Sport nutritionists may have earned a bachelor's degree in dietetics, nutrition, food service systems management, or a related area and been licensed by a state; or they may have earned a master's degree in exercise physiology with a specialization in nutrition. They may be hired by an intercollegiate athletic program or a professional athlete or team. The salary range for this position is $30,000–$90,000.

Cardiac rehabilitation specialists help clients identify and reduce the risk factors, such as high blood pressure, high blood cholesterol, obesity, and smoking, that can lead to cardiovascular disease as well as help heart disease patients regain their health. Those served could include individuals recovering from coronary artery bypass surgery, angina, heart attack (myocardial infarction), heart failure, heart transplant, and other heart-related conditions. Cardiac rehabilitation specialists educate clients about their risk factors and how to address them; they develop plans for clients making lifestyle changes, such as healthy eating and stopping smoking, incorporating appropriate physical activities into their lives, and providing support and encouragement for enhancing quality of life by reducing symptoms and risk factors. Working under the medical supervision of physicians, cardiac rehabilitation specialists help establish realistic and safe goals for clients to engage in regular exercise programs that will enhance the quality of their lives. Cardiac rehabilitation specialists may earn starting salaries around $40,000 and progress to make over $80,000 depending on location and work setting, like a hospital or clinic.

RECREATION AND LEISURE SERVICES

Programming and Instruction

Recreation and leisure services are allied fields with physical education, exercise science, and sport. Recreation and leisure services professionals provide activities and programs for individuals of all ages and ability levels. The private sector provides millions of jobs in commercial recreation. Many physical education and recreation graduates obtain their first jobs in the following areas:

- Lodging—management, operation, and programming for individuals associated with housing services, such as resorts, cruise ships, and camps
- Recreation—planning, management, and operation of recreational programs, facilities, and areas for agencies such as commercial/private, governmental, volunteer, industrial, outdoor, and therapeutic institutions
- Entertainment services—management, operation, and programming for such organizations as theme parks, racetracks, and video game manufacturers
- Culture services—management, operation, and programming for institutions that deal with fine arts, such as sport halls of fame, historical sites, and national and state parks
- Sports—management, operation, and programming for athletic areas and facilities, such as water parks and tennis complexes, health and fitness clubs, and professional athletic organizations

Although numerous opportunities exist in these areas, the sport sub-cluster probably appeals to most individuals, with instructional and program operations being the major types of jobs available. Tennis, golf, and swimming are among the popular types of specific sport clubs; multisport complexes also exist. Health and fitness clubs are examples of these general and specific types of leisure-service organizations.

All of these activity-related clubs or businesses require membership, thereby excluding a segment of the population. Most individuals who work for sport and fitness organizations are encouraged, if not required, to sell memberships as one of their responsibilities. Hours vary by club but are usually in the early mornings, afternoons, evenings, and on weekends, since these are most members' leisure hours. Job security varies with each person's expertise; however, potential for advancement into management and even ownership is good. Benefits include working with people and seeing their improvement, as well as having opportunities to maintain personal healthy lifestyles in these settings. Social skills, sales ability, and sports expertise are more important than a college degree, although being knowledgeable about the components of physical fitness and having expertise in skill analysis are quite helpful. Attaining a national certification in exercise testing or as a personal trainer can increase career options and lead to higher salaries.

The lodging subcluster includes resorts, condominium complexes, retirement centers, and camps that are increasingly hiring specialists in golf, tennis, swimming, and other sports to organize and instruct groups and individuals. For these recreation directors, hours vary to meet the needs of the guests, but the pleasant work environment may compensate for not having a typical schedule.

The thrill of activities like rock climbing attracts many enthusiasts to careers in recreation.

Courtesy Aram Attarian

City and county recreation departments offer a broad spectrum of activities, from instructional classes to league play to excursion trips and special events. Teachers are especially needed early mornings, afternoons, and evenings, but also throughout the day. Recreational classes are offered in a wide variety of activities such as water aerobics, rock climbing, massage, cross-country skiing, a variety of martial arts, arts and crafts, parent and child aerobics, and various types of dance. During the summers and evening hours, competitive and recreational leagues abound in basketball, baseball, football, volleyball, softball, soccer, tennis, and other popular sports.

Sponsored trips to museums, art events, state and national parks, zoos, and other attractions especially appeal to retirees and families. Fun runs, road races, and triathlons attract serious competitors as well as weekend athletes. The availability of facilities for private swimming, weight-training sessions, spinning classes, or for pickup basketball games also falls under the responsibility of recreation departments. Therefore, program supervisors and administrators have major responsibilities for providing and scheduling facilities to ensure that events operate smoothly and safely. In the future, recreation departments will increasingly be charged with the preservation of green space in cities to ensure park areas are available for use during leisure hours. Recreation professionals who teach can anticipate starting salaries around $25,000. These salaries will grow as management responsibilities increase.

Rehabilitative

An outgrowth of the desire for a healthy lifestyle is the proliferation of specialized clinics and counseling centers, including those for weight control, massage, nutrition counseling, and stress management. Weight control centers sometimes promote a particular diet or system and usually provide information about nutrition and encourage safe exercise. **Massage** is the systematic and scientific manipulation, such as through kneading, rubbing, and tapping, of body tissues to therapeutically enhance the functioning of the nervous, muscular, and circulatory systems. Wellness programs emphasize the development of nutritional, exercise, and attitudinal lifestyle changes through counseling and participatory sessions. The proliferation of stress management classes, clinics, seminars, workshops, and counseling centers reflects the demand for information and preventive and corrective strategies. Since these are fee-based businesses, salaries vary dramatically.

ATHLETIC TRAINING AND PHYSICAL THERAPY

Athletic trainers serve individuals of all ages and skill levels, especially in the rehabilitation of sport injuries. From the youth sport participant to the professional athlete to the senior citizen who wants to continue to be active, athletic trainers help prevent, treat, and rehabilitate injuries. In preparation for practices and games, athletic trainers tape, wrap, or brace ankles, knees, shoulders, or other body parts for protection. After workouts, athletic trainers prescribe the use of modalities, such as massages, ultrasound, and whirlpools, to help relieve soreness and treat muscle strains. When injuries occur, athletic trainers assess the severity and provide emergency first aid, if needed, and treatment, such as ice and the application of splints. Working with physicians, they establish the proper rehabilitation program that will enable the athlete to safely return to play as soon as appropriate. Athletic trainers help develop training and exercise programs that will enable athletes of all ages and skill levels to get into good condition and ready to play. This can include showing individuals how to train aerobically, stretch properly, and develop muscular strength and endurance. Athletic trainers can assist athletes with eating nutritiously, the administration of physical examinations, and the selection and use of proper exercise and sports equipment. Athletic trainers work with athletes on sport teams at all levels and with individual athletes, often in health clubs and clinical settings.

Most athletic trainers work with interscholastic, intercollegiate, and professional sport teams. Athletic trainers also work in physicians' offices, rehabilitation and therapy clinics, the military, or with individual athletes. Because they often work when others are physically active, athletic trainers work many evenings and weekends and must travel to sporting events. The job prospects for athletic trainers continue to expand because of increased awareness of sport-related injuries. For example, concerns about concussions and permanent complications in the absence of proper assessment and monitoring of concussed athletes prior to their return to practice or competition contribute to the demand for athletic trainers. Entry-level salaries can begin less than $25,000 while experienced athletic trainers in some settings can earn 2 or 3 times this amount.

Physical therapists, who sometimes work with athletic trainers in the rehabilitation of sport injuries, treat patients with a variety of medical conditions and injuries with the goal of improving patients' movement and managing their pain. Physical therapists serve important roles in the rehabilitation and treatment of patients with chronic conditions or injuries. Their typical duties include diagnosing patients' dysfunctional movements through observation and by listening to their concerns. Physical therapists establish treatment plans that incorporate exercises, stretching movements, hands-on therapy, and equipment to help ease patients' pain and increase their abilities to move. As patients make progress, treatment plans are modified and new treatments prescribed as appropriate. Within any constraints identified by physicians and each patient's physical situation, physical therapists enable their patients to increase muscular strength, endurance, coordination, and range of motion, while accepting and adjusting to the limitations of their injuries or chronic conditions. Physical therapists also educate patients, family members, and other care givers about what to expect regarding recovery from injuries and illnesses along with coping strategies to deal with limitations.

Physical therapists provide care to individuals of all ages who may be suffering from amputations, arthritis, back and neck injuries, birth conditions, fractures, sport-related injuries, sprains, strains, strokes, and work-related injuries. They also may specialize in an area, such as sport physical therapy, or with preferred age groups, such as pediatrics (working with children). Physical therapists are licensed to use a variety of modalities in caring for their patients such as massage, administration of heat and cold, and use of assistive equipment and devices, such as prosthetics. A challenge for physical therapists is getting patients to persist during treatment and convalescence when progress is slow and setbacks inevitably occur. The goal for patients and physical therapists is to enable patients to learn how to execute daily living activities so they can live healthier and more active lives. In addition, physical therapists must maintain documentation of treatments provided, progress made, and services provided, so patients can obtain medical insurance coverage for their treatments.

Physical therapists typically work in offices of health practitioners, hospitals, and nursing and residential care facilities, although some provide home health care services and may be self-employed. One attraction of this field is the opportunity to work varied hours, including part-time.

While some academic programs award a Master of Physical Therapy degree, the Doctor of Physical Therapy degree from other institutions specifies completion of 3 years of study and practice. To qualify for admission, an applicant must have achieved excellent grades as an undergraduate student (over a 3.5 grade point average for the most competitive degree programs) while completing courses required for admission and having gained experience observing or assisting in physical therapy settings. Physical therapy degree programs typically require courses in anatomy, biomechanics, neuroscience, pharmacology, and physiology as well as clinical rotations in acute care, orthopedic care, and others. Passing a national or state-administered examination is required by all states for licensure to practice as a physical therapist.

Physical therapists can expect to begin their careers, depending on location and setting, earning at least $40,000 with the potential to increase their pay to over $100,000. Aging baby boomers who are more physically active as well as those who suffer more debilitating conditions will increasingly demand the services of physical therapists. Job opportunities are strong in all settings. Additionally, advances in medical technology will help physical therapists serve their patients better as well as increase the percentage of trauma victims who survive and need rehabilitative care.

Another option that may interest exercise science students is becoming a chiropractor. To become a chiropractor, a person must complete a four-year Doctor of Chiropractic degree and obtain a state license to practice. Treating patients with health problems of the musculoskeletal system, which is made up of bones, muscles, ligaments, and tendons and using spinal manipulation to treat patients' ailments, such as back or neck pain, is the work of a chiropractor. After assessing a patient's medical condition and especially analyzing the spine, a chiropractor provides musculoskeletal therapy by adjusting the patient's spinal column and other joints by hand. While concerned about overall health, many chiropractors believe that misalignments of the spinal joints interfere with and cause health problems. In addition to manual therapy on spinal column, some chiropractors also use acupuncture, massage therapy, ultrasound, and heat and cold treatments as well as devices like braces or shoe inserts to alleviate patients' pain. Chiropractor may operate in general practice or specialize in areas such as neurology, pediatrics, orthopedics, or sports injuries. Job prospects are positive for chiropractors with pay ranging from around $40,000 to over $150,000 as they gain experience and build a client base.

ATHLETICS

Schools and Colleges

A second career aspiration of many secondary school and some elementary school physical educators is coaching the numerous teams provided for boys and girls. Many schools have coaching vacancies, but no teaching positions in physical education because of the resignations of some physical educators from coaching but not from teaching and because of the increased number of girls' teams. If licensed in and willing to teach in a second subject area, the teacher-coach is automatically more marketable. Coaching positions in the more visible sports of basketball and football are not as easy to obtain as those in other sports, and more openings typically exist for coaches of girls' sports than for boys' teams.

Coaches are expected to provide educationally sound learning opportunities for their athletes. The National Standards for Athletic Coaches identify the skills and knowledge that coaches should possess. Its eight domains are philosophy and ethics, safety and injury prevention, physical conditioning, growth and development, teaching and communication, sport skills and tactics, organization and administration, and evaluation.

In many schools, coaches are expected to work with more than one team and sometimes may have to assist with as many as three teams. Some states allow nonteachers or substitute teachers to coach; others allow only employees of the school system to be hired. Monetary supplements (ranging from $1,000 to over $100,000 for a few football coaches) are minimal compared with the long hours and innumerable demands placed on coaches. In some high schools, job security for football and basketball coaches does not exist unless winning teams are consistently produced. Victories are not as critical to job retention for coaches of most other sports.

Other athletic opportunities within schools include athletic training, sport officiating, and administration. High school sport officials normally work at other jobs and umpire or referee only as a hobby or a second job. A former coach or current coach usually serves as the school's athletic director. This individual coordinates team schedules, budgets, and facilities, and supervises the overall athletic program.

Athletic programs vary dramatically depending on the size of a college. In community colleges and small four-year colleges, many coaches teach in physical education or in other departments, with coaching remaining a secondary responsibility. These individuals receive coaching supplements to their salaries and/or reduced teaching loads. Most sports at these institutions are non-revenue producing, although for some teams recruiting is expected, since athletic grants-in-aid may be awarded. At larger universities, coaches of non-revenue-producing sports usually hold full-time positions in athletics, although some may also carry out assigned administrative responsibilities.

The teacher-coach, administrator-coach, part-time coach, or full-time coach frequently works day and night. Seldom is there an off-season or free time. While most college coaches have earned master's degrees, this is not a prerequisite, and the major field does not have to be physical education. Ways of gaining entrance into college coaching vary. For example, you may volunteer to serve as an assistant or as a graduate student assistant coach, you may earn an assistant coach's position after a successful high school coaching career, or you may get selected for a coaching job because of outstanding achievements as a collegiate or professional athlete. In most cases, future head coaches, even those at small institutions and for non-revenue-producing sports, must get experience serving as successful assistant coaches.

Once jobs are obtained, most coaches retain them as long as they abide by the rules, keep their athletes content, maintain their desire to coach, and develop successful programs; or they may choose to move to positions of greater prestige or institutions competing at higher levels. In larger institutions, most football and basketball coaches have job security only when they win and show that they can handle the pressures of the job without violating institutional, sport governance organization, or other rules. For these coaches, the long hours and pressures are compensated for by the material benefits and the prestige. Most coaches derive satisfaction from helping their athletes improve their skills and in seeing them mature as individuals.

Coaches' salaries depend on the sport; the competitive divisions in which their teams play; whether or not their sports are revenue producing; their years of experience; their past won-lost records; and additional benefits such as sport camp revenues, shoe contracts, and radio and television shows. Assistant coaches may receive no salaries, only tuition and fee waivers as graduate students, or may receive starting salaries around $30,000. Part-time coaches, who teach or hold other jobs, can

Sport promotions specialists work to fill stadiums for college football games.
© Gallo Images/Getty Images RF

expect stipends of a few thousand dollars, depending on the factors listed above. Full-time, head coaches' salaries range from $30,000 to hundreds of thousands of dollars. Entire salary packages for many football and basketball coaches with winning records at large universities exceed $1 million.

At small colleges, coaches are often the directors of athletics. As larger universities' athletic programs grew, however, they entered the entertainment business and required administrators to direct them. Athletic directors, associate and assistant directors, fund-raisers, and ticket managers often have earned master's degrees in sport management to prepare them for these careers. Money and personnel management skills are crucial, as is expertise in public relations, since skyrocketing budgets have made fund-raising vital. When skillfully achieved, all of these factors mesh into successful athletic programs that bring prestige and lucrative benefits to their directors. Security is based on the institution's overall program rather than on one team's performance, although the successes of the revenue-producing sports are certainly most important.

Associated with intercollegiate athletics and vital to their programs are numerous career options. Assistant and associate athletic directors assume responsibility for facility management, compliance with rules such as those of the National Collegiate Athletic Association (NCAA), grants-in-aid, business affairs, fund-raising, and coordination of non-revenue-producing sports. These positions may be filled by coaches, former athletes, or people trained in sport management. Job security is not guaranteed; continuation is based on successful completion of assigned duties. A major benefit is the association with a successful athletic program and its reflected glamour. Individuals in these management positions earn from $30,000 to over $500,000, depending on level of responsibility, experience, and the institution served.

For individuals who wish to combine writing skills with athletics, sports information is an exciting career choice. This vital component of the athletic program is responsible for compiling statistics and personal information about athletes, coaches, and teams to publicize upcoming events and provide postgame data as well as develop and maintain websites. Press releases and team brochures further publicize the intercollegiate program. A degree in journalism or sport communication would be appropriate, but volunteer experience and a willingness to start at the lowest level and work upward may be necessary to gain entrance into this athletic career. Travel, personal contacts with players and coaches, and contributing to the success of a program are among the benefits.

Sport promotions specialists are responsible for filling the stadium and arena through advertising and various promotional strategies. At a small college, one person may handle both sports information and sport promotions, or each coach may have to fulfill these additional responsibilities for his or her team. Large institutions have promotions specialists who frequently share in activities to raise funds for grants-in-aid and facilities. Public relations skills are usually more important than a particular educational degree. Development officers' or fund-raisers' primary efforts are directed toward bringing money into the athletic department through gifts and donations. Salaries for athletic administrators are directly linked to their ability to market their teams, resulting in increased ticket sales and donations.

Strength and conditioning coaches design and implement training programs for athletes. Frequently these positions are filled by exercise scientists with strong exercise physiology and biomechanics backgrounds and those who hold certifications from the National Strength and Conditioning Association. Helping athletes reach their athletic potential is a significant reward for these individuals.

Some college athletic departments hire sport psychologists to work individually with athletes. Because the athletic skills of all elite athletes are superior, many believe that the key to athletes' achieving optimal performances is mental. Sport and exercise psychologists use biofeedback, relaxation, imagery, and various coping mechanisms to help athletes handle the pressures of competition, achieve their potential, and enjoy their experiences.

Nonschool

More than 20 million children participate on youth sports teams sponsored by recreation departments, private clubs, community service organizations, national sport associations, and churches as well as in after-school physical activity programs. In most cases, the coaches are volunteers; the officials and the league, program, and association directors are professionals with experiences and expertise in physical education, recreation, or sports. However, in sports like baseball, gymnastics, soccer, and volleyball, independent programs have been established by coaches and funded by parents to provide advanced skill development and competitive opportunities. Public recreation departments provide athletic competitions for adults, such as softball and basketball leagues, master's swimming events, and road races. Experience gained as a volunteer coach, program administrator or assistant, or official may lead to a full-time job in a recreation-related career.

Sport managers are responsible for the operational logistics for sports competitions, such as a triathalon.
© Royalty-Free/Corbis

Professional

Prior playing experience in college and as a professional is an asset for coaches of professional teams, although not necessarily a prerequisite. Coaches are hired on the basis of demonstrated success with high school, college, or professional teams and are fired for not producing winning teams. Lucrative salaries, many in excess of $1 million, help compensate for the pressures to win and time demands.

Professional sports require hundreds of people working behind the scenes to ensure that events take place as scheduled. A commonality of many of these positions is the need for experience in business and marketing. Responsibilities of the ticket sales staff include season ticket packaging, selling tickets for individual events, and selling to and serving corporations that purchase luxury suites. Correspondence and direct contacts with fans are extensive, with the greatest challenge always remaining trying to satisfy as many fans as possible. Customer satisfaction is essential. No formal educational background is required, but a sport management degree is highly desirable.

Chief financial officers are responsible for planning budgets and administering the expenditures to support sport teams. Although accountants and secretaries may actually handle the daily transactions, financial officers oversee multimillion-dollar budgets and personnel who work in this area. A business background is essential, but on-the-job training in a small program or as an intern may be equally valuable in obtaining an entry-level job in this field.

Marketing directors serve various functions, depending on the situation. With teams needing to maintain or increase fan support, their primary responsibility focuses on increasing ticket sales and revenues. Radio or television commercials, newspaper advertisements, exciting upcoming events or opponents, or winning records may be used to generate greater spectator and sponsor interest. Season ticket sales are keys to success, since they stabilize income for advertising and ticket sales and indicate consistent fan support. Marketing directors also may help promote sales of team merchandise. These marketing specialists are hired for their proven ability to fulfill job responsibilities rather than for any educational degree.

Professional sport officiating provides many part-time and some (mostly in baseball and basketball) full-time careers. No specific educational background is required, but years of experience are necessary. As early as possible, such as in recreational youth leagues, anyone interested in officiating should start learning the rules and techniques while gaining experience and expertise. There may be some reflective glamour and prestige, but officials often are the "villains" and are only begrudgingly accepted as vital to sports. After years of success in the high school and college ranks and completion of several training programs, the best-qualified officials may get opportunities to officiate in the professional leagues. Most officials, however, hold other jobs and officiate as a hobby or a second career. Unusual hours and travel are inherent characteristics, but salaries for professional officials are quite good.

SPORT MANAGEMENT

Business and Industry

Golf courses, bowling lanes, gymnastics schools, tennis camps, swimming centers, ice rinks, and health spas all require managers who have administrative skills in addition to knowledge about the development of physical skills. Directors in each of these settings must possess budgetary skills, personnel management abilities, planning knowledge, and supervisory capabilities. Since these organizations are interested primarily in producing profits and thus maintaining high enrollments or large attendance, they must hire qualified instructional staff. Individuals working in these settings may earn $20,000 to over $100,000 a year.

Corporate fitness programs also hire managers with management, motivational, and supervisory skills. Exercise and sport science and fitness specialists who possess knowledge in public relations and marketing can advance more easily into management positions within corporate fitness programs. Since employers want the dollars spent for fitness programs to result in enhanced worker productivity, the goals are to motivate workers to adhere to fitness programs and increase their active participation.

Theme parks and resorts have become multimillion-dollar ventures providing leisure-time entertainment for people of all ages. Recreation administration and sport management degrees could prepare you to handle the budgetary, facility management, and personnel aspects of these businesses.

More than 150 sport halls of fame and museums each year host millions of people who view sport memorabilia and photographs and recall stars of the past. These tourist attractions highlight achievements of former heroes and heroines, and periodically elect new enshrinees; some host events to promote their respective sports. Sport historians and administrative curators are needed for positions in these settings.

Facility managers are associated with arenas and stadiums at universities, in communities, and with professional teams. To be cost effective, large facilities usually are multipurpose because audiences often are attracted to several different sporting events as well as to concerts, other types of entertainment, and conventions. Facility managers must have planning and organizational abilities as well as personnel management skills. Facility managers work for either a university, a governmental agency, a private corporation, or a professional team. They schedule events around the major team(s) or work for a municipality that rents its venue to teams. Depending on the size of the facility and the number of scheduled events, the individuals managing them may earn salaries of $40,000 to over $100,000.

Schools and Colleges

Administration is another career possibility for physical educators in schools. This position may be as a department chair who accepts management responsibilities, resulting in a reduced teaching load, or as a principal, headmaster, or superintendent. Advancement can result from successful service to the school, advanced education, or interest and demonstrated competence in these positions. In these jobs, increased salaries parallel longer hours and greater responsibilities.

Colleges have many administrative positions, ranging from program director to department chair to college dean. These careers are open to individuals with doctoral degrees, years of experience, expertise in working with people, and management skills. Administrative challenges, such as personnel problems, tight budgets, and day-to-day operational demands, are offset by opportunities to make enhancements in programs, lead faculty in the attainment of professional goals, and positively influence students' education.

Intramural and recreational sports and campus recreation programs are popular components of collegiate life. Directors, assistant directors, facility supervisors, and program coordinators constitute the staff. Job responsibilities vary from publicity to facility management and from personnel to programming. Intramural and recreational programs are administered through either the physical education department or the office of student affairs. In the first context, the staff also may teach; in the second, they seldom do. Most intramural, recreational sports, or campus recreation professionals have earned at least master's degrees in physical education, exercise science, sport, management, or recreation. Increasingly, the trend is to make these positions nonfaculty, with job security based solely on fulfillment of assigned responsibilities. Rather than the usual school-day hours, these programs operate in the afternoons and evenings and on weekends, the leisure hours of the students they serve. Student interactions in nonacademic activities and opportunities to administer fun-filled programs attract people to these positions. Entry-level program coordinators may earn around $30,000; assistant directors' salaries range from $40,000 to $50,000; directors are paid between $50,000 and $150,000, depending on program size and scope. (See the Research View Competencies of Sport Managers.)

RESEARCH VIEW

Competencies of Sport Managers

As an emerging field of study, sport management is continuing to define itself and the role it should play in the pervasive and competitive business of sports. Because sports on the professional, intercollegiate, interscholastic, youth, and recreational levels are multi-billion-dollar businesses, professionals in this field are responsible for upholding sport in the public trust. That is, sport managers are expected to fulfill their duties in accordance with the highest level of professional conduct. The ethical standards of this field, as found in codes of ethics, require accountability for meeting the performance expectations of the public being served. These expectations include integrity, honesty, and the equitable and respectful treatment of all individuals.

In addition to these personal traits, sport managers should be competent in fulfilling all of their job responsibilities. Knowledge and skills are needed in these areas:

- Budgeting
- Communicating effectively
- Complying with organizational rules and laws
- Decision-making skills
- Financing (corporate and private funds)
- Hiring, supervising, and evaluating staff
- Managing daily operations
- Marketing and promotions
- Organizing and managing time
- Managing risk
- Setting long- and short-range goals

Developing these competencies will help sport managers prepare for and perform well throughout their careers.

Sport Marketing

Individuals in sport marketing and promotions are in the business and entertainment side of sports. Professional teams receive millions of dollars from television, corporate sponsorships, and ticket sales. Sport marketers play essential roles in generating this cash flow. Their work extends from the conceptualization of sporting events through obtaining sponsorships and managing promotional campaigns to ensuring that a huge audience is entertained so that they will buy more tickets and merchandise in the future. Sport marketers are employed by professional teams and large collegiate athletic programs to conduct market research; produce print and electronic promotional materials; negotiate contracts for advertisements and sponsorships; plan and coordinate sporting events; help develop new team, sport, and athlete merchandise and products; and generate innovative approaches to ticket sales and fan entertainment.

Working with large corporations that have an interest in using sports to sell their products, sport marketers manage promotional campaigns and sponsorships of domestic and international sporting events as well as obtain millions of dollars from the corporations that will pay for title sponsorship of a stadium or football bowl game. Sport marketers may work as agents in negotiating and preparing contracts for athletes as well as in obtaining endorsements for them and managing their finances. Sport marketing is an expanding field because of increased interest in sports with more athletes, venues, and sponsors. The results of other marketing efforts include advertising and promotional campaigns built on the endorsement of sport stars and fantasy camps for fans and corporate sponsors. Sport marketers are in the sales business, so they need excellent communication skills, including the ability to persuade, creativity, business sense, competitiveness, and strong skills in networking.

Sport marketers extend their work beyond the entertainment business of sport into the business side of goods and services. Sporting attire is popular for everyone, whether for exercising, going out on the town, or working. From cross-training shoes to designer warm-up suits to team logo jackets and caps, millions are wearing sport clothing for its comfort and style. Billions of dollars of athletic and sport clothing and shoes are sold annually. Regardless of skill level, it seems only the most technologically advanced tennis rackets, custom-made golf clubs, and autographed baseball gloves are good enough for aspiring athletes. Therefore, jobs are and will continue to be plentiful in the sales and marketing of sporting goods. Expertise in sports is an advantage for people in sales, marketing, and management. Individuals choosing sales may enjoy flexible hours, travel, rapid advancement, and job security if they are good at what they do.

Most managers and many instructors in health and sport clubs are expected to sell memberships. Those who are especially adept at this task frequently advance into management positions with increased marketing responsibilities, such as initiating special promotions.

Enhanced equipment design and facility innovations require a great deal of research. Some of this research involves exercise physiologists, biomechanists, and athletic trainers who, because of their expertise and experience, help improve and make new equipment and facilities safer. Safety and improved performance

NASCAR has an outstanding record of promoting auto racing because sport managers have been successful in connecting sponsors with loyal fans.

U.S. Air Force photo by Master Sgt Michael A. Kaplan

motivate these efforts to produce the best ball or surface. Inventors or innovative designers will reap financial benefits if their products gain the same kind of wide acceptance that the makers of specialized golf clubs, for example, have seen.

Sport Communication

The interdependence of the media and sports has created numerous opportunities in the glamour careers of sport broadcasting, sport journalism, and sport photography. Broadcasting opportunities vary from prime-time, national telecasts to special events coverage to sport reporting for a local network. On-the-air experience, an expertise in play-by-play announcing, an aptitude for interviewing, and a smooth delivery in reading sports news overshadow an educational degree. Willingness to start in small markets at a salary just above minimum wage is a key to advancement. Cable networks provide another avenue for aspiring sport broadcasters on a variety of dedicated sport channels.

Since sports sell newspapers and magazines and increase television ratings, thereby selling commercial time, professional and college teams are especially sensitive to the media as a significant source of revenue. The sportswriting field attracts a large number of people. Many sportswriters have earned college degrees in journalism, but some secure newspaper or magazine jobs because of their past experiences in college sports information offices, their own sport careers, or their background in physical education, exercise science, or sport management. A sportswriter must possess an inquiring mind, a desire to talk with people, the ability to listen, and the willingness to work unusual hours while under the pressures of deadlines and space limitations.

A sport photographer may start by taking pictures for a college newspaper or yearbook and progress to assignments with a major publication. A thorough understanding of the intricacies of various sports provides a photographer with the insight necessary to capture the essence and meaning of sports as well as the outcome of a particular event. Long hours, low compensation, and little glamour may eventually be rewarded with extensive travel for a national publication.

OTHER RELATED CAREERS

In addition to the aforementioned broad categories of jobs open to physical education, exercise science, and sport management majors, several other specific careers are available. Many of these, however, require specialized education, training, or certification. For the medical doctor with an interest in sports, there are specializations in exercise physiology, orthopedic surgery, and sports podiatry, as well as the option to serve as a team physician. Sport nutrition and sport and exercise psychology are growing fields for both private practice and consultation with college and professional athletes. Lawyers may choose to emphasize the ever-expanding area of sport law or work as sport agents.

Dance careers include not only those of performing artists with national and regional companies but also those of artistic directors, managing directors, development officers, public relations agents, booking agents, dance journalists, and dance photographers. Limited jobs and long hours, though, deter some people from pursuing careers as dancers or in dance-related jobs. No educational degree is required for these positions or for those of studio teachers, yet all who pursue them have spent years developing their expertise.

Rather than viewing the sky as falling, a young professional should view the sky as the limit. Box 5.4 provides an overview of some potential careers, lists the necessary preparation, and indicates salary ranges. Knowing these alternatives should help you focus on one or more broad areas of interest as you choose a career pathway. See Box 5.5 for suggestions about how to locate more information about careers.

BOX 5.4   EXAMPLES OF JOBS MATCHED WITH EDUCATION AND SALARY RANGES

Job	Required Education and/or Experiences	Salary Range*
Academic counselor	Master's degree in any field	$30,000–$50,000
Assistant and associate athletic director	Bachelor's degree in any field; master's degree preferred	$40,000–$200,000
Athletic director	Bachelor's degree in any field; master's degree preferred	$50,000–$1,000,000
Athletic trainer	Bachelor's degree in athletic training with NATABOC certification; master's degree preferred	$30,000–$100,000
College coach	Bachelor's degree in any field; master's degree if also teaching	$40,000–$8,000,000
College professor	Master's degree in physical education or equivalent in smaller institutions; doctoral degree in one of the exercise or sport sciences or pedagogy in larger institutions	$45,000–$150,000
Compliance officer (college)	Master's degree in any field	$60,000–$90,000
Fitness instructor	Expertise in physical activities; fitness leader or equivalent certification preferred	$20,000–$90,000

(continued)

BOX 5.4   EXAMPLES OF JOBS MATCHED WITH EDUCATION AND SALARY RANGES (continued)

Job	Required Education and/or Experiences	Salary Range*
Intramural coordinator	Master's degree in recreation or equivalent	$30,000–$50,000
Official	Expertise and experience in officiating a specific sport	$5,000–$150,000
Personal trainer	Expertise in cardiorespiratory endurance training; personal trainer certification preferred	$20,000–$100,000
Physical education teacher	Bachelor's degree in physical education and state certification or licensure	$20,000–$90,000
Physical therapist	Master's or doctoral degree in physical therapy; state licensure	$50,000–$110,000
Recreation supervisor	Bachelor's degree in recreation or equivalent	$30,000–$60,000
School coach	Bachelor's degree and teacher certification; some states require coaching certification	$1,000–$80,000
Sports information director in a college	Bachelor's degree, preferably in journalism	$30,000–$100,000
Sport psychologist with a professional or college team or athlete	Doctoral degree in sport psychology	$50,000–$100,000
Strength and conditioning coach	Master's degree in exercise physiology or equivalent; personal trainer certification preferred	$40,000–$100,000

*Salaries are based on education, experience, expertise, specific job expectations, and location. Almost everyone begins at the lower end of the salary range. Pay increases and career advancement depend on hard work, competence in completing job responsibilities, continuing growth and development in knowledge and skills, networking, and enthusiasm for the job.

Teachers are needed for aerobics classes in health and fitness clubs as well as in public recreation programs.
© Jeff Maloney/Getty Images RF

BOX 5.5   INFORMATION ON CAREERS IN SPORTS

JobMonkey at www.jobmonkey.com/sports/ describes sports jobs and careers in sport journalism, sport broadcasting, health and fitness, coaching, intercollegiate athletics, professional sports, recreational sports, physical education teaching, professional sports, sporting goods, and in many more areas.

A subscription to Sports Careers (www.sportscareers.com) provides access to job listings in marketing and sales, media and public relations, fitness, coaching, scouting, finance, promotions, events, facilities, operations, agent, retail, and manufacturing as well as internship opportunities.

At www.jobsinsports.com/, if you choose to subscribe, you can search job data bases from thousands of employers, look for an internship, locate sports and industry contact information, and post your resume.

By subscribing to Work in Sport (www.workinsports.com), you have access to hundreds of current jobs and internships in sports; you can submit resumes and find contact information of organizations in the sport industry.

TeamWork Online's Sports Jobs (www.teamworkonline.com/) is a job board and applicant tracking system that assists in recruiting and identifying candidates for open positions in sports. You also can learn what characteristics and abilities sport executives are looking for, examine current positions, and ask to be notified of future vacancies that meet your interests.

By signing up for SportsCareerFinder (www.sportscareerfinder.com), you have access to extensive information about employers in collegiate, professional, and recreational sports, and you can post your resume for employers to search when filling open positions.

Women Sports Jobs at www.womensportsjobs.com/default.htm is an online career center in sales, marketing, broadcasting, public relations, coaching, officiating, health and fitness, athletic administration, event management, journalism, sporting goods, and much more. By joining, you can search jobs, post your resume, and find a job.

Career Cast (www.careercast.com) allows you to search for jobs as well as provides job seeking advice, if you pay for this service. ESPN Careers (espncareers.com) allows you to explore opportunities for your dream job working for ESPN.

Monster (www.monster.com/sports-careers) allows you to learn about the sport job market, salaries, and job opportunities.

SUMMARY

In today's rapidly changing, technological world, career changes as often as every 10 years or less have become the norm rather than the exception. Instead of looking at one specialty, you need to become a multispecialist who can make different applications of your knowledge. Young people entering the workforce need to bring creativity and imaginative reasoning to their jobs, as well as an adventuresome willingness to accept risks and failures while bouncing back to try again. Your first challenge is to assess your preferences and interests. Factors that influence your career choice(s) include family, role models, knowledge about career alternatives, opportunities to work with certain age groups, ease of entry, salary range, career advancement, time compatibility, job security, and location. Career opportunities abound in physical education, exercise science, and sports in teaching, inside and outside of educational institutions; in developmental and rehabilitative fitness; in school, college, and professional sports; and in sport management, marketing, and communication. After matching your aspirations and abilities with career characteristics, you can select one or more as the focus for your college preparation and initial and subsequent careers.

CAREER PERSPECTIVE

KELLY MCFARLAND
Founder, Owner, and Physical Therapist
Premier Rehab, Physical Therapy, and Aquatics
North Richland Hills, Keller, and Fort Worth, Texas

EDUCATION
B.S., exercise and sports sciences, Texas Tech University
M.S., physical therapy, Texas Woman's University
DPT, physical therapy, Texas Woman's University

Courtesy Kelly McFarland

JOB RESPONSIBILITIES AND HOURS

As the owner of Premier Rehab, with three locations, Kelly works closely with area orthopedic surgeons to provide high-quality patient care specializing in advanced ortho-pedics. She is committed to providing the best possible care to her patients with the goal of helping them return to work, activity, and normal routines of life. Premier Rehab has worked closely with the Dallas Diamonds Women's Professional Team in getting injured players back to the field as soon as possible and provides the inpatient therapy care for a local hospital. In addition to her commitment to total patient care and service, Kelly's primary job responsibilities include supervising staff, completing insurance uti-lization reports, marketing to physicians, building a reputation in the area for complete physical therapy care, maintaining a positive flow of daily tasks and duties, ordering equipment and supplies for the clinic, and keeping up with Medicare guidelines. The salary for beginning physical therapists is around $55,000. After 4–6 years of experi-ence, this could increase to $70,000–$90,000 depending on employment setting and responsibilities.

SPECIALIZED COURSE WORK, DEGREES, AND EXPERIENCES NEEDED FOR THIS CAREER

Each physical therapy school has specific admission and academic course work require-ments. Most physical therapy schools are now doctoral degree programs, and they often require the Graduate Record Exam with a minimum score of 1,000 on any two sections. Given the competitiveness for admission into a physical therapy program, the grade point average during a baccalaureate program usually must exceed 3.5 (on a 4.0 scale). In addi-tion, admission requirements typically include previous volunteer work in physical therapy settings, letters of recommendation, certification in cardiopulmonary resuscitation, comple-tion of prerequisite courses, and an interview. In her studies, Kelly found studying gross anatomy and the student rotations as most fulfilling. While her program of study was very difficult, she would not eliminate or change the requirements because everything she learned is relevant and helpful in the fulfillment of her job responsibilities.

SATISFYING ASPECTS

Kelly especially enjoys helping people learn what their bodies can and cannot and should or should not do. She is committed to getting people back to the everyday aspects of their lives with a caring attitude and to being the person whom they trust to make them better. She takes great satisfaction in analyzing physical problems and helping clients address and resolve these, yet always is disappointed if she cannot help lessen someone's pain and get him or her back to a fully functioning life. Kelly and members of her staff provide pain relief and injury rehabilitation services for sports injuries; postsurgical rehabilitation; treatment for back, neck, knee, shoulder, and arm pain; and rehabilitation for work, automobile accident, and personal injuries. In addition, her clinic provides aquatic exercise using the Hydroworx® underwater treadmill pool to reduce the stress on the spine and joints and aid in accelerated recovery for muscle injuries.

JOB POTENTIAL

Advancement for physical therapists can be limitless as long as there are vacancies, such as in administrative positions to supervise clinics, oversee continuing education, and conduct marketing. Individuals moving into these administrative positions could earn as much as $95,000, depending on the number of clinics supervised and scope of responsibilities. A physical therapist can also teach educational seminars, write for newsletters or other publications, and conduct research with university faculty. Physical therapists have the opportunity to work in a plethora of settings, such as hospitals; sports rehabilitation clinics; centers for neurological rehabilitation, rehab centers specializing in traumatic brain injury and spinal cord injuries; pain management clinics; pediatric therapy centers; skilled nursing or extend day rehab centers treating the geriatric population; aquatic therapy programs; schools; and research centers.

SUGGESTIONS FOR STUDENTS

Kelly recommends that students decide as early as possible during their college years on a career in physical therapy so they can take the classes required for admission into a doctoral program in this field, volunteer in various physical therapy settings, and assess whether this is the right profession based on their interest and abilities. It is very important, she suggests, that students have a strong commitment to this career choice so they will be willing to dedicate themselves to learning during volunteer hours and completing difficult course work.

KEY POINTS

Factors influencing career choices	You should examine the most important factors that will influence how possible career options are evaluated and the relative priority placed on these factors.
Lifestyle preferences	You should assess personal preferences for the unique characteristics of careers being considered.
Teaching	Careers in teaching exist in schools, clubs, camps, recreation programs, and colleges.
Fitness	Careers in fitness may include leadership, instruction, and exercise prescription in clinical, club, and specialized settings.

Sport management	Careers in sport management exist in schools, colleges, public programs, and professional sports and may include finance, event and facility management, marketing, public relations, sales, and other commercial and sport applications.
Sport communication	Careers are available in sport broadcasting, journalism, and photography.
Recreation	Careers in recreation include public and private physical activity and sport programs in a variety of settings.
Athletic training and physical therapy	These fields require certification or licensure in addition to educational degrees to prepare the specialists who help individuals rehabilitate from sport injuries and debilitating conditions.
Interviews	Students should talk formally or informally with professionals in careers of interest to them, so they can learn more about the scope of responsibilities, working conditions and hours, educational requirements, salary range, and other unknown areas and begin networking.

REVIEW QUESTIONS

1. What are several factors that may influence your career choice?
2. What factors may outweigh the importance of your salary?
3. What are several careers that involve teaching?
4. What are several careers in professional sports?
5. What is the job potential for careers in recreational services for senior citizens?
6. In what types of careers would a sport management background be beneficial?

STUDENT ACTIVITIES

1. Complete the self-assessment inventories in Boxes 5.1 and 5.2 on pages 127–128.
2. Make a list of your professional and personal career goals.
3. Compile a list of the abilities and characteristics needed for success in your prospective career.
4. Talk with one person in each of the following careers: (a) one you think you definitely would like to pursue; (b) one you think you might like to pursue; (c) one you know little or nothing about.

5. Investigate the educational and work backgrounds of two individuals in two different careers in physical education, exercise science, or sport.

6. Using the sample interview questions on page 131, conduct a formal interview of a person in a career that you are considering.

7. Using the Internet, find and briefly describe five career options discussed in this chapter or identify five emerging physical education, exercise science, and sport careers.

REFERENCE

Bureau of Labor Statistics, U.S. Department of Labor. *Occupational Outlook Handbook, 2014 Edition.* Retrieved from www.bls.gov/ooh/

WEB CONNECTIONS

1. www.jobsinsports.com
    Explore the Jobs in Sport website for internship opportunities, thousands of entry-level positions, and advancement opportunities in all areas of sport management.

2. www.exercise-science-guide.com
    Learn more about exercise science education, salaries, and career options.

3. www.jobs2careers.com
    Find jobs in whatever career interests you may have from fitness to recreation and exercise science to sport management including jobs where you live.

4. http://ncaamarket.ncaa.org/jobs
    The National Collegiate Athletic Association provides "The Market" for finding career openings in college athletics.

5. www.indeed.com
    This site claims to have all jobs for all interests. Insert your search terms and explore dozens of possibilities.

6. www.careerbuilder.com/
    Go to the Career Builder website, type in key words describing your career interest and preferred location and begin searching for the right job.

7. www.teamworkonline.com/career.cfm
   TeamWork Online provides a comprehensive listing of job opportunities in sports.

8. www.apta.org/apta/jobbank/index.aspx?navID=10737422765
   Go to this site to search for physical therapy jobs, post your resume, and sign up for job alerts.

6

PREPARATION
FOR A CAREER

LEARNING OUTCOMES

- Students will be able to articulate the importance of setting and striving to achieve short- and long-term goals as they work toward their dream jobs.
- Students will be able to explain the importance and value of participating in volunteer activities, internships, and other extracurricular activities while they are undergraduate students.
- Students will be able to describe the importance of and process for obtaining certifications, such as becoming a certified personal trainer.
- Students will be able to distinguish among various graduate degree programs as they relate to their fields of interest.

Professionalism is based on knowledge. Thus far, you have learned about the objectives, disciplinary content, philosophy, and professional structure of physical education, exercise science, and sport. You have begun to learn more about various careers through the career perspectives in each chapter. Now, with a career targeted, you are getting ready to learn more about your intended work. The information in this chapter should help you get the most out of your college years. As your knowledge increases, take advantage of various activities in the field and obtain certifications. You are not just joining a profession; you are becoming a professional. Your professionalism will demonstrate itself through a commitment to learning and desire to develop your capabilities to the fullest.

While this chapter introduces you to various career alternatives, at this point you will want to focus on learning more about each career and as much as you can about those of greatest interest to you. The end of this chapter provides information about writing application letters, developing a résumé, and preparing for interviews.

THE CHALLENGE

Everyone's existence depends on self-worth. We all have varying degrees of this basic need that relate directly to our personal levels of happiness. Self-worth is developed by participating and achieving success in different activities. This may include feeling confident in your sport skills, as well as in leadership skills acquired as a volunteer youth coach, a camp counselor, or an intern in a health and fitness club. An enhanced feeling of competency comes from taking on responsible roles like team manager, lab assistant, Special Olympics or Senior Games volunteer, and sport reporter for a college newspaper. Most people want to feel satisfied with and successful in their lives. Each person, however, defines these concepts uniquely. Many factors contribute to this "satisfaction factor" in our lives. Listed below are some characteristics that people value personally. Select any of these that can help you establish a sense of direction for the personal, social, and professional goals you will be setting. It will help if you can identify one or more individuals who you think personify those traits you wish to emulate and follow their examples.

Analytical	Motivated	Respectful
Assertive	Organized	Responsible
Benevolent	Outgoing	Sensitive
Competent	Patient	Serious
Considerate	Persevering	Sincere
Cooperative	Poised	Sociable
Creative	Polite	Spontaneous
Determined	Practical	Tactful
Energetic	Progressive	Tenacious
Enthusiastic	Prudent	Thorough
Friendly	Quiet	Thoughtful
Fun	Rational	Tolerant
Helpful	Reflective	Trustworthy
Honest	Reliable	Understanding
Loyal	Resourceful	Versatile

Once you have observed some of these traits in others, you are encouraged to learn how you can develop these characteristics. People who have been praised as good role models are usually willing to share how they developed their unique abilities. These same individuals are often eager to share strategies that have worked to make them successful.

Setting goals helps you seek and work to achieve a desirable end state. Written goals focus attention on the relevant factors that may facilitate progress or reduce distractions. When you take the time to thoughtfully set realistic and personally meaningful goals, you will most likely have a vested interest in their achievement, resulting in increased motivation and effort. Persistence is aided by breaking down goals that will take considerable time and effort to achieve (long-term goals) into a series of short-term goals that can help decrease boredom and maintain focus and intensity. These short-term goals can be stated as behavioral objectives, which should be written in measurable terms, so there is a standard by which to verify accomplishment. Evaluations or assessments should substantiate when objectives

Maintaining personal fitness is one vital aspect of preparing for a career in physical education, exercise science, and sport.

© Pixtal/agefotostock RF

have been achieved. Thus, goals serve as a road map—providing a sense of direction that in turn helps prevent your getting side tracked and helps point in the desired direction for greater efficiency and a feeling of success.

When you set goals, use the acronym SMART to optimize the probability of achieving them. Goals should be:

- **S**pecific—establish a definite goal that is important and write it down
- **M**easurable—identify specific criteria that will verify progress in achieving the goal
- **A**ttainable—establish a challenging, yet realistic, path to achieving the goal
- **R**elevant—identify the reasons why this goal is personally important and visualize how it will feel when this goal is accomplished
- **T**ime-bound—set a specific time limit, so you will know the price to be paid will be worth it when the goal is accomplished

Goal setting also helps in assessing abilities and interests and establishing immediate and future expectations. Goal setting helps you establish your personal philosophy, as described in Chapter 4. Short-term goals are accomplishments that can occur within a day, week, month, or another not-too-distant time period. Such goals could include attending a weekend workshop, starting a personal exercise program, or joining a professional association. It is important that short-term goals are readily achievable, positively reinforcing, and related to or leading to the attainment of long-term goals. Long-term goals are larger in scope and are often composed of numerous short-term goals. Continual self-assessment and reaffirmations of goals are essential, since interests and aspirations change. Before establishing some professional goals, it may be easier to start with personal and performance goals. To facilitate this process, respond to the questions in Box 6.1.

Associated with developing positive character traits and goal setting is the skill of networking. **Networking** is connecting with others on a personal basis in ways that will expand your professional opportunities. As you decide what you want to do and determine the type of person you want to be, you can be helped by others who have experienced the same process through which you are progressing. Associating yourself with others who can serve as your mentors and who can introduce you to others in your chosen career can be valuable. These individuals can help you obtain internship experiences and possibly get an entry-level job. They are tremendous resources for information, guidance, and personal development.

BOX 6.1   PERSONAL AND PERFORMANCE GOAL SETTING

Personal

1. What is your personal long-term career goal or dream?
2. Is it possible to achieve this goal if you work hard and motivate yourself the next few years?
3. What intermediate goals must you fulfill in the next few months to make progress toward your dream?
4. What are immediate (today/this week) goals that you can accomplish that will help you advance toward your long-term career goal?

Performance

5. What is one academic goal that you can achieve within 6 months?
6. How can you improve your academic performance during this academic year?
7. What is one athletic or fitness goal that you can achieve within 6 months?
8. How can you improve your athletic or fitness performance during this academic year?
9. What is one leadership goal that you can achieve within 6 months?
10. How can you improve your leadership performance during this academic year?

EDUCATIONAL BACKGROUND

Academic success in college can greatly facilitate the achievement of your goals. Try to benefit as much as possible from these educational opportunities to learn and develop your skills and abilities. This does not mean that all you need to do is to study, although lifelong learning certainly is vital.

Everyone needs to develop basic academic competencies in reading, writing, speaking, listening, mathematics, critical thinking, studying, and computer literacy. Basic academic competencies and general education course work constitute most liberal arts programs through which institutions provide students with the broad knowledge base for their lives and careers. Advocates of a liberal arts education think all students should be educated to function effectively in a culturally diverse world, regardless of their career choices. In today's interconnected world, cultural competency and being culturally competent are essential. Such an education potentially helps the research scientist interact with the practitioner, assists the coach in understanding family backgrounds and pressures on their athletes, provides insights about other people and their languages in our multicultural society, and develops appreciation for the arts, history, and philosophy.

Some students may fulfill these core requirements by taking a conglomeration of courses without much thought or direction. Whether you take general education courses during the first 2 years at a community college or throughout a four-year collegiate program, you should seriously consider your selection and sequence of course work to maximize career preparation. Your major or specialized studies normally hold greater interest because they tend to relate more directly to your chosen career. Nevertheless, you still need to make a serious commitment to learning the most you can from each class (see Box 6.2 for information about how an academic advisor can help you on your academic journey).

Experiential learning, which describes the knowledge, skills, and abilities developed through involvement in actual work, expands and completes the learning that occurs through your academic studies. Experiential learning and internships are

---

BOX 6.2   HOW AN ACADEMIC ADVISOR CAN HELP YOU

Here are several benefits you can gain through seeking out and meeting regularly with your academic advisor:

- Learn information about student services, academic policies, course offerings, scholarships, majors, career services, internships, research opportunities, graduate school options, and career opportunities.
- Connect you with other faculty and students.
- Empower you to take active and responsible roles in your learning to help you achieve your academic and career goals.
- Help ensure that you meet requirements for general education courses, major programs, and graduation.
- Provide letters of recommendation for study abroad, internships, graduate schools, or jobs.

valuable for career preparation. Some majors' programs require students to observe in the schools each week, complete an internship, design practicum experiences for their career choices through independent study courses, or take a laboratory course that offers practical experiences. Often courses for the prospective teacher require observation and mini-teaching experiences, many as early as the first year of college.

Several curricula allow students to earn college credits while receiving pay for work completed while learning, such as being a recreation leader for a community, camp counselor, sport club instructor, or personal trainer. An independent study option allows students to earn college credit for developing research projects or for work experiences specific to their areas of interest. Other curricula have experiential courses as a part of their requirements. Each of these options allows students opportunities to gain valuable experiences while they are selecting and preparing for their careers.

GETTING INVOLVED

During your years in college, considerable career-relevant learning occurs outside the classroom. Experiential learning is important. For example, by serving as a team manager, sport official, or event coordinator in intramurals or recreational sports, you can learn about personnel management, scheduling, and rules. Working with a sport club, such as karate or rugby, you may get an opportunity to coach or manage the club's financial affairs. Of course, you can learn many things just by participating in various college extracurricular activities or as a varsity athlete. The time to start is now.

Volunteer Activities

While the knowledge gained in college courses introduces content and provides the foundation for a career choice, experiences and practical applications solidify learning. Participating in volunteer activities while a student offers valuable opportunities to gain experience. If a career in fitness appeals to you, you may start by attending aerobics classes or joining a health club before volunteering to assist instructors in a class or club. Later you may enhance your learning to become an instructor. Or, if becoming a personal trainer is your career aspiration, you could observe a personal trainer working with clients, assist a personal trainer, obtain a personal trainer certification, and work as a personal trainer while a student. Other volunteer possibilities in this field include conducting fitness classes for children in after-school programs, senior citizens at retirement centers, other students in residence halls, or volunteering to serve as an intramural manager, sport club manager, or fitness leader within your campus recreation program.

Student athletic trainers should volunteer to work under the supervision of a certified athletic trainer at least several hours each week while completing their undergraduate studies so they can learn, develop, and practice the skills required for success in this career. As their skills improve, student athletic trainers will get opportunities to work with multiple athletic teams to gain the requisite skills they will be required to demonstrate to qualify for licensure.

Volunteering to help teach children sport skills can be rewarding as well as help advance your career.

© McGraw-Hill Education/Gary He, photographer

Students planning to pursue an advanced degree in physical therapy must have experience observing physical therapists work with their clients. Ideally, shadowing physical therapists in hospitals, physical therapy clinics, or other settings will introduce students to a range of skills and knowledge they will be required to learn and develop, and it will make them more qualified applicants for physical therapy programs.

Exercise science majors often choose to volunteer to work in commercial or corporate fitness programs or clinical settings. You could help exercise physiologists, fitness leaders, and physicians assess the fitness levels of clients, prescribe exercise programs, and monitor progress. You could observe and learn how to measure various fitness parameters and help participants adhere to their prescribed programs.

Exercise science students who aspire to earn graduate degrees could volunteer to serve as subjects in research studies. As an undergraduate laboratory assistant working with one of your professors, you can gain tremendous experience using exercise physiology, biomechanical, and other scientific instrumentation. You will quickly learn whether the research process—hypothesis, design, data collection, statistical analysis, and interpretation—appeals to you.

The sport management major can seek out volunteer opportunities both on and off campus. Your college's intramural or recreational sports program needs students to serve as team managers for residence units, sport club officers, and facility and activity supervisors. Opportunities may also be available to organize special events, such as fun runs, orientation sessions, or all-night activities. Volunteers provide

Internships are available in a wide variety of settings where interns can gain valuable professional experience.
© Chris Ryan/agefotostock RF

valuable assistance working with Special Olympics, family recreational centers, Senior Games, private sport leagues, and State Games. After successfully completing minor tasks, you may qualify for the responsibility of coordinating sport competitions during these events. Volunteer coaches are needed in youth sport leagues and recreation programs. Experiences gained in these settings may lead to opportunities to serve as an assistant coach in a middle or secondary school.

Officiating

Officiating opportunities abound in intramurals, within recreational leagues, and in middle schools; some colleges offer classes in officiating. These learning experiences may result in advancement into the high school, college, and professional ranks. The National Federation of State High School Associations, through its state associations, requires interested individuals to attend clinics and take written examinations to become certified as sport officials. Following successful completion of these requirements, individuals earn ratings that qualify them to officiate high school athletic contests. The most proficient officials receive the top rankings, earn the honor of working in championships, and may get an opportunity to advance to the next competitive level. Several single-sport organizations, such as USA Volleyball, offer training and education programs for officials.

Internships

An **internship** is a supervised period of apprenticeship, related to a student's degree program and career plans, when a student works under supervision to learn practical applications of disciplinary and professional content. Most fields associated with

⌕ RESEARCH VIEW

Importance of Internships

In today's competitive job market, especially in physical education, exercise science, and sport careers, it is vital that students realize the value of internships and seek them out. According to numerous research studies, students who participate in internships during their undergraduate and graduate programs gain the following advantages:

- Get more extensive learning experiences.
- Benefit from extensive hands-on experiences.
- Obtain better preparation for employment.
- Gain a competitive edge when seeking employment.
- Network with potential employers.
- Learn from other employees and build good relationships with them.
- Impress your internship supervisor, making it more likely you will be hired as full-time employee.
- Position yourself for more job offers.
- Qualify for higher starting salaries.
- Advance through more frequent promotions.

Additional information can be obtained online using your favorite search engine, contacting departmental offices or career services offices, or reviewing books such as *Getting Your Ideal Internship, The Internship Bible,* and *The Vault Guide to Top Internships.*

Timeline for Pursuing an Internship or Job
First Year in College

- Learn about available resources on campus, such as exploring possible majors and careers with your academic advisor.
- Talk with professors about possible majors and careers.
- Make an appointment at the career development center to assess your interests as well as your areas of strength through available inventories.
- Participate in at least one extracurricular club or activity related to your potential career.
- Record your activities and experiences for your résumé.
- Apply for a part-time or summer job related to your possible career choice.

Second Year in College

- Take an introductory course for a major in which you are interested.
- Join a professional organization as a student member.

(continued)

- Prepare a draft of a résumé.
- Learn more about various careers by finding and reading the career backgrounds of individuals in careers of interest to you.
- Select a major and meet with an academic advisor to plan the sequence of your course work.
- Interview a person in a career in which you may be interested.
- Participate in at least two extracurricular clubs or activities related to your potential career.

Third Year in College

- Add entries about your academic achievements and collegiate experiences to your résumé.
- Meet with the internship advisor and explore options.
- Participate actively in a majors' club in your area of interest.
- Attend job fairs or career events and seek out possible internships.
- Attend a meeting of a state, regional, or national professional organization to begin networking for possible internships.
- Explore internship opportunities online, via the print media, and through campus resources.
- Investigate your college's program for connecting students with alumni for internships.
- Attend seminars offered by the career development center.

Fourth Year in College

- Attend a meeting of a state, regional, or national professional organization to continue networking.
- Participate actively in a majors' club in your area of interest.
- Prepare letters of application for internships and make contacts with potential internship sites.
- Complete the internship application process and attend the internship orientation meeting.
- Add entries about your academic achievements and collegiate experiences and complete your résumé.
- Complete a mock job interview through the career development center.
- Continue to network at career events and job fairs.
- Identify individuals who might be willing to write letters of recommendation for you and ask them to do so.

physical education, exercise science, and sport require one or more internships, in which students enhance their skills and abilities and link the theory from their course work with actual practice in their future careers. The aspiring sport manager has to participate in on-the-job experiences, such as in sport marketing and facility and event management, to help prepare for future jobs. Exercise scientists who aspire to prescribe exercise programs in a variety of settings need to experience through internships how to administer fitness assessments and assist individuals with personal programs to gain the knowledge and skills needed to succeed. In most programs, these internships are a part of degree requirements, with associated academic expectations. Some internships permit students to receive pay; others must be completed without pay. The Research View Importance of Internships provides additional information about internships. Go to the National Internship Directory to find internships in sport management, health/fitness/wellness, marketing, and much more (www.internsearch.com).

These experiences associated with your potential career choice may help confirm your interests or indicate that another field may be preferable. Another valuable learning experience is shadowing a person who agrees to mentor you as you learn more about a potential career. As a volunteer or intern, you will help others while developing your abilities. Each time you participate in one of these activities, add this to a list of your extracurricular experiences. Later, when you apply for a job, you can include these activities on your résumé. Volunteer and internship experiences will help differentiate you from other applicants.

BEGINNING YOUR CAREER INVOLVEMENT

While you are a student, get involved in career-related activities. Most colleges and universities have majors' clubs in physical education, exercise science, and sport. Majors' clubs often sponsor faculty-student colloquia, invite leaders in the profession to give presentations, and interact academically and socially. These organizations also frequently organize trips to state, district, and national conferences or workshops where students learn about the profession, hear about current developments, and listen to research reports. Service projects, such as working with Special Olympics and conducting fund-raising events for charities, also are popular ways for young professionals to help others by sharing their expertise; at the same time, you gain valuable experience. Following are some questions to assist you in your career development:

1. What would I like to do immediately following graduation? After 5 years? 10 years? 20 years?

2. What experiences and learning opportunities can I take advantage of while in college to help me achieve my immediate, short-, and long-term career goals?

3. What resources and people on my campus can help me achieve my immediate, short-, and long-term career goals?

4. What objectives and action plans have I established to help me explore various aspects of my career development while in college?

5. How will the development of a portfolio (describing work experiences, internships, volunteer experiences, and class activities) help demonstrate what I have learned in my career preparation?

6. How will what I have learned in my college courses help me make better decisions in my career?

7. How are my personal, academic, and social strengths matched to the potential career for which I am preparing?

8. How can others help me evaluate and understand my abilities and develop strategies to work on areas in need of strengthening?

9. How will I use feedback from experiences and from others to better prepare myself to make decisions relative to my career choice?

10. How motivated am I to devote the time and effort needed to be successful in and satisfied with my career choice?

Certifications

An important demonstration of professional growth and development is the attainment of certifications. Earning a specialized certification is an important career step for the following reasons:

- Confirms the attainment of a high level of competence and the achievement of the standards of the profession, such as becoming a Certified Athletic Trainer by the NATA Board of Certification.
- Shows a willingness and commitment on the part of certification applicants to enhance their career preparation, such as by obtaining a Health Fitness Specialist certification from the American College of Sports Medicine.
- Provides potential clients and the general public with a quality control measure that reassures them that the certified person possesses a level of competence, such as completing coaching certification courses through the American Sport Education Program.
- Enables potential employers to differentiate among applicants based on a known standard of knowledge and skills, such as becoming a Certified Personal Trainer through the National Strength and Conditioning Association.

Before describing the general steps for obtaining certifications, a word of caution is needed. Unfortunately, there are certification mills that will provide you with pieces of paper, inevitably at a significant cost, that appear to certify your knowledge and skills without any examination of whether you are knowledgeable in an academic area or skillful in a specific endeavor. Potential employers realize this and will only be impressed with you and the certifications you hold if these have been obtained from reputable professional organizations and agencies that stand behind the competence of those they certify.

An excellent starting point for obtaining a certification is to do a Web search, such as by typing in "certification programs in fitness," click on an organization of interest, and follow the instructions specific to that organization. In general, the steps you will need to follow to obtain a certification include the following:

- Review the available certifications in your area of interest and select the one you think is right for you.
- Determine that you meet the required prerequisite knowledge and skills for seeking this certification.
- Review any study materials about the examination.
- Take a practice examination or complete the sample questions, if provided.

- Read carefully the policies and procedures about the certification and application processes and any other information provided so you are fully informed.

- Complete the application for the certification, making sure all the required information is provided.

- Submit your completed application and payment to the certifying agency or organization.

- Complete successfully all aspects of the certification examination.

- Add to your résumé only after the certification has been awarded.

The American Red Cross offers certifications for lifeguards and instructors in water safety, first aid, cardiopulmonary resuscitation, automated external defibrillator, and other health and safety services courses. The YMCA of the USA also certifies lifeguards and swimming instructors. These certifications can lead to employment as pool and beach lifeguards and as swimming teachers. The YMCA also offers several fitness certification programs.

In certifying health and fitness professionals, the American College of Sports Medicine (ACSM) requires a rigorous level of knowledge and skill. ACSM believes certified professionals set the best possible performance examples, provide safe and caring environments, and show a greater incidence of client and patient success in achieving health and fitness goals. ACSM offers several types of certification.

Table 6-1 provides examples of and information about these and other certifications in health, fitness, sport, and coaching.

The American Sport Education Program (ASEP) certifies coaches and officials for youth and interscholastic sport programs and provides volunteer coaching

Certified exercise leaders can help individuals of all ages develop physically.
© Sven Hagolani/fstop/Corbis RF

TABLE 6-1

EXAMPLES OF AND INFORMATION ABOUT PROFESSIONAL CERTIFICATIONS

Certification	Description
Aerobics and Fitness Association of America (http://www.afaa.com/certification_and_specialty_workshops.htm)	
KickBoxing	To become certified, candidates must be able to apply the principles of biomechanics, exercise physiology, and injury prevention in the teaching and learning of kickboxing techniques.
Personal Trainer	To become certified, candidates must demonstrate knowledge of anatomy, kinesiology, nutrition, and weight management, the ability to conduct fitness assessments, and the ability to lead exercise and weight programs.
Primary Group Exercise	To become certified, candidates must demonstrate knowledge of the basic exercise sciences and the ability to lead group exercise.
Step	To become certified, candidates must demonstrate scientific background in physiology and biomechanics, injury prevention, verbal and visual cueing skills, and pattern choreography and sequencing.
Military Fitness Specialist	To become certified, candidates must demonstrate knowledge and skills of personal fitness trainers and group exercise instructors; designed to assist active duty members and civilians with fitness knowledge and programming skills.
American College of Sports Medicine (http://certification.acsm.org/get-certified)	
ACSM Certified Group Exercise Instructor	These professionals instruct groups or individuals in the fundamentals of fitness and exercise activities and meet performance domains in participant and program assessment, class design, leadership and instruction, and legal and professional responsibilities.
ACSM Certified Personal Trainer	These professionals conduct basic pre-participation health screening assessments, develop and implement safe and effective methods of exercise, recommend appropriate healthy behaviors based on the fundamental principles of exercise science, and motivate healthy populations and those individuals with medical clearance to begin and continue exercise programs.
ACSM Certified Health Fitness Specialist	These health and fitness professionals, who must have earned a minimum of a bachelor's degree in exercise science, conduct and interpret fitness assessments, construct appropriate exercise prescriptions, implement exercise programs for apparently healthy clients, and demonstrate the ability to effectively counsel individuals regarding lifestyle modification and motivate them to maintain positive lifestyle behaviors.
ACSM Certified Clinical Exercise Specialist	These degreed professionals, who hold a bachelor's degree in exercise science, exercise physiology, or kinesiology, conduct and interpret clinical exercise tests and electrocardiograms for individuals with controlled cardiovascular, pulmonary, and/or metabolic disease.
ACSM Registered Clinical Exercise Physiologist	A candidate must have a master's degree in exercise science, exercise physiology, or kinesiology. These certified professionals perform clinical exercise testing, data interpretation, and exercise prescriptions and counseling for individuals with cardiovascular, pulmonary, metabolic, orthopedic, musculoskeletal, neuromuscular, and/or immunological/hematological disease.
ACSM/ACS Certified Cancer Exercise Trainer	These professionals perform fitness assessments and recommend exercise programs for individuals with cancer diagnosis, treatment, and recovery status.

(continued)

TABLE 6-1 (continued)

EXAMPLES OF AND INFORMATION ABOUT PROFESSIONAL CERTIFICATIONS

Certification	Description
ACSM/NCPAD Certified Inclusive Fitness Trainer	These professionals lead and demonstrate safe, effective, and adapted exercises for individuals with disabilities to help them begin and continue healthy lifestyles.
ACSM/NSPAPPH Physical Activity in Public Health Specialist	These professionals, who must hold a bachelor's degree in a health-related field and have at least 1,200 hours of related experience promoting physical activity, healthy lifestyle management, or other health promotion, conduct needs assessments and plans, develops and coordinates physical activity interventions at local, state, and federal levels.

American Council on Exercise (http://www.acefitness.org/fitness-certifications/default.aspx)

Medical Exercise Specialist	The candidate must demonstrate the ability to provide post-rehabilitative fitness programming to individuals recovering from cardiovascular, pulmonary, metabolic, and musculoskeletal conditions to overcome these and prevent recurrence.
Group Fitness Instructor	The candidate must demonstrate the knowledge and skills to teach an array of group fitness programs safely and effectively based on foundational knowledge in the exercise sciences, instructional techniques, cueing, and injury prevention.
Health Coach	The candidate must demonstrate the knowledge and skills to help clients create healthier behaviors through sound nutrition, appropriate exercise, and lifestyle change.
Personal Trainer	The candidate must demonstrate knowledge of risk factor screening, fitness assessment, nutrition, exercise science, exercise programming, instructional and spotting techniques, and lifestyle modification.

Cooper Institute (www.cooperinstitute.org/certified-personal-trainer/)

CI-Certified Personal Trainer	These certified professionals provide personal training and fitness guidance to assess fitness needs and abilities and develop and implement individualized programs that are safe, effective, and motivational.

National Strength and Conditioning Association (http://www.nsca.com/Certification/)

NSCA-Certified Personal Trainer	The candidate must demonstrate the knowledge and skills to work with active and sedentary physically healthy individuals and design individualized, safe, and effective exercise programs to help them achieve their personal health and fitness goals.
Certified Strength and Conditioning Specialist	These professionals apply scientific knowledge to train athletes, conduct sport-specific testing sessions, design and implement safe and effective strength training and conditioning programs, and provide guidance regarding nutrition and injury prevention for the primary goal of improving athletic performance.
Certified Special Population Specialist	These fitness professionals, using an individualized approach, assess, motivate, educate, and train special population clients of all ages, including those with chronic and temporary health conditions, regarding their health and fitness needs.
Tactical Strength and Conditioning	These professionals apply scientific knowledge to physically train protective services personnel (military, fire, rescue, law enforcement, and other emergency personnel) to improve performance, promote wellness, and decrease injury risk.

education (www.asep.com/). Coaches in high school can complete online courses on coaching principles and sport first aid as well as coaching sport-specific techniques and tactics courses. Officials can complete online courses in officiating principles.

The National Federation of State High School Associations (www.nfhslearn .com/) offers the opportunity to become an Accredited Interscholastic Coach (AIC). This online program is comprised of four courses for this Level I certification. The Fundamentals of Coaching course provides a student-centered curriculum to help coaches create a healthy and age-appropriate athletic experience that supports the educational mission of schools and includes content from all eight domains contained in the National Standards for Sport Coaches. First Aid, Health and Safety for Coaches course teaches American Red Cross first aid in the context of sport and the prevention of sport-related injuries. The Level 2 Certified Intercollegiate Coach builds on the AIC through completion of online courses in creating a safe and respectful environment, strength and conditioning, teaching and modeling behavior, engaging effectively with parents, sportsmanship, two additional courses of choice, and a sport-specific course of choice.

Recreation and leisure services professionals may choose to seek national certification through the National Recreation and Park Association. To be certified, applicants must meet educational and experience requirements as well as demonstrate a high level of professionalism in their work. The Certified Park and Recreational Professional has enhanced credibility and contributes to the status of the field, as does the Certified Park and Recreation Executive, Aquatic Facility Operator, and Certified Playground Safety Inspector (see www.nrpa.org/certification/). The challenge for recreation and leisure services specialists is to create programs with activities that match each person's interests and needs.

Some institutions offer students the option to complete coursework in tracks, specializations, concentrations, or minors in addition to their majors. For example, students majoring in exercise science might choose to use their electives to specialize in a corporate fitness track. Students in physical education might choose to take a coaching minor to better prepare for a teaching-coaching position in a school. Other students might choose to major in sport management while completing a concentration in marketing or a business minor through the business school. Although each institution uses its own terminology for these programs, each allows students to take undergraduate courses in areas directly relevant to their chosen careers or as preparation for a graduate program for which knowledge in both areas of emphasis would be beneficial.

Undergraduate education is enriched when students learn how to read scholarly articles, conduct research, and share their research and scholarship in written and verbal formats. Students can enhance their preparation for graduate studies and some careers by independently or collaboratively working with faculty mentors or classmates on research projects to create and disseminate knowledge. Through their research experiences, students will develop their research and teamwork skills as they expand their abilities to think creatively.

GRADUATE EDUCATION

Your career objective may require advanced study in physical education, exercise science, or sport management at an accredited institution. Master's degree programs usually take 1 to 2 years to complete; doctoral degree programs typically require 3 to

5 years beyond the master's degree. Master of Science (M.S.), Master of Arts (M.A.), Master of Education (M.Ed.), and Master of Arts in Teaching (M.A.T.) are the typical offerings. They normally require 30 to 36 semester hours for completion, although the actual coursework taken varies from institution to institution. The M.S. and M.A. degrees generally emphasize more discipline-oriented study and may allow for specialization in athletic training, exercise physiology, sport management, or sport psychology, as shown in Table 6-2. Completion of these degrees usually requires a thesis, an original research project, or an internship in addition to a comprehensive examination or other summative assessment. Oriented toward education and teaching, the M.Ed. and M.A.T. degrees lead to advanced licensure for individuals working in the schools and usually require an internship or practicum experience (see Box 6.3). Many institutions offer licenses in advanced study beyond the master's degree in special education, supervision, counseling, and administration. Increasingly, schools expect teachers to obtain master's degrees or higher as they continue their lifelong learning.

TABLE 6-2

EXAMPLES OF COURSE WORK AND INTERNSHIPS ASSOCIATED WITH MASTER'S DEGREE PROGRAMS IN FOUR EXERCISE AND SPORT SCIENCES

Athletic Training	Sport Management
Athletic Training Administration	Personnel Management in Sport Organizations
Head, Neck, and Spine Evaluation	Sport Law
Human Anatomy	Sport Finance
Lower Extremity Evaluation	Social Issues in Sport
Management and Prevention of Injuries	Applied Statistics and Research Methods
Pathophysiology	Sport Marketing
Pharmacology	Sport Ethics
Research Methods	Sporting Event and Facility Management
Therapeutic Exercises and Strength Training	Applied Sport Marketing Research
Clinical Experience I, II, III, and IV	Internship in Sport Management
Therapeutic Modalities	
Upper Extremity Evaluation	

Exercise Physiology	Sport and Exercise Psychology
Exercise Physiology	Psychological Aspects of Sports
Applied Statistics and Research Methods	Applied Statistics and Research Methods
Assessment of Physiological Functions in Exercise	Motivation in Sport
Exercise Testing and Prescription	Social-Psychological Issues in Sport
Nutritional Aspects of Exercise	Issues in Sport and Exercise Psychology
Planning Health Promotion in Medical and Worksite Settings	Stress Management
Cardiovascular Disease Epidemiology	Counseling and Interviewing Skills
Seminar in Exercise Physiology	Social Cognition
Practicum in Exercise Physiology	Personality Assessment and Research
Thesis in Exercise Physiology	Practicum in Sport Psychology

BOX 6.3   EXAMPLES OF COURSEWORK FOR A MASTER'S DEGREE EMPHASIZING PHYSICAL EDUCATION

Curriculum and Instruction
Educational Psychology
Educational Research
Educational Statistics
Issues and Trends in Physical Education
Legal Issues in Education
Motor Learning in Physical Education
School and Program Management
Scientific Foundations of Physical Education
Internship or Practicum Experience

The highest academic degrees are the Doctor of Philosophy (Ph.D.) and the Doctor of Education (Ed.D.). The Ph.D. is oriented toward research in an exercise or sport science, such as exercise physiology, sport history, sport management, motor learning, or sport and exercise psychology. The focus of most Ed.D. programs is advanced study in curriculum and instruction, with physical education forming one portion of the program.

Before deciding whether to enroll in a prospective graduate program, determine whether advanced education is needed for your career. If so, you will need to find out which accredited universities offer the type of program that meets your area of interest. For example, only a few institutions offer a specialization in athletic training at the master's degree level. Although some institutions require an area of specialization for a master's degree, others offer a general physical education, exercise science, or sport program.

Most admission requirements include an undergraduate degree in physical education or related exercise or sport science emphasis, a minimum of a 3.0 (on a 4.0 scale) grade point average, and a better-than-average score on the Graduate Record Examination (GRE) or Miller Analogies Test (MAT). Since institutions are free to set their own admissions standards, review the requirements of the institutions offering the program you desire. You may write for information or check out multiple institutions and their programs by visiting their Web sites, some of which offer online applications. Applications should be completed during the middle of the senior year or at least 6 months prior to the expected entrance date. Required admission materials include college transcript(s), letters of recommendation, application forms, and test scores (such as GRE or MAT results).

For careers that do not require advanced degrees, additional and ongoing education is beneficial. Employers sometimes provide this on the job; otherwise, employees need to attend workshops, conferences, or continuing education classes. Keep current with and stimulated by career changes and developments. These often result in greater job productivity and can lead to career advancement. Remember, career development is a lifelong process.

One important component of graduate education is participation in research projects.
© John A. Rizzo/Getty Images RF

GAINING EXPERIENCE

Your exploration of career options is enhanced when you gain experience through volunteer work, internships, extracurricular activities, and summer or part-time jobs. When you do such work, you are able to investigate what is involved in a position as well as develop job-related skills. Through these experiences, you will find out what you do or do not enjoy, which may result in your pursuing a career enthusiastically or rethinking your future career. Exploring career options while a student gives you an advantage in your postcollege job search because potential employers will be impressed by the skills and knowledge you already have as well as by your accomplishments while completing these experiences. In reality, many entry-level positions for graduates grow out of networking, internships, and volunteer contributions because students have already demonstrated the quality of their work.

While you are still a first- or second-year college student, it is important to investigate the job market by talking with older students, faculty members, or individuals in the career(s) you are considering, maybe by asking them the questions listed in Box 6.4. Reflect on their responses as you continue to narrow or broaden your career possibilities and make the most of your education. By carefully selecting your elective courses, you may be able to obtain a double major or specialize in an area such as corporate fitness. Through certain courses you may qualify for an internship, a summer work experience, or a part-time job, or you may have an opportunity to gain valuable experience as a volunteer in intramurals or intercollegiate athletics.

Why should you be concerned about preparing a résumé early in your collegiate career? The most pragmatic reason is having one may help you get a part-time job or volunteer experience that might even give you the opportunity to learn more about a potential career and begin to network in this field. Another reason is that it is easy with technology to keep up with your activities, experiences, and achievements, lest you forget some of these, as you move through your college years. Having complete information for the preparation of a résumé will definitely help when you begin to seriously apply for the first job in your chosen career. Box 6.5 provides tips for preparing an effective résumé. Tables 6-3 and 6-4 show sample résumés, and Box 6.6 shows a sample application letter for a part-time job. Box 6.7 illustrates a sample cover letter for a full-time job. You may want to visit your college's placement center to learn about the services it offers. Professionals there can help you get a summer job as well as your first job after graduation. Numerous online resources also can provide assistance.

It has been said that "it's not what you can do, but who you know" that determines whether or not you get certain jobs. Many good jobs are obtained through

---

BOX 6.4   POSSIBLE QUESTIONS TO ASK ABOUT YOUR PROSPECTIVE CAREER

1. What is the educational background required?
2. How much prior experience is needed?
3. What are the typical work hours?
4. What is the daily routine and the average time spent on each of these activities?
5. What is the starting salary and salary range?
6. How much vacation time is provided?
7. What are the fringe benefits?
8. To what extent will the job responsibilities affect my personal life?
9. What are the requisite skills and knowledge for this job?
10. What personal characteristics, such as creativity, problem-solving ability, or enthusiasm, are necessary for being successful in the job?
11. What is the potential for employment in this career?
12. In what regions or states is this job available?
13. What is the potential for advancement in this career?
14. Is on-the-job training or advanced education required to maintain employment or to advance in this career?
15. What are the specific work responsibilities of this type of job? How much time is spent doing each?
16. What criteria are used to evaluate job performance?
17. What are the most satisfying or advantageous aspects of this job?
18. What are the most frustrating or disadvantageous aspects of this job?
19. What has been your biggest disillusionment?
20. What has been your most rewarding or enjoyable experience?

BOX 6.5   TIPS FOR PREPARING AN EFFECTIVE RESUME

- Assume your resume is a one-of-a-kind marketing communication about YOU (with the goal of convincing the employer that you are a superior candidate who should be granted an interview)
- Target your resume to the specific job for which you are applying
- Grab the interest of the reader in the top half page of the resume by making honest statements about your abilities, qualities, and achievements that elicit interest and excitement about you (be sure to focus on your college, not high school, years)
- Provide evidence by listing jobs held, scope of responsibilities in each, and successes in these positions
- List jobs and experiences in reverse chronological order, with an emphasis and more detail about more recent or relevant jobs and experiences
- Show that you meet the requisite job requirements, such as education and experience
- List education in reverse chronological order and include any licenses and advanced professional training
- Use powerful, action verbs
- Demonstrate your excellent writing skills by ensuring that your resume is clearly written, well-organized, concise, consistent in format, error-free, and visually appealing
- Include a summary statement that describes your expertise and skills, breadth and depth of experiences and accomplishments, one or more personal or professional characteristics, and your professional interest or objective

Go to http://rockportinstitute.com/resumes/ for more tips for preparing an effective resume.

personal contacts. Why not let this work for you? Notify friends, relatives, former employers, and other people you have met that you are looking for a part-time or summer job or an internship. Follow up on all leads, because sometimes getting a good job results from "being in the right place at the right time." Initiate contact with anyone you think can help you. Networking is extremely important. You can begin to establish a network of acquaintances in your chosen career through your extracurricular activities, internships, volunteer experiences, and summer jobs and by attending workshops and conferences. The people you meet, interact with, and impress can help you get your initial or a subsequent job. Networking includes expanding your number of friends in the field and building positive relationships with them.

Another way to lead potential employers to view your job application favorably is to provide them with a portfolio that describes and illustrates your educational accomplishments, work experiences, and unique abilities. A **portfolio** is a representative collection of a student's work that demonstrates performance, achievements, and experiences. This portfolio could be provided in a looseleaf notebook for the interviewer to review, shared on an electronic file submitted at the time of application for review prior to the personal interview, or via a Web page you design and maintain. Box 6.8 provides an outline for a portfolio.

TABLE 6-3

SAMPLE RÉSUMÉ FOR A PROSPECTIVE TEACHER

LEWIS RAY KNIGHT

School Address:
1234 Drake Lane
Columbus, FL 38281
Phone: (915) 437-4921

Permanent Address:
567 Swinging Bridge Boulevard
Norlina, TX 72802
Phone: (173) 548-2183

Education:
University of South Miami, Miami, Florida, May, 2016
Bachelor of Science in Physical Education

Experiences:
Student Teacher, East Junior High School, Miami, Florida (Spring 2016)
Teacher's Aide, West Junior High School, Miami, Florida (Fall 2015)
Miami Boys' and Girls' Club volunteer basketball coach (2012–2016)
Counselor at Norlina, Texas, summer sports camp (2013–2015)

Honors and Awards:
Residence Hall Intramural Manager of the Year (2014)
Dean's List (2013–2016)

College Activities:
Chairperson of the Physical Education Majors' Club Social Committee (2013–2015)
Intramural and Boys' Club basketball official (2013–2016)
Intramural participant in basketball, touch football, softball, and tennis (2012–2016)
Student member of SHAPE America

Availability:
Available for employment, August, 2016

References:
Dr. Samuel R. Wilson
Department of Physical Education, Exercise Science, and Sport
University of South Miami
South Miami, FL 38281

Dr. Mary S. Vine
Department of Physical Education, Exercise Science, and Sport
University of South Miami
South Miami, FL 38281

Mr. Timothy Z. Miller
Director, Miami Boys' and Girls' Club
11890 West Lakeland Avenue
South Miami, FL 38282

TABLE 6-4

SAMPLE RÉSUMÉ FOR A PROSPECTIVE CORPORATE FITNESS LEADER

MARY ANN SMITH

School Address:
8923 Amigo Drive
Northridge, CA 90324
Phone: (412) 901-4413

Permanent Address:
7421 Langley Road
San Antonia, CA 97181
Phone: (433) 821-0431

(continued)

TABLE 6-4 (continued)

SAMPLE RÉSUMÉ FOR A PROSPECTIVE CORPORATE FITNESS LEADER

Personal Strengths:
- Integrity
- Responsible
- Loyalty
- Hardworking
- Good communication skills
- Excellent technology skills

Experiences:

Intern exercise leader with Jones & Jones Company in Newark, New Jersey (summer 2016)
- Designed an aerobics program for 125 employees
- Organized a family-oriented fun run
- Initiated a company-wide incentive program for weight reduction

Volunteer at Redwood Convalescent Center, Northwest, California (2013–2015)
- Developed a recreation program for non-ambulatory patients

Sales person, The Sports Shop, Northwest, California (2012–2014)

College Activities:

Vice President of the university's Racquetball Club (2015–2016)

Member of Exercise Science Majors' Club (2013–2016)

Volunteer assistant in department's exercise physiology laboratory (2014–2016)

Education:

California State University, Northridge, California, May, 2016

Bachelor of Science in exercise science

Overall GPA: 3.5; Major GPA: 3.8

Special Skills:

Certified Health Fitness Specialist (American College of Sports Medicine)

Certified in first aid and cardiopulmonary resuscitation

Affiliations:

Student member of the American College of Sports Medicine

Student member of the National Strength and Conditioning Association

References:

Dr. Sally R. Eaton
Department of Kinesiology
California State University
Northridge, CA 90324

Dr. Philip D. Stanton
Department of Kinesiology
California State University
Northridge, CA 90324

Dr. Cameron F. Baylor
Department of Kinesiology
California State University
Northridge, CA 90324

BOX 6.6   SAMPLE APPLICATION LETTER FOR A PART-TIME JOB

Ms. Terry Ann Cowan
Manager, Sports Unlimited
1902 Smithfield Road
Helena, MO 61102

October 1, 2016

(continued)

BOX 6.6   SAMPLE APPLICATION LETTER FOR A PART-TIME JOB (continued)

Dear Ms. Cowan:

As a sophomore at Western State University majoring in sport management, I am interested in finding a part-time job related to my prospective career. Specifically, I would like to learn about retail sporting goods sales by working 10 to 12 hours per week, in the evenings and on weekends.

My previous work experience includes three summers as a camp counselor teaching racket sports to boys and girls ages 6 to 16, and 9 months as a clerk in a fast-food restaurant. My immediate supervisors for these two jobs have agreed to provide you with an evaluation of my work.

At the university, I am a member of a social sorority, the jazz dance club, and the Sport Management Majors' Club. My commitments to these would not interfere with whatever hours you might assign me to work. I have enclosed my résumé, which provides you with additional information about my work experiences and campus activities.

If you have an opening for a sales clerk or anticipate one in the near future, I would appreciate your calling me at 371-9882 or contacting me at msm22@wsu.edu. In the event that you cannot reach me within one week, I will call you to follow up on this inquiry. Thank you for your consideration.

Sincerely,

Mary Sue Markam

BOX 6.7   SAMPLE COVER LETTER FOR A TEACHING AND COACHING POSITION

April 12, 2015

Mr. Raymond C. Van Meter
Personnel Director
Guilford City Schools
329 West Broadway
Guilford, GA 67941

Dear Mr. Van Meter:

(This paragraph explains why you are writing.) I read with great interest that the Guilford City Schools is looking for a middle school physical education teacher and assistant football and assistant track and field coach at the high school level. I am writing to apply for this position.

(This paragraph explains what you have to offer.) In May of 2016 I will be graduating from the Eastern Georgia University with a bachelor's degree in physical education with a coaching minor. Currently, I am completing my student teaching internship under the supervision of John R. Williams at Westside Middle School. I also have served as his volunteer assistant coach with the South Guilford High School track team. During the summers while in college, I worked as a camp counselor for King Brothers' sports camp in Kennesaw and taught girls and boys ages 10–14 skills in archery,

(continued)

BOX 6.7   SAMPLE COVER LETTER FOR A TEACHING AND COACHING POSITION (continued)

badminton, softball, tennis, and volleyball. I have served as a volunteer youth sport coach in football for 3 years with the Griffin Parks and Recreation Department. Also while an undergraduate student, I volunteered with the Eastern Georgia University track and field team for 2 years.

(This paragraph explains how you will follow up.) I would appreciate the opportunity to meet you in person and discuss the experiences and abilities I would bring to the Guilford City Schools. I will contact you within one week to answer any questions you may have about my qualifications. Please do not hesitate to contact me before this time using the contact information provided below. Thank you very much for taking the time to review my application.

Sincerely,

Andrew G. Barnes
546 Morrow Drive
Guilford, GA 67941
agbarnes44@yahoo.com

BOX 6.8   OUTLINE FOR A PORTFOLIO

Professional Philosophy
- Provide a brief profile about yourself.
- Describe your personal values.
- Share your short-term professional goals specifically as they relate to this career.

Educational Background
- List colleges attended, degrees earned, and major.
- Describe academic honors earned and recognitions received in college.
- Explain how your collegiate studies prepared you for a career in this field.
- Identify memberships held in professional organizations and describe how your past participation has helped enhance your professional development.
- List any professional certifications and licenses and explain their significance relative to the position sought.

Work Experiences
- List all work experiences that helped prepare you for the position sought.
- Describe the scope of your work responsibilities in each job.
- Include commendations and illustrations of the quality of your work.

Extracurricular Activities
- Describe your participation in nonacademic clubs and organizations during your college years and how what you learned and experienced helped increase your abilities and knowledge.
- Explain the importance of each aspect of your volunteer work.

(continued)

BOX 6.8   OUTLINE FOR A PORTFOLIO (continued)

Examples of Your Professional Abilities
- Include copies of awards, dean's list citations, and thank-you letters for service.
- Illustrate your competence, such as through publication of student research, a videotape of a professional presentation, samples of lesson plans, or internship evaluations.
- Provide examples of your commitment to lifelong learning, such as workshops or conferences attended.

Professional Goals
- Share your long-term career aspirations and your current plans for achieving them.

SUMMARY

As you prepare for your career, you need to begin to set short- and long-term goals. These will help you make incremental progress toward the achievement of your career aspirations. Your choices of courses to fulfill requirements, your selection of a major, and your use of electives will determine the quality of your education and career preparation. The quantity, quality, and diversity of your extracurricular activities will enrich your college years and possibly assist in your career choice. Internships and volunteer activities, especially those enabling you to gain valuable experiences related to your interest area, are important additions to your under-graduate years. It is beneficial to obtain any appropriate certification prior to seeking your first job, since many positions require this for employment. In addition, completing an advanced degree in an area of specialization will enhance your knowledge and marketability. The process of getting a job begins with the courses you take, the experiences you gain, and the abilities you demonstrate as a young professional. Build on this base of knowledge and experience by examining various career options, developing a résumé, writing application letters, and interviewing for a part-time or summer job.

CAREER PERSPECTIVE

PEEWEE ROBERSON
Managing Director, Recreational Sports
Texas Tech University
Lubbock, Texas

EDUCATION
B. S. in physical education, Texas Tech University
M. Ed., Texas Tech University
Ph. D. candidate in higher education, Texas Tech University

Courtesy PeeWee Roberson

JOB RESPONSIBILITIES AND HOURS

PeeWee plans and directs the overall operation, including maintenance improvements and capital development, of the Recreational Sports Department. He develops and oversees the budget, establishes and leads in the accomplishment of short, medium, and long-term goals, and manages all large-scale projects. PeeWee leads and manages the professional and classified staff including hiring, supervising, and evaluating. He administers and oversees the operation of all Recreational Sports programs and facilities, including the Student Recreation Center, Aquatic and Leisure Pool, Turf Complex, and all associated fields and outdoor areas. He also represents Recreational Sports on university committees. PeeWee typically works Monday through Friday between 7:30 am to 5:30 pm, but as the managing director, he at times works on weekends and nights when many events and activities are happening as well as responds to any administrative need associated with accidents, weather issues, and other emergency situations. A salary range of $70,000 to $150,000 depends on years of experience, job performance, and the size and operational complexity of each university's recreational sports program.

SPECIALIZED COURSE WORK, DEGREES, AND EXPERIENCES NEEDED FOR THIS CAREER

Experience working in recreational sports with increasing levels of responsibility is essential for advancement through the ranks and a prerequisite for becoming a managing director. Working in areas like intramurals, outdoor activities, facilities, fitness, and open recreation help younger professionals understand the organization and operations better. More directors come from facility management more than any other area. Understanding how construction works as well of how to maintain equipment and work with maintenance issues are important areas of competence as well. Pee Wee believes that gaining knowledge about sport management, recreation and leisure services, construction and facility management, sport programming, officiating sports, and cardiopulmonary resuscitation have been helpful to him as he fulfilled his responsibilities. PeeWee found principles of leisure programming, facilities management, funding in higher education, leadership in higher education, administration of higher education, higher education law, student development, and other leadership courses were important in preparing him for his responsibilities. He added, it is essential to never stop learning even if you are a department head.

SATISFYING ASPECTS

PeeWee enjoys most seeing and contributing to the growth and development of his young professional staff and working with student employees. Seeing students develop and grow to become mature individuals makes his job especially rewarding. Being fair and consistent when dealing with inevitable personnel issues and disciplinary problems are challenges that can be resolved positively in most cases.

JOB POTENTIAL

Since most college recreational sport programs exist in public universities linked with state funding constraints, salaries increases are often limited. If an individual starts out at the bottom of an organization, he or she must remember that working hard and performing competently will impress your supervisor and are the keys to advancement. Hard work and competent performance are career-long expectations because everyone has a supervisor to impress. PeeWee stresses the importance of lifelong learning and doing what is right. Ethical conduct, integrity, and being a leader will lead to higher salaries, expanded responsibilities, and promotions.

SUGGESTIONS FOR STUDENTS

PeeWee advises that working in recreational sports affords bountiful opportunities to build relationships with people and make a difference in the lives others, especially if you like working with students. The friendships you make can last forever. Since student employees change over the years, recreational sport administrators must change with them, thus making everyone better. The training, developing, and learning you embrace will always make you a better person. PeeWee emphasizes the importance of working hard and learning continuously. He concludes that you will make a difference if you care and respect the individuals around you.

KEY POINTS

Setting goals	Goals should be specific, measurable, attainable, relevant, and time-bound.
Volunteer activities	Gaining experiences related to a potential career is an invaluable way to learn which and to what degree activities are personally rewarding and enjoyable.
Internship	A formal supervised period of work in a position related to a potential career provides an excellent opportunity to expand one's knowledge, learn more about career options, network, and help prepare for working in a selected field.
Certification	Through demonstrating more extensive knowledge, one can show greater expertise and commitment while setting oneself apart from other applicants for positions.
Undergraduate research	Students should take advantage of participating in research projects with their professors and expanding their scholarly knowledge in their areas of interest.
Graduate degrees	Since graduate degrees are often required for entry into some fields, and for advancement in many fields, students should examine the job requirements of their potential careers and explore options for obtaining any required or desired advanced degrees.

Experiential learning	Learning is optimized whenever knowledge, skills, and abilities can be developed and enhanced through related work experiences.
Résumé	The development of a résumé should be an ongoing process that includes a record of all relevant activities and achievements during the undergraduate years.
Networking	Meeting and building relationships with individuals in potential careers may be the most important factor in obtaining an entry-level position or advancement opportunity.
Portfolio	This representation of a student's or professional's work can help differentiate a person from other applicants for positions because of how its contents illustrate or describe personal accomplishments, experiences, and unique qualities.

REVIEW QUESTIONS

1. What are goals? Why is establishing long- and short-term goals important?

2. What are several reasons why working as a volunteer in activities related to your intended career is important?

3. Why is completing an internship important?

4. What are the various types of graduate degree programs offered by universities? What are examples of the programs of study offered?

5. Describe the process for obtaining a certification related to your intended career.

6. What should a résumé include?

7. What is the purpose of developing a professional portfolio?

STUDENT ACTIVITIES

1. Talk with students who have completed internships in intramurals, in campus recreation, in athletics, with a community group, in a corporate fitness program, or with a sport business. Ask them about the positive and negative aspects of their experiences.

2. Get involved in one professionally related extracurricular activity. Evaluate your experiences to determine what you learned and how they could help you in the future.

3. Find out about your institution's majors' club in your field of study and become actively involved with it.

4. Select a certification, such as one in health and fitness, and set short- and long-term goals for achieving it.

5. Shadow an individual in a career that interests you. Ask this person's advice about how best to prepare to enter that career.

6. Write a letter of application for a position in your chosen career. In one paragraph, highlight your most significant qualities.

7. Using the Internet, obtain information about three graduate programs that interest you.

 WEB CONNECTIONS

1. www.mindtools.com/page6.html
    This site provides toolkits on leadership skills, strategy, problem solving, decision making, time management, stress management, communication skills, learning skills, and career skills.

2. www.cooperinstitute.org/pub/courses.cfm
    Learn about the personal trainer certification program, personal training courses, online courses, and specialty courses offered by the Cooper Institute.

3. certification.acsm.org/get-certified
    Learn more about the certification programs offered by the American College of Sports Medicine and how to become certified.

4. www.acefitness.org/getcertified/default.aspx
    Check out this site for information about fitness certifications offered by the American Council on Exercise.

5. www.nsca.com/Certification/
    Learn about the certifications offered by the National Strength and Conditioning Association.

6. www.strategicbusinessnetwork.com/about/importance
    This site provides a wealth of information about the importance of networking.

7. www.internships.com/sports
    Search for internships in professional sports, broadcasting, marketing, nutrition, psychology, and sport science, with the option to search by company, such as Disney or ESPN.

8. www.internsearch.com/
    At this site, students can search for internships in sports, fitness, and recreation.

HISTORY AND DEVELOPMENT OF PHYSICAL EDUCATION, EXERCISE SCIENCE, AND SPORT

GYMNASIA AND PLAY-GROUND OF THE CHILDREN OF THE HOME AND COLONIAL INFANT SCHOOL SOCIETY, GRAY'S-INN-LANE.

© Chronicle/Alamy

CHAPTER

7

EARLY HERITAGE IN SPORTS AND GYMNASTICS

LEARNING OUTCOMES

- Students will be able to explain the contributions of the Greek and Roman civilizations to sport programs in the United States.
- Students will be able to describe the contributions of the knights, Renaissance, Reformation, and naturalism to physical education, exercise science, and sport programs in the United States.
- Students will be able to explain the contributions of German gymnastics and Swedish gymnastics to physical education, exercise science, and sport programs in the United States.
- Students will be able to describe the impact of British sports on sport programs in the United States.

Throughout history, people have participated in various physical activities. Integral to early civilizations' survival tasks of seeking food, clothing, shelter, and protection were the utilitarian skills of running, jumping, throwing, wrestling, climbing, and swimming. Before formal educational programs emerged, tribal leaders and parents mandated that children learn and practice survival skills through imitation. Communal requirements stressed physical prowess for both aggressive and defensive purposes.

Modern programs of physical education in the United States borrowed primarily from the philosophies, activities, and developments of Europeans from prehistoric times through the 1800s. The Greeks valued optimal physical prowess, and Greek athletics laid the foundation for subsequent physical education and sport programs. In Europe, military training served utilitarian purposes. After social conditions stabilized, the philosophy of naturalism stressed development of the body to help educate the whole child. Gymnastics that stressed nationalistic goals borrowed the apparatus and activities of earlier naturalistic programs. Sports and games in England offered an alternative to formalized gymnastics systems.

EARLY CULTURES

The earliest known hieroglyphic writing and formation of the Egyptian state occurred around 3100 B.C. with Egypt unifying into one kingdom under the pharaohs around 2650 B.C. The next few 100 years saw the building of the great pyramids and tombs with their extensive inscriptions. The classical period of art, manifested in painting, carving, sculpting, and literature, occurred between 1975 and 1640 B.C. This era also was characterized by extensive knowledge about the body, antiseptics, and surgery. After tumultuous times of disunity and foreign rule, the Egyptians subsequently defended their state, which was ruled by military generals and pharaohs until it was conquered by the Persians in 525 B.C. After Alexander the Great captured Egypt from the Persians in 332 B.C., thus making it part of his empire, he built a fortified city and named it Alexandria. This city dominated the eastern Mediterranean world culturally, politically, and economically for more than 900 years due to its location, which served as a geographical and political bridge between Europe and Africa. Alexandria was enriched by maritime trade, the Greek intellectual tradition, and its status as the capital of Egypt and seat of rule for the Ptolemaic dynasty.

The Egyptians have been recognized more for their alphabet and their scientific, agricultural, and engineering prowess than for their educational achievements. Although the Egyptians did not have health objectives related to physical activity, they showed interest in physical development if it achieved a vocational, recreational, or religious objective. The warrior class physically trained for hunting, charioteering, warfare, and wrestling. For recreation, people of all classes swam, hunted, and played ball games. Dancing, like wrestling, was a form of entertainment. Dancing also was important in religious rituals.

Scholars have divided the history of China, one of the earliest civilizations in the world, into a series of dynasties. During the Shang Dynasty between 1500 and 1000 B.C., the bronze culture enabled China to achieve unprecedented advancements in politics, economy, industry, culture, art, medicine, transportation, astronomy, and written communication. The subsequent Zhou Dynasty, which reigned until 221 B.C., was noted for its brilliant achievements in culture. Under the Qin Dynasty, which lasted only 15 years, China was unified into the first multinational, autocratic state in Chinese history. This beginning of the imperial history of China saw the initiation of the construction of the Great Wall. The Tang Dynasty, which lasted between 618 and 907 A.D., elevated China into arguably the largest, richest, and most sophisticated state in the world at that time as its people spearheaded cultural exchange between the East and the West in politics, economics, military power, foreign relations, literature, and poetry. Between 960 and 1279, China flourished economically and enjoyed such great artistic and intellectual achievement that this era has been called the Chinese Renaissance. The Yuan Dynasty, which lasted 98 years, emerged in 1271 following the defeat of much of China by nomadic fighters from Mongolia led by Genghis Khan. The Mongols established Beijing as a political, economic, and cultural center. The prosperous Ming Dynasty was characterized by advances in the arts and sciences, an agrarian-centered society, growth in industries, the refurbishing of the Great Wall, and a strong and complex central government.

Although in earlier eras physical training had been valued, the religions of Taoism, Buddhism, and Confucianism emphasized the contemplative life. The defense-minded Chinese maintained a military class who participated in archery, boxing, chariot racing, football, and wrestling, but these activities were never popularized for the masses. Many Chinese flew kites, played chess, practiced light exercises called *Kung Fu,* hunted, did acrobatics, and fished. For the Chinese, literary studies and moral and religious training were valued most.

The geography of India has shaped its history, with its location an attraction to invaders from the East and West. The first invaders, the Aryans, with their strong cultural traditions, introduced the caste system. Local Hindu kingdoms, however, survived numerous invasions and perpetuated their culture and religion. While the Persians and the Greeks invaded India, their influence was limited in time and in scope. The Maurya Empire, beginning around 300 B.C., conquered nearly the entire subcontinent, and one of its kings introduced Buddhism throughout much of central Asia. Although Arab (Muslim) armies had previously conducted raids in India, they returned in 1192 under Mohammed of Ghor and devastated the city of Delhi and its Buddhist temples, and this time they did not leave. Numerous Muslims vied for dominance until 1527 when the Mughal (Persian for Mongol) monarch Babur came into power. While ruling India, his descendants established a tradition of cultural acceptance that contributed to their success and left behind several colossal monuments, including the Taj Mahal. Subsequently, Europeans began their imperialistic forays into India, led by the Portuguese in 1510, who were displaced by the British in 1610.

In India, Hinduism renounced pleasure and individualism and was characterized by asceticism in preparation for the next life. Spiritual well-being led to healthful practices and participation in physical exercises such as yoga, a system of meditation and regulated breathing. Buddhism, which deemphasized physical activities, sought to reform the excesses of the Indian caste system.

For various reasons, the Egyptians, Chinese, and Indians engaged minimally in physical activities. Not until the Greeks did a civilization openly stress physical prowess and prescribe organized methods for its development.

Greece, regarded as the birthplace of Western civilization, produced a rich heritage of art, drama, history, mathematics, oratory, philosophy, poetry, science, and sculpture, as well as the earliest recorded athletic or sport activities. This progressive society, which recognized the importance of educating the whole individual, evolved through four eras: (1) the Homeric era, from prehistoric times until the first recorded Olympic Games in 776 B.C.; (2) the era of the totalitarian city-state of Sparta, from 776 B.C. to 371 B.C.; (3) the early Athenian era, which emphasized democracy and individual freedom, from 776 B.C. to the end of the Persian Wars in 480 B.C.; and (4) the later Athenian era, from 480 B.C. until 338 B.C., which grew out of heightened intellectual curiosity (Van Dalen & Bennett, 1971).

HOMERIC GREEKS (BEFORE 776 B.C.)

The Homeric era was named for the Greek poet Homer, who is credited with composing *The Iliad* and *The Odyssey,* which include the earliest records of athletic competitions. Book XXIII of *The Iliad* describes the funeral games held in honor of Patroclus, Achilles' friend who was killed in the Trojan War. The contests included a chariot race, boxing, wrestling, a footrace, a duel with spears, a discus throw, archery, and a javelin throw. Athletes of the period competing in individual events like these fought fiercely to win. In *The Odyssey*, Homer chronicled the wanderings and return of Odysseus from the Trojan War. Illustrative of these adventures was one episode in Book VIII in which Odysseus, taunted by the Phaeacians, responded by throwing the discus beyond the distances achieved by their athletes.

The predominant philosophy that developed during the Homeric era became known as the **Greek Ideal,** which stressed the unity of the "man of action" and "man of wisdom." This all-around mental, moral, and physical excellence was called **arete** and was believed to be personified by the Greek gods. Revered as part deity and part human, the 12 major gods of the Olympic Council were worshiped as the personifications of the Greek Ideal, with superior intellectual and physical capacities, such as strength, endurance, agility, and bravery. In funeral games held in honor of both respected soldiers killed in battle and the gods, Greek warrior-athletes competed to prove their arete. Success, or winning to prove one's athletic superiority, was valued more highly than prizes, although lucrative prizes were awarded. Prior to competing, many athletes sought the favor of the gods.

SPARTANS (776 B.C. TO 371 B.C.)

The Greeks organized themselves into small governmental units known as city-states. The two dominant, though dramatically contrasting, city-states were Sparta and Athens. By the eighth century B.C. Sparta had begun its military conquests. As Sparta conquered land and took captives, a strict code of discipline, rather than adherence to the Greek Ideal, was imposed on its people. The **agoge,** an educational system that ensured the singular goal of serving the city-state, evolved. Mandating complete submission, the Spartan civilization became stagnant because everything, including education, was controlled by the government.

At birth, a child was examined by a council of elders. If healthy and strong, the child was spared. Weak or sickly children were exposed to the elements to die. The mothers' roles in raising children resembled those of state nurses; they had to suppress tender and maternalistic feelings. While sons were taught to value their roles as obedient soldiers, daughters learned about their responsibility to bear healthy children.

To prepare themselves physically for this duty, girls participated in state-prescribed gymnastics in addition to wrestling, swimming, and horseback riding. Dancing also was important in the education of girls and boys as a means both of physical conditioning and honoring the gods.

The boys' educational system, the agoge, was highly structured and formalized. Boys were conscripted by the state at 7 years of age and remained in military service until death. Spartan boys began their military training with running and jumping for conditioning. They progressed to swimming, hunting, wrestling, boxing, playing ball, riding horses bareback, throwing the discus and the javelin, and competing in the **pancratium,** a contest combining wrestling and boxing skills.

Young boys were trained to endure hardships and pain. Discipline reigned supreme; youths who failed to develop valor, devotion to the state, and military skill were punished, often severely.

Beginning at 20 years of age, youths engaged in intensive military maneuvers and actual warfare. These Spartan soldiers, who had been conditioned to fight until death, repeatedly demonstrated their superiority over neighboring city-states and other foes. Not only did the Spartans dominate militarily during this time, but they also won more Olympic victories than athletes from any other city-state. Spartan men, at the age of 30 years, qualified for citizenship and were expected to marry; however, their obligation to the state continued as they trained youth in the public barracks. The Spartan military machine, with its focus on physical prowess and disregard for intellectual development, contributed to its inability to rule its innumerable captives and lands. Although they made excellent soldiers, the people were trained not to think for themselves but to perform on command. The Spartans also were few in number due to their strict practices. These factors contributed to the end of their domination as a city-state.

EARLY ATHENIANS (776 B.C. TO 480 B.C.)

Athens differed sharply from Sparta. The Greek Ideal became the Athenian Ideal as this city-state sought to provide an educational system that encouraged boys to develop their physical and mental abilities. Within a framework of democracy, liberalism, and the popularization of various philosophies, physical prowess flourished in Athens as an integral part of the preparation of boys for war and as a means to depict beauty and harmony.

Girls remained at home under the care of their mothers and received little or no formal education. Once married, they lived secluded lives. Unlike the physically trained women in Sparta, the Athenian women's social role typically was very different from the men's role. Boys in the lower classes, though, were as uneducated as girls.

The Athenian educational system, which valued the all-around citizen, dominated the lives of upper-class boys, who, under the guidance of their fathers, learned about their future responsibilities. Usually beginning at age 7 and lasting until 14 to 18 years, young boys were formally educated at privately owned schools. The time when each boy started, the length of time he attended, and the time when he ended this phase of his education were determined solely by the father, since no governmental regulations existed. Not all boys could attend these schools, since fathers had to pay for their sons' education.

The importance attached to the all-around-development ideal was evident in each boy's attendance at two schools. A music school provided instruction in arithmetic, literature, and music, while at a **palaestra,** called a wrestling school, boys trained physically. Both schools were equally valued, as the unity concept prevailed. Palaestras were owned and directed by **paidotribes,** the first physical education teachers. Palaestras were not elaborate athletic facilities but varied from sparse rooms to simple buildings where the boys practiced wrestling, boxing, jumping, and dancing. Some palaestras also included playing fields and a place for swimming.

At the age of 18 years, Athenian boys became eligible for citizenship. For 2 years thereafter they were subject to military service, if the state needed them, although no mandatory conscription existed. From 20 years of age onward, upper-class Athenian men did not work but instead spent much of their time at government-furnished **gymnasiums,** sites for intellectual and physical activities for Greek citizens. There they practiced athletics to maintain their readiness as warriors in case they were needed by their city-state. Intellectual discussions, dealing with political issues, and social interactions were equally important facets of days at the gymnasium.

Greek dancing provided one means of honoring the gods as part of religious worship. It also enhanced physical conditioning and demonstrated the symmetry and beauty adored by the Athenians. Athletics played a similar role, as festivals honoring the gods gave Greek males the opportunity to display their physical prowess and aesthetically pleasing bodies. The importance of honoring the gods eventually led to a proliferation of festivals throughout Greece.

LATE ATHENIANS (480 B.C. TO 338 B.C.)

The Athenian-led victory over the Persians in 480 B.C. set the stage for several cultural changes. Economic expansion, self-confidence, increased leisure time, intellectual curiosity, and expansion of political power combined to shift educational goals away from devotion to the state and toward a heightened pursuit of individual happiness. This rampant individualism led to a deemphasis on the physical aspects of education because, as members of the dominant city-state, citizens no longer saw the need to train as soldiers. The Athenian warrior-athletes were replaced by mercenary soldiers and professional athletes.

The gymnasiums became more like pleasure resorts than places for exercise. They provided sites for philosophical discussions and the training of professional athletes. The Golden Age of Athens (the fifth century B.C.) was highlighted by a flowering of democracy and intellectual curiosity led by the Sophists, a class of teachers of rhetoric, philosophy, and the art of successful living, and by the Athenian statesman, Pericles. Warning cries from some philosophers about the undermining of the Athenian society went largely unheeded. As a result, the Athenians were militarily unprepared and fell to the Macedonians in 338 B.C.

PAN-HELLENIC FESTIVALS (776 B.C. TO A.D. 400)

Festivals honoring the gods during the Homeric period led to the establishment of regular celebrations, which expanded dramatically in the fifth century B.C. Warrior-athletes, who were expected to perfect their skills for warfare, used these religious festivals to demonstrate their physical prowess, especially since this proved their allegiance to the Greek Ideal as personified by the gods. Some of these **Pan-Hellenic** (meaning for all Greeks) **festivals** also included musical events and aquatic displays (see Table 7-1 for a list of the four major Pan-Hellenic festivals). The Pan-Hellenic festivals were exclusively for males with one exception: the Heraean Games, which were held for maidens who competed in a footrace.

TABLE 7-1				
PAN-HELLENIC FESTIVALS				
Name	*Frequency*	*Honoring*	*Location*	*Wreath for Victor*
Olympic Games	Every 4 years	Zeus	Olympia	Olive leaves
Pythian Games	Every 4 years (third year of each Olympiad)	Apollo	Delphi	Bay leaves
Isthmian Games	Every 2 years (second and fourth years of each Olympiad)	Poseidon	Isthmia	Pine
Nemean Games	Every 2 years	Zeus	Nemea	Wild celery

The ancient Olympic Games were unmatched in prestige among these festivals. They were held every 4 years at Olympia, in honor of Zeus, the chief Greek god. These events began at least by 776 B.C. (the date of the earliest existing artifact of a victory at Olympia), but probably started much earlier. The sacrifices to Zeus, feasting, and athletic contests lasted 5 days in August and attained such prestige that the perennially warring city-states would guarantee safe passage to travelers to the games. Box 7.1 lists when it is believed that each event became a part of the games at Olympia and provides a probable outline of how events were organized during the 5 days. This sequence of events, with sacrifices and other tributes to Zeus, reinforced the link between religious service and athletic competition.

To be eligible for the games at Olympia, a prospective athlete had to be male, Greek born, and free (not a slave), and had to train for 10 months before the contests (with the last month of training at Olympia under the guidance of the judges). Although the games were open to males from all social classes, the training requirement precluded participation by most poor Greeks, who had to work. Athletes were required to take an oath of fair play. Victors received a wreath of olive branches to symbolize their highly respected victory. Honored by a hero's welcome when returning home, a victor reveled in triumphal processions and banquets, special privileges, and monetary rewards. Initially Olympia provided no accommodations for either spectators or athletes, as neither a stadium nor a site for the contests existed. The games were scheduled in open spaces with spectators sitting wherever they could. Later construction of a stadium (for footraces) and the hippodrome (for horse and chariot races) provided space for about 40,000 spectators.

The **stade race** was named because it was a footrace the length of the stadium, although the dirt running area was nothing like a track or stadium of today with seating for spectators. This race of about 200 meters was probably the only event in the first games at Olympia. A two-stade race, a longer race of about 12 laps, and a race in armor were later added to this phase of the athletic contests. Marble slabs with toe grooves may have served as starting blocks, and either a trumpet blast or

BOX 7.1   ANCIENT OLYMPIC GAMES

Chronology

776 B.C.	Stade race
724 B.C.	Added the two-stade race
720 B.C.	Added the longer distance race
708 B.C.	Added pentathlon and wrestling
688 B.C.	Added boxing
648 B.C.	Added pancratium and horse race
632 B.C.	Added events for boys
520 B.C.	Added the race in armor
472 B.C.	Festival set as a 5-day event and the sequence of events listed below:
408 B.C.	Two-horse chariot race
384 B.C.	Four-colt chariot race

First Day
Oath-taking ceremony
Contests for heralds and trumpeters
Contests for boys
Sacrifices, prayers, singing of hymns,
and other religious observances

Second Day
Chariot race
Horse race
Pentathlon (discus, javelin, long jump,
stade race, and wrestling)

Third Day
Main sacrifice to Zeus
Footraces

Fourth Day
Wrestling
Boxing
Pancratium
Race in armor

Fifth Day
Prize-giving ceremony
Service of thanksgiving to Zeus
Banquet

a starting gate was probably used to start these events. In the longer distance races, the athletes rounded posts at the opposite end of the stadium.

Hand-to-hand combat events included boxing, wrestling, and the pancratium. Since no weight categories existed, boxing pitted two athletes of any size against each other until one raised a hand to admit defeat. No gloves were worn; the boxers' hands were wrapped with pieces of leather. Blows were confined primarily to the head, often resulting in severe injuries. Wrestling was one of the most popular events because its competitors displayed agility, gracefulness, and strength (see Research View for one example). The objective was to throw the opponent to the ground 3 times. The pancratium borrowed from boxing and wrestling to become an "almost-anything-goes" combat. Except for biting and gouging, an athlete could employ any maneuver, such as tripping, breaking fingers, and strangleholds, to force an opponent's admission of defeat.

Long jump

Discus throw

Javelin throw

Stade race

Wrestling

FIVE EVENTS IN THE PENATHLON

(Long jump, javelin throw, wrestling) © ACE STOCK LIMITED/Alamy; (Discus throw) © Lev Tsimbler/Alamy RF; (Stade race) © Picture Post/Hulton Archive/Getty Images

Chariots, two-wheeled vehicles pulled by four horses, raced, as did horses, at the hippodrome, a narrow field about 500 meters long. These races were limited to the wealthy, who could afford to maintain the horses and hire the charioteers.

RESEARCH VIEW

The Strength of Milo of Kroton

Milo of Kroton was a legendary Greek athlete and 6-time renowned Olympic champion in wrestling (once as a boy, and after 8 years he won five consecutive titles). Numerous real, or possibly mythical, accounts added to his reputation of unrivaled strength. For example, Milo did not develop his strength by lifting a bull each day as the bull grew. However, Milo's development of strength affirms the principle of training known as progression, increasing gradually the stress on the muscles so the body can adapt. According to ancient sources, Milo could tie a cord around his forehead, hold his breath, and break the cord with his bulging forehead veins. He could stand with his right elbow against his body and arm outstretched, hold out his right hand with the thumb pointed upward with his fingers spread, and no one could bend any of his fingers. Milo carried an ox for several miles and then killed it with one blow of his fist, cooked it, and immediately ate it all. On another occasion, he held up a falling roof so others could escape and then ran out of the house himself.

The victors were the owners, not the charioteers or jockeys. The chariot race consisted of 12 laps.

The winner of the **pentathlon** was recognized as the best all-around athlete. Although the order of events and the method of determining the victor have been lost in antiquity, the discus throw, the javelin throw, the long jump, the stade race, and wrestling constituted the pentathlon. Like the long jump and the javelin throw, the discus throw existed only as a pentathlon event. In the discus throw, the athlete hurled a circular piece of stone or bronze about 1 foot in diameter and weighing 4 to 5 pounds. In the long jump, jumpers were aided by handheld weights, called **halteres,** which were swung to enhance their performances. The javelin was thrown for both distance and form as a test of skill and strength. A leather thong was wrapped around the 8- to 10-foot javelin, giving it a rotary motion upon release, thereby increasing accuracy. The stade race and the wrestling match probably concluded the pentathlon, although these may not have been held if one athlete had already won the first three events.

Two developments ushered in a change in attitude toward the Pan-Hellenic festivals. Intellectual curiosity and a search for knowledge in Athens replaced the Greek Ideal and hence lessened interest in physical development. Within the games themselves, lucrative prizes increasingly overshadowed the earlier motive of honoring the gods through displays of athletic prowess. Professional athletes who trained under coaches at the gymnasiums and specialized in certain events now dominated the contests. Expensive prizes led to cheating, corruption, and bribery. Although officially ended by Roman decree around A.D. 400, the Olympic Games or other Pan-Hellenic festivals continued at sporadic intervals for many years.

Before leaving the Greeks, take the challenge to answer the questions in Box 7.2.

ROMAN REPUBLIC (500 B.C. TO 27 B.C.)

Roman civilization began as a small tribal community near the Tiber River during the height of the Greek civilization. By extending its rule over neighboring tribes, the Roman nobles, who were landowners, succeeded in establishing a republic

---

BOX 7.2 GAINING A BETTER UNDERSTANDING OF THE HISTORY OF SPORT AND PHYSICAL ACTIVITY IN GREECE

Students: Why did the Greeks do the following? (If you do not know the answer, see if you can find the answer in your textbook or do an online search to find the answer.)

1. Why did boys and men train for and compete in athletic contests in the nude?
2. Why did Spartans leave some of their children on mountains to die?
3. Why did Spartan females train physically and Athenian females did not?
4. Why did the Greeks have no weight categories for competitions in wrestling, boxing, and the pancratium?
5. Why did the Greeks crown only the victors (there were no second- or third-place awards) in the Olympics and other Pan-Hellenic festivals?

around 500 B.C. Soon the common people, who had been given land for their military service, demanded and received greater voice in the government. Thus, through this democratization process, many Romans attained higher degrees of political and economic freedoms.

Roman life during this era focused singularly on serving the state, even though the home provided education for youths without government involvement. Fathers and mothers taught their sons to become **citizen-soldiers,** including in their education a mental and physical readiness for war, respect for the law, and reverence for the gods. Accompanying their fathers to the Campus Martius or other **military camps,** boys learned military skills such as archery, fencing, javelin throwing, marching, riding, running, swimming, and wrestling; they developed bodily strength, courage, and obedience to commands as they trained. Conscripted into the military at 17 years of age, men were available for active duty, if needed, until age 47. During these 30 years, men were expected to fulfill their business and political duties as well.

Daughters were educated to assume a vital role in raising children and were expected to instill in their sons the importance of fighting, and even dying, for Rome. Roman women were more highly respected and socially active than Athenian women, although they did not usually train physically.

Festivals honoring the gods held as prominent a place in Roman society as they had in Greek society. However, the Romans did not participate in athletic contests or dance; rather, they offered sacrifices to their gods and preferred to watch others compete. These festivals provided leisure-time relief from strenuous military training, but served no educational purposes. Table 7-2 compares Greek and Roman athletic programs.

TABLE 7-2
COMPARISON OF ATHLETIC PROGRAMS

Early Athens	Late Athens	Roman Republic	Roman Empire
Participants			
Aristocratic citizens	Professional athletes	Citizen-soldiers	Professional gladiators and charioteers
Motivation			
All-around development	Profit	Preparation for war	Profit
Training			
Gymnasiums and palaestras	Gymnasiums under trainers	Military camps and fathers	Specialized schools
Events			
Archery, boxing, chariot races, discus, footraces, javelin, and wrestling	Boxing, chariot races, footraces, horse races, pancratium, pentathlon, and wrestling	Archery, fencing, javelin, marching, riding, running, swimming, and wrestling	Chariot races and gladiatorial contests

(continued)

TABLE 7-2 (continued)			
COMPARISON OF ATHLETIC PROGRAMS			
Early Athens	*Late Athens*	*Roman Republic*	*Roman Empire*
Organization			
Festivals	Scheduled games and festivals	Festivals	Frequent, organized festivals
Number of Stadiums or Arenas			
Few	Many	Few	Many

ROMAN EMPIRE (27 B.C. TO A.D. 476)

The economic and political freedoms gained by citizens during the Republic eroded during the century before the Empire was established in 27 B.C. under Augustus Caesar. The peasants, who had received land in exchange for military service, were ravaged by years of war and subsequent debts and taxes. Powerful landowners seized this opportunity to expand their estates and gain greater political influence. The poorer citizens, who were forced off their land, migrated to Rome, where they lived off the public dole or handouts. Replaced by a professional army and denied political freedoms and personal dignity, the common people spent their days attending festivals and games sponsored by upper-class senators or the emperors who sought the support of the masses. Gambling on the outcomes of these contests became a favorite pastime.

At least 200 days per year were public holidays and provided opportunities for festivals. Around 150,000 spectators watched **chariot races** at the Circus Maximus, attesting to the popularity of these contests. Professional charioteers hired by the teams (the blues, the greens, the reds, and the whites) raced their low, lightweight chariots drawn by four horses in seven-lap races, for a distance of about three miles. The Colosseum became the favorite site for the **gladiatorial contests,** where, to the pleasure of as many as 90,000 spectators, animal fights featured elephants, bulls, tigers, lions, panthers, and bears. Condemned criminals, social undesirables, and Christians were forced to combat lions, tigers, and panthers. Massive sea battles in the Colosseum provided additional bloody, gory entertainment. Gladiators, armed with shield and sword, buckle and dagger, or net and spear, fought each other for freedom or for money.

Gladiators and charioteers trained physically, but most other Romans lost interest in developing their bodies because they were no longer expected to serve as soldiers. Spending time at the thermae, baths of varying water temperatures, filled the leisure hours for upper-class men and women (with separate hours reserved for the women). At the numerous **thermae,** Roman men participated in health gymnastics or ball play to overcome indolent lifestyles that featured gluttonous feasts and drinking bouts.

Gladiatorial contests occurred in the Colosseum. These remains in Rome show the massive size of this arena and the openings for animals beneath the floor of the arena.
© Ingram Publishing/agefotostock RF

Claudius Galen, born in Pergamum in Greece and educated in Alexandria in Egypt when it was the greatest medical center in the ancient world, became a physician to emperors and gladiators. His public demonstrations of anatomy enhanced his stature as a physician, despite the prevailing taboo against human dissection that resulted in his conducting most of his anatomical studies using animals. Galen's writings were circulated widely during his lifetime, and translations of his original Greek manuscripts formed the basis of medical education in medieval universities.

The physical abilities of the Romans dissipated rapidly during an era characterized by governmental upheavals, power struggles, and an apathetic and dependent populace. In A.D. 476, with the deposition of the last Roman emperor by the Visigoths under Odoacer, the Roman Empire ended. As was true of the demise of the city-state of Athens, a lack of emphasis on physical development contributed to the decline of a once powerful civilization.

MEDIEVAL EUROPE (500 TO 1500)

The years following the fall of the Roman Empire represented a low point physically and intellectually. During the Middle Ages, many church leaders, such as St. Augustine, spoke against dancing. Church leaders also opposed frivolous activities that might detract from piety, proper commitment to worship, and godly living. The Catholic church, in seeking a higher level of morality than displayed by most Romans, regarded the body and anything that benefited it as sinful. Asceticism, a doctrine that renounces the comforts of society and espouses austere self-discipline, especially as an act of religious devotion, was practiced by monks during medieval times.

The only schools existing during this time were at the monasteries, which restricted intellectual education to those who served the church. The monks, however, preserved many aspects of Greek culture.

European society in the eleventh to the sixteenth centuries was feudalistic; that is, the economic, political, and social aspects of life centered on ownership of land and the military power to maintain or expand territory. The monarch, at least theoretically, owned the land. Unable to rule diverse properties successfully, the king divided the territory among nobles who, in turn, promised military service. As vassals to the king, they similarly divided their holdings among lesser vassals, with the same reciprocal protection guarantees. At the bottom of this pyramidal structure were the serfs, or peasants, who toiled in the fields. Their labors were meagerly rewarded with protection provided by those they served.

The vassal landowners, who were **knights,** were the ones in feudal society who valued physical training, although the peasants engaged in various recreational pursuits. At 7 years of age, sons of nobles left their homes to go to the manors of other knights. Under the guidance of ladies of the castles for the next 7 years, these **pages** were educated through stories about chivalry, with its code of moral and social duties of knighthood. **Squires,** beginning at 14 years of age, learned archery, climbing, dancing, fencing, jousting, riding, swimming, and wrestling. As a valet for a knight, the squire served meals, cleaned armor, cared for the knight's horse, played chess and backgammon, and accompanied the knight into battle. Following 7 years of extensive training as a squire, the youth became eligible for knighthood. Once knighted, these nobles engaged in hunting and hawking and continued their training for battle.

In the isolation of the manorial system of the Middle Ages, few opportunities existed for social interaction and entertainment, so tournaments grew in popularity to fill this void. Although festive occasions, these tournaments included combat between knights, who divided into two teams and fought under conditions similar to war in the **grand tourney,** or **melee.** Although strict rules and blunt weapons supposedly limited the injuries, fatalities frequently occurred in the melee, leading to its demise. Another event at the tournaments was **jousting,** which pitted two mounted knights armed with lances in a head-on attempt to unseat each other. Since weapons were blunt and the objective was not to kill the opponent, the joust gradually became the primary event of the tournaments.

Because war served as an adventurous solution to boredom, and because service to God was required of the knights, many willingly volunteered for the eight Crusades between 1096 and 1270. Instigated by the Catholic church, these military expeditions attempted to expel Moslems and Turks from the Holy Lands and to establish papal control in that region. The knights profited from the captured spoils of war, and some took part mainly for this reason.

Interaction with people from other civilizations through the Crusades contrasted markedly with the isolated lifestyle of the feudalistic period, which peaked between 1250 and 1350. As the importance of the knights lessened because of the invention of gunpowder, towns became established as trade centers. The emergence of a strong merchant class in these towns started the transition to a period of intellectual, cultural, and social reawakening.

Knights were outfitted in armor for battle, jousts, and grand tourney or melee.
© Joshua Ets-Hokin/Getty Images RF

RENAISSANCE AND REFORMATION (1450 TO 1650)

A renewed appreciation for classical culture grew out of the intellectual void of the Middle Ages. Intellectual curiosity and creativity were encouraged rather than stymied as education came to be highly valued by people of all social classes. During the Middle Ages, several allied yet diverse philosophies developed; these blossomed from the fifteenth to seventeenth centuries, marked by a renewed appreciation for classical culture called the **Renaissance.** They directly influenced attitudes toward physical education, although most often the mind and the body were viewed as two separate entities. Scholasticism, based on the authority of church leaders and the writings of the Greek philosopher Aristotle, placed intellectual development in a revered position alongside a fixed religious dogma.

Humanistic education in Italy stressed the harmonious and holistic development of human beings, embracing the Greek Ideal of unity. A sound mind in a sound body described this philosophy, which implemented the principles of humanism and emphasized the physical as well as the intellectual development of students. Humanists stressed the importance of a healthy body as preparation for intellectual endeavors rather than stressing a dichotomous relationship between mind and body.

Realism, which grew out of humanism, emphasized the importance of understanding the Greek classics and educating for life. The development of health (through exercise and play) and scientific thinking became critical educational outcomes for the realists.

During the Protestant Reformation of the 1500s and 1600s, educational moralism developed as religious fervor combined with nationalism. Although initially wanting only to purify the Catholic church, reformers such as Martin Luther and John Calvin became catalysts for widespread religious and cultural change. Their doctrines stressed personal salvation, moral responsibilities, and state duties. Most of the Protestant sects deemphasized physical development as a distraction from these objectives. One religious group, the Puritans, was especially vehement in opposing what they deemed frivolous activities and tried to enforce its strict doctrines on others. While humanism and realism furthered the Renaissance theme of a sound mind in a sound body, moralism hindered its acceptance as an educational goal.

Throughout the Renaissance, the 1700s, and most of the 1800s, education was valued for boys, especially those from the upper class, who attended boarding schools or were taught privately by tutors. Seldom was education provided for girls.

AGE OF ENLIGHTENMENT (1700s)

The Renaissance set the stage for the Age of Enlightenment, during which two additional philosophies influenced physical education. Englishman John Locke wrote about educational disciplinarianism. He said that character, especially valued for upper-class boys, required a sound mind in a sound body and developed best through moral and physical discipline. Jean-Jacques Rousseau, a French philosopher, led the rebellion against the devaluation of the individual. In his book *Emile,* Rousseau described the ideal way to educate a boy, stressing **naturalism,** or everything according to nature. That is, each child possessed a unique readiness to learn in a natural developmental process that should dictate when a child was exposed to various types of knowledge. The child, free to explore nature while recreating, thus prepared physically for later intellectual pursuits and therefore learned optimally. The Age of Enlightenment provided additional insights into how to educate a child, thereby laying the foundation for European gymnastics programs.

German gymnastics included jumping, climbing, vaulting, and other physical exercises.
© INTERFOTO/Alamy

NATURALISM (1770 TO 1830)

Although the French were not receptive to Rousseau's educational theories, Johann Basedow, a German teacher, was. In establishing a school for boys called the Philanthropinum in 1774, Basedow sought to implement naturalistic principles that focused on meeting individual needs; he also stressed the importance of readiness to learn. At his school, he allotted 3 hours each day to instruction about and participation in recreational activities, such as gymnastics, sports, and games, and 2 hours to manual labor. While Basedow advocated dancing, fencing, riding, and vaulting, the teacher hired to direct the program, Johann Simon, introduced Greek activities like jumping, running, throwing, and wrestling. Simon utilized natural settings to provide the needed apparatus, such as balance beams, high-jumping poles, jumping ditches, and tree swings. Johann Du Toit, Simon's successor, added archery, skating, swimming, marching, gardening, and woodworking to Basedow's original curriculum and Simon's Greek activities.

In 1785, Christian Salzmann patterned the program at the Schnepfenthal Educational Institute after Basedow's naturalistic lessons in games and gymnastics. Johann GutsMuths, who taught at Schnepfenthal for 50 years, was strongly influenced by Basedow's writings and provided similar activities and pieces of apparatus. GutsMuths's 3- to 4-hour daily program consisted of the following:

- Natural activities, such as jumping and running
- Greek athletics, such as throwing and wrestling
- Military exercises, such as fencing and marching
- Knightly activities, such as climbing and vaulting
- Manual labor, such as gardening and woodworking

GutsMuths influenced many people through two significant books: *Gymnastics for the Young,* which not only described Schnepfenthal's program but also laid the theoretical foundation for modern programs, and *Games for Exercise and Recreation of the Body and Spirit,* which described the skills developed in 105 games or activities and provided illustrations of the apparatus used, such as climbing masts, hanging ladders, rope ladders, and wooden horses.

NATIONALISM (1800s)

Friedrich Jahn, a German educator and an ardent patriot, visited the Schnepfenthal Educational Institute and borrowed many aspects of GutsMuths's program. But, Jahn's purpose for **German gymnastics** was nationalistic rather than naturalistic. He sought to develop fitness and strength in German youth with the goal of helping in the re-unification of all German people. After encouraging his students to climb trees, jump over ditches, run, and throw stones on half-holiday excursions from classes, he established the first turnplatz near Berlin in 1811. A **turnplatz** was an outdoor exercise area where boys, who became known as **Turners,** trained using balance beams, ropes and ladders for climbing, high-jumping standards, horizontal bars, parallel bars, pole-vaulting standards, broad-jumping pits, vaulting horses, a figure-eight-shaped track, and a wrestling ring. Jahn also promoted **nationalism** through patriotic speeches and stories and group singing of patriotic songs. First boys and then, as the Turner system of gymnastics expanded, males of all ages and social classes participated in the increasingly popular gymnastic exercises. Jahn explained Turner gymnastics in his book *German Gymnastics.*

The Turners vigorously advocated for a unified Germany, and many local turnplatz initially received government subsidies. After the Congress of Vienna realigned Germany into a confederation of 38 independent states in 1815, though, the Turners' single-minded goal of a unified nation was viewed as threatening. Finally, in 1819, government leaders succeeded in banning Turner gymnastics. Not until 1840 was it again legal to participate in Turner gymnastics, although underground programs continued during the intervening years. Jahn's Turner gymnastics never gained widespread popularity in other nations because of its nationalistic appeal and emphasis on strength, although Turner gymnastics were practiced by Germans in other nations, including the United States.

In the 1840s, Adolph Spiess borrowed from his training in Turner gymnastics to devise a system of German school gymnastics. Approval of his program in the public schools hinged on his defense of gymnastics as a subject equal to all others and one that offered progressions for various ages, boys and girls, and all ability levels and required trained teachers and equipped indoor and outdoor facilities. Although influenced somewhat by Jahn's and GutsMuths's programs, Spiess devised a school system that stressed discipline and obedience and included diverse activities such as marching, free exercises, and gymnastics with musical accompaniment.

Nationalism became the dominant theme of **Danish gymnastics** in the early 1800s, too. Fitness, strength, and military competence emerged as the goals of Franz Nachtegall. In 1799, he established a private gymnasium in Copenhagen, the first of its kind. Nachtegall's curriculum, which borrowed extensively from the apparatus and exercises of GutsMuths, gained popularity and, in 1809, helped

Denmark initiate the first European school program in physical education for boys. His *Manual of Gymnastics,* published in 1828, provided the curriculum for the schools. Teachers for the schools were initially educated alongside military men at the Military Gymnastic Institute, founded in 1804 by the king of Denmark, with Nachtegall as its director. Danish gymnastics in the military and schools was based totally on command-response exercises, with rigid, mass drills associated with a nationalistic theme.

Patriotism raged in Sweden in the late 1700s and early 1800s due to Sweden's loss of territory to Russian and Napoleonic forces. This nationalistic fervor initially influenced Per Henrik Ling to study and write about the Scandinavian heritage. While pursuing this objective in Denmark for 5 years, he learned gymnastics from Franz Nachtegall and engaged in fencing, through which he improved an arthritic arm. The personal therapeutic benefits Ling experienced led him to promote gymnastics throughout his career. Returning to his homeland in 1804, Ling became a fencing master and an instructor of literature and history, while also teaching gymnastics.

Ling's theory that the knowledge of Norse literature and history combined with gymnastics training could make Sweden a stronger nation influenced the king, who provided financial support to establish the Royal Gymnastics Central Institute in Stockholm in 1814 under Ling's direction. As a training institute for military men, Ling's program allowed Swedes to stress precise execution of movements on command, mass drills, posture-correcting movements, and specific exercises on specially designed exercise apparatus. Swedish apparatus developed by Ling included stall bars, booms, vaulting boxes, and oblique ropes. England, Denmark, Belgium, Greece, and other countries adopted Swedish gymnastics for military training.

Class of female students engaged in Swedish gymnastics. Stall bars, which are attached to the walls on the left and rear, were used for hanging and moving activities.

Photo: Nordiska museet

In addition to Ling's primary emphasis on nationalism through military training, he also emphasized three other themes through his **Swedish gymnastics** program: medical, educational, and aesthetics. Ling developed exercises that had a therapeutic or medical emphasis, so that through movement health could be restored to injured or weak parts of the body. He is credited with devising a system of massage to treat ailments involving joints and muscles. As military men were trained, Ling valued the preparation of leaders of the gymnastics movements and thus emphasized the use of proper pedagogy or educational methodology. Ling's aesthetics involved the expression of feelings through movement. Even though Swedish gymnastics focused on movement on command, rigidly held positions, and posture, it offered exercises that were viewed as appropriate for females, as well as males.

When Hjalmar Ling, Per Henrik Ling's son, began teaching at the Royal Gymnastics Central Institute, he initiated the development of Swedish school gymnastics. Borrowing from his father's program the principles of progression and precise execution of movements on command, Hjalmar Ling devised the **Day's Order,** systematized, daily exercises that progressed through the whole body from head to toe. These lessons were appropriately graded for the age, ability, and gender of each child and used apparatus designed for children. Mass drills under a teacher's direction remained paramount.

Figure 7.1 provides a time-line for the significant periods. Table 7-3 compares the three major gymnastics systems in Europe. Figure 7.2 on page 216 illustrates how European philosophies and innovators influenced subsequent programs. The Research View Strength Training adds information about the influence of early cultures on strength training.

SPORTS IN GREAT BRITAIN (1800s)

The nationalistic fervor for German, Danish, and Swedish gymnastics never gained prominence in Great Britain, other than through minimal usage of Ling's Swedish gymnastics by the British military. As the dominant world power, Great Britain had not faced territorial decimation as many other European nations had; therefore, nationalism failed to undergird a gymnastics program in that country. Instead, the British legacy to both European and worldwide physical education has undoubtedly been its sports.

Englishman John Locke's sound mind and sound body concept resembled the Greek Ideal. The **British Amateur Sport Ideal** of "playing the game for the game's sake" was similar to the Greek love of athletic supremacy. Frenchman Pierre de Coubertin, who has been credited with founding the modern Olympic Games in 1896, was highly influenced by the British Amateur Sport Ideal and the role of sports in British public schools.

Sports and recreational pastimes have traditionally been divided along class or socioeconomic lines in Great Britain. Given few alternatives due to their socioeconomic status, working-class males were especially attracted to pugilism (bare-knuckle boxing), blood sports (such as cockfighting), and varieties of football (soccer). These "poor man's sports" required little equipment, usually encouraged gambling, and were often banned by the church.

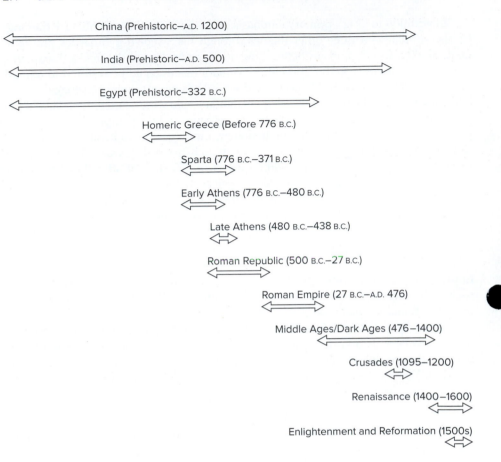

FIGURE 7.1

Timeline from Prehistoric to Modern Times.

🔍 RESEARCH VIEW

Strength Training

Long before strength training became a scientific discipline, soldiers and others in ancient China, India, and Egypt lifted weights to develop strength. Greeks and Romans also exercised with weights. According to Mel Siff in *A Short History of Strength and Conditioning,* the first books on weight training were published in the sixteenth century in Europe. Weight training was included in some early educational programs in England, France, and Germany. As espoused by Per Henrik Ling, muscular exercise was believed to offer therapeutic benefits. Building on these concepts in the mid-nineteenth century, Archibald MacLaren developed a system of physical training with barbells and dumbbells for the British Army.

TABLE 7-3				
COMPARISON OF EUROPEAN GYMNASTICS SYSTEMS				
System	*Theme(s)*	*Participants*	*Program*	*Apparatus*
German	Nationalism; physical activities used to develop strong, sturdy fearless youth	Initially only upper-class boys; then all boys and males of all ages	Individualized under Jahn and vorturners (teachers)	Vaulting horses; parallel bars; ropes and ladders for climbing; balance beams; running tracks
Danish	Nationalism	Soldiers; teachers	Formalized exercises on command; no individual expression	Hanging ladders; rope ladders; masts and poles for climbing; balance beams; vaulting horses
Swedish	Nationalism; therapeutic or medical; pedagogical or educational; aesthetics	Soldiers; teachers	Movement on command; posture correcting	Stall bars; vaulting boxes; climbing poles; oblique ropes; Swedish booms

British upper-class sports, such as cricket and rugby, were popularized at private boys' boarding schools, called public schools, in the 1800s. Thomas Arnold, headmaster at Rugby School, praised the role of sport according to Thomas Hughes in *Tom Brown's Schooldays*. Arnold regularly advocated sport participation as a means for boys to learn moral virtues such as cooperation, leadership, loyalty, self-discipline, and sportsmanship. These public schools stressed participation in a variety of sports rather than specialization in one, playing the game rather than training in skills and fitness, and competition between boys in various residences. Public school boys often demonstrated greater learning through sport than in their scholastic efforts. Since graduates of these public schools were future leaders of the nation, lessons learned in sports were acclaimed for preparing better citizens.

Cricket, rowing, association football (soccer), track and field, athletics (track and field), rugby, and field hockey became the most popular sports at Oxford and Cambridge Universities despite faculty disfavor. The British Amateur Sport Ideal of playing the game for the game's sake rather than for remuneration prevailed in these sport competitions, especially since these upper-class men did not need to play for money.

Muscular Christianity traces its history to at least the Victorian era in Great Britain. This movement emphasized vigorous masculinity, such as achieved through sports, in combination with development of character. For example, Thomas Hughes described the importance of males who attended public schools and universities developing their physical strength and health along with moral principles and ideals, which would serve them well in their personal lives and as political leaders. Team sports were viewed as ideal for nurturing the physical and moral health of boys and men.

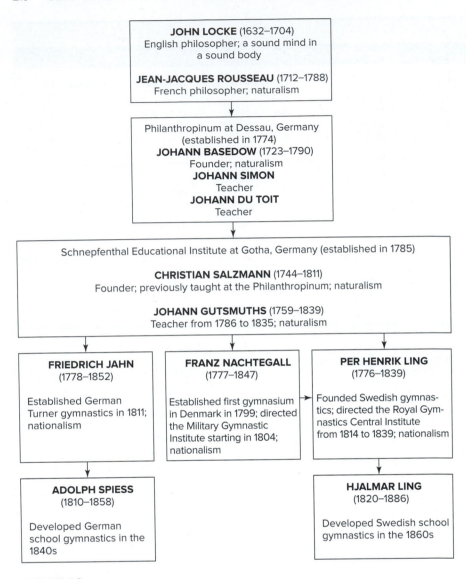

FIGURE 7.2

Significant European influences on physical education, exercise science, and sport programs in the United States.

While not linked directly with organized religion, which often was associated with women and feminization in the late nineteenth century, upper-class males used muscular Christianity to reflect masculine values, such as manliness and discipline. As a result, religion and sports for males in Great Britain peacefully coexisted as long as ethical conduct remained important. Fair play, honorable victories, and respect for opponents came to be expected outcomes of British sports for schoolboys, university men, and upper-class gentlemen.

The British first popularized rugby in boys' boarding schools in the 1800s.
© Jeff Maloney/Getty Images RF

Many sports started in Great Britain spread throughout the world during their years of colonization (see Table 7-4). Sometimes these sports were welcomed by indigenous people; at other times they were rejected outright. Horse

TABLE 7-4		
SELECTED SPORTS AND THEIR ORIGINS		
Wrestling	China	c. 2000 B.C.
Boxing	Mesopotamia	c. 1500 B.C.
Track and field	Greece	c. 776 B.C.
Soccer (association football)	Great Britain	1200s
Ninepin bowling	Great Britain	1200s
Golf	Scotland	1400s
Cricket	Great Britain	1600s
Lacrosse	North America	1700s
Baseball (rounders)	Great Britain	1700s
Gymnastics	Germany	late 1700s
Field hockey	Great Britain	mid-1800s
Water polo	Great Britain	1870
Badminton	India	1870s
Tennis	Great Britain	1873
Table tennis	Great Britain	1880s

> **BOX 7.3   GAINING A BETTER UNDERSTANDING OF THE HISTORY OF GYMNASTICS AND SPORT IN EUROPE**
>
> Students: Why did these occur? (If you do not know the answer, see if you can find the answer in your textbook or do an online search to find the answer.)
>
> 1.   Why did the lady of the castle train the page?
> 2.   Why was naturalism a popular theme for the teaching of physical skills?
> 3.   Why was German (Turner) gymnastics banned in Germany?
> 4.   Why was nationalism such an important theme for gymnastics systems?
> 5.   Why did the British affirm the belief that sports build character?

racing, tennis, golf, soccer, badminton, field hockey, and rugby are among the most prominent of these sports. Most sports in the United States were introduced by British colonists. Before concluding this chapter, take the challenge to answer the questions in Box 7.3.

SUMMARY

The European legacy of athletics, gymnastics, and sports laid the foundation for physical education and sport programs in the United States. The Greeks provided a rich heritage of mind-body unity and glorified the aesthetically developed, all-around athlete. Varying dramatically from this ideal were Spartan soldiers and the specialized, professional athletes of the later Athenian era. The Roman Republic illustrated the utilitarian goal of a fit military force. During the next 1,000 years, it was primarily the knights who developed their bodies, but they did so primarily for military conquest rather than for any inherent value. Church leaders discouraged frivolous activities. During the Renaissance, philosophers and educators emphasized physical development for overall education and grappled with whether the mind and body should be educated separately or simultaneously. Naturalism and nationalism directly influenced the development of gymnastics systems in Germany, Denmark, and Sweden. British sports and games, with their associated emphasis on moral values, laid the foundation for physical education and sport programs in the United States. Figure 7.3 provides a concept map that shows the relationships among the various eras and individuals whose programs of gymnastics and sports impacted similar programs in the United States, which is the subject of the next chapter.

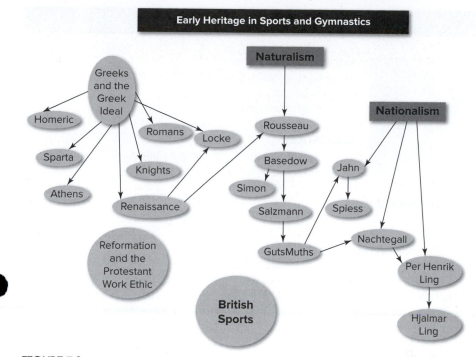

FIGURE 7.3

This concept map depicts interrelationships among eras of time and key leaders in gymnastics and sports that impacted programs in the United States.

CAREER PERSPECTIVE

Courtesy Michael DeLong

MICHAEL DELONG
Head Football Coach (retired)
Springfield College
Springfield, Massachusetts

EDUCATION
B.S., physical education, Springfield College
M.A., physical education, University of North
Carolina at Chapel Hill

JOB RESPONSIBILITIES AND HOURS

The responsibilities of college and university coaches vary tremendously, depending on the
emphasis placed on the institution's program and the sport. Mike organizes and administers
an NCAA Division III football program, including directing a staff of two full-time assistant
coaches and 12 graduate assistants, recruiting student athletes, planning games and
practices, working directly with admissions, raising funds, developing community support,
and carrying out on- and off-field coaching duties. Of these responsibilities, recruiting may
be the most time consuming and challenging. He also teaches four semester hours in-season
and six to eight semester hours out-of-season, and advises physical education majors—a
typical work load at a smaller institution. As with most coaches, Mike's weekly hours,
which vary from 85 in-season to 70 off-season to 30 during the summer, are demanding.
Salaries are based on each coach's experience and won–lost record, the institution and its
reputation, and the sport. At the NCAA Division III level, the salary range is $40,000 to
$80,000 for head coaches and $20,000 to $40,000 for assistant coaches.

SPECIALIZED COURSE WORK, DEGREES, AND WORK EXPERIENCES
NEEDED FOR THIS CAREER

Although college or university coaching does not require a master's degree, teaching at
smaller institutions may require attaining this degree. Physical education is the most common major for coaches at both the undergraduate and graduate levels, although many
coaches have degrees in other disciplines. Opportunities to become head coaches usually
follow years of coaching high school teams, serving as effective graduate assistants or full-
time assistant coaches, or completing successful college or professional playing careers.
Volunteering to coach a youth, school, or club team may provide an entry into this career.
Mike recommends that prospective coaches emphasize exercise physiology, oral and written communication skills, problem-solving techniques, organizational skills, motivational
strategies, and theory and technique courses. He encourages prospective coaches, as well as
those already in positions, to visit successful programs and to learn from others.

SATISFYING ASPECTS

People may choose this career because they love a particular sport, want to continue
associating with it, enjoy teaching its skills and strategies, like to help athletes develop
their talents to their optimal levels, or any combination of these and other reasons. Mike
especially enjoys player-coach relationships, coach-to-coach interactions, and the feeling of

accomplishment as the team improves. Coaching can be tremendously satisfying, not only in terms of wins and losses but also in watching teams and players grow and mature. For Mike, helping individuals reach their goals is the most rewarding part of coaching.

JOB POTENTIAL

Mike states that to be secure in a college or university coaching position, winning is essential. If you perform within the rules, he says, you will be secure; if you do not perform within the rules, you can expect to be relieved of your duties. Promotion is also based on performance. Coaches who are proven workers have a good chance for advancement in the profession. Politics also plays a role, so it helps to know people. Since getting your foot in the door is difficult and highly competitive, a major part of the initial hiring process is knowing someone who can help you secure a full-time position. Once you have proven your abilities and made connections with people, things generally go a little easier. The job market is extremely competitive, especially for the best jobs. Patience and perseverance are two characteristics essential for success.

SUGGESTIONS FOR STUDENTS

Mike states that coaching is a wonderful career because of the fun and excitement. Coaches are surrounded by great people who like to work and play hard. The rewards of developing players and a team to perform to their fullest potential are tremendous. Mike advises that prior to becoming a coach, be sure you are ready to make a full commitment, because the players you will coach deserve your best effort. Your family also must be aware of the sacrifices they will have to make to the time demands of this career. He adds that you need to be flexible and ready to overcome obstacles and setbacks; there are both extreme highs and extreme lows with which you must cope. The rewards of coaching are directly proportional to the effort you put into the team. If you give your best, coaching is well worth the effort in the long run.

KEY POINTS

Egypt	Warriors trained; dancing was valued in religion
China	Only the military class valued physical development
India	Participated in yoga, a system of meditation and regulated breathing
Greece	Characterized by the Greek Ideal of the "man of action" and "man of wisdom"
Homeric Era	Upper-class males, who were warriors, competed in funeral games in boxing, chariot racing, wrestling, foot racing, and throwing the javelin and discus
Spartans	Emphasized military supremacy; boys and girls trained physically
Early Athenians	Emphasized the Greek Ideal; upper-class boys attended wrestling schools and music schools; girls had no physical training; upper-class adult males trained physically at gymnasiums
Late Athenians	Lost interest in physical development as they emphasized the man of wisdom

Characteristics of Olympic Games	Honored Zeus; olive wreath for each winner; required to be a Greek citizen; could be from any social class; required to train 10 months and last month at Olympia; pledged an oath of fair play; competed in the nude
Roman Republic	Males trained for war at military camps
Roman Empire	People entertained at chariot races and gladiatorial contests
Middle Ages	Squires learned skills in riding, swimming, archery, climbing, jousting, wrestling, and fencing and knights competed in jousts and the grand tourney or melee
Renaissance	Health stressed to overcome epidemics; embraced the classical ideal of "a sound mind in a sound body"
Reformation	Protestant sects relegated physical education to an inferior position; led to the Protestant work ethic in United States
Jean-Jacques Rousseau	Stressed "everything according to nature" and a readiness to learn physical activities in and through nature
Johann Basedow	Established school for boys based on the naturalistic principles from Rousseau
Johann GutsMuths	His school program was based on naturalism and included natural activities, Greek-type athletics, knightly activities, military exercises, and manual labor
Friedrich Jahn	Developed German or Turner gymnastics to develop strong youth based on nationalism
Adolph Spiess	Developed German school gymnastics by adapting Jahn's program for boys and girls
Franz Nachtegall	Developed Danish gymnastics for military (nationalism) and children in schools
Per Henrik Ling	Developed four areas of Swedish gymnastics—military (nationalism); medical; educational; and aesthetics—with an emphasis on formal movements and posture
Hjalmar Ling	Developed Swedish school gymnastics based on the progressive, precise execution of movements on command
English sports	Emphasized for upper-class boys to learn values, and believed in "playing the game for the game's sake"

REVIEW QUESTIONS

1. What is the Greek Ideal, and why was it important to the Greeks?
2. What were the training programs for boys and girls in the city-states of Sparta and Athens?
3. What were the regulations for competitors and the events in the ancient Olympic Games?
4. What were the three favorite pastimes of the Romans during the Empire?
5. What activities did a squire train in and why?

6. What is naturalism, and how did it impact European systems of gymnastics?
7. What were the five types of activities that comprised the physical development program at the Schnepfenthal Institute under GutsMuths?
8. What was the theme for Jahn's Turner gymnastics program and why?
9. What were Per Henrik Ling's four themes or areas of emphasis for Swedish gymnastics, and why was each important?
10. What is the legacy of the British emphasis on sports on programs in the United States?

STUDENT ACTIVITIES

1. As a class project, reenact the ancient Olympic Games by having each student participate in an appropriate athletic contest. Each student is expected to research the specifics about the assigned or selected event before competing against classmates.

2. Select one activity or area of training for a squire during medieval times. Prepare a 5-minute oral report and demonstration of how the boys were taught and how they practiced the necessary skills.

3. Along with several classmates, prepare a demonstration of German, Danish, and Swedish gymnastics, and then lead the class in a 5-minute lesson.

4. Write a five-page paper about the early history and development of any sport that is associated with the British Amateur Sport Ideal or that was founded in Great Britain.

5. Challenge yourself to find 20 people or terms from the ancient world and European heritage in the puzzle below. Define or describe each one found.

```
GB HUI T CZ D WOP ACF J MNB R OS HUPK CE S T UPL B AS DE
N OQE WE F R NT F Y S HUE K E I HOC S P K B OL J OR S J R E P T G
R E A P E R H E N R I K L I N GON R T S J D WF WGL C N HWS P I E S S
C Z V A B GNE MC L R K N P E HWN A T I ON A L I S ME BR P R S N GB
E MCL NT UL HT E I Y A J H OI GF Y D S V A S WA QWOH T T DT A U
AUN ACHE T A L L I B B E OZ V B S D V Z F HS GHI U X P T Y F A OP
T C WE P VL T OR P V E T P DMN T C GE C Y DX MA P C I E R HP T A W
L H OS GON MR Y DT A Y S T ADE R ACE L S A T Y Z Y NR T OOH C R
D A E T X T T U Y T UR NE R T C F Y MVC A D F T F N HT GY E K OL A N
UR S R MGE N P DNOMI B A E T R J B X E V B I D S L OE WA R H OL B
E I K AE L WV Y E R A DUL N OE L OY T OK HCE P OT UNMO S N AM
NOCT S I R OK C GAT H WOH P Y P R E N AI S S A N CE E GU T I OP
R T S E CE NR WC S I E U AT WMT K B UT S B UB R D C Y I C S R C I R
HR L DGS I K I NMJ X T R I B C HAI C B UL H OT I B ONE S E D S R
E AMO AT H P GE DAME C A R L N GR E E K I DE A L U WT OE D B OS
WCNT YOMP Y S I C GA VOL D S Y GDN WCGWN P GI R K AT I E O
F E T N P Y GT D L P B AMR GD I P I S R D P N N Y S N L B H S U OR X L
D S CE L A E A Y L S R D P D S UN S OP R F DHOU I N N S D F T I CK Y
T I J ODY T WA C B H K T H X P T B MMI A R D P MA DR N P MN P I T M
D P T R P WS B R I T I S H AMAT E UR S P ORT I DE A L L T B S GB T
```

6. Conduct a class debate about the similarities and differences among the early and later Athenians, the Roman Republic and Empire, and modern-day sporting activities and competitions.

7. Identify 10 contributions to or influences on American physical education and sport described in this chapter.

REFERENCE

Van Dalen, D. B., & Bennett, B. L. (1971). *A world history of physical education* (2nd ed.). Englewood Cliffs, NJ: Prentice-Hall.

WEB CONNECTIONS

1. www.penn.museum/sites/olympics/olympicintro.shtml
    This site at the Penn Museum provides a plethora of historical facts and information about the history and events of the ancient Olympic Games.

2. www.perseus.tufts.edu/olympics/sports.html
    Students visiting this site can learn more about ancient Olympic sports, take a virtual tour of ancient Olympia, gain an understanding of the context and spirit of the ancient Olympic Games, and read stories about Olympic athletes of that time.

3. www.roman-empire.net/
    Learn more about the Roman Empire through the brief descriptions of the early and late Republic, the Emperors, the army, society, and religion, as well as through the pictures and video clips provided on this site.

4. www.vroma.org/~bmcmanus/arena.html
    This site provides information about gladiators and their contests.

5. www.knight-medieval.com
    This site describes everything you want to know about knights, their weapons, and the era of chivalry.

6. www.ibiblio.org/wm/paint/glo/renaissance/
    Learn about the rebirth of knowledge or Renaissance.

7. plato.stanford.edu/entries/enlightenment
    This site describes the Enlightenment, a period between the middle of the seventeenth through the eighteenth century. It explains the scientific, philosophical, societal, and political revolutions that impacted the modern western world.

8. www.iep.utm.edu/rousseau/

   Jean-Jacques Rousseau was a French eighteenth-century philosopher. This biography of Rousseau includes a description of his philosophy of education explained in *Emile*.

CHAPTER

8

EARLY AMERICAN PHYSICAL EDUCATION AND SPORT

LEARNING OUTCOMES

- Students will be able to describe the influence of Native American, colonists, calisthenics, and light gymnastics on early school and nonschool physical education and sport programs in the United States.
- Students will be able to explain how German and Swedish gymnastics contributed to the development and spread of school and nonschool physical education and sport programs in the United States.
- Students will be able to assess and articulate the impact of Edward Hitchcock, Dudley Sargent, William Anderson, and Delphine Hanna on college physical education and sport programs in the United States.
- Students will be able to describe how and why children's play and men's amateur sports gained supporters and participants in the late 1800s.

The early colonists brought with them a love for sporting pastimes. Once survival was assured, time was spent bowling, racing horses, skating, wrestling, and playing various ball games. Formalized exercises comprising the German gymnastics and Swedish gymnastics systems appealed to a few, but neither won full acceptance as a unified, national approach to physical education appropriate for residents in the United States. People from Great Britain, through worldwide colonization (including North America), spread their love of sports and games. Hygiene, the science of preserving one's health, was the focus of many early school programs in the United States. These programs were often called physical culture or physical training. Emphasizing health, strength, and bodily measurements, physical training programs in the 1800s were added to school and college curricula primarily under the direction of physicians. Leaders established teacher training institutes that offered coursework in the theoretical aspects of the emerging profession of physical education. Sports and play activities drawn from a European, and mostly British, heritage continued to grow in popularity as college students and upper-class clubs sponsored competitions. Many towns provided playgrounds, further stimulating interest in physical activity and sport.

Before examining the major programs and developments that contributed to early American physical education and sport programs, it is important to explain their significance. The emerging field of physical education was built on a heritage of German gymnastics, Swedish gymnastics, hygiene, medicine, strength development, play, and sports. Early leaders in physical education established teacher training institutions to prepare teachers for schools and colleges. Many individuals contributed to the solid foundation laid prior to the twentieth century that led to subsequent developments in physical education, exercise science, and sport, described more fully in Chapter 9.

PHYSICAL ACTIVITIES IN THE COLONIES

Sports, physical activities, and dance occupied a prominent role in the lives of most Native Americans when colonists from other countries arrived in North America. These activities were associated with religious ceremonies, festive celebrations, and social relaxation. However, differences in language, lifestyles, geographic regions, livelihoods, and overall cultures verify that one cohesive vision for a national program did not exist. Many tribal nations contributed to the popularity of sporting pastimes.

According to Oxendine (1988), some of the most important factors characterizing traditional Native American sports included the following:

- A strong connection between sport and other social, spiritual, and economic aspects of daily life
- The serious preparation of mind, body, and spirit of participants and the community as a whole prior to major competition
- The assumption that rigid adherence to standardized rules and technical precision in sporting activities was important
- Strong allegiance to high standards of sportsmanship and fair play
- The prominence of males and females in sports and physical activities, but with different expectations
- A special perspective on team membership, interaction, and leadership styles
- The role of gambling as a widespread and vital component in all sports
- The importance of art as an expression of identity and aesthetics (pages 3–4)

The most popular Native American sport was lacrosse, also called baggataway, meaning ball game or the game of ball. The competitors displayed grace, adroitness, and dexterity, often in honor of their gods. The courage, ruggedness, skill, speed, and endurance required to play this game helped train males for war. The rules, size of the playing field, equipment, and clothing varied widely.

Native Americans, including many girls and women, played shinny, a ball-and-stick game similar to modern field hockey. Women also actively participated in double ball, in which a stick was used to propel two balls attached by a string.

Footraces among Native Americans served as a source of motivation and pride. Besides children's play and ceremonial uses by adults, running skills benefited males in war, the pursuit of game animals, and the delivery of messages. The sacred ball race combined kicking a ball along a prescribed 25-mile course and running after it.

Other sports of major interest to Native Americans included archery, swimming, fishing, canoeing, and snow snaking, which involved sliding a pole a great distance across a frozen path. Ritualistic dances and games of chance also were popular.

The first colonists came to North America in search of a new life, adventure, and religious freedom. During the 1600s, the prime motivator for physical activity was survival: men hunted, fished, and grew crops; women performed domestic chores. What little time existed for relaxation was frequently spent in work-related recreation, such as barn raisings, corn huskings, or quilting bees. Dancing and games were often a part of these gatherings, although some religious groups forbade dancing.

The sporting heritage brought to this country by Europeans became increasingly popular in the 1700s. In spite of Puritan-initiated laws forbidding gambling, card playing, and mixed dancing, New Englanders relaxed by bowling, fishing, fowling, or playing cricket, rugby fives (a game similar to handball), and marbles.

Led by the Dutch in New York, settlers in the middle colonies, free from many of the religious prohibitions imposed on their northern neighbors, eagerly engaged in merriments such as pulling the goose (snapping off the head of a greased goose while riding horseback or standing in a moving boat); played games, such as skittles (in which a ball or flat disk is thrown down an alley at nine skittles, or pins); and participated in outdoor amusements, such as boating, fishing, hunting, horse racing, and sleighing. These activities were enthusiastically pursued by the upper class. Interestingly, when nine-pin bowling was prohibited by law because of its association with gambling, a tenth pin was added to allow bowlers, and soon gamblers, to participate legally in their favorite pastime. The Quakers of Pennsylvania favored fishing, hunting, and swimming as diversions while banning many other leisure pursuits.

Virginia, strongly influenced by the British, emerged as the leading Southern colony. Emulating the gentry across the ocean, Southern plantation owners sought to acquire all the trappings befitting their aristocratic status, including sporting pastimes. Cockfighting, bowling, and card playing were engaged in at taverns, which initially were exclusively for men. Fox hunting, horse racing, hawking, and watching boxing matches found many enthusiasts.

Participation in various physical activities increased throughout the 1700s as an emerging nationalism placed emphasis on the development of health and strength. Benjamin Franklin, Noah Webster, and Thomas Jefferson were among those who supported physical activities for healthful benefits. At the same time, sport involvement continued to win new adherents because sports offered competition, freedom, and fun.

In the late 1700s, as the colonists prepared for a confrontation with the British, military days provided opportunities for marching and drilling with weapons, but also offered opportunities for social interaction and game playing. The military training was utilitarian in purpose, though, and did not lead to an emphasis on physical fitness in the post–Revolutionary War years. This trend repeated itself throughout the history of the United States as each war signaled a need to have trained soldiers; aside from these times of emergency, there was little emphasis in this country on physical fitness programs.

Following the War of 1812, nationalism became a dominant force in American life, setting the stage for a gradual extension of democratic rights to more people and the provision of education to more children. Beginning in the 1800s, free, public education for boys and girls consisted primarily of the three Rs (reading, writing, and arithmetic). Educators in public schools initially showed little interest in physical education, although in 1853 Boston became the first city to require daily exercise for children. In private academies and schools in the early 1800s, though, the belief that physical

---

BOX 8.1   GAINING A BETTER UNDERSTANDING OF EARLY SPORTS IN THE UNITED STATES

Students: Why did Native Americans or early settlers in this country do the following? (If you do not know the answer, see if you can find the answer in your textbook or do an online search to find the answer.)

1. Why did Native Americans play the game of baggataway?
2. Why did early settlers change the Dutch game of nine-pin bowling to a game with ten pins?
3. Why did early settlers fight roosters (i.e., cockfighting) against each other?
4. Why did early settlers claim baseball was invented in the United States?
5. Why did early settlers box without gloves?

---

activities contributed to health led to children's participation in sports. Prior to the Civil War, few colleges provided for their students' physical development; however, academies and private schools for boys and occasionally for girls (such as Mt. Holyoke Female Seminary beginning in 1837) included physical exercises in their curricula.

Early experiences in physical activities and sports for minority groups in this country could be described as either isolated or they were assimilated due to an emerging nationalist spirit. African Americans, whether enslaved or free, valued their cultural heritage in music and dance but, due to prejudicial attitudes, remained largely excluded from organized sport programs. While William Lewis became an All-America football star at Harvard University in 1892–1893, and Moses and Welday Walker briefly played professional baseball in the late 1800s, they were notable exceptions to segregated sports. German, Irish, Italian, Jewish, and other European immigrants during this time engaged in dances, games, sports, and gymnastics brought from their homelands. Some immigrants chose to pursue sports like baseball and boxing as a way to become more like their American playmates.

Early American physical education and sport was influenced by European gymnastics, the development of normal schools and a national organization, the provision of play for children, and amateur sports for men and women. Each of these contributed to the content and structure of physical education and sport programs, which are an amalgam of a variety of exercises, gymnastics, formalized educational curricula, play, and sports. Before concluding this section, take the challenge to answer the questions in Box 8.1.

EARLY GERMAN GYMNASTICS IN THE UNITED STATES

The first private school to initiate required physical education in the United States was the Round Hill School, founded in 1823 in Northampton, Massachusetts. Table 8-1 lists this school's establishment, along with other highlights in the development of physical education in the nineteenth century. The founders of Round Hill School scheduled time each day for sports and games even before they employed Charles Beck, a German Turner, to instruct boys in the German system of gymnastics. Beck established an outdoor gymnasium, taught the first Turner exercises on apparatus in this country, and translated Friedrich Jahn's treatise on gymnastics into English.

TABLE 8-1

A FEW SIGNIFICANT EVENTS IN EARLY AMERICAN PHYSICAL EDUCATION

1823	Round Hill School is established with physical education in its curriculum
1824	Hartford Female Seminary, directed by Catharine Beecher, included calisthenics in its curriculum
1837	Mount Holyoke Female Seminary opened with calisthenics listed as part of the school's program
1851	First national German Turnfest held in Philadelphia
1853	Boston became the first city to require daily exercises for school children
1865	First women's physical education program started at Vassar College
1866	California passed the first state physical education law
1872	Brookline, Massachusetts, became the first community in America to use public funds to establish a playground
1885	Association for the Advancement of Physical Education founded in Brooklyn, New York
1889	Boston Conference on Physical Training held
1892	Ohio became the second state to pass a physical education law
1893	Harvard became the first college to confer an academic degree in physical education

In addition, Harvard students and Bostonians were taught Turner gymnastics by German immigrants in the 1820s. The interest in Turner gymnastics dissipated when these instructors ceased to teach and because this system's emphasis on developing strength failed to appeal to sports-minded Americans.

When a second wave of political refugees fled Germany beginning in 1848, they too brought their love of gymnastics to the United States, where they established Turner societies (beginning in 1848 in Cincinnati) and Turner festivals (in 1851). These **Turnfests** featured thousands of Turners who exhibited their physical prowess on German apparatuses and through running and jumping activities. In 1866, they founded the Normal School of the North American Gymnastic Union in New York City to

German gymnastics in the United States in the late 1800s.
© Corbis

prepare teachers of German gymnastics. When most German immigrants migrated to the Midwest, they settled in isolated communities and maintained their national identity, including their gymnastics programs. Gradually these Turner societies broadened their programs to include social functions and exercises appropriate for the entire family. Later in the 1800s, they introduced the Turner system into several schools, although it was modified with Adolph Spiess's school gymnastics principles. The influence of German gymnastics on programs in the United States was limited because of their ethnic isolation and the emphasis on strength development and nationalism. However, during the late 1800s and early 1900s, many schools and colleges incorporated exercises on German apparatuses into their programs. Some of these apparatuses, such as the parallel bars, rings, and balance beam, remain vital parts of the sport of gymnastics.

EARLY AMERICANS WHO INFLUENCED PHYSICAL EDUCATION PROGRAMS

Catharine Beecher, the first American to design a program of exercises for American children, tried to get daily physical activity incorporated into schools. As director of the Hartford (Connecticut) Female Seminary beginning in 1824 and later, when she founded the Western Female Institute in Cincinnati in 1837, she introduced girls to **calisthenics.** At the latter school, she set aside 30 minutes per half-day for this program of exercises, which was designed to promote health, beauty, and strength. Beecher's objective was to aid girls in improving their vitality so that they could better fulfill their missions in life as wives and mothers. She expanded her concepts from a *Course of Calisthenics for Young Ladies,* which she wrote in 1832 primarily for girls, to *A Manual of Physiology and Calisthenics for Schools and Families,* published in 1856, in which she advocated the introduction of physical training in American schools for all children. Borrowing from the therapeutic concepts of Swedish gymnastics as developed by Per Henrik Ling, Beecher, through her writings and school programs, emphasized exercises that could be executed at home without a teacher, using diagrams from her books as guides.

Although Beecher's efforts did not achieve widespread results, she did influence another American. Dioclesian Lewis was a promulgator of causes of the day, including the abolition of slavery, temperance, women's rights, and health. At the convention of the American Institute of Instruction in 1860, Lewis had the opportunity to bring his concept of **light gymnastics** to the attention of educators from around the country and, especially, Boston. For his program, Lewis borrowed from Beecher's calisthenics, adding light apparatus such as bean bags, dumbbells, Indian clubs, and wands. He also borrowed from Swedish gymnastics its special emphasis on treatment of curvature of the spine and other chronic maladies. As a result of his promotional efforts, Boston adopted his system in its elementary schools. To prepare teachers to instruct children in light gymnastics, he founded the Normal Institute for Physical Education in 1861, the first of its kind. A **normal school** was a specialized institution for preparing students to become teachers.

The 10-week program of study at the Normal Institute for Physical Education included instruction in anatomy, physiology, hygiene, and gymnastics. Seemingly ahead of his time, Lewis believed in equity between the genders, cardiorespiratory conditioning, and conducting measurements to demonstrate the success of his program in improving the health of students. He also emphasized that exercises done to the accompaniment of music would result in more activity and greater enjoyment.

In 1860, the first required college physical education program began at Amherst College because its president was concerned about the health of the students. This paramount concern led to the hiring of Edward Hitchcock, who, as director of the Department of Hygiene and Physical Education, gave health lectures, served as college physician, and supervised the required physical exercises for all students. As was true of most of the early physical educators, Hitchcock's primary credential for the job was a medical degree. Borrowing from Lewis's light gymnastics, Hitchcock's program, led by squad captains, included class exercises to the accompaniment of music. Students had class 4 days per week and were allowed to use a portion of their class time to practice sport skills or exercise on the horizontal bars, rings, ropes, and vaulting horses. Hitchcock also administered a battery of bodily, or **anthropometric,** measurements, such as height, weight, chest girth, and lung capacity, to evaluate the effects of the program on students and compare their progress from year to year.

A second noteworthy college physical education program was developed by Dudley Sargent at Harvard College beginning in 1879, when he was hired to direct the newly opened Hemenway Gymnasium. Since no required physical education program existed at Harvard, Sargent, who also was a physician, used an individualized approach to encourage students to exercise. Based on numerous anthropometric measurements, Sargent prescribed a series of exercises to meet each student's physical needs, using chest expanders and developers, leg machines, rowing machines, and other apparatuses he had designed. Opposed to strict German gymnastics and light gymnastics programs, Sargent encouraged students to participate in baseball, bowling, boxing, fencing, rowing, and running in addition to their individual conditioning programs.

Examples of movements and handheld apparatus used in Dioclesian Lewis's light gymnastics program.
© A2Z Collection/Alamy

Class exercises at Amherst College. Note the dumbbells used and the squad captain leading the class.

© The Granger Collection, New York

Box 8.2 on page 234 provides a brief summary of the contributions of the early leaders in physical education in the United States. The Research View describes the contributions of the "father of physical culture."

🔍 RESEARCH VIEW

The Father of Physical Culture

Bernarr Macfadden (1868–1955) has been called the "father of physical culture." He was a lifelong advocate of physical fitness, eating fresh, all-natural food, and promoting bodybuilding and outdoor exercise. He advocated the natural treatment of disease and stressed the avoidance of drugs and stimulants. Macfadden wrote over 100 books and became a millionaire publisher of *Physical Culture,* a magazine for women called *Beauty & Health,* and other magazines and newspapers that inspired millions to live healthy, vigorous lives. Although only 5' 6" and weighing around 145 pounds, he developed amazing physical strength, including powerful upper body muscles, a strong chest, and incredible stamina and energy. After reading William Blaikie's *How to Get Strong and How to Stay So* (published in 1879), Macfadden became a highly skilled gymnast, champion wrestler, and showman who liked to demonstrate his muscles, which he did by illustrating and posing (wearing limited or no clothing) for his books and magazines. *Physical Culture,* begun in 1899, focused on bodybuilding but also became the most popular health magazine of the time and was the forerunner of today's health and bodybuilding publications. Macfadden advocated bodybuilding for men and women. He conflicted with societal standards of his time by encouraging women to exercise, participate in outdoor sports such as tennis and swimming, and discard restrictive clothing. For more about the enigmatic life of Bernarr Macfadden, visit www.bernarrmacfadden.com.

BOX 8.2 EARLY LEADERS IN PHYSICAL EDUCATION IN THE UNITED STATES

Charles Follen (1796–1840)
Established gymnasium in Boston (1826)
Taught German gymnastics to Harvard College students (1826–1828)

Charles Beck (1798–1866)
Hired as first physical education teacher in the United States (1825)
Taught at Round Hill School (1825–1830)

Catharine Beecher (1800–1878)
Taught at the Hartford Female Seminary (1824)
Started the Western Female Institute (1837)
Promoted calisthenics in American schools for boys and girls

Dioclesian Lewis (1823–1888)
Developed light gymnastics with handheld pieces of apparatus
Started the Normal Institute for Physical Education (1861)

Edward Hitchcock, M.D. (1828–1911)
Served as Professor of Hygiene and Physical Education at Amherst College (1861–1911)
Elected first president of the Association for the Advancement of Physical Education (1885)
Led in the development of anthropometric measurements of males

Amy Morris Homans (1848–1933)
Directed the Boston Normal School of Gymnastics (1889–1909)
Directed the Department of Hygiene and Physical Education at Wellesley College (1909–1918)
Founded the Association of Directors of Physical Education for College Women (1915)

Dudley Sargent, M.D. (1849–1924)
Directed the Hemenway Gymnasium at Harvard College (1879–1919)
Led in the development of anthropometric measurements of males
Founded and directed the Sargent School for Physical Education (1881)
Founded and directed the Harvard Summer School (1887)

Edward Hartwell, M.D. (1850–1922)
Instructed (1882) and directed (1885–1890) the gymnasium at Johns Hopkins University
Directed physical training for the Boston public schools (1890–1897)

William Anderson, M.D. (1860–1947)
Initiated the meeting that led to the formation of the Association for the Advancement of Physical Education (1885)
Founded the Chautauqua Summer School of Physical Education (1886)
Founded and directed the Brooklyn (Anderson) Normal School (1886)

Hartvig Nissen (1856–1924)
Introduced Swedish gymnastics at the Swedish Health Institute in Washington, DC (1883)
Served as assistant director (1891–1897) and director (1897–1900) of physical training for the Boston public schools
Taught at the Harvard Summer School and Sargent Normal School and directed the Posse-Nissen School

Nils Posse (1862–1895)
Graduated from the Royal Gymnastics Central Institute in Stockholm, Sweden
Led in instruction of Swedish gymnastics in the United States (1885–1895)
Taught at the Boston Normal School of Gymnastics (1889)
Founded and directed the Posse Normal School (1890)

Delphine Hanna, M.D. (1854–1941)
Taught at Oberlin College (1885–1920)
Became professor of physical education (1903)
Initiated anthropometric measurements of females
Taught Luther Gulick, Thomas Wood, Jay Nash, and Jesse Williams

EARLY SWEDISH GYMNASTICS IN THE UNITED STATES

The first American introduction to Swedish gymnastics as a complete system occurred in 1883, when a Norwegian, Hartvig Nissen, opened a Swedish Health Institute in Washington, DC. Two years later Nils Posse, a graduate of the Royal Gymnastics Central Institute in Stockholm, introduced Swedish gymnastics in Boston. Impressed by Posse's program, philanthropist Mary Hemenway volunteered to furnish the Boston School Committee free teacher training in Swedish gymnastics if the schools would offer this program to children. This led Hemenway to finance the establishment of the Boston Normal School of Gymnastics in 1889. Hemenway selected Amy Morris Homans as the school's director; Nils Posse became the first instructor. The graduates of this school taught in the Boston schools and nationally, especially in women's colleges, spreading Swedish gymnastics. Edward Hartwell, director of physical training for the Boston public schools beginning in 1890, was also a strong supporter of Swedish gymnastics. Previously he had directed the Johns Hopkins University gymnasium, where he experimented with many of the principles Dudley Sargent advocated.

BATTLE OF THE SYSTEMS

Between 1885 and 1900, a leading topic for discussion among physical educators was which system of gymnastics could provide a unified, national program for the United States. This controversy became known as the **Battle of the Systems**. Although there was some overlap between programs, in general the German and Swedish systems and those advanced by various Americans developed and vied for supporters (see Figure 8.1 and Table 8-2).

In an attempt to introduce Swedish gymnastics to the general public and leaders in physical training and thus gain its acceptance as the program for American schools, Mary Hemenway financed the Boston Conference on Physical Training in 1889. Under the direction of Amy Morris Homans, this conference was highly successful and one of the most important conferences in physical education ever held in the United States. Its significance can be attributed to the exposure given to the various programs existing at that time. German gymnastics, Swedish gymnastics, Hitchcock's program, Sargent's system, and others were explained, and the merits of each were discussed. After explaining his program, Sargent proposed this solution to the search for an American system:

> What America most needs is the happy combination which the European nations are trying to effect: the strength-giving qualities of the German gymnasium, the active and energetic properties of the English sports, the grace and suppleness acquired from French calisthenics, and the beautiful poise and mechanical precision of the Swedish free movement, all regulated, systematized, and adapted to our peculiar needs and institutions. (Barrows, 1899, page 76)

Although the leaders in physical education at this conference were exposed to the various systems, no one system was found to meet completely the needs of Americans because each seemed to have weaknesses. Still, the Boston conference provided an opportunity for leaders to learn about the various systems and exchange ideas for the future promotion of American physical education.

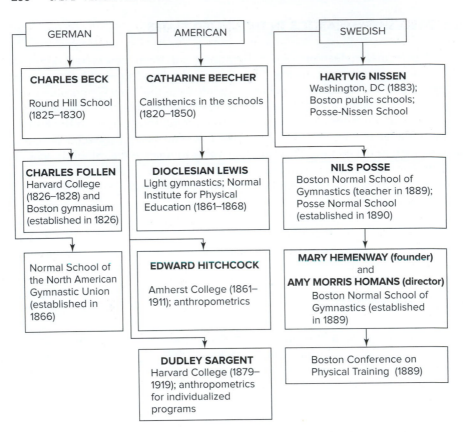

FIGURE 8.1

Concept map showing relationships among and contributions of leaders in early American physical education.

TABLE 8-2		
BATTLE OF THE SYSTEMS		
System	*Purpose*	*Advocates*
German gymnastics	Developed individual abilities and healthy, strong youth for war or emergencies using apparatus	German Turners, including Carl Betz, C.G. Rathman, George Brosius, and William Stecher
Swedish gymnastics	Promoted health, correct expression, and beauty of performance using exact movement patterns	Hartvig Nissen; Nils Posse; Amy Morris Homans; Edward Hartwell
Hitchcock's program	Emphasized hygiene through required exercises with light apparatus	Edward Hitchcock
Sargent's system	Provided individualized exercises on exercise machines	Dudley Sargent; Delphine Hanna
Association gymnastics	Contributed to the development of the all-around man	YMCA directors

Although German gymnastics were widely accepted in the Midwest as were Swedish gymnastics in the Northeast, few states mandated physical education. In 1866, California passed a law providing for twice-a-day exercises for a minimum of 5 minutes to promote health and bodily vigor, but it was short-lived. Ohio's 1892 law was the first lasting physical education law. Louisiana (in 1894), Wisconsin (in 1897), North Dakota (in 1899), and Pennsylvania (in 1901) passed similar legislation. In the late 1800s, most colleges included German and Swedish gymnastics in their physical education programs, but they also borrowed from Hitchcock's program and Sargent's principles and exercise machines. Before concluding this section, respond to the review items in Table 8-3.

TABLE 8-3

GAINING A BETTER UNDERSTANDING OF THE BATTLE OF THE SYSTEMS

The Battle of the Systems occurred as individuals in the United States participated in various types of European gymnastics or sports, designed new programmatic approaches unique to their specific settings, and sought to decide what should be included in school and college physical education and sport programs. Match the statements in the middle column with the system in the right column to help you better understand each of these systems and how or why they influence future programs. (Items on the right may be used more than once or not at all.)

	Review Questions	System
1. _____	1. Used an individualized approach in prescribing exercises	A. Anderson's system
2. _____	2. Borrowed from other programs for a more general approach	B. Association gymnastics
3. _____	3. Focused on posture and movement on command	C. British sports
4. _____	4. Advocated for schoolchildren by Edward Hartwell	D. Calisthenics
5. _____	5. Emphasized the use of machines to develop the body	E. Danish gymnastics
6. _____	6. Included practice for sports in its required program	F. German gymnastics
7. _____	7. Associated with the development of character	G. Hitchcock's program
8. _____	8. Emphasized the development of strength	H. Light gymnastics
9. _____	9. More popular for schoolchildren and females	I. Sargent's system
10. _____	10. Had as its goal the development of the all-around man	J. Swedish gymnastics
11. _____	11. Focused on exercises for developing health, beauty, and strength	
12. _____	12. Used Indian clubs and other apparatuses during exercise	
13. _____	13. Used anthropometrics to determine the effect of the program on students	
14. _____	14. More popular regionally and among immigrants	
15. _____	15. Influenced Delphine Hanna's program at Oberlin	
16. _____	16. Required class exercises 4 days a week for all students	
17. _____	17. Influenced other programs through a normal school	
18. _____	18. Influenced Mabel Lee's program at Nebraska	
19. _____	19. Had very few advocates in the United States	
20. _____	20. Emerged as the primary content in today's school programs	

ESTABLISHMENT OF NORMAL SCHOOLS FOR PHYSICAL EDUCATION

One means by which the various programs were promoted was the development of normal, or teacher training, schools. The 1880s were especially noteworthy: Six institutions were established to prepare physical education teachers either in a specific system or in an eclectic program that borrowed from several systems. In 1881, Dudley Sargent began teaching women from Harvard Annex and other women and men who were interested in his exercise machines and methodology. At the resultant Sargent School for Physical Education, he provided a curriculum based on a theoretical, scientific foundation along with various activities of a practical nature.

Delphine Hanna took courses from Dioclesian Lewis, Nils Posse, and Dudley Sargent; she attended both the Sargent School for Physical Education and Harvard Summer School of Physical Education. The program she initiated at coeducational Oberlin College in 1885 closely resembled Sargent's. Besides using many pieces of apparatus he designed, Hanna emphasized anthropometric measurements of female students to assess their individual development. The scope of her work included teaching a class to train men to instruct their male classmates. Among her first students were Thomas Wood and Luther Gulick, later luminaries in physical education. Table 8-4 summarizes the early teacher training institutions in the United States and their curricula.

A unique normal school established in 1885 in Springfield, Massachusetts, was the Young Men's Christian Association (YMCA) Training School. The YMCA's goal, through its association gymnastics, was to develop the all-around man and send

TABLE 8-4

NORMAL SCHOOLS FOR PHYSICAL EDUCATION

Years	Founder	Name	Program
1861–1868	Dioclesian Lewis	Normal Institute for Physical Education	Light gymnastics
1866–1951	Turners	Normal School of the North American Gymnastic Union	German gymnastics
1881–1929	Dudley Sargent	Sargent School for Physical Education	Theoretical and practical curriculum
1885–today	Young Men's Christian Association	YMCA Training School (Springfield College)	Association gymnastics
1886–1920s	William Anderson	Chautauqua Summer School of Physical Education	Advanced theoretical and practical curriculum
1886–1953	William Anderson	Brooklyn (Anderson) Normal School	Theoretical and practical curriculum
1887–1932	Dudley Sargent	Harvard Summer School of Physical Education	Advanced theoretical and practical curriculum
1889–1909	Mary Hemenway and Amy Morris Homans	Boston Normal School of Gymnastics	Swedish gymnastics
1890–1942	Nils Posse	Posse Normal School	Swedish gymnastics

him out as a physical director to the increasing number of YMCAs, both nationally and internationally. (The first YMCA gymnasiums had opened in 1869 in New York City, San Francisco, and Washington, DC.) The YMCA was a leader in promoting physical development and sports nationally and internationally (see Table 8-5).

In 1886, William Anderson established two normal institutions. While teaching in New York, he started the Brooklyn Normal School; later, when he became the director of the Yale College gymnasium, he moved this school to New Haven, Connecticut, and renamed it the Anderson Normal School. Anderson, along with Jay Seaver, also worked with leaders in the Chautauqua movement to set up the Chautauqua Summer School of Physical Education. The curricula at both schools focused on a generalized approach with theoretical and practical coursework.

In 1887, Dudley Sargent gained approval to open the Harvard Summer School of Physical Education, which provided opportunities for teachers already in the field to start or continue their professional training in physical education. This summer school was particularly important in the expansion of knowledge in physical education, since at this time no graduate degree programs existed. The diversity and breadth of the offerings, along with its outstanding faculty, made attendance at the Harvard Summer School prestigious; a certificate from the school was highly respected.

Swedish gymnastics was initially taught at the Boston Normal School of Gymnastics in 1889 and continued to be taught following the school's affiliation with Wellesley College beginning in 1909. Amy Morris Homans directed the programs at both institutions. In 1890, Nils Posse established the Posse Normal School, which also promoted Swedish gymnastics.

TABLE 8-5
BRIEF HISTORY OF THE YOUNG MEN'S CHRISTIAN ASSOCIATION (YMCA)

1844	Founded in England by George Williams to help address the unhealthy social conditions in cities during the Industrial Revolution
1851	Began initially in the United States in Boston for a similar reason
1866	New York YMCA began its advocacy for the improvement of the spiritual, mental, social, and physical conditions of young men
1885	YMCA Training School established in Springfield, Massachusetts, to train directors who could develop the all-around man in YMCAs that served all social classes
Late 1800s	YMCAs built gymnasiums and swimming pools, organized summer camps for boys, and conducted exercise programs for males; they also promoted the new games of basketball (1891) and volleyball (1895)
1890s	Luther Gulick's equilateral triangle of spirit, mind, and body depicted the YMCA's purpose
Mid-1800s to mid-1900s	Dwight L. Moody and John Mott guided the American YMCA movement as thousands of foreign work secretaries carried out an evangelical missionary outreach
Since 1950s	YMCAs admitted females and expanded to offer programs for family members of all ages

Source: See www.ymca.net/history for a comprehensive history of the YMCA in the United States.

Executing a synchronized Indian club routine.
© E. Phillips/Fox Photos/Getty Images

Beginning in the late 1800s, normal schools were replaced with teacher preparation programs that offered undergraduate college degrees. In 1885, Delphine Hanna initiated a physical education teacher curriculum for women students at Oberlin College; it became a four-year degree program in 1900. Only programs at Stanford University, the University of California, the University of Nebraska, and Harvard College preceded it.

This country's first degree program in physical education (a Bachelor of Science in Anatomy, Physiology, and Physical Training) was established in 1891 at Harvard College. Carl Fitz, a physician, worked with Dudley Sargent in the development and delivery of this program, which was designed to prepare gymnasium directors to teach and provide general preparation for individuals wishing to pursue the study of medicine. Working at the Physiological Laboratory, which was associated with the Lawrence Scientific School, Fitz focused on the importance of research in the relatively new field of physical education and was one of the foremost researchers in the experimental study of physiology of exercise in the 1890s.

FOUNDING OF A NATIONAL ASSOCIATION

In the late 1800s, physical education programs offered a potpourri of activities reflecting the philosophies and interests of their leaders. As a young teacher, William Anderson recognized this diversity and the fact that few opportunities existed for the exchange of curricula and philosophical ideas among individuals interested in physical training. After seeking support from two recognized leaders in the field, Edward Hitchcock and Dudley Sargent, Anderson invited gymnastics teachers, ministers, journalists, school principals, college presidents, and others engaged in the promotion of physical training to meet at Adelphi Academy in Brooklyn, New York, on November 27, 1885, to discuss their various programs and decide whether sufficient interest existed to regularly provide a forum for professional interchange. Of the 60 people who attended, 49 responded positively, resulting in the formation of the Association for the Advancement of Physical Education, today's SHAPE America.

PROMOTION OF PLAY FOR CHILDREN

While organized school programs were being established, the **playground movement** outside the schools gained support and momentum. The industrialization of the United States directly influenced this development. Immigration and the massive influx of Americans into urban areas resulted in overcrowded cities with crowded brick tenements. In an effort to provide suitable play space for children in this environment, the first sand boxes were built in Boston in 1886. In 1888, New York passed the first state legislation that led to an organized play area for children. By 1899, the Massachusetts Emergency and Hygiene Association sponsored 21 playgrounds.

Jane Addams's Hull House, a Chicago settlement house started in 1894, included a model playground. Settlement houses engaged children in playing sports and games popular in the United States. They also helped children and their parents learn English and adopt the ways of their new home. Boston constructed the Charlesbank outdoor gymnasium in 1889. Religious leaders, school administrators, philanthropists, and social workers worked together or independently in the late 1800s to ensure children were provided places and opportunities to play. In part, these efforts demonstrated a genuine concern for the welfare of children and society as a whole. These playgrounds also served as a method of social control, to assimilate immigrants into a new culture to replace their past ethnic or cultural connections. That is, the early leaders in the playground movement sought to use play to "Americanize" the myriad immigrants streaming into the cities.

DEVELOPMENT OF AMATEUR SPORTS FOR MALES

Americans' love for sports preceded the founding of the United States but blossomed after the Civil War as baseball became the national sport for men of all ages and amateurs as well as professionals. Races between cyclists, horses, runners, and yachts, with associated gambling, were especially attractive to the upper class. Normally these races, as well as sports such as cricket, golf, and tennis, were organized or played by members of elite social clubs. The New York Athletic Club, founded in 1868, led in the formation of the Amateur Athletic Union (AAU) in 1879. This organization sought to promote amateur sports for upper-class males, similar to the British ideal of the pure amateur who played sports for the love of the game. Paid, professional athletes were disrespected because it was believed they played for the money and money impacted the outcomes of competitions. The AAU sought to check the evils associated with professionals playing sports.

In 1853, Scottish immigrants, through their Caledonian games, began to promote their native sports, such as hammer throwing, putting stones, and tossing the caber (lifting a large wooden pole and flipping it end over end). The Czechoslovakian Sokols also promoted physical activities through mass displays in national festivals, such as the first held in 1879 in New York City. Table 8-6 lists many of the sport organizations that helped promote amateur sports during the late 1800s.

Frenchman Pierre de Coubertin, through persistent promotional efforts, established the modern Olympic Games and the spirit of amateurism that honored the integration of mind, body, and spirit. The classical restoration of the Panathenaic Stadium, in pure white marble, provided an awe-inspiring setting for the first Olympic

Tossing the caber was a popular event at the Caledonian games.
© Lawrence M. Sawyer/Getty Images RF

TABLE 8-6	
FOUNDING DATES OF AMATEUR SPORT ORGANIZATIONS	
1871	National Rifle Association
1875	National Bowling League (no longer exists)
1878	Cricketer's Association of the United States (no longer exists)
1879	National Archery Association (no longer exists)
1879	Amateur Athletic Union
1880	League of American Wheelmen (cycling) (today League of American Bicyclists)
1880	National Canoe Association (American Canoe Association)
1881	United States National Lawn Tennis Association (United States Tennis Association)
1882	National Croquet Association (no longer exists)
1884	United States Skating Association (no longer exists)
1887	American Trotting Association (no longer exists)
1894	United States Golf Association

Men's intercollegiate basketball was a slower-paced game years ago when a center jump followed each basket scored. Note the very small center jump circle and the area between the free throw line and the end line, which became known as the "key" because of its shape.
© ClassicStock/Alamy

Games of the modern era in Athens in 1896. Male athletes (241) representing 14 countries competed. While track and field, called athletics, occupied center stage, athletes also competed in cycling, fencing, gymnastics, tennis, shooting, swimming, weight lifting, and wrestling. None of these sports were open to female athletes.

James Connolly, one of the 13 athletes representing the United States, captured the first victory in the modern Olympic Games in the triple jump. Athletes from the United States dominated the track and field events, with first-place medals in the 100-meter, 400-meter, and 110-meter hurdles, long jump, high jump, pole vault, shot put, and discus throw. Greek athletes placed in swimming, cycling, fencing, gymnastics, and shooting and won the marathon. Germans captured most of the gymnastics medals.

The YMCA developed and promoted two sports. In 1891, at the YMCA Training School, Canadian James Naismith developed the rules for basketball and initiated the first game. This game was designed as an indoor sport to fill the void between football and baseball seasons. Five years later, William Morgan, at a YMCA in Holyoke, Massachusetts, originated volleyball as a less vigorous indoor game. Both sports met a need and found more early adherents in YMCAs than in private clubs and colleges. The YMCA also promoted both sports internationally and urged American youth to play basketball.

Gambling had been associated with sports since colonial times when owners and spectators bet on the outcomes of horse races. Americans from all levels of society wagered on cockfights, wrestling bouts, boxing matches, walking contests, and baseball games throughout the 1800s. One of the evils the AAU sought to eliminate in its promotion of amateur athletics was gambling. Baseball promoters had to overcome the perception that all players and fans bet on the outcomes of professional games. Nevertheless, many college students enthusiastically gambled on their sport competitions, especially football.

COLLEGIATE SPORTS FOR MEN

Sports on college campuses were initially organized by students as extracurricular activities, to the displeasure of administrators and faculty who viewed them as extraneous to the mission of higher education. The first intercollegiate event, in 1852, matched Harvard and Yale in rowing. The two early favorites in collegiate sports were baseball, which first matched Amherst against Williams in 1859, and football, which actually began as a soccerlike game between Princeton and Rutgers in 1869. Students founded organizations to standardize rules for competitions in rowing, baseball, football, and track.

College faculties paid little attention to sports until they began to infringe on students' academic work. Missed classes, decreased academic performances, injuries, gambling, property damage on campus and in nearby towns during victory celebrations, playing against professional teams, commercialization, and a general overemphasis on athletics compelled faculties to take action. For example, in 1882, a group of Harvard faculty members recommended that a committee of three faculty members oversee athletics. Three years later, this committee was expanded to include two students and one alumnus. In 1888, it again expanded to an equal representation of three faculty, three students, and three alumni. In 1883, representatives of eight eastern colleges met and proposed that colleges should not compete against professional teams; no professional athletes should coach college teams; students

Baseball was a popular intercollegiate sport beginning in the 1800s.
© Kirn Vintage Stock/Corbis

should be permitted only 4 years of participation in athletics; contests should take place only on campuses; and faculties should control athletics. Because only 2 colleges ratified them, these regulations failed to take effect.

In 1895, the Intercollegiate Conference of Faculty Representatives (today's Big Ten Conference), composed of one faculty member from each of 7 midwestern institutions, adopted rules requiring all players to be enrolled in college, all transfer students to wait 6 months before being eligible to play on a team, players who were paid were ineligible, games were prohibited against professional teams, and all athletes delinquent in their studies were not eligible to play. These efforts, however, did not control the overwhelming growth of student-initiated and student-administered intercollegiate athletics in the late 1800s. Table 8-7 chronicles the initiation of collegiate sport organizations and competitions.

TABLE 8-7
DEVELOPMENT OF COLLEGIATE SPORTS FOR MEN

1843	First collegiate rowing club started at Yale
1844	Harvard forms a rowing club
1852	First intercollegiate sport competition in rowing occurs as Harvard defeats Yale by four lengths
1859	College Union Regatta Association established by Harvard, Yale, Brown, and Trinity
1864	Haverford beats Pennsylvania 89–60 in the first intercollegiate cricket competition
1869	Rutgers outscores Princeton (6–4) in the first intercollegiate football game
1871	Rowing Association of American Colleges formed
1873	First intercollegiate track and field competition held in conjunction with the intercollegiate rowing regatta
1876	Intercollegiate Football Association established
1876	Intercollegiate Association of Amateur Athletes of America formed to govern track and field
1877	Harvard shoots 20 points better than Yale in the first intercollegiate rifle competition
1877	New York University defeats Manhattan (2–0) in the first intercollegiate lacrosse contest
1883	Intercollegiate Lawn Tennis Association founded
1883	Harvard's J. S. Clark wins the singles and the doubles (with P. E. Presbrey) events during the first intercollegiate tennis tournament
1883	Intercollegiate Athletic Conference established by Harvard, Princeton, and Cornell
1884	Pennsylvania defeats Wesleyan (16–10) in the first intercollegiate polo contest
1890	First intercollegiate cross country competition occurs as Pennsylvania beats Cornell
1894	Harvard outscores Columbia (5–4) in the first intercollegiate fencing meet
1895	Brown beats Harvard (4–2) in the first intercollegiate ice hockey game
1896	Yale beats Columbia by 35 holes in the first intercollegiate golf event with six-man teams
1896	First intercollegiate swimming meet with Pennsylvania defeating Columbia and Yale
1899	Pennsylvania surpasses Columbia (2–0) in the first intercollegiate water polo contest
1899	Intercollegiate Cross Country Association of Amateur Athletes of America established
1899	Yale's gymnastics team defeats competitors from 19 institutions in the first intercollegiate gymnastics meet

SPORTS FOR WOMEN

In the late 1800s, archery, croquet, and tennis were among the first sports to attract female participants because these activities did not require revealing clothing and were non-vigorous. Male and female attitudes about proper feminine behavior and medical opinion that vigorous activity would irreparably harm women's reproductive capabilities combined to prevent women from engaging in aggressive and highly competitive sports. Bicycling introduced a radical change in attire with the bloomer costume, or divided skirt, which allowed freedom from the appropriate attire of the day, which included voluminous skirts with petticoats and tightly laced corsets. Bloomers and middy blouses became the accepted costume for gymnastics and other physical activities; students at the Sargent School for Physical Education were among the first to wear them.

Societal attitudes toward women in the 1800s closely paralleled the Victorian perception that females were weak, objects to be placed on pedestals for admiration but not to be taken seriously because they were incapable of mental achievements. Females who sought schooling, especially college attendance, encountered ridicule and suspicions about their femininity. Their roles as wives and mothers were viewed as contradictory to the development of their minds.

Catharine Beecher's calisthenics and Swedish gymnastics with their therapeutic emphasis, became acceptable because they were believed by many to complement the feminine role. When many college women enthusiastically participated in baseball, basketball, and rowing, some physicians and women strongly opposed vigorous exertion. They argued that although mild activity such as walking, gardening, or moderate exercise could benefit women, an overexpenditure of energy might leave them infertile, hopelessly depleted of the energy needed to survive childbirth or motherhood. Not until medical opinions gradually changed in the twentieth century did restrictive opinions dissipate as women began to be viewed as capable of physical and mental achievement.

Some women in the upper socioeconomic strata shared their husbands' and fathers' desires to engage in conspicuous consumption. In flaunting their wealth, the rich popularized sports such as archery, golf, tennis, and yachting. In each case, these sports were organized at private clubs or in settings where social interaction between the sexes usually was a desired outcome. Following the lead of men, upper-class women began to compete nationally in archery (1879), tennis (1887), and golf (1896). Because of societal expectations, they always dressed in the latest fashions, many of which severely limited their mobility and skill development.

Women eagerly adopted basketball but adapted and modified its rules to make the game less strenuous and rough. The Committee on Women's Basketball was established by the American Association for the Advancement of Physical Education to standardize these rules. In 1896, the first intercollegiate contest between women, from the University of California and Stanford University, occurred. In addition to basketball, field days for track events and a few other sports became popular in women's colleges in the 1890s.

TABLE 8-8
TIMELINE FOR THE 1800s IN THE UNITED STATES

	Significant Events		*Firsts*
1823	German gymnastics introduced in the United States		
1824	Calisthenics introduced by Catharine Beecher		
		1837	Calisthenics program for college women
		1851	National German Turnfest
		1852	Intercollegiate athletic competition for males
		1853	Required daily exercise for school students
1860	Light gymnastics introduced by Dioclesian Lewis	1860	Required college physical education program
		1861	Normal school for gymnastics
		1879	National amateur sport organization
1883	Swedish gymnastics introduced in the United States		
		1885	Meeting of today's SHAPE America
		1885	YMCA Directors trained
		1886	Sand boxes provided for urban children
1889	Hull House (settlement house) opened		
1889	Boston Conference on Physical Training held		
		1891	Degree program in physical education
		1892	Lasting physical education law
		1896	Female full professor of physical education
		1896	Modern Olympic Games
		1896	Intercollegiate athletic competition for females

SUMMARY

Early physical education in the United States evolved from recreational sports and games into organized school and college programs that emphasized one system of gymnastics or combined exercises from various systems. Swedish and German gymnastics had their advocates, since health and strength were favored outcomes, but neither found widespread national acceptance because they did not satisfy Americans' emerging love of sports. Prior to 1900, teachers of physical education had completed programs in normal schools; a fledgling national association existed; but an accepted curriculum had not emerged nationally. With the popularization in the late 1800s of children's play and sports in amateur clubs and on college campuses, the stage was set for the development in the 1900s of American programs based primarily on playing sports. The Timeline in Table 8-8 will help you review a few key events that impacted physical education and sport during the 1800s.

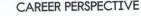

CAREER PERSPECTIVE

Courtesy Dean Diersing

DEAN DIERSING
Supervisor (Exercise Physiologist)
Cardiac & Pulmonary Rehabilitation
University Medical Center
Lubbock, Texas

EDUCATION
B. S. in exercise and sport sciences, Texas Tech University
M. S. in exercise and sport sciences (emphasis in clinical exercise
physiology), Texas Tech University

JOB RESPONSIBILITIES AND HOURS

Dean provides instruction, guidance, and motivation to patients and employees under the
general supervision of the medical directors of cardiac services and pulmonary services in
a hospital-based cardiac and pulmonary rehab program. He is responsible for day-to-day
operations including hiring, training, and supervising all personnel, financial management,
and the administrative services associated with providing quality care in the rehabilitation
of cardiac and pulmonary patients. Dean leads his team in the development of short- and
long-term goals and delivery of services to meet these objectives. Through his oversight,
staff members comply with all professional codes and hospital and departmental policies
and procedures. Daily, Dean and his staff develop and supervise exercise prescriptions
and educate cardiac and pulmonary patients in their rehabilitation and recovery. This
includes evaluating patients, identifying risk factors, and developing individualized goals
and treatment plans. These plans are based on assessments and interventions dealing with
blood pressure measurement, nutrition habits, lipid management, diabetes management,
physical activity monitoring, weight management, psychosocial interventions, exercise
programming, comorbid condition management, and medication management. Dean typically works from 7 am to 4 pm with others working 8 am to 5 pm with patients served at
a variety of times. Occasionally he may provide weekend inpatient therapy if other staff
members are unavailable, since his program operates 6 days a week. Dean and his staff are
actively involved with community outreach including marketing their cardiac and pulmonary rehabilitation services. Additionally, Dean assists with cardiac diagnostic stress testing on an "on call" basis. The starting salary range of individuals working in this career is
$28,000–$50,000.

SPECIALIZED COURSE WORK, DEGREES, AND EXPERIENCES
NEEDED FOR THIS CAREER

To qualify for his supervisor position, Dean needed to have earned his master's degree in
clinical exercise physiology. While not required at the time, possessing this degree set him
apart from other applicants while demonstrating his knowledge, dedication to learning,
and passion for serving others in this field. Dean's undergraduate and graduate internships in clinical exercise physiology not only strengthened his application but also helped
prepare him for his career. Since only one state (i.e., Louisiana) recognizes a licensure
process for exercise physiologists, certifications are not required. Dean, like many leaders
in cardiac and pulmonary rehabilitation, has become a Certified Exercise Physiologist and
Registered Clinical Exercise Physiologist through the American College of Sports Medicine.

After gaining experience and expertise, Dean earned the Certified Cardiac Rehab Professional certification from the American Association of Cardiac and Pulmonary Rehabilitation. Dean believes that most of his exercise science courses, such as exercise testing and prescription, exercise physiology, cardiopulmonary exercise physiology, and electrocardiography, have had direct application in helping his patients manage essential lifestyle changes.

SATISFYING ASPECTS

Dean values the opportunity his career choice provides to make a change in people's lives after they have experienced a heart attack or open heart surgery. The rewards of helping individuals improve their health are offset when patients fail to take control of lives through preventive activity. To Dean, observing the remarkable outcomes benefiting patients who maximize their cardiac rehabilitation sessions is awesome. Other satisfying aspects of Dean's work are the interactions with his team. He takes great pride in helping each staff member increase his or her clinical skills through educational and experiential opportunities and seeks to develop his team to become one of the best. Dean wishes he could help all individuals with chronic lung disease or heart disease benefit from education, lifestyle modifications, and secondary preventions.

JOB POTENTIAL

Dean's employer offers a career ladder that allows an exercise physiologist through professional growth and development, longevity, and goal attainment to earn additional merit increases and advancement into positions with greater responsibility and leadership opportunities.

SUGGESTIONS FOR STUDENTS

Dean believes strongly that everyone should "let your passions drive you." Individuals do not choose this career based on its income potential but on their passion for helping others become motivated to change their lifestyle choices. He enjoys what he does every day because he is passionate to help others experience healthier lives.

KEY POINTS

Native Americans	Sport closely aligned with social, spiritual, and economic aspects of life with gambling often associated with sports, such as lacrosse
Colonial Americans	Engaged recreationally in bowling, sleighing, fox hunting, horse racing, hawking, cockfighting, rounders, cricket, and boxing
German gymnastics	Introduced at Round Hill School, spread from New York City to the Midwest in isolated enclaves of Germans; not adopted because of its emphasis on nationalism and development of strength using apparatus
Catharine Beecher	Offered calisthenics, a course of exercises designed to promote health and thus to secure beauty and strength, especially for females

Dioclesion Lewis	Taught light gymnastics, exercises with wands, rings, bean-bags, dumbbells, and Indian clubs accompanied by music, at the Normal Institute for Physical Education
Swedish gymnastics	Taught by Hartvig Nissen and Nils Posse at the Boston Normal School of Gymnastics, primarily to females and children, and Posse-Nissen School
Edward Hitchcock	Gave lectures on health, initiated the light gymnastics program for students, and used anthropometrics to find the average, ideal college male at Amherst College
Dudley Sargent	Designed individualized programs for Harvard students using exercise machines he designed, taught primarily females at his normal school, and directed the advanced teacher training program in the Harvard Summer School
Delphine Hanna	Took anthropometric measurements of college women and instructed Luther Gulick, Thomas Wood, Jay Nash, and Jesse Williams at Oberlin College
William Anderson	Founded two normal schools for physical education and was pivotal in establishing the Association for the Advancement of Physical Education
YMCA	Established a training school to prepare physical directors for developing the all-around man (intellectual, physical, and spiritual)
Men's amateur sports	The socially elite engaged in horse racing, yachting, and gambling, played tennis, golf, and cricket, and formed athletic clubs for track and field
Women and sports	Some engaged in horseback riding (sidesaddle), walking, dancing, croquet, cycling, or tennis

REVIEW QUESTIONS

1. What were some of the characteristics of Native Americans' sport and what were their popular sports?
2. What were the differences between sporting activities of the Puritans, Dutch, and English settlers?
3. How and why were German gymnastics spread in this country?
4. What program of exercises did Catharine Beecher develop and why?
5. What was Lewis's system of gymnastics and how was it spread?
6. Which system of gymnastics was most popular with females in the late 1800s and early 1900s and why?
7. What were the components of Edward Hitchcock's program at Amherst College?
8. What were the two primary characteristics of Dudley Sargent's program at Harvard?

9. What was the purpose of the YMCA Training School?
10. What was the Battle of the Systems, and what was the outcome?

STUDENT ACTIVITIES

1. As a class, reenact a portion of the Boston Conference on Physical Training (1889) by having each student report on one of the following systems: Swedish, German, Edward Hitchcock's, or Dudley Sargent's.

2. Read about the founding of the first professional organization in physical education (today's SHAPE America), and report your findings to the class orally or in a two-page paper.

3. Research the name(s) and starting date(s) of the oldest normal school(s) for physical education for males and for females in your state.

4. Investigate which college(s) in your state offered the first intercollegiate athletic competitions for men and for women. In which sports did these competitions occur?

5. Research any one of the individuals, events, or topics discussed in this chapter. Write a two-page paper about the major contributions of this individual, event, or topic to the history and growth of physical education and sport.

REFERENCES

Barrows, I. C. (1899). *Physical training.* Boston, MA: George H. Ellis Press.

Oxendine, J. B. (1988). *American Indian sports heritage.* Champaign, IL: Human Kinetics.

WEB CONNECTIONS

1. www.history.org/foundation/journal/winter10/lacrosse.cfm
   This site provides an article about the history of Native American lacrosse as well as links to articles about colonial sports and activities.

2. sacramentoturnverein.com/history/
   This site provides a history of the Turner movement from its beginnings in Germany through the immigration and impact of Turners in the United States.

3. www.faqs.org/childhood/Pa-Re/Playground-Movement.html
   This brief article describes the beginning of the playground movement and provides related links for additional information. See also these sites for addition information about playgrounds: www.nycgovparks .org/about/history/timeline/playgrounds-public-recreation; www.encyclopedia.chicagohistory.org/pages/976.html; www.vigorousnorth.com/2010/09/natural-history-of-playgrounds.html

4. www.aausports.org
   The Amateur Athletic Union, one of the largest, multi-sport, volunteer sports organizations in the United States, offers amateur sports competitions including the AAU Junior Olympic Games.

5. http://www.infoplease.com/spot/womeninsportstimeline.html
   Check out this site for an extensive timeline of the significant events in women's sports.

6. www.ymca.net/history/
   This history of the Young Men's Christian Association explains its contributions to the promotion of physical activities and sports in the United States.

7. www.musarium.com/kodak/olympics/olympichistory/
   Visit this site for a timeline with superb photographs that capture the essence of competition and athletic excellence in the modern Olympic Games.

8. http://files.eric.ed.gov/fulltext/ED261990.pdf
   This site provides a reprint of the yearly chronicle of the American Alliance for Health, Physical Education, Recreation and Dance between 1885 and 1985.

CHAPTER

9

TWENTIETH AND TWENTY-FIRST CENTURY PHYSICAL EDUCATION, EXERCISE SCIENCE, AND SPORT

LEARNING OUTCOMES

- Students will be able to articulate the influence of Luther Gulick, Thomas Wood, Clark Hetherington, Jay Nash, and Jesse Williams on play, physical education, recreation, and sports in the United States.
- Students will be able to describe the expansion of men's intercollegiate athletic programs, from their interclass origins to today's commercialized businesses in the United States.
- Students will be able to explain how women's sport programs evolved from an emphasis on mass participation to competitive sports, especially in recent years, due to federal legislation.
- Students will be able to reconstruct the transition of participants and programs from play to recreation to fitness in the United States.

Professional discussions concerning which system of gymnastics would best meet the needs of students in the United States continued into the early twentieth century. Beginning in the 1920s, school physical education moved from formalized exercise programs to curricula that included sports, games, aquatics, and outdoor activities with educational outcomes stressed. Two themes emerged in the middle of the twentieth century: Education "through" the physical and education "of" the physical vied for advocates and influenced school physical education and sport curricula. The popularity of sports at all levels and for both sexes expanded tremendously. Nonschool programs from mid-century until today have offered sport competitions for individuals of all ages and skill levels, lifetime recreational activities, and a wide range of fitness programs. Federal legislation mandating equal opportunity for participation in sports and physical activities for females and individuals with special needs led to dramatic changes in school and nonschool programs. Today people participate in physical activities to develop and maintain fitness and in lifetime sports for fun, fitness, and competition.

THE NEW PHYSICAL EDUCATION

By the end of the nineteenth century, no gymnastics system had been adopted in the United States. The formal nature of German and Swedish gymnastics and other alternative programs failed to appeal to a broad base of physical educators and their students, who were seeking activities that offered competition, fun, and more freedom of expression. Speaking at the International Congress on Education sponsored by the National Education Association in 1893, Thomas Wood articulated his vision to address this need by calling for a new approach to physical education:

> The great thought in physical education is not the education of the physical nature,
> but the relation of physical training to complete education, and then the effort
> to make the physical contribute its full share to the life of the individual,
> in environment, training, and culture. (page 621)

Delphine Hanna's influence helped bridge the transition from the nineteenth to the twentieth century. A student of Dioclesian Lewis, Nils Posse, and Dudley Sargent, she taught at Oberlin College, which is the oldest, continuously operating coeducational institution in the United States. In addition to directing the physical education program for female students at Oberlin, she taught Luther Gulick, Thomas Wood, Jay Nash, and Jesse Williams. These four men, along with Clark Hetherington, were instrumental in developing and promoting programs that moved away from formalized gymnastics systems and were appropriate for individuals of all ages.

This **new physical education** beginning in the 1920s focused on developing the whole individual through participation in play, sports, games, and natural, outdoor activities. The curriculum and philosophy of the new physical education was heavily influenced by and consistent with educational and psychological theory developing at that time.

Faculty at Teachers College also contributed to the integration of educational developmentalism and social education into the new physical education. Thomas Wood taught there for 31 years. Rosalind Cassidy took a Teachers College degree, as did hundreds of physical educators in the middle decades of the 1900s. For 27 years, Jesse Williams influenced Teachers College students to advocate for education through the physical as also supported by Wood and Cassidy. Williams was the primary advocate for seeking to achieve social outcomes through physical education and sport.

LEADERS IN THE NEW PHYSICAL EDUCATION

Luther Gulick and his roommate, Thomas Wood, likely discussed their mutual interest in physical education while attending Oberlin College, where they were influenced by Delphine Hanna. In 1887, Luther Gulick became an instructor at the YMCA Training School in Springfield, Massachusetts, and, 2 years later, was named superintendent. While at the YMCA Training School, he emphasized sports in the physical directors' curriculum and started the YMCA's Athletic League to promote amateur sports. Stressing unity in the development of body, mind, and spirit, he designed the YMCA triangle (see Figure 9.1), emblematic of the all-around man. He then moved to New York and taught before accepting the position of director of physical training for the New York City public schools. Although Gulick supported gymnastics as the basis of school curricula, he founded the Public Schools Athletic League (PSAL) to provide after-school sports opportunities for boys, especially in track and field activities.

Another Gulick legacy was his promotion of play. In 1906, he helped establish the Playground Association of America (PAA) and served as its first president. He also advocated for the provision of playgrounds and public recreation in this country, initiated (with his wife) the Campfire Girls in 1913, and led in the camping movement. In *A Philosophy of Play,* he articulated the importance of play as an educational force and helped begin the play movement within physical education.

For 2 years, Thomas Wood directed the gymnasium work for men at Oberlin College. After receiving a medical degree at Columbia, he developed the undergraduate teacher training curriculum in physical education at Stanford University, beginning in 1891. Ten years later, he joined the faculty of Teachers College of Columbia University, where he led the establishment of the first master's (1910) and doctor's (1924) degree programs in physical education. He also was instrumental in the development of health education as a separate field of study. *The New Physical Education,* which he co-authored with Rosalind Cassidy in 1927, provided the philosophical foundation for refocusing school programs from gymnastics to sports, games, dance, aquatics, and natural activities.

Rosalind Cassidy helped broaden and clarify the tenets of the new physical education during her professional career at Mills College in California. She helped develop and promote an understanding that physical education could uniquely contribute to the education of the whole person through physical activities. Through her voluminous writings, she also redefined physical education as the study of human movement.

Clark Hetherington was taught and greatly influenced by Wood at Stanford University. This influence was evident from Hetherington's coining of the term **new physical education** and from his advocacy of organic, psychomotor, character, and intellectual development as descriptive of physical education's objectives. G. Stanley

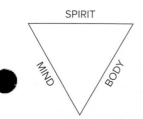

FIGURE 9.1
YMCA emblem designed by Luther Gulick.

Hall, a second mentor for Hetherington, emphasized educational developmentalism, which paralleled Hetherington's philosophy that play is a child's chief business in life. At the University of Missouri, the University of Wisconsin, New York University, and Stanford University, Hetherington helped establish an undergraduate physical education program. At New York University, he led to the development of a graduate degree program.

One of the first graduates of New York University's Ph.D. program in physical education was Jay Nash. Nash had served as assistant supervisor of physical education in California under Hetherington before joining the faculty at New York University in 1926 as Hetherington's replacement. Nash stressed that recreational skills should be learned early in life and could provide enjoyment throughout life. Fearing an overemphasis on sport spectating in the United States, Nash stated that school programs should teach carryover, or lifetime, sports to encourage people to adopt active lifestyles; that is, people should be educated for leisure.

Building on the concept of complete education espoused by Thomas Wood and Rosalind Cassidy, Jesse Williams led in the promotion of **education through the physical.** This theme stated that physical education as a field uniquely contributed to the education of the whole person because it included learning through the physical realm. This was a vitally important approach during the years of the Depression when funds for education were severely cut. Williams stressed that physical education programs should be retained because they, more than all school curricula, uniquely contributed to the physical development of students as well as the education of the total child. Williams also was influenced by John Dewey's social education theories. Williams applied these to physical education by stating the social and intellectual interactions occurring during physical activities helped educate children for living in a democratic society. Through his 41 books and the students he influenced in the highly regarded graduate physical education programs at Teachers College of Columbia University, he helped physical education programs gain a strong position in schools during the middle decades of the twentieth century.

Figure 9.2 summarizes the influence of these new physical educators on each another. It is interesting that Nash signaled a change in the professional training of physical educators: Whereas Hanna, Gulick, Wood, and Williams held medical degrees, Nash earned a Ph.D. in physical education.

The European gymnastics systems had failed to appeal to a broad spectrum of individuals in the United States. These systems were either too structured or too focused on strength or posture. Even the prgrams advocated by Edward Hitchcock, Dudley Sargent, William Anderson, and the YMCA did not fully meet the needs of educating school and college students physically. This set the stage for the development of the new physical education, which sought to incorporate play, sports, games, and outdoor activities into the curriculum. The inclusion of a variety of movement forms appealed to individuals of all ages much more than had any of the gymnastics systems. Just being physically active, however, was not enough. Rather, the new physical educators sought to expand on the importance of physical development within education by linking it directly with the education of the whole child. Thus, the logical extension of the new physical education was the emphasis on education through the physical.

DELPHINE HANNA
Anthropometrics
Individualized program

LUTHER GULICK
Play and boys' athletics

THOMAS WOOD
Complete education and
The New Physical Education

JESSE WILLIAMS
Education through the
physical

CLARK HETHERINGTON
Play is a child's chief
business in life

ROSALIND CASSIDY
The New Physical Education
and study of human movement

JAY NASH
Recreation, especially
in lifetime sports

FIGURE 9.2

Delphine Hanna directly influenced four of the new physical educators as they emphasized play, sports, games, recreation, and meeting educational outcomes. These men and women influenced the thinking and programs of each other as depicted through the connecting lines and arrows.

Source: Photo slides provided by Angela Lumpkin

MAJOR DEVELOPMENTS IN PHYSICAL EDUCATION AND EXERCISE SCIENCE

Several parallel movements built on the advances of the new physical education, expanding this educational curriculum even further. These developments included the play movement; the growth of women's physical education; the education of the physical movement; the emergence of exercise science; the focus on human movement; and the influence of the scientific movement, educational developmentalism, and social education in the schools. Box 9.1 highlights many of the leaders in these developments.

The Play Movement

Luther Gulick proclaimed the importance of play for children, especially outside the schools. In New York, he established the PSAL's sports competitions for boys and the Girls' Branch of the PSAL, which provided opportunities for girls to participate in folk dancing. Elizabeth Burchenal directed the Girls' Branch of the PSAL before founding and presiding over the American Folk-Dance Society.

As supervisor of physical culture in the Detroit public schools for 14 years, Ethel Perrin stressed informal, coeducational classes that emphasized play rather than formalized gymnastics. Under her leadership, Detroit led the nation in the provision of specially trained physical educators at all levels of instruction.

The play movement also influenced nonschool programs. Following the passage of child labor laws, children were taken out of the sweat shops and returned to their neighborhoods, where playgrounds and parks were provided for them. Children of immigrants were assimilated into the American culture, made friends, learned social skills, and learned how to win and lose as they perfected their baseball, basketball, football, softball, and ice hockey skills. Cities and towns prioritized offering sport competitions and recreational activities, first for children and later for adults, to meet this inherent need to play.

Women's Physical Education

Not until the 1970s did most college physical education programs end their practice of separation by gender. Throughout most of the 1900s, women's physical education

Mabel Lee, the first female president of the American Physical Education Association.
Source: Photo slide provided by Angela Lumpkin

BOX 9.1   TWENTIETH-CENTURY LEADERS IN PHYSICAL EDUCATION IN THE UNITED STATES

Delphine Hanna, M.D. (1854–1941)
Taught at Oberlin College (1885–1920)
Used anthropometrics to prescribe exercise programs for college women
Established a four-year degree program (1900)
Named professor of physical education (1903)
Instructed Luther Gulick, Thomas Wood, Jay Nash, and Jesse Williams

Luther Gulick, M.D. (1865–1918)
Served as instructor (1887–1900) and superintendent (1889–1900) of the Department of Physical
    Training at the YMCA Training School
Directed physical training for the New York City public schools (1903–1908)
Established the Public Schools Athletic League in New York City (1903)
Helped establish the Playground Association of America (1906)
Influenced by Delphine Hanna and Thomas Wood

Thomas Wood, M.D. (1864–1951)
Taught at Stanford University (1891–1901)
Taught at Teachers College of Columbia University (1901–1932)
Helped formulate the philosophical cornerstone for the new physical education
Appointed the first professor of health education at Teachers College of Columbia University
Influenced by Delphine Hanna, Luther Gulick, and Rosalind Cassidy

Clark Hetherington (1870–1942)
Directed physical training and athletics at the University of Missouri (1900–1910)
Established a Demonstration Play School at the University of California at Berkeley (1913)
Taught at the University of Wisconsin (1913–1918)
Served as state supervisor of physical education for California (1918–1921)
Taught at New York University (1923–1929)
Taught at Stanford University (1929–1938)
Influenced by Thomas Wood and G. Stanley Hall

Jay Nash (1886–1965)
Taught at New York University (1926–1953)
Promoted recreation and carryover sports
Influenced by Clark Hetherington and extended his theories as well as those of Luther Gulick
    and Thomas Wood

Jesse Williams, M.D. (1886–1966)
Taught at Teachers College of Columbia University (1911–1916; 1919–1941)
Stressed educational values, social education, and education through the physical
Became a dominant influence in physical education (1930–1960)
Influenced by John Dewey

(continued)

BOX 9.1   TWENTIETH-CENTURY LEADERS IN PHYSICAL EDUCATION IN THE UNITED STATES (continued)

Rosalind Cassidy (1895–1980)

Taught at Mills College in California (1918–1947)

Taught at the University of California at Los Angeles (1947–1962)

Led in writing about and promotion of the new physical education, education through the physical, and physical education as human movement

Influenced by Thomas Wood

Elizabeth Burchenal (1876–1959)

Served as executive secretary of the Girls' Branch of the Public Schools Athletic League (1906–1916)

Founded and served as first president of the American Folk-Dance Society (1916–1929)

Became first chairperson of the Committee on Women's Athletics of the American Physical Education Association (1917)

Influenced by Luther Gulick and Melvin Gilbert (in dance)

Ethel Perrin (1871–1962)

Supervised physical culture in the Detroit public schools (1909–1923)

Provided leadership with the executive committee of the Women's Division of the National Amateur Athletic Federation (1923–1932)

Served as assistant/associate director of health education for the American Child Health Association (1923–1936)

Influenced by Amy Morris Homans

Tait McKenzie, M.D. (1867–1938)

Taught (1891–1904) and served as medical director of physical education (1896–1904) at University Medical College (Canada)

Taught as professor on medical faculty and directed physical education (1904–1931) and served as professor of physical therapy (1907–1931) at the University of Pennsylvania

Depicted hundreds of athletic events in works of sculpture that showed the aesthetic harmony of bodily proportion and expression

Mabel Lee (1886–1985)

Directed physical education for women at the University of Nebraska (1924–1952)

Elected first woman president of the American Physical Education Association (1931)

Led the profession as a proponent of wholesome sports for women

Influenced by Amy Morris Homans

Charles McCloy (1886–1959)

Worked for the YMCA in the United States and internationally (1908–1930)

Served as a research professor in physical education at the University of Iowa (1930–1954)

Stressed the development of skills and organic vigor (education of the physical) as the primary objectives of physical education

(continued)

BOX 9.1   TWENTIETH-CENTURY LEADERS IN PHYSICAL EDUCATION IN THE UNITED STATES (continued)

Eleanor Metheny (1908–1982)
Taught at Wellesley College and at the Harvard Fatigue Laboratory (1940–1942)
Taught at the University of Southern California (1942–1971)
Led in the study of meaningful movement experiences
Influenced by Charles McCloy

---

focused on preparing teachers, with strict disassociation from competitive athletics. Curricula remained somewhat formalized, were centered on minimal skill development for all rather than on enhancement of the abilities of the highly skilled, and focused on value development through sport, rather than winning.

Only gradually did women gain acceptance as equals within the physical education profession, possibly because most early male leaders were physicians and few females had the opportunity to pursue medical degrees in the early years. Two exceptions were Eliza Mosher and Helen Putnam, who served as vice presidents in the national organization. Mabel Lee was elected the first woman president of the American Physical Education Association (APEA) 46 years after it was established. Within the APEA, Lee, Burchenal, and other women worked to preserve an educational model for women's participation in sport.

Education of the Physical

Charles McCloy led the campaign against a primary emphasis on educational outcomes as advocated by Wood, Cassidy, and Williams. Instead of supporting Williams's claim that physical education merited inclusion in the schools because it helped attain social, emotional, and intellectual goals, McCloy affirmed his commitment to **education of the physical,** a belief that physical education's unique contribution within education should be to develop individuals' physical fitness and sport skills. During his more than 20 years with the YMCA, and especially during his tenure at the University of Iowa, McCloy stressed organic and psychomotor development as the most important objectives for physical education. He stated the uniqueness of physical education depended on the development of physical skills. He also encouraged the teaching of sport skills and the measurement of progress through standardized assessments.

An extension of this philosophical approach to physical education was the growth in the use of tests and measurements, which paralleled the scientific movement in education. Built on the importance of anthropometric measurements in the late 1800s, early twentieth-century physical educators developed numerous physical tests. The PSAL initiated achievement tests to reward boys' successful performances. College achievement tests measured cognitive knowledge, motor ability, endurance, and sport skills. David Brace's Motor Ability Test, Frederick Cozens's test of general athletic ability, Frederick Rogers's Strength Index and Physical Fitness Index, and Charles McCloy's

Motor Quotient were among the most notable measures developed and used in school and college physical education programs.

Exercise Science

Dudley Sargent, a leader in anthropometrics (discussed in the previous chapter), included measurements of the strength and power of his students at Harvard in his prescriptions for individualized programs. His use of dynamometers and the various exercise machines he designed made him a pioneer in combining data of physical performance with exercise prescription and sport involvement. Through the Harvard Summer School and Sargent School for Physical Education, his influence was pervasive. In 1892 George Fitz, who, like Sargent, held an M.D., established the Physiology Laboratory as a part of the Lawrence Scientific School at Harvard. Advanced students completed physiological research, some of the first conducted in this country. The Harvard Fatigue Laboratory (interestingly, located within the School of Business) was directed by David Dill during its operation from 1927 to 1947. The breadth of the exercise and environmental research included clinical studies in physiology as well as investigations involving nutrition, physical fitness, and heart and lung function.

Fitness activities, such as exercising in water, are offered by recreation departments, YMCAs and YWCAs, and health clubs.

© Keith Brofsky/Getty Images RF

Researchers in this laboratory, as well as the Institute for Environmental Stress at the University of California at Santa Barbara, the Laboratory for Physiological Hygiene at the University of Minnesota, and the Human Physiology Laboratory at Indiana University, became prolific publishers of their research findings, providing the foundation for today's exercise physiology programs.

During the 1900s, four researchers were particularly noteworthy for translating exercise physiology research into practice for the enhancement of physical fitness. At George Williams College in Chicago, Arthur Steinhaus trained students for laboratory-based research and was a prolific author. Peter Karpovich at Springfield College helped link physical education with exercise physiology. Thomas Cureton at Springfield and the University of Illinois became a leading spokesperson for the importance of physical fitness through his writings and the students he taught. Kenneth Cooper, an Air Force physician, developed the aerobics fitness scoring system that helped spawn the popularity of jogging and other fitness activities in the 1970s. Cooper established a research institute in Dallas that continues to promote scientifically based educational and research programs.

Human Movement

Rosalind Cassidy and Eleanor Metheny helped revolutionize the conceptual base of physical education. Metheny, a student of Charles McCloy, was acclaimed for her insightful writings and inspirational speeches on this topic.

Movement education, especially as influenced by Rudolf Laban in England, significantly influenced elementary school curricula. Movement education, a child-centered curriculum, emphasized presenting movement challenges to students and encouraging them to use problem solving through guided discovery to learn fundamental skills. Some educators believed developmentally appropriate subject matter for children should focus on their free expression of movements in response to challenges or problems. Advocates favored individualized learning of locomotor, nonlocomotor, and perceptual-motor skills.

AMATEUR AND COLLEGIATE SPORTS

The popularization and commercialization of sports in the twentieth and twenty-first centuries have been phenomenal. In addition to becoming the nucleus of physical education programs, sports are organized for competition inside and outside schools and colleges.

Youth Sport Programs

In the 1920s, the popularity of sports in the United States led many people to expect the schools to provide competitive sports for children. Some junior and most senior high schools assumed this responsibility because physical educators believed students in these age groups were physiologically and psychologically prepared for competition. For elementary-age children, educators widely believed the negative outcomes from competitive sports outweighed the benefits. This belief did not prevent the development of youth sports programs, however. Communities, private associations, and civic organizations stepped in to fill the void, seeing sports as a deterrent to delinquency, a tool for social control, a means of developing self-discipline and cooperation, and an outlet for exercise and fun. Local as well as national programs, such as Little League Baseball and Pop Warner football, expanded to the point that today they involve millions of young athletes and adult organizers and billions of dollars.

Although many physical educators philosophically disagree with highly competitive youth leagues, these sport enterprises are deeply entrenched in American society. Parents have favored youth sport programs for several reasons:

- Their children have fun through participation.
- The programs offer opportunities for learning sport skills.
- These experiences enhance socialization abilities such as cooperation and teamwork and development of values.
- Sport involvement contributes to physical development and fitness.
- Youth sport programs provide children with wholesome alternatives for the use of their time, thus lessening misbehavior or unattended hours at home watching television, playing video games, or surfing the Web. In addition, many value youth sports because the whole family can participate together—as players, coaches, and cheerleaders and in various other volunteer capacities.

Children have varying reasons for participating in youth sports. Mostly they want to have fun, learn or improve sport skills, stay in shape or get exercise, associate with friends, or merely have something to do. Unfortunately, some youth join a team or participate in sports just to please their parents. After years of success as a young athlete, winning, seeking rewards or awards, maintaining popularity, or qualifying for college grants-in-aid or professional careers may become the primary motivations for participating in sports.

When youth sport programs remain focused on children's aspirations, and when parents' attitudes and behaviors are kept in perspective, millions benefit. When winning surpasses all other goals, exploitation of young athletes and an erosion of values reign. For example, exposure to the media, such as the televising of the Little League World Series, has served only to intensify the pressures on young competitors as well as raise the expected levels of performance to adult and even professional levels. As a result, children are no longer allowed to be children or play just for fun of it. When adults rudely dispute officials' calls and berate their children for not performing well enough, they become part of the problem. These adults rob children of the many benefits of playful participation in sport. Adult domination also prevents children from learning in and through sport the art of negotiation, how to make decisions, communication skills, and how to lead and follow.

Numerous occurrences in youth sports call attention to the prevalence of exploitation. Pressures to win, commercialization, elimination of lesser-skilled players, injuries resulting from excessive play or practice, violence, overspecialization, cheating, and lack of value development are but a few examples. As more and more educators promote and provide coaching education programs, these problems are ameliorated. Parent orientation sessions also are important deterrents to adults misbehaving and placing excessive pressures on children.

Intramurals

In the late 1800s and early 1900s, most college athletic teams and some physical education programs evolved out of interclass competitions organized by male students. As athletics and physical education developed separate programs, a need still existed for recreational activities for students. In 1913, the University of Michigan and The Ohio State University appointed the first intramural directors. At Michigan, beginning in 1919, Elmer Mitchell led in the development of sport opportunities for students who were not varsity athletes but wanted more competition than was available in physical education classes. Originally in the colleges and after the mid-1920s in the schools, intramurals offered league and class (or homeroom) competitions in individual and team sports. In the 1940s, coeducational activities were introduced and became popular. The greatest expansion in combined male and female activities occurred in the 1970s and 1980s.

Today many intramural programs operate as campus recreation programs, having greatly expanded the scope of their activities. In addition to competitive leagues and coeducational recreation, club sports, faculty/staff programs, instructional clinics, fitness classes, special events and tournaments, and free-play opportunities have been offered. Over the years, many intramural and recreational sports programs changed from receiving funds from athletic departments and physical education departments to being supported by students' fees. At the school level, where intramural activities vary from traditional competitions to a variety of leisure-time events and are scheduled throughout the day and night, physical educators normally provide the expertise while school budgets provide the equipment.

Outside the schools, the same concept of intramurals, or sport competitions within the walls, has provided innumerable opportunities for physical activity. Many corporations offer or sponsor sport leagues and competitions in volleyball, bowling, softball, and other sports for their employees at all levels of the organization. These leisure-time activities help build camaraderie among employees as well as help them adopt healthier lifestyles.

Collegiate Sports for Men

In the early 1900s, concerns in collegiate sports focused on football, primarily because of the injuries and deaths that occurred with shocking regularity. While President Theodore Roosevelt expressed concern, college presidents threatened to ban intercollegiate football. As a direct result of football injuries and deaths, the National Collegiate Athletic Association (NCAA) was formed in 1906. Although composed of a small group of faculty representatives with power only to make recommendations, the NCAA attempted to control the roughness and brutality of football by revising the rules. Gradually football overcame these problems and emerged as the major collegiate sport. Baseball in colleges, though rivaled by the professional major leagues, retained a degree of popularity secondary to the professionals and to football, while intercollegiate competitions in boxing, golf, tennis, track and field, wrestling, and other sports have never seriously challenged the supremacy of football. Basketball emerged as the second leading collegiate sport, but not until the 1950s.

The NCAA continued as the sole voice of and controlling organization for college athletes until 1938, when the National Junior College Athletic Association (NJCAA) was founded to provide competitive opportunities for students in two-year institutions. Then, in 1952, the National Association of Intercollegiate Athletics (NAIA) began to sponsor championships for small colleges (it sponsored an annual basketball tournament for men starting in 1940). Table 9-1 lists these and other major sports organizations for men and women.

Today collegiate athletics for men are quite different from what they were in the 1940s. Under faculty control by representative vote, the NCAA remained primarily an advisory organization during its first 40 years. Control rested with each institution, where most frequently athletic councils composed of alumni, faculty, and students exercised authority over athletics. Institutions that held membership in conferences agreed to follow additional regulations and guidelines. Other than standardizing the rules and providing championships, the NCAA had not been granted power by the

TABLE 9-1

FOUNDING DATES OF SPORT GOVERNANCE ORGANIZATIONS

Boys and Men

1888	Amateur Athletic Union (AAU)
	*1879—National Association of Amateur Athletes of America
1910	National Collegiate Athletic Association (NCAA)
	*1906—Intercollegiate Athletic Association of the United States
1922	National Federation of State High School Associations (NFHS)
1938	National Junior College Athletic Association (NJCAA)
1952	National Association of Intercollegiate Athletics (NAIA)
	*1940—National Association of Intercollegiate Basketball

Girls and Women

1974	National Association for Girls and Women in Sport (NAGWS)
	*1917—Committee on Women's Athletics
	*1927—Women's Athletic Section
	*1932—National Section of Women's Athletics
	*1953—National Section for Girls and Women in Sport
	*1958—Division for Girls and Women in Sport
1971	Association for Intercollegiate Athletics for Women (AIAW)
	*1966—Commission on Intercollegiate Athletics for Women

First Championships Offered for Girls and Women

1916	Amateur Athletic Union
1976	National Junior College Athletic Association
1980	National Association of Intercollegiate Athletics
1981	National Collegiate Athletic Association

*Earlier name of the same organization.

College football in the 1930s.
© University of Georgia/Collegiate Images/Getty Images

institutions to legislate or to mandate eligibility or academic rules. Beginning with the national acceptance of athletic grants-in-aid in the 1950s and throughout the following decade, the role of the NCAA changed dramatically as institutions became willing to relinquish some of their autonomy to the NCAA to ensure that other institutions would comply with the regulations governing grants-in-aid and recruiting. A second development began with the first negotiation of a television contract in 1951, thus providing the NCAA with enforcement leverage. That is, the NCAA could penalize an institution economically for rule violations by disallowing television appearances.

During the last quarter of the twentieth century, the NCAA once again experienced dramatic change. In its Division III programs, students not awarded grants-in-aid continued to compete for the love of their sports, cheered on by a few friends and family and with minimal hope of continuing their athletic careers beyond graduation. While students competing in Division II programs received grants-in-aid, most realized their talents were limited and therefore focused more on the educational opportunities provided them. It was at the Division I level that highly commercialized sports exploded in popularity. Corporate sponsorships, donations from enthusiastic fans (in return for priority seating and other perks), and television contracts became essential to funding the multimillion-dollar budgets needed to support athletic programs at the highest level. Athletic administrators at the approximately 100 "big-time" football and basketball programs finally admitted to being in the entertainment rather the education business. Coaches with multimillion-dollar contracts were hired to win and fired for losing. Athletes received an educational opportunity that was too often not pursued successfully, while universities reaped millions for their performances in the most prestigious bowl games or for making it to the Final Four in basketball. In recent years, with a budget in the hundreds of millions of dollars, primarily from its television contract for the men's basketball championship, the NCAA became the most powerful amateur sports organization in the United States.

Over the years several issues have threatened the integrity of intercollegiate athletics for men, primarily at the NCAA Division I level but increasingly at all levels. Scandals in basketball began to occur in the 1950s and have continued sporadically since then whenever gamblers have been able to entice athletes to affect the point spread of games. Today, the biggest gambling concern is the amount of money that is gambled illegally on collegiate sports. The commercialization of intercollegiate athletics is illustrated by athletic administrators who eagerly seek corporate dollars as they sell logos on uniforms and signage in stadiums and arenas. Will corporate sponsorship of teams be next? Despite mandatory testing, drug use and abuse by college athletes threatens to undermine equity between competitors as some athletes seem to be seeking every advantage to win. Another major issue today is the inordinate influence of television, which often determines dates for competitions, starting times, and sometimes even locations for intercollegiate competitions. Disruption to the educational pursuits of the athletes, who play games during the academic week and arrive back on campus shortly before classes begin the next day, seems irrelevant to institutions reaping the financial revenues promised by national and cable networks.

The two persistent blights that have long plagued men's college sports, however, have been academic problems and recruiting issues. In academics, the use of nonstudents in the late 1800s has been replaced today by preferential admissions, athletes not attending classes, athletic personnel writing athletes' papers, athletes receiving unearned grades, changing of grades to maintain the eligibility of athletes, lack of progress toward degrees, and failure of athletes to graduate. Regarding recruiting, the issues include having someone else take a recruit's SAT or ACT test, making too many contacts with high school athletes, alumni and other athletic supporters giving money or other benefits to prospects and/or their families, and providing sex and alcohol to high school seniors during recruiting visits to college campuses. Despite these issues and the scandals that frequently are exposed, many would argue men's intercollegiate athletics has achieved its highest level of popularity ever and will continue to attract more and more fans.

Collegiate Sports for Women

During the early 1900s, sports for women were strictly controlled by women physical educators, who consistently followed the societal expectations for their gender. Caution about a potential overemphasis on competition or unladylike behavior led to modified rules in several sports. Mass participation in class exercises, field days, play days, and sports days, rather than competitive athletics, became the norm. Because of its healthful benefits, physical education was stressed for girls in schools and women who attended colleges. Outfitted in middy blouses and bloomers, the traditional gymnasium costume of the day, women exercised in mass drills, engaged in Swedish gymnastics, and enjoyed sports such as archery, basketball, field hockey, rowing, and tennis. Some girls and women competed on teams, especially in basketball, until these teams were eliminated by physical educators who believed competitive sports were harmful to females physically, emotionally, and mentally.

In women's colleges, **field days** were normally conducted once or twice a year on campus, and all students were urged to participate. **Play days,** beginning

Basketball, played in bloomers, was the most popular college sport for women in the 1890s and early 1900s.
Source: Library of Congress, Prints and Photographs Division [LC-USZ62-130220]

in the 1920s, provided for social interaction as female students met and formed teams composed of representatives from several institutions. These teams played one or more sports before reassembling for a picnic or other social event. Evolving from these play days were **sports days,** during which college teams competed, frequently in only one sport, but still with the emphasis on social interaction and fun. **Telegraphic meets** enabled females to compete in sports on their own campuses such as swimming, bowling, and archery and compare their times or scores with females from other institutions.

In 1917, the Committee on Women's Athletics was established by the APEA to implement standards and policies that advocated mass participation while vigorously opposing varsity competition. Between 1923 and 1942, the Women's Division of the National Amateur Athletic Federation also opposed highly competitive sports, including those in the Olympic Games, claiming they were inappropriate for women.

In the late 1960s, a gradual change in societal attitudes regarding girls and women in sports paralleled a liberalized philosophy displayed by female leaders in physical education. As long as athletes' welfare was guaranteed and high standards were maintained, competitions were permitted and even encouraged, especially beginning in 1969, when the Commission on Intercollegiate Athletics for Women began sponsoring national tournaments. Two years later, the Association for Intercollegiate Athletics for Women (AIAW), an institutional membership organization, assumed this responsibility. During the next 11 years, the AIAW sponsored championships and established standards and policies governing women's intercollegiate athletics. With equal opportunity mandated by Title IX of the 1972 Education Amendments, colleges and schools financed increased sport competitions for girls and women. In 1976 the NJCAA and in 1980 the NAIA began offering national championships for college women; smaller institutions benefited financially from having one membership fee, one governance structure and set of rules, and similar sport schedules for all athletes.

The NCAA initially opposed Title IX of the 1972 Education Amendments, claiming that its requirement for equal opportunity in all educational programs would adversely affect men's intercollegiate athletics. The NCAA lobbied the Department of Health, Education and Welfare (HEW) for exclusion of athletics from Title IX; they campaigned in support of the Tower Amendment in the U.S. Senate to exclude revenue sports from Title IX jurisdiction; and they turned to the courts, arguing the inapplicability of Title IX to athletics on constitutional grounds. Each of these approaches was unsuccessful (see A Brief History of Title IX in Table 9-2).

Claiming Title IX mandated that the NCAA govern both men's and women's athletics, the NCAA began in 1981 to offer national championships for women in what amounted to a takeover of women's intercollegiate athletics. Even though in the previous decade the AIAW had grown to 960 members and sponsored 42 championships in three competitive divisions in 19 sports, it could not match the NCAA's large financial base, out of which it paid the expenses for women's teams participating in NCAA championships. The NCAA also waived its membership dues for women's athletic teams if its institution was already a member

TABLE 9-2

A BRIEF HISTORY OF TITLE IX

1972	Congress enacts Title IX of the Education Amendments of 1972	Prohibits sex discrimination in any educational program or activity in an institution receiving federal financial assistance
1974	Attempt to exclude revenue-producing sports from Title IX	Senator John Tower introduces legislation (which was not adopted) to exempt revenue-producing sports from inclusion in determining whether an institution was in compliance with Title IX; other, similar attempts fail in 1975 and 1977
1974	Javits Amendment	Senator Jacob Javits's amendment (which was adopted) requires the Department of Health, Education, and Welfare (HEW) to issue Title IX regulations that include specific reference to particular sports
1975	HEW issues final Title IX regulations	Higher education institutions and secondary schools have 3 years to comply with Title IX
1979	HEW issues final policy interpretation on Title IX and intercollegiate athletics	This policy interpretation requires institutions to provide equal opportunity and specifies 3 areas required for compliance: financial assistance (athletic grants-in-aid); program areas such as coaching, facilities, travel and per diem, and tutoring; meeting the interests and abilities of male and female students
1980	Department of Education (DOE) is established	DOE is given oversight of Title IX through the Office for Civil Rights (OCR)
1984	*Grove City vs. Bell*	The Supreme Court rules that the applicability of Title IX in athletic programs is limited to only those programs or activities that receive direct federal financial assistance
1988	Civil Rights Restoration Act	This congressional act overrides *Grove City vs. Bell* and mandates that all educational institutions receiving federal financial assistance, whether direct or indirect, must comply with Title IX

(continued)

TABLE 9-2 (continued)	
A BRIEF HISTORY OF TITLE IX	
1992	*Franklin vs. Gwinnett County Public Schools*	The Supreme Court rules that under Title IX, plaintiffs may receive punitive damages when noncompliance with Title IX is intentional
1993	Gender Equity Study	The National Collegiate Athletic Association publishes its first Gender Equity Study
1996	Policy clarification	OCR issues clarification about how institutions can provide effective accommodations in intercollegiate athletics
1996	First EADA report due	The Equity in Athletics Disclosure Act requires all institutions to make available specific information about their intercollegiate athletic programs
1998	Further clarification about financial aid to athletes	OCR issues clarification about the meaning of substantially equal relative to providing financial aid to male and female athletes
2003	Commission examines how Title IX applies to athletics	In 2002, the Secretary of Education appoints The Commission on Opportunities in Athletics. Its report recommends weakening the application of Title IX to athletics. No changes are made, however, due to a minority report opposing these recommendations and public criticism of the recommendations
2003	Further clarification of intercollegiate athletics policy	OCR reaffirms the regulations and policies of Title IX
2005	Further clarification on the 3-part test	OCR issues clarification that permits the use of a Web survey to determine whether there is sufficient interest to support an additional varsity team for the underrepresented sex; creates a presumption of compliance with part 3 of the 3-part test
2008	Further clarification on participation opportunities	OCR issues clarification about how to ensure that male and female students are provided equal participation opportunities in intercollegiate athletic programs
2010	Further clarification on the 3-part test—part 3	OCR issues clarification that reverses the 2005 clarification on the 3-part test. Specifically, colleges cannot rely on surveys to show they are providing equal athletic opportunities for members of both sexes
2011	DOE policy guidance	DOE clarified that Title IX included protection against sexual harassment and sexual violence applied to all students, including athletes

for its men's programs, and it contracted to televise the women's basketball finals (directly opposite the AIAW's title game). Despite the AIAW's espoused educational model for athletics, which was specifically designed to avoid problems associated with the commercialized male sports model, the AIAW ceased to exist in June 1982. Although a few women have gained some status in the NCAA, such as Judith Sweet, the first female to serve as president, the NCAA is governed predominantly by men. Men hold most coaching and administrative positions in women's athletics within the NCAA as well as in the NAIA and NJCAA.

Jesse Owens won gold medals in the 100-meter, 200-meter, and 400-meter relay races and long jump the 1936 Berlin Olympic Games.
Source: Library of Congress, Prints and Photographs Division [LC-USZ62-27663]

Amateur Sports

The amateur sports scene in the United States outside the colleges remained largely under the direction of the AAU through the 1970s, since this organization sponsored diverse sports competitions for people of all ages. Basketball, boxing, swimming, and track and field especially attracted thousands of participants. Because championships in these sports were offered by NCAA institutions, the 2 organizations frequently clashed. Repeatedly, when the time came for the selection of Olympic teams, controversies raged. In 1922, the National Amateur Athletic Federation was formed to mediate this dispute, with few positive results. The conflicts inevitably affected the athletes because the 2 associations often refused to sanction events, certify records, or permit athletes to participate in each other's events. The Amateur Sports Act, passed in 1978, resolved some of these problems by requiring that each Olympic sport has its own governing body and establishing guidelines governing the selection of these organizations.

For the most part, the spirit of the Olympics promoted by Pierre de Coubertin, founder of the modern games, and perpetuated by the governing International Olympic Committee prevailed during the first half of the twentieth century. The 5 interlocking rings symbolized friendship among the athletes of the world. Competitive superiority remained the ideal until the Olympic Games became the stage for displaying the supremacy of one's national ideology. The boycotts of 1980 and 1984 confirmed the power of politics in international sport competitions.

Commercialism, with its product displays and lucrative television contracts, forever changed the image of these competitions. Media attention and the potential for leveraging medals into athletic endorsements also played significant roles in the commercialization of the Olympics. The 1984 Los Angeles Olympic Games were the first to be commercially successful. Scandals associated with site selection and perks for International Olympic Committee members substantiated the influence of money on these games.

The Olympic Games dramatically changed when Israeli athletes and coaches were captured by Arab terrorists and subsequently killed at the Munich Games in 1972. Security measures costing millions of dollars in each Olympic Games thereafter disrupted the friendly interactions among athletes of the world as well as ease of attendance for spectators, especially following the explosion of a bomb in Centennial Park during the Atlanta Olympic Games in 1996.

The original events of the modern Olympic Games paralleled the popular activities of the turn of the century, such as track and field, gymnastics, fencing, and tennis. While many Olympic sports were associated with elitist clubs for men, including shooting, rowing, yachting, and equestrian clubs, the entry of college males in track and field, swimming, and wrestling broadened the composition of the teams from the United States and thus attracted participants from throughout society. Few women, primarily in swimming (starting in 1912) and track and field (starting in 1928), competed in the Olympics, until the number of sports opened to them increased. The popularity of gymnastics and figure skating, especially for women, has been enhanced through the showcasing of Olympic competitions.

The Olympic Games have been held each 4 years since 1896, except for 3 times during World Wars I and II, and have continued to increase in the number of events offered for males and for females. For example, in the Olympic Games in London in 2012, 10,568 athletes (including 4,676 females) competed in 302 events, quite an increase from the 241 male athletes who competed in 43 events in the first modern Olympic Games in Athens.

Beginning in 1924 in Chamonix, France, the Winter Games provided nations where sports on snow and ice were more popular the opportunity to demonstrate the superiority of their athletes. At the first Winter Games in 1924, 258 athletes

Mildred (Babe) Didrikson won gold medals in the 800-meter hurdles and the javelin throw and a silver medal in the high jump in the 1932 Los Angeles Olympic Games.
© Getty Images

(including 11 females) competed in 16 events; in the 2014 Sochi Winter Games, 2,780 athletes, with over 40% of these athletes females, from a record of 88 countries competed in 98 events. While the Winter Games initially were held in the same year as the summer Olympic Games, in 1994 they were offset by 2 years so each would have a more independent identity.

PLAY TO RECREATION TO FITNESS

Play

The playground movement spread in the early 1900s as the PAA, founded in 1906 by Luther Gulick and Henry Curtis, provided the necessary leadership. Gulick was instrumental in the publication of its monthly magazine, *The Playground.* The provision of adequate playgrounds throughout the country was also enhanced by the support of President Theodore Roosevelt. Clark Hetherington supervised the writing of *The Normal Course in Play* in 1910, which was used to prepare recreation leaders. Joseph Lee, as president of the PAA, helped expand the play concept to include the value of play and recreation for all ages, leading to the reorganization of the PAA in 1911 and its new name, the Playground and Recreation Association of America (PRAA).

Recreation

In 1930, the PRAA became the National Recreation Association (which became the National Recreation and Park Association in 1965), verifying the importance and worth of everyone engaging in recreational activities during leisure hours. The Depression years suddenly gave people large amounts of free time, but many had limited financial resources. The federal government helped in two ways. Federal agencies, such as the Works Progress Administration, provided jobs by funding

Backpacking is one of many popular outdoor activities.
© Royalty-Free/Corbis

construction of camping sites, golf courses, gymnasiums, playing fields, and swimming pools. Once completed, these were opened for mass recreational use. Especially popular sports during the 1930s were bowling and softball.

Wartime production brought the United States out of the Depression. At the same time, sport competitions and recreational programs were initiated to revive the spirits and bodies of soldiers and factory workers. While the armed services used sports for training and conditioning soldiers, industries began to provide sport teams and competitive opportunities for employees, realizing that such activities positively affected productivity and morale. Industrial recreation continued to expand, even after the war ended.

Outdoor education emerged as the recreational thrust of the 1950s. As the country became more mechanized and technological, the appeal of camping, hiking, and similar back-to-nature activities provided people with the chance to get away from daily routines and stress. Some schools and colleges began to offer backpacking, rock climbing, spelunking, winter survival, ropes courses, and orienteering, all of which have maintained their popularity.

As early as the 1930s, Jay Nash promoted carryover, or lifetime, sports within the curriculum. By the 1960s, this philosophy had gained numerous supporters. Led by the Lifetime Sports Foundation with joint sponsorship of the American

High-adventure activities such as white water rafting are exciting pursuits during leisure hours.
© Getty Images RF

Alliance for Health, Physical Education, and Recreation (AAHPER), today's SHAPE America, archery, badminton, bowling, golf, and tennis were introduced into many schools. Slowly programs expanded from offering only team sports to the inclusion of these and other lifetime sports.

Fitness

Historically, fitness as a curricular emphasis surfaced during wartime or times when peace was threatened. Certainly this characterized physical education during the years surrounding World Wars I and II. One of the greatest advocates for physical training for the war effort was Tait McKenzie. Although recognized more for his outstanding sport sculptures, McKenzie used his training as a physical educator and physician in England, his native Canada, and the United States to rehabilitate soldiers injured during World War I. Many other male and female physical educators served as physical training instructors or consultants to the armed forces.

During World Wars I and II in schools and colleges, mass calisthenics and the development of fitness formed the basis of curricula. In peacetime, fitness was seldom emphasized in the educational curriculum. However, during the Cold War years of the late 1950s, all that changed, as many people felt threatened by the rising prominence of the Union of Soviet Socialist Republics (USSR).

The fitness mania began in the 1970s, with joggers leading the craze. In 1970, the lonely runner was suddenly joined by thousands of marathoners and road racers of all ages and males and females, while tennis participants multiplied and swimming became more popular. The pervasiveness of this fitness mania was evident not only by the sport paraphernalia that enthusiasts used and wore but also by the popularity of sporting attire for everyone. However, the people most involved in getting and keeping in shape have come from the middle and upper classes rather than being drawn equally from all economic levels. Also, many school-age children, rather than becoming fitness advocates, have preferred to watch television, play video and computer games, surf the Web, or become sport spectators.

Fitness for Children   The United States was embarrassed by the 1954 results of the Kraus-Weber Minimal Muscular Fitness Test, which indicated that European children demonstrated greater fitness (only 9% failed) than children in the United States (57.8% failed).

As an immediate response to this report and following a national conference on the topic, President Eisenhower established the President's Council on Youth Fitness. This council promoted a minimum of 15 minutes a day of vigorous activity for all children and distributed thousands of copies of *Youth Physical Fitness: Suggested Elements of a School-Centered Program.*

Since the Kraus-Weber Minimal Muscular Fitness Test measured primarily flexibility and abdominal strength (and thus received criticism that it inaccurately assessed overall fitness), the physical education profession developed the AAHPER Youth Fitness Test. To the dismay of professionals, the 1958 results of this 8-item test battery showed that children in the United States had low levels of fitness. Between 1958 and the second national administration of this test in 1965, teachers promoted fitness through daily physical education classes, periodic testing, and

Muscular strength and endurance
can be measured using sit-ups.
© D. Berry/PhotoLink/Getty Images RF

an increased emphasis on the importance of fitness. These efforts were rewarded with improvement by all age groups in all skills, except on one item for 1 gender and age. Unfortunately, these vigorous efforts lapsed, so poor fitness levels among school-age children were reported in the 1980s.

In response to widespread criticism that the AAHPER Youth Fitness Test failed to measure the major components of physical fitness, the AAHPERD (D for dance was added to AAHPER) introduced the Health-Related Lifetime Physical Fitness Test in 1981. While more accurately measuring the recognized components of fitness, these test norms only reconfirmed the lack of fitness among school-age children in the 1980s.

In 1994, AAHPERD joined the Cooper Institute in a collaborative and comprehensive physical fitness education and assessment program. Physical Best, the educational component of the program, helps students develop the knowledge, skills, and attitudes for a healthy and fit life and tries to motivate them to engage in regular, enjoyable physical activity. Physical Best seeks to educate all children about health-related fitness concepts, regardless of their athletic talent and physical and mental abilities. FITNESSGRAM is a computerized reporting system of a health-related physical fitness assessment. FITNESSGRAM allows physical education teachers to easily report their students' fitness levels to parents. (See Table 9-3 for a timeline for youth fitness testing and programs.)

Available data show that the youth fitness goals in *Healthy People 2010* were not achieved. In the wake of the 1996 publication of the Surgeon General's report on *Physical Activity and Health* and the identification of physical inactivity as a primary risk factor contributing to coronary heart disease, the nation's interest in the physical well-being of parents and children alike has never been stronger. Increased concern has been expressed about the rising incidence of obesity in children. Schools, public recreation programs, and private businesses need to combine their efforts to provide greater opportunities for physical education and sport activities for children. Increased funding is needed to provide daily physical education classes for all children, as well as to purchase equipment such as aerobic machines and heart rate monitors. (See the Research View Dispelling Myths Through the Exercise Sciences, which lists a few misconceptions about fitness that have been dispelled through the years.)

TABLE 9-3
TIMELINE FOR YOUTH FITNESS TESTING AND PROGRAMS

1954	Publication of the minimum muscular fitness test of schoolchildren
1956	President Eisenhower creates the President's Council on Youth Fitness
1958	American Alliance for Health, Physical Education and Recreation (AAHPER) Youth Fitness Test published
1965	Update of AAHPER Youth Fitness Test
1976	Update of AAHPERD Youth Fitness Test
1980	AAHPERD Health-Related Physical Fitness Test released
1985	National Children and Youth Fitness Study I results published
1987	National Children and Youth Fitness Study II results published
1987	National FITNESSGRAM developed
1988	Publication of AAHPERD Physical Best
1994	Combination of FITNESSGRAM and AAHPERD Physical Best programs
2012	Presidential Youth Fitness Program launched as a partnership between the President's Council on Fitness, Sports and Nutrition, American Alliance for Health, Physical Education, Recreation and Dance, Amateur Athletic Union, Cooper Institute, and Centers for Disease Control and Prevention

Fitness for All Ages The emphasis on aerobic fitness for individuals of all ages was aided by the 1968 publication of Kenneth Cooper's *Aerobics*. This book outlined a program for helping every adult attain and maintain physical fitness by compiling a certain number of points each week while participating in physical activities. Since the 1970s, many Americans have renewed regular physical activity by playing tennis, softball, and golf; running roadraces and marathons; engaging in skating, wind surfing, and skiing; and purchasing millions of dollars' worth of home exercise equipment. Women, many for the first time, have joined classes in aerobic dance, step aerobics, water aerobics, Pilates, and other variations of exercise combined with music. Health and fitness clubs now offer a variety of aerobics conditioning classes; individualized weight-training programs provided by personal trainers; aerobic machines such as elliptical machines, stair climbers, treadmills, stationary bikes, and rowing machines; and instruction in tennis, racquetball, and golf. Many clubs also offer various sport leagues and tournaments, massage, sports medicine consultation, and nutritional counseling. Some people have suggested that such clubs have replaced social events and bars as the preferred places for meeting and interacting with others. The appearance of fitness is certainly apparent in fashions; many Americans are trying to achieve a level of fitness that both looks and feels good. Unfortunately, this glamorizing of ideal body images may be pushing females into unhealthy exercise and diet habits that can lead to amenorrhea, anorexia, and osteoporosis.

FEDERAL LEGISLATION

Although early leaders of this country, such as Benjamin Franklin and Thomas Jefferson, were promoters of physical education, the federal government did not

RESEARCH VIEW

Dispelling Myths Through the Exercise Sciences

Date	Misconception	What the Research Has Shown
1900s–1950s and earlier	Endurance exercise is harmful to females.	Activities that increase cardiorespiratory endurance are important for females' health.
1950s	Diseases are not related to inactivity.	Heart disease, high blood pressure, obesity, and some types of cancer are directly related to a lack of regular physical activity.
1950s	Exercise is not useful for older individuals.	Older individuals can greatly enhance the quality of their lives through cardiorespiratory, muscular, and flexibility activities.
1900s–1950s and earlier	Weight training will slow an athlete and should be banned.	Strength training is highly effective in enhancing performance as well as helping to prevent injuries.
1900s–1950s and earlier	Endurance training is bad for the heart.	Cardiorespiratory training strengthens the heart and increases its capacity.
1970s	Water should not be consumed during vigorous physical activity and sports.	Fluid replacement is essential in preventing heat-related illness.
1980s	Anabolic steroids are harmless and will have only a minimal effect on the development of strength.	Anabolic steroids have many harmful and irreversible health risks even though they significantly contribute to strength development.
1990s	Children and adolescents are getting enough physical activity through nonschool-based sports programs.	12.7 million children (approximately 17%) and adolescents ages 2 to 19 are obese resulting in increased risks for serious and long-term health problems.
2000s	Sports teach character.	The higher the level and number of years of competition, the greater the likelihood that athletes will act in unethical ways and rationalize their behaviors as the way the game must be played to win.
1950s to present	American children are physically fit.	American children are increasingly obese, and many participate in insufficient regular physical activity.

become involved in physical education issues until recent years. Legislation that directly influences physical education includes mandates for equal opportunity for both genders and for students with special needs.

Coeducational Physical Education

Title IX of the 1972 Education Amendments required equal opportunity in all educational programs and stated as its basic principle that "no person in the United States shall, on the basis of sex, be excluded from participation in, be denied the benefits of, or be subjected to discrimination under any education program or activity receiving federal financial assistance." In relation to physical education, this statement meant it was illegal to discriminate against either gender in curricular content, equipment and facility usage, teacher quality, or other program areas. One specific impact of this legislation was to make school physical education classes coeducational. Boys and girls could be separated by gender for contact sports (such as wrestling). They could also be taught separately in sex education units within health education classes.

Females who learn to lift weights in physical education classes are more likely to continue this strength-development activity outside of school; especially as they learn that lifting weights does not make them masculine, but rather helps build muscle tone and enhance their appearances and self-images as being healthy and fit.
© Nice One Productions/Corbis RF

Although physical education classes comprised of both genders, except in contact sports, was the law, some physical educators and adolescents resisted change. For example, some teachers maintained class rolls that included students of both genders but refused to teach the opposite gender. When classes were comprised of both genders, some teachers favored boys with their instruction or time because they were perceived to be more highly skilled, while other teachers ignored or provided limited instruction to girls. Also, many adolescent boys resisted, such as by not passing balls to girls, having to learn and compete in classes that included both genders.

Despite resistance or personal preferences, Title IX has led to substantial changes. Elementary school children accept classes composed of both girls and boys as the norm. As they participate with and against each other during the developmental years, the differences in their levels of performance lessen. Teachers assess abilities and evaluate performances to ensure fair standards and groupings. Increasingly, students in the secondary schools are accepting of combined classes, learning respect for the capabilities of members of the opposite gender. Gradually acceptance and appreciation of girls and women actively participating in sports have led to recreation and fitness programs that welcome all who seek to enjoy physical activity and develop their physical capabilities.

Adapted Physical Education

Historically, students with special needs were not given opportunities to participate in physical education classes or were assigned to corrective or remedial classes, with a resulting social stigma. The development of adapted programs led to a more individualized approach. **Adapted physical education** is intended for exceptional students who are so different in mental, physical, emotional, or behavioral characteristics that, in the interest of quality of educational opportunity, special provisions must be made for their proper education. Yet not all schools made such provisions for students' special needs; therefore, the federal government became involved.

Section 504 of the Rehabilitation Act of 1973 specified that "no otherwise qualified handicapped person shall, on the basis of handicap, be excluded from participation in, be denied the benefits of, or otherwise be subjected to discrimination under any program which receives or benefits from Federal financial assistance." Thus, every student was guaranteed access to the entire school program, including physical education. The Education Amendment Act of 1974 mandated that all children must be placed in the least restrictive environment, or the setting in which their optimal learning and development could occur.

The Education for All Handicapped Children Act of 1975 (Public Law 94-142) was the first law to specifically mandate physical education in its guidelines. Generally, it required that physical education, specially designed if necessary, be provided for every child with special needs in the public schools within regular physical education classes, unless the student had unusual restrictions; any unusual restrictions were to be provided for through the development of an Individualized Education Program (IEP).

The basic tenets of the Individuals with Disabilities Education Act (IDEA) have remained intact since the original passage of the law in 1975, even though each

Through adapted physical education, individuals with special needs can develop physically as they achieve their individual goals.
© Digital Vision RF

set of amendments strengthened the original law. This legislation fostered significant changes in the lives of children with special needs and their families, and in the roles of schools and teachers who educated children with special needs. The 6 principles of IDEA include free, appropriate public education; appropriate evaluation; an IEP; the least restrictive environment for each child; parent and student participation in decision making; and procedural safeguards. Special education and related services, including the initial evaluation, must be provided at public expense, under public supervision and direction, and delivered by appropriately trained personnel. (In addition, the Americans with Disabilities Act [passed in 1990] sought to eliminate barriers that prevented individuals with special needs from fully participating in society.)

The IEP must be a written plan designed by a representative of the public agency (school) who is qualified to provide or supervise special education and may include the input of the child's teacher, one or both of the child's parents, the child (when appropriate), and other individuals selected at the discretion of the parent or school. One problem in the development of IEPs has been the frequent failure to involve physical educators, even though IDEA specifies that the child's physical activity needs must be met.

An IEP for a student with special needs must include the following as also depicted in Figure 9.3:

- Current performance levels
- Annual goals
- Special education and related services to be provided
- Participation with non-disabled children
- Participation in state and district-wide tests
- Dates and places for services (when, how often, where, and how long)

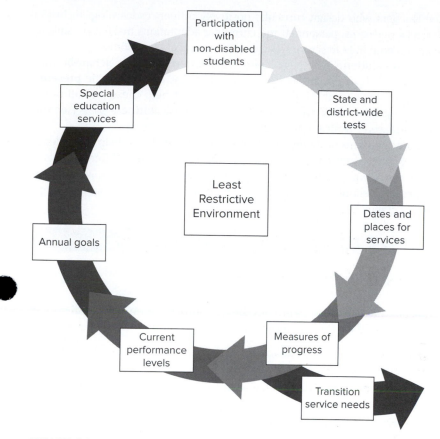

FIGURE 9.3

Least restrictive environment.

- Transition service needs
- Measures of progress

Inclusion is the placement of students with physical, mental, behavioral, or emotional limitations or special needs into regular classes with their peers.

Full inclusion means that even though there may be individual adaptations in class assignments, a child with special needs is placed in a regular educational setting if this is believed to be the best placement. Advocates of full inclusion emphasize that being near and interacting with peers, primarily to foster social skills and build self-esteem or self-image, far outweigh any liabilities. The principles of full inclusion rest on the rights of children to attend their local schools instead of being isolated in special programs. Critical to the success of inclusive classrooms are well-prepared teachers, supplementary aids and services, and support personnel.

Adapted physical educators can work with other physical educators to reap the benefits of teaching in inclusive classrooms. Students can potentially gain respect for classmates with differing abilities. Teachers can create an environment of social acceptance and attempt to foster changed attitudes. The collaboration among students, as well as among the teachers who design curricula, positively influences learning. Inclusion implies that special resources, personnel, and curricular adaptations make it possible to educate all children with mild to severe special needs in regular classrooms.

The inclusion of students who have hearing limitations, are wheelchair-bound, have attention deficit disorder, suffer from cerebral palsy, or are autistic presents significant challenges to the physical educator, who must help these and all other students achieve cognitive, affective, motor skills, and physical fitness goals (see the Research View Adapted Physical Education).

Individualized programs or modified activities may be needed to help all students have successful learning experiences. To make this approach effective, differently sized and weighted pieces of equipment, choices in task dimensions and goals, and variety in evaluation measures should be used. Peer tutors, collaborative teaching, and cooperative learning activities have proven effective in inclusive classes.

RESEARCH VIEW

Adapted Physical Education

Adapted physical educators seek to provide instructional programs for individuals with special needs based on the answers to research questions such as these:

- What are the most effective adaptations that can be made for the wheelchair-bound student during a softball unit of study?
- How can instructional strategies be used to accommodate students with attention deficit disorder?
- What curricular planning and implementation methods should the adapted physical educator utilize to meet the needs of children with emotional and behavioral disorders?
- Why are equipment adaptations essential for children with developmental delays? Which of these are most effective for learning fundamental movement skills?
- What types of evaluations and assessments should be used with children with learning disabilities who are placed in inclusive physical education classes?
- How can learning outcomes other than those associated with physical development be designed so children with special needs can experience success?
- What are the most effective instructional strategies for the physical education curriculum portion of an Individualized Education Program for a child with cerebral palsy?
- What curricular adaptations should be made to help an intellectually gifted child who is obese become physically fit?
- What are the pros and cons of pairing students with special needs with students without physical limitations during physical education classes?

The key approach that complies with federal legislation is the use of the **least restrictive environment.** Each child is placed into the educational setting most appropriate for his or her learning and development. Placement and curricular decisions are based on individuals' abilities and needs, with a continuum of alternatives available from full inclusion to one-on-one instruction. Special classes, such as adapted physical education, should be provided, if needed, to enhance the learning of each child. Although students may learn from one another, students with special needs may also negatively affect the academic environment of other students by increasing class sizes or making the teacher's job more difficult. Rather than automatically including all children with special needs in a regular classroom, each child should be placed in the setting where optimal learning can occur. This least restrictive environment varies from child to child. Whether mentally challenged, learning disabled, emotionally disturbed, or physically limited, all children can benefit from programs appropriate for their developmental levels.

SUMMARY

Today's curricula in physical education provide a blend of gymnastics, play, fitness, health, intramurals, recreation, and sports. The new physical education, beginning in the 1920s, led in this transition, demonstrating that physical education contributes to the complete education of students. Table 9-4 and Box 9.2 highlight many of the significant occurrences in physical education and sport, including the play movement; the growth of women's physical education; the education of the physical movement; the focus on human movement; and the influence of the scientific movement, educational developmentalism, and social education, as well as the establishment of standards and accountability. Leadership from the national association, such as through professional journals or at conferences, and standards for teacher preparation helped solidify physical education into a recognized profession.

Youth sports were organized, yet desirable outcomes at times were threatened by the emphasis placed on winning. Intramural programs were developed to meet the needs of students desiring sport competitions outside of physical education classes but at a lower level than varsity athletics. Collegiate sports for men expanded from their student-organized status into multimillion-dollar business enterprises with extensive regulations and media exposure. Women's sports in the colleges focused on a philosophy of mass participation until the 1970s, when the AIAW encouraged competition and Title IX mandated equality of opportunity. The most visible amateur sport competitions were the Olympic Games.

The play movement for children expanded into recreational activities and then fitness for workers and families. Despite sporadic emphasis on fitness, throughout the twentieth century, many American children did not achieve optimal fitness. Nevertheless, instilling in children a commitment to health-related fitness should be a primary goal of education in the twenty-first century. The federal government has attempted to ensure all Americans have equal educational opportunities by legislating that all schoolchildren, including those with special needs, have the right to physical education.

TABLE 9-4

SIGNIFICANT EVENTS IN PHYSICAL EDUCATION, EXERCISE SCIENCE, AND SPORT

1900	Grammar School Athletic League of Philadelphia created
1903	Public Schools Athletic League formed in New York by Luther Gulick (Girls' Branch began in 1905)
1906	Playground Association of America founded
1910	Teachers College of Columbia University offered the first master's degree with a specialization in physical education
1913	First departments of intramural sports started at the University of Michigan and The Ohio State University
1916	New York became the first state to appoint a Director of Physical Education, Thomas Storey
1924	Teachers College of Columbia University conferred the first Ph.D. with a specialization in physical education
1927	Harvard Fatigue Laboratory established
1930	First publication of the *Journal of Health and Physical Education* and the *Research Quarterly*
1931	Mabel Lee elected first woman president of the American Physical Education Association
1937	The American Physical Education Association merged with the Department of School Health and Physical Education of the National Education Association to form the American Association for Health and Physical Education
1950	National Intramural-Recreational Sports Association established
1954	Results of the Kraus-Weber Minimal Muscular Fitness Test published
1956	President's Council on Youth Fitness established
1958	Administration of the AAHPER Youth Fitness Test began
1965	Lifetime Sports Foundation established
1971	Association for Intercollegiate Athletics for Women established
1972	Title IX of the Education Amendments passed
1975	The Education of All Handicapped Children Act passed
1978	Amateur Sports Act passed
1985	American Alliance for Health, Physical Education, Recreation and Dance celebrated its 100th anniversary
1990	*Healthy People 2000* released by the U.S. Department of Health and Human Services
1991	*Keeping Faith with the Student Athlete: A New Model for Intercollegiate Athletics* issued by The Knight Commission on Intercollegiate Athletics
1996	The Surgeon General's Report on *Physical Activity and Health* published
1996	The centennial Olympic Games held in Atlanta
2000	*Healthy People 2010* released by the U.S. Department of Health and Human Services
2001	*A Call to Action: Reconnecting College Sports and Higher Education* issued by the Knight Commission on Intercollegiate Athletics

(continued)

TABLE 9-4 (continued)
SIGNIFICANT EVENTS IN PHYSICAL EDUCATION, EXERCISE SCIENCE, AND SPORT

2004	*Challenging the Myth* issued by the Knight Commission on Intercollegiate Athletics
2006	The Centers for Disease Control and Prevention issued the School Health Policies and Programs Study, a comprehensive assessment of school health policies and programs in the United States
2006	National Collegiate Athletic Association celebrated its 100th anniversary
2008	The U.S. Department of Health and Human Services issued the *2008 Physical Activity Guidelines for Americans*
2010	*Healthy People 2020* released by the U.S. Department of Health and Human Services
2010	*Dietary Guidelines for Americans* issued
2010	*Restoring the Balance: Dollars, Values, and the Future of College Sports* issued by the Knight Commission on Intercollegiate Athletics
2012	The National Association for Sport and Physical Education issued the *Shape of the Nation Report: Status of Physical Education in the USA*

BOX 9.2   TIMELINE FOR KEY THEMES IN PHYSICAL EDUCATION AND SPORT

To help you frame this century more clearly, a few key events in each decade in the categories of physical education, sports, and physical activity are highlighted in this chart.

1900–1909	**Physical education**—normal schools prepare most teachers
	Sports—increased sports competitions for males between colleges; founding of the National Collegiate Athletic Association (NCAA)
	Physical activity for all—founding of the Playground Association of America (PAA)
1910–1919	**Physical education**—colleges and schools emphasize fitness in response to the war
	Sports—first intramural programs established in colleges
	Physical activity for all—PAA expands to include recreation programs for all ages
1920–1929	**Physical education**—colleges increasingly prepare teachers, who now earn degrees; *The New Physical Education* helps broaden school and college curricula in physical education
	Sports—numerous college football stadiums built or expanded; publication of *American College Athletics*, which exposes problems of commercialization and loss of educational values
	Physical activity for all—the Golden Age of Sports attracts new sports fans; increased interest in recreational activities
1930–1939	**Physical education**—popularity of "education through the physical"; numerous physical education programs cut due to the Depression

(continued)

BOX 9.2   TIMELINE FOR KEY THEMES IN PHYSICAL EDUCATION AND SPORT (continued)

Sports—founding of the National Junior College Athletic Association; founding of Pop Warner Football and Little League Baseball for boys

Physical activity for all—President Franklin Roosevelt's plan for recovery from the Depression results in the construction of numerous playing fields, parks, gymnasiums, and other recreational areas; the inexpensive sports of softball and bowling become popular

1940–1949   **Physical education**—colleges and schools emphasize fitness in response to the war

Sports—return of veterans leads to growth in the popularity of college football, including extensive recruiting and the widespread awarding of athletic grants-in-aid

Physical activity for all—industrial recreation programs popular with men and women

1950–1959   **Physical education**—youth fitness testing and programs to develop fitness are initiated

Sports—founding of the National Association of Intercollegiate Athletics (NAIA); founding of the American College of Sports Medicine

Physical activity for all—the Kraus-Weber Minimal Muscular Fitness Test reports that European children are more fit than children in the United States; outdoor education activities like hiking and backpacking gain in popularity

1960–1969   **Physical education**—the Lifetime Sports Foundation promotes lifetime sports in school curricula

Sports—first Super Bowl in National Football League; increase in popularity of college basketball for men

Physical activity for all—Kenneth Cooper's *Aerobics* launches the popularity of jogging and other aerobic activities for adults

1970–1979   **Physical education**—federal legislation mandates that persons with special needs must have access to physical education

Sports—Congress passes the 1972 Education Amendments, which include Title IX; founding of the Association for Intercollegiate Athletics for Women (AIAW); Congress passes the Amateur Sports Act

Physical activity for all—participation in racquetball, tennis, swimming, and golf increases

1980–1989   **Physical education**—the *National Standards for Physical Education* influence quality of school programs

Sports—NCAA and NAIA offer championships for women; AIAW ceases to exist; National Senior Games begin

Physical activity for all—recreation programs for senior citizens begin to increase dramatically as the population in the United States ages

1990–1999   **Physical education**—school programs, which are threatened by elimination, reductions in class time, and erosion in financial support, emphasize fitness activities to attempt to address the rise in obesity in youth

(continued)

BOX 9.2   TIMELINE FOR KEY THEMES IN PHYSICAL EDUCATION AND SPORT (continued)

Sports—extreme, high risk, and adventure sports, such as rollerblading and snowboarding, become popular

Physical activity for all—Surgeon General's report on *Physical Activity and Health* urges everyone to engage in moderate activity on a regular basis

2000–2010   **Physical education**—programs include challenge activities, use of technologies like heart rate monitors and exergaming, and traditional and non-traditional games, movements, and sports to encourage students to become more physically active to combat the increased prevalence of youth who are obese and overweight

Sports—independent sport organizations offer increased number and levels of competitions for highly skilled young athletes, while professional athletes earn millions of dollars as their popularity grows

Physical activity for all—The *2008 Physical Activity Guidelines for Americans* urges children and adolescents to daily engage in at least 60 minutes of aerobic or strengthening physical activity and adults to engage each week in at least 150 minutes of moderate-intensity or 75 minutes of vigorous-intensity aerobic physical activity

CAREER PERSPECTIVE

Courtesy Michael Nelson

MICHAEL NELSON
Owner: Bodyworks Family Sports Centers, Freedom Fitness
Lubbock, Texas

EDUCATION
B. S., creative writing through the general studies program,
Texas Tech University
M. S., sports medicine/sports health, Texas Tech University

JOB RESPONSIBILITIES AND HOURS

Michael owns his own company, so he is the visionary, leader, steward of resources, and ultimately responsible for everything. As a champion of servant leadership, Michael empowers his employees to ensure they are performing their tasks and roles to optimally serve members, guests, and teammates. His 6 locations and 300 staff serve 23,000 members, so his days are filled with problem solving, and especially resolving people problems, even though there are seldom easy resolutions. As a small business owner, he acknowledges that work hours co-mingle with all other hours since it seems like almost everything he does in some form or fashion has something to do with business. Michael chooses to work Mondays through Fridays between 9 AM and 6 PM and on Saturdays from 9 AM to noon. He keeps office hours, attends meeting, and maintains a presence in his centers in addition is always working on his business even when he is not physically present in one of his locations. More specifically, Michael manages the mail, pays bills, consultants with accountants, and meets with many people like corporate staff, the chief operations officer, marketing folks, vendors, bankers, and community members. As a business owner, he can make between $0 and hundreds of thousands of dollars. He has grown his business through competitive challenges to be successful after over 20 years in operation.

SPECIALIZED COURSE WORK, DEGREES, AND EXPERIENCES NEEDED FOR THIS CAREER

Michael does not believe that coursework or degrees are the keys to success. Rather, he needed the inability to take "no" for answer, willingness to work hard regardless of the cost or time demands, ability to work with and inspire people, and willingness to do whatever it takes, for however long it takes, to achieve his goals. For him, there were no required certifications or specific degrees required, just determination. Michael began as a personal trainer, and while doing this earned 11 certifications specific to this field to establish and enhance his credibility. To earn these credentials, he found anatomy, physiology, and exercise physiology courses beneficial. He wished he had learned more about business operations required of an owner. Nothing can compare, however, with gaining experience and learning growing on the job.

SATISFYING ASPECTS

To Michael, the most satisfying aspects of his career are fulfilling his spiritual mission in life which is to love and serve God by loving and serving people. His dedication to helping people achieve their health and fitness goals, literally saving lives and saving families, is a huge source of personal satisfaction. Helping team members achieve their potential, helping them find their mission in life, and watching how much they grow individually are highly satisfying, too. It has been fun and gratifying to receive accolades from the community, such as being on the cover of *Lubbock Magazine* or the *Texas Techsan,* but being a provider of health and fitness that is helping the community certainly is more important. Of course, there are some stressors, such as paying the bills and knowing his decisions impact the livelihoods of hundreds of individual people and their families. He does not enjoy dealing with dishonest and mean-spirited people.

JOB POTENTIAL

For business owners like Michael, the possibilities and potential are limitless. He believes that since he provides a needed service to the public at a competitive price and convenient time, he will be successful. Since this is not guaranteed, however, Michael continually seeks wisdom, listens, and remains humble.

SUGGESTIONS FOR STUDENTS

Just like Jesus said, if you're going to follow Him, you must count the cost. If you're going to be a small business owner, you must realize that it is going to take more money, hours each day, many years, and tireless effort than you anticipate it will. Others may doubt you, and the challenges and obstacles will at times seem insurmountable. Michael did not issue himself a paycheck the first 6 months he was in business, take a day off for 2 years, and have a vacation for 10 years. He wants students to understand that owning and operating your own business is really hard. Michael advises students to surround yourself with the best people possibly could with expertise in different areas.

KEY POINTS

Luther Gulick	Directed physical training for the New York City Public Schools and established the Public Schools Athletic League (i.e., interscholastic sports)
Thomas Wood	Established physical education and health undergraduate programs at Stanford University and Teachers College of Columbia University and emphasized educational goals achieved through natural activities
Clark Hetherington	Established the four phases of the educational process—organic education, psychomotor education, character education, and intellectual education; emphasized play for children
Jay Nash	Advocated for recreation and lifetime sports as a part of total life experiences for all ages
Jesse Williams	Emphasized education through the physical and the use of physical development as a means to achieving educational objectives
Charles McCloy	Advocated for education of the physical and organic or physical development

Playground movement	Provided public playgrounds for children as a means of social control and assimilation and socialization of immigrant youth into American culture
Recreation movement	Expanded leisure-time pursuits to all ages with decade-long popularity of industrial recreation, outdoor activities, lifetime sports, and fitness activities
Physical fitness	Because of poor results on the Kraus-Weber Minimal Muscular Fitness Test in the mid-1950s, the national association developed a series of fitness tests for school-aged children, with each successive test more representative of the components of physical fitness
Adapted physical education	From a history of exclusion and few opportunities, federal law mandated that a student with any special learning need must be integrated into regular classes, provided with the least restrictive learning environment, and given appropriate accommodations as specified in an Individualized Education Program
Men's intercollegiate athletics	Students promoted, financed, and controlled rowing, baseball, football, and other sports until abuses such as injuries, property damage, class absences, rule confusion, gambling, drunkenness, professionalism, commercialism, and loss of values resulted in faculty and administrative control; the NCAA was formed to 1906 to reform football to address rampant injuries and deaths
Intramurals	Leisure-time activities among students, and funded by students; have expanded to include all types of campus recreation activities
Women's sports	Basketball players restricted to thirds or halves of courts were representative of the perceptions of females as physically and emotionally too fragile for competition; play days and sports days precluded varsity teams; the Association for Intercollegiate Athletics for Women offered national championships for female students
Title IX	Prohibited discrimination by gender in any educational program, including athletics

REVIEW QUESTIONS

1. What was the programmatic theme of Luther Gulick as well as his primary contributions to the field?

2. What was the programmatic theme of Thomas Wood as well as his primary contributions to the field?

3. What was the programmatic theme of Clark Hetherington as well as his primary contributions to the field?

4. What was the programmatic theme of Jay Nash as well as his primary contributions to the field?

5. What was the programmatic theme of Jesse Williams as well as his primary contributions to the field?

6 What was the programmatic theme of Charles McCloy as well as his primary contributions to the field?

7. How and why did the playground movement begin and then evolve into the recreation movement?

8. What is the importance of Section 504 of the Rehabilitation Act of 1973 and The Education for All Handicapped Children Act of 1975 (Public Law 94-142), which today is the Individuals with Disabilities Education Act?

9. Why did faculty initially oppose men's collegiate athletics and subsequently allow them?

10. What philosophy permeated and dominated women's approach to physical activity in the 1920s–1960s and how did this change with the establishment of the Association for Intercollegiate Athletics for Women?

STUDENT ACTIVITIES

1. Interview someone in the sports information office, athletic department, library, or news bureau who can help you learn about the earliest intercollegiate men's and women's sports programs at your institution. Based on this and on information you can obtain from other sources, write a two-page description of each program.

2. Write a three-page comparison of the philosophies and major contributions of the "new physical educators."

3. Learn about the test items of the FITNESSGRAM. Divide into groups and administer these test items to classmates.

4. Select one person discussed in this chapter. Write a three-page description of his or her contributions to physical education, exercise science, and sport.

5. Conduct a class debate about whether the most appropriate theme for physical education should be "education through the physical" or "education of the physical."

6. Write a five-page paper comparing the major developments in men's and women's intercollegiate sports in the twentieth century.

REFERENCE

National Education Association. (1894). *NEA Proceedings, 32,* 621.

WEB CONNECTIONS

1. www.ncpad.org/

   A plethora of information about adapted physical education and physical activity awaits the visitor to the Web site of the National Center on Physical Activity and Disability.

2. www.ncaapublications.com/p-4039-in-the-arena-the-ncaas-first-century.aspx

   This site provides a link to a comprehensive history of the NCAA that can be downloaded. The title is "In the Arena: The NCAA's First Century."

3. www.active.com/

   This site can help individuals of all ages live actively by using its resources about training and fitness, healthy living, outdoor adventure, and summer sports camps.

4. www.ed.gov/pubs/TitleIX/index.html

   The Department of Education provides a 25-year description of the progress in equal opportunity in educational programs achieved as a result of Title IX of the 1972 Education Amendments.

5. www.fitness.gov/

   Learn about the work of the President's Council on Fitness, Sports and Nutrition as it seeks to educate and empower Americans through regular physical activity and good nutrition.

6. www.fitnessgram.net

   This site provides information about the FITNESSGRAM, a fitness assessment and personal physical activity management program for schools.

7. www.ed.gov/parents/needs/speced/iepguide/index.html

   A Guide to the Individualized Education Program is designed to assist educators, parents, and state and local educational agencies in implementing the requirements of Part B of the Individuals with Disabilities Education Act.

8. www.nrpa.org/

   Find a wealth of resources at this site of the National Recreation and Park Association, which is dedicated to advancing parks, recreation, and environmental conservation efforts to enhance the quality of life for everyone.

IMPORTANCE OF PHYSICAL EDUCATION, EXERCISE SCIENCE, AND SPORT FOR EVERYONE

3

© Comstock Images RF

CHAPTER

10

OPPORTUNITIES AND CHALLENGES IN PHYSICAL EDUCATION AND EXERCISE SCIENCE

LEARNING OUTCOMES

- Students will be able to explain how exercise and sport scientists have expanded their research and the application of knowledge to help address fitness and other quality of life issues for individuals in the United States.
- Students will be able to differentiate among the curricula and methodology of elementary, middle, and secondary school physical education programs.
- Students will be able to describe the instructional and operational challenges facing physical educators and exercise and sport scientists as they serve students and clients.
- Students will be able to articulate how to prevent or ameliorate career burnout.

Being physically active is an important key to an enhanced quality of life for individuals of all ages. Providers of recreational and leisure services must adapt to changing demographics, family structures and schedules, work patterns, and economic realities while enhancing the quality of their programs. Fitness specialists and exercise scientists in various settings work with adults to help them establish and maintain lifelong activity programs. Specialization, research, technology, and the scholarly pursuit of knowledge are significant factors in the expansion and recognition of careers associated with physical activity. Changes in school programs should guarantee opportunities for all people to meet their unique needs while engaged in progressively challenging experiences. Daily physical education for students, changes in certification requirements, and increased teacher competencies, are related efforts to improve the quality of education for students. Challenges confronting school physical educators include limited equipment and facilities, lack of parental support for education, and disciplinary problems.

VALUE OF PHYSICAL ACTIVITY FOR EVERYONE

Physical activity is for everyone. But convincing people of this fact remains a major challenge. However, as listed in Box 10.1, significant and lasting values result from participating regularly in physical activity.

From students' perspectives, the intrinsic rewards of physical activity and sport are having fun and the pure excitement and pleasure of moving. Added to these, the objectives of physical education in the schools include learning and applying fitness concepts, learning motor and fundamental sport skills, encouraging lifetime fitness, gaining knowledge about sport rules and strategies, and enhancing social and emotional development. As discussed in Chapter 1, teachers can meet these objectives only by making them a central focus of their work and teaching them consistently to ensure their achievement. Teachers must provide quality programs and promote their value to school administrators, policy makers, and parents.

BOX 10.1   VALUE OF PHYSICAL ACTIVITY

According to the American Heart Association (AHA), physical inactivity is a major risk factor for coronary artery disease and contributes to obesity, high blood pressure, high blood cholesterol, and diabetes. The AHA recommends getting the equivalent of at least 150 minutes of moderate intensity aerobic physical activity each week by incorporating 30 minutes a day of physical activity on at least 5 days. This physical activity should include flexibility and stretching exercises and muscle strengthening activity at least 2 days each week.

The AHA stresses the importance of physical activity because it

- Improves blood circulation, which reduces the risk of heart disease
- Keeps weight under control
- Helps in the battle to quit smoking
- Improves blood cholesterol levels
- Prevents and manages high blood pressure
- Prevents bone loss
- Boosts energy level
- Helps manage stress
- Releases tension
- Promotes enthusiasm and optimism
- Counters anxiety and depression
- Helps you fall asleep faster and sleep more soundly
- Improves self-image
- Increases muscle strength
- Reduces risk of stroke
- Establishes good heart-healthy habits in children and counters the conditions that lead to heart attack and stroke later in life
- Helps delay or prevent chronic illnesses and diseases associated with aging and maintains quality of life

Children and youth must learn healthful living habits while in school because many will not attend college or be able to afford fitness club memberships or personal exercise equipment. During the critical elementary years, students need to learn how to develop cardiorespiratory endurance, with a focus on frequency, intensity, and duration of exercise along with participating in a variety of physical activities. They need to learn to walk, jog, swim, cycle, and jump rope as alternative ways to develop aerobic endurance. They need to learn how to attain and maintain muscular strength, endurance, and flexibility because these health-related fitness components will enhance not only how they feel but also their ability to study, work, and play more easily and productively. Closely aligned with these needs is the importance of teaching children how to enhance their basic motor skill development, which will be beneficial throughout life. Basic throwing, catching, striking, and loco-motor movements are easily transferable to tennis, golf, bowling, dance, and other lifetime activities. Teachers should demonstrate and positively reinforce development of cooperative behaviors, teamwork, fair play, and the ability to be a follower and a leader. Individually, students will nurture self-confidence and self-worth by successfully achieving personal goals. Concurrent with these psychomotor and affective outcomes, teachers should ensure children are provided information about nutrition, diseases, environmental concerns, and the harmful effects of drugs.

Teachers should invite school administrators, policy makers, and parents to observe how their physical education classes are achieving these objectives. Hosting Parent-Teacher Association or Organization (PTA/PTO) programs, parents' nights, mall demonstrations, and other special events shows physical education is vital to the health and well-being of students.

At the high school level, the emphasis on fitness development, lifetime sports, and health issues such as not smoking or using drugs, sex education, and nutrition should continue. At this level, it is especially important to give students some options for what sports and activities they want to learn. Although some consumer information may be relevant at an earlier age, the teen years lend themselves well to consumer education. Adolescents need to learn how to differentiate between the facts and fallacies of fitness ads. Although some home exercise equipment, such as elliptical trainers or exercise bicycles, can improve one's fitness if used properly, machines that supposedly help a person lose weight without effort blatantly misrepresent the truth. What are the caloric and nutritional components of the average fast-food meal? Are any diet centers or diet programs safe or worth the money? Should a person smoke cigarettes or marijuana? What are the effects of alcohol on the body and its fitness? Given the need for answers to these questions and the potential benefits of school physical education, it is imperative schools fund physical education and health education curricula.

Opponents of such funding claim that physical education is nonessential. According to the Centers for Disease Control and Prevention, between 1976–1980 and 2007–2008 obesity increased from 5.0% to 10.4% among preschool children aged 2–5, from 6.5% to 19.6% among youth aged 6–11, and from 5.0% to 18.1% for adolescents aged 12–19. Others argue community programs and interscholastic athletics

Outdoor activities are popular for fitness and fun.
© Liquidlibrary/Dynamic Graphics/Jupiterimages RF

can provide students with adequate sports and fitness opportunities. However, due to the cost and additional time, many students (especially those who drop out of school) will never participate in these programs. In addition, most community-sponsored programs stress competition rather than instruction.

The American Academy of Child and Adolescent Psychiatry reports that children in the United States watch an average of 3 to 4 hours of television each day. This professional organization states that children who watch a lot of television are more likely to have lower grades, read fewer books, exercise less, and be overweight. Given the negative outcomes associated with excessive television watching and inactivity, parents need to realize the importance of stressing an activity-filled life for their children, as well as modeling this for them. Parents also need to work with schools to ensure children and adolescents are learning movement, fitness, and sport skills, so they will be more likely to continue to engage in a variety of physical activities outside of school.

Many colleges in the United States have eliminated their required physical education programs because of budget limitations and an increasing emphasis on general education and requirements of specialized majors. In many of the programs at institutions where physical education is an elective, these programs have had to become entirely self-supporting. Students may elect any activity course available, but they must pay instructional, facility usage, and equipment rental fees. On other campuses, this pay-as-you-participate approach applies only to certain off-campus or non-traditional courses. This type of program is limited to those who are genuinely interested in a particular activity or sport and who can afford to enroll in it. Unfortunately, at universities with elective programs, those who need physical education the most may not choose to enroll.

Exercise and sport scientists may prescribe walking as part of an aerobic conditioning program for clients.

© Dan Tremain/Getty Images RF

In 1992, the American Heart Association (AHA) added physical inactivity to high blood pressure, smoking, and high blood cholesterol as a significant contributor to heart disease. Despite this focus, the majority of adults in the United States do not participate in a regular physical activity program. As a result, 35% of adults are obese. (See www.cdc.gov/obesity/data/adult.html for a graphic representation of the dramatic increase in obesity in the United States between 1985 and the present.) Some inactive, overweight adults, however, are changing their habits. As middle-aged and senior citizens join the millions of others who are walking to stay fit, these segments of the population reinforce the importance of being physically active. To help avoid becoming the next coronary statistic, many older Americans are quitting smoking, reducing alcohol consumption, ridding their diets of many sources of cholesterol, and exercising. Popular exercise and recreational activities include walking, swimming, fishing, camping, aerobics, and bowling. For those with physical limitations, many retirement homes, recreation departments, churches, and hospitals are providing opportunities for movement, sports, and recreational pastimes. Providing for the leisure needs of older Americans may become the largest segment of new physical activity-related jobs in this century.

BOX 10.2   PROGRAM ADHERENCE FACTORS

The transtheoretical model describes how individuals acquire positive behaviors; it is based on the premise that behavioral changes occur over time and progress sequentially through five stages. In stage one, people are unmotivated or resistant to engaging in regular physical activity. In stage two, while people are thinking about the costs and benefits of engaging in some type of physical activity, they also may continue to be ambivalent or procrastinate. In stage three, people are beginning to make preparations for changing their inactive lifestyles, such as by joining a fitness class, getting a physical examination, or buying a self-help book. In stage four, people begin to engage in regular physical activity, yet they must be vigilant against relapse into inactivity by using one or more of the program adherence factors listed below. In stage five, people are maintaining their regular physical activity program as they become more committed to making it a permanent part of their lives.

- Set realistic exercise goals and commit to achieving them.
- Tailor your exercise program to fit your current fitness level and lifestyle.
- Meet your physician's expectations for addressing a health concern through exercise.
- Implement a safe, individualized, and progressive program.
- Participate in fun and satisfying activities.
- Ensure access to facilities at convenient times.
- Ensure proper supervision that includes education about exercise and helps with motivation.
- Develop a positive feeling about exercise and how it can affect your health.
- Keep records of your exercise program and periodically reward yourself for making progress.
- Get periodic assessments and associated feedback about your fitness level.
- Receive support and encouragement from family members, friends, and peers.
- Build your self-efficacy, or the optimistic assessment that you can cope with the demands of life by continuing your exercise program.
- Develop a strong belief that you can overcome barriers and succeed with your exercise program.
- Include periodic social functions with others in your exercise group.
- Be patient because developing fitness takes time.
- Ensure that your exercise program has meaning by connecting with a personal need.

See also the special issue, Adherence to Exercise and Physical Activity (2001). *Quest 53*(3), 277–387.

Once people are convinced regular exercise is not only important but essential for an enhanced quality of life, the next challenge is how to get those who have begun exercise programs to continue them. Adherence is a pervasive problem for everyone who prescribes exercises and activities. Whether a corporation or an individual is paying for the exercise program, the goal is positive, lasting outcomes. Box 10.2 lists several factors that contribute to activity adherence. Most adult exercise programs emphasize similar strategies to enhance lasting and positive lifestyle changes. Most important, all people need appropriately designed programs they can understand; goals that are feasible, measurable, and monitored; and positive experiences that will encourage them to adhere to their programs.

BOX 10.3   PHYSICAL ACTIVITY TIPS

General Suggestions

- Schedule a time for daily physical activity of at least 30 minutes.
- Vary your physical activities to maintain enthusiasm and interest.
- Find a partner to join you so you can help each other adhere to your physical activity programs.
- Set realistic goals, measure your progress, and reward yourself when you are successful.
- Include physical activities that contribute to all-around physical fitness including to develop and maintain cardiorespiratory endurance, muscular strength and endurance, and flexibility.
- Use time while engaged in physical activity to socialize with others.
- Make sure your equipment and exercise area are safe.
- Combine physical activity with healthier eating patterns.
- Have fun and enjoy being physically active.

Build Exercise into your Daily Life

- Walk to work or school and walk when doing errands.
- Park your car farther away from your destination so you will walk more.
- Take the stairs instead of the elevator or escalator.
- Take short fitness breaks during the day to walk around or execute a few exercises at or beside your desk.
- Schedule times to play with your children or walk your pets.
- Exercise while watching television, such as by lifting hand weights, riding a stationary bicycle, walking on a treadmill, or stretching.
- Exercise while listening to music or work out with an exercise DVD.

Physical activity should be a part of everyone's life regardless of age or capability as stated in the *2008 Physical Activity Guidelines for Americans*. Some physical activity suggestions are provided in Box 10.3. The earlier in life people learn the value of being physically fit and begin exercising regularly, the greater the quality of their lives.

RECREATION AND LEISURE SERVICES

Demographic changes, altered family and work patterns, environmental concerns, and shifts in the economy have transformed contemporary recreation and leisure services. An increasingly diverse ethnic mix in the population of the United States makes business as usual no longer acceptable. African Americans, Native Americans, Asian Americans, Hispanics, and other ethnic groups are demanding recreational and artistic programs that appeal to their unique cultural backgrounds. The former melting pot concept has given way to an appreciation and promotion of diversity throughout society, which means these changes must be reflected in leisure programming.

Demographics indicate a graying of America. The older segment of the population possesses considerable political clout and financial resources. As life expectancies increase, older adults want to have their recreational needs met along with those of younger groups. Senior citizens are often physically vigorous. While some may require only passive activities in a retirement center, other retirees robustly play golf and tennis, walk and hike, travel and tour, and swim and cycle. In this century, serving the recreational and leisure needs of this population will become more widespread and demanding. Seniors want more opportunities for:

- Masters competitions in sports such as tennis, swimming, golf, and running
- Senior Games in numerous sports
- Age- and ability-appropriate activity classes at health and fitness clubs
- Age- and ability-appropriate activity programs sponsored by recreation departments
- Walking clubs
- Sport leagues, such as in bowling, golf, and softball
- Therapeutic programs sponsored by senior citizen programs, retirement centers, and hospitals
- Intergenerational after-school activity programs for children and senior citizens

The traditional 1950s family of a working father, a homemaking mother, and two or three children characterizes fewer than half of today's families with school-age children. Divorced parents, broken homes, and absent fathers leave approximately one out of every two children in single-parent homes before they reach adulthood. The cost and quality of child care have become major issues for these parents. Meeting the developmental play needs of preschool children challenges those who offer in-house or commercialized child-care services. Currently schools, places of worship, and public centers offer after-school care for children, which may or may not include developmentally appropriate play opportunities.

Many adolescents (and some preadolescents) have become latchkey kids—children who come home from school to empty houses. These unattended children are told to lock themselves in their houses because playing outside is considered unsafe. This setting seems to foster unending hours of watching television and eating junk food. Lack of supervision may also permit youthful experimentation with alcohol, tobacco, illegal drugs, sex, and law-breaking activities.

In most cities and towns, schools, recreation departments, and private clubs provide numerous alternatives to unsafe, inactive, and delinquent behaviors. Competitive youth sports teams, children's fitness clubs and programs, adventure activities, cooperative games, and creative playground opportunities are just a few of the options available. While some parents can afford to enroll their children in private dance, gymnastics, swimming, or tennis lessons, many rely on public programs for facilities, equipment, and instruction.

Threats to the environment also jeopardize the resources available for recreation and leisure. Outdoor enthusiasts are increasing their efforts to protect natural resources and open spaces from abusive individuals and encroaching real estate developers. Rock climbers, hikers, and campers are expected to leave nature exactly as they found it. Industries are expected to stop polluting the air, water, and land. Despite limited resources, cities and states continue to dedicate land to meeting the recreational needs of present and future generations.

Like many public programs, recreation and leisure services have experienced increased budgetary constraints. Although people are taxed for municipal services, including recreation, there never seems to be enough money, space, or programs. To meet their budgets, many recreation departments must charge entry or participation fees, which excludes those unable to pay. In addition to the rising cost of

Outdoor education activities, such as rock climbing, can be learned and practiced in publicly provided settings.

© Valerie Loiseleux/Getty Images RF

programming, these agencies have increased expenses due to vandalism, lawsuits, and security. In addition, bringing programs and facilities into compliance with the Americans with Disabilities Act is costly. To adequately serve individuals with limitations, facilities must be accessible, have specialized recreational equipment, and have qualified, trained personnel.

Recreation and leisure services are among the human services industries that have proliferated in recent decades. Individuals pursuing careers in national and state parks, boys' and girls' clubs, commercial and corporate fitness, sport clubs, and recreation must focus on customer or client satisfaction. To accomplish this, they must determine the personal goals of those they serve. For example, those who choose careers offering backpacking, rock climbing, and canoeing may have the following goals in mind for program participants:

- To learn outdoor skills
- To challenge the limits of one's ability
- To enjoy risk-taking achievements
- To develop cooperative or self-reliant behavior
- To appreciate nature

Knowing these goals, professionals can propose suitable programs to meet participants' goals or help them design individualized or group programs.

EXERCISE SCIENCE

More and more students are pursuing careers related to physical activity outside educational settings. Many prepare for these careers by studying exercise science, where one studies human movement along with the body's adaptations to movement. The exercise scientist seeks to understand the scientific foundations of physiological responses to exercise. This field has grown more specialized as the quantity and quality of knowledge have expanded.

In the 1970s and 1980s, colleges responded to the decrease in physical education majors preparing to teach by offering specializations. Students were attracted to these majors because they sought careers in the emerging fields of athletic training, corporate and commercial fitness, exercise physiology, and sport psychology. Most of these graduates sought positions that allowed them to work with adults participating in fitness and sport programs. The diversity of career options and opportunities for advancement, travel, economic security, research, and management also appealed to many.

In recent years, career options in exercise science have increased due to the media-reinforced appeal of cosmetic fitness; concern about health conditions related to lifestyle, such as coronary heart disease and obesity; and skyrocketing health care costs. Those most likely to participate in fitness programs are upper-income individuals, young adults, males, Caucasians, suburban residents, and the more highly educated, although fitness enthusiasts occupy every demographic stratum. Fitness specialists find their greatest challenge is trying to motivate individuals to initiate and maintain activity programs through self-discipline. The two most

Exercise scientists investigate how to help athletic teams improve their flexibility, strength, and endurance, which in turn can help improve performance.
© Juice Images/Alamy RF

frequent explanations for not exercising are lack of time and poor motivation or self-discipline.

Fitness programs have expanded in private and public health and sport clubs, recreation departments, retirement homes, work sites, rehabilitation clinics, hotels, and resorts. Many people have joined clubs specifically to receive instruction and encouragement from fitness leaders and personal trainers in aerobics and weight training. Besides teaching, individuals in these careers are expected to prescribe safe exercise programs, monitor members' progress, provide nutritional guidance, manage the facility, and sometimes supervise other personnel. Fitness specialists and exercise scientists are expected to conduct smoking cessation classes, provide information about injury prevention and care, teach exercises to reduce low back pain, conduct assessments of various fitness parameters, prescribe exercise programs for rehabilitation, and conduct clinical research. Undergraduate students need to be prepared to handle these diverse responsibilities. Increasingly, graduates of exercise science curricula are working with adults (and sometimes children) in health and fitness programs. As described in previous chapters, these professionals are challenged to direct and manage programs that help unfit Americans develop and maintain personal fitness, provide recreational opportunities in a wide variety of sports and games, and offer leisure-time activities that may include spectator events, cruises, and trips to theme parks.

College graduates may need to obtain certifications to work in exercise science positions. More and more health and fitness clubs are expecting their employees to hold certifications as personal trainers, aerobics leaders, and fitness program directors. Almost all individuals responsible for providing emergency care to athletes in sport competitions are expected to have training in basic first aid and cardiopulmonary resuscitation. Athletic trainers in colleges, in clinics, and with professional teams must be certified. States and employers are increasingly requiring higher levels of expertise to ensure that only qualified individuals work in physical activity situations. Exercise scientists working in clinical settings, such as hospitals, research laboratories, and rehabilitation clinics, need to demonstrate competencies in areas such as the following:

- The structure and function of the human body and its systems
- The operation of muscles and joints through various movements, such as supination, pronation, flexion, extension, adduction, and rotation
- The major components of skill-related physical fitness, including agility, balance, coordination, power, reaction time, and speed, and the biomechanical principles underlying these components
- The biomechanical principles associated with striking, throwing, catching, running, walking, and jumping
- The ability to accurately measure body fat, blood pressure, heart rate, and oxygen consumption during exercise
- The ability to explain, demonstrate, and prescribe the physiological principles associated with warm-ups and cool-downs
- The ability to explain, demonstrate, and prescribe appropriate cardiorespiratory endurance activities
- The ability to explain, demonstrate, and prescribe exercises designed to increase muscular strength and endurance
- The ability to explain, demonstrate, and prescribe appropriate flexibility exercises
- The care and prevention of common exercise injuries
- The genetic and cellular basis of disease
- The prevention and treatment of chronic illnesses
- The determinants of oxygen consumption under differing conditions of exercise

Most people who seek the services of an exercise scientist want to develop all-around wellness. Physical activity is only one component of all-around wellness; increasingly, people are also seeking emotional, spiritual, intellectual, and social benefits. Many want to find balance through their workouts, leading to stress reduction, increased self-esteem, friendships, and peace of mind. This means program and exercise leaders must prepare themselves to address the whole person, not just the body. The expansion in program offerings in health and fitness clubs to include massage, yoga, Pilates, nutrition counseling, stress management workshops, and musical and artistic outings along with personal fitness programs reflects this broadening focus.

INTERDISCIPLINARY RESEARCH

The knowledge explosion in recent years has influenced research in the exercise and sport sciences. Expanded research efforts, technological advances, and computer-assisted data analyses have aided this proliferation. The quality and quantity of information have led to increasing specializations for two primary reasons. First, the sheer volume of books, research, reports, resources on the web, and scholarly papers, many of which can be accessed electronically, makes it difficult for individuals to gain extensive knowledge. Second, a greater understanding of a discipline encourages people to specialize in an area of particular interest to create and disseminate new knowledge. In turn, this greater understanding may lead to enhanced sport performances or strategies to improve health.

The quantity of scholarly publications and presentations in physical education and the exercise and sport sciences continues to increase. Responding to institutional mandates, specialists with Ph.D.s are dedicating themselves to expanding knowledge in their areas of specialization. They pursue research questions such as how to improve athletic performance, how to enhance the process of teaching and learning movement skills, and how to maximize muscle mass and flexibility using certain types of exercise equipment. Exercise and sport science professionals in clinical settings, corporate fitness centers, recreation programs, and fitness and health clubs conduct research on various fitness programs, training regimens, and success rates among their clientele.

A growing area of research in physical education focuses on student learning. Pedagogical studies include teaching observations such as analyses of time-on-task and academic learning time, student performance, and teacher expectations, and how these factors are interrelated. Research about collaborative learning strategies has the potential to dramatically affect the quality of student learning.

Technology also has contributed to the proliferation of research in the exercise and sport sciences. Athletes can now recover from injuries faster through advanced surgical techniques and computer-monitored rehabilitation programs. Data collection on the incidence and causes of injuries has been used to redesign conditioning and practice drills to both reduce injury and enhance rehabilitation. Sport psychologists use biofeedback and relaxation techniques to positively affect performance. Biomechanists apply computer technology to skill execution to both improve technique and reduce the risk of injury. Computer analyses of blood lactates, oxygen exchange, workloads, and drug effects are invaluable to the exercise physiologist's understanding of how the body functions under the stress of exercise. Sport sociologists and sport historians collaboratively examine the role of sport in society relative to race, gender, and other cultural factors.

Library retrieval systems and Web search engines help researchers in all disciplines keep abreast of current research, trends, and experimental data. Access to information available electronically allows researchers to replicate studies or build on the findings of their colleagues. Various technologies help researchers collaborate in a timely manner. The use of personal computers for word processing, data analyses, and information retrieval through the Internet, and the productivity of today's college, corporate, and community researchers facilitate greater collaboration and interdisciplinary research. Physicians, sport psychologists, sport biomechanists, exercise physiologists, and athletic trainers share their expertise and research electronically to the benefit of students, world-class athletes, and the general public. The federal government provides funding for interdisciplinary research because of its far-reaching applications and potential benefits.

Exercise and sport scientists are frequently criticized for failure to apply their findings. Technology can partly alleviate this problem by emphasizing practical as well as theoretical studies, disseminating new information more widely, and focusing on specific situations in need of change. For example, those participating in various weight loss programs could be outfitted with heart rate monitors to ensure they are exercising within their target heart rate zones. Careful record-keeping with regard to heart rates, diets, frequency and duration of exercise, and types of activities, exercise and sport scientists, along with athletic trainers, aerobics instructors, and fitness program directors, not only would add to the base of knowledge concerning weight loss but also has more scientific measures by which to compare various weight loss programs. Exercise and sport scientists who benefit from such findings have a responsibility to work with researchers in applying new information.

It is incumbent on fitness, exercise, and sport professionals to remain current with the latest research. (See the Research View Conducting Research in the Exercise and Sport Sciences, which provides guidance for this process.) Regardless of position held, the knowledge explosion has made the half-life of information learned in college, graduate school, or certification courses short-lived. That is, the relevancy and even accuracy of information you acquire while obtaining your physical education or exercise science degree may be wrong, dangerous, or questionable a decade after you graduate. A few examples follow. Once-popular exercises such as squat thrusts are now contraindicated. Withholding fluid replacement from athletes, which was once thought to build stamina or toughness, is very dangerous; such an action today would be the basis for a wrongful-death lawsuit if an athlete died after being denied fluids. Some drugs taken to enhance performance or build muscular strength may be legal today but banned tomorrow if new research determines they are harmful to the body. Thus, lifelong learning is imperative, particularly with regard to research in your specialty.

ELEMENTARY SCHOOL PROGRAMS

Since the early 1900s, elementary school physical education programs have focused on teaching fundamental movement skills that lead directly to the ability to play sports and games. As curricula evolved, greater emphasis was placed on a balanced and varied range of activities that progressed from simple to complex in keeping with learning developmental skills of the various grade levels. These activities included simple games and relays, rhythmic activities, basic sport skills, lead-up games, and game play. Professional preparation courses and textbooks stressed the importance of progressions, allotments of time for each major category of activity, and instructional methodology.

🔍 RESEARCH VIEW

Conducting Research in the Exercise and Sport Sciences

When searching for research-based articles in the exercise and sport sciences, start with an index into which you enter a subject area or a few keywords. The indexes below are recommended:

- **Medline Plus** (www.nlm.nih.gov) is the U.S. National Library of Medicine journal citation database. The world's most comprehensive source of life sciences and biomedical bibliographic information provides over 22 million reference citations.
- **Academic Search Premier** (www.ebscohost.com/academic/academic -search-premier/) is the world's largest scholarly, multi-discipline, full-text database designed specifically for academic institutions.
- **ABI/INFORM** (http://www.proquest.com/products-services/abi_inform_ complete.html) is a business research database that includes content from newspapers, working papers, business cases, dissertations, and much more.
- **SPORTDiscus** (https://www.ebscohost.com/academic/sportdiscus-with-full -text) is considered the world's leading sport, fitness, and sports medicine bibliographic database and included full-text articles from most journals.
- The **Physical Education Index** (http://www.proquest.com/products -services/pei-set-c.html) searches coaching, health, history, physical education, physical fitness, physical therapy, recreation, sports, sports medicine, teaching methods, and training.

Additional Helpful Information

See this reference from the American Psychological Association (APA) for how to cite electronic documents (http://www.apastyle.org/learn/tutorials/basics-tutorial.aspx).

In the 1960s, an alternative elementary physical education curriculum, called movement education, was introduced in the United States. It was based on the concepts of spatial and body awareness; movement qualities of flow, force, space, and time; and relationships to others or objects. Students learned about their own space relative to body size, movement task, and equipment, thereby gaining insights into their own capabilities and becoming more skillful movers. Movement education stressed the following:

- Lessons were activity centered and student centered.
- Specific movement patterns were determined by each child within parameters established by teachers, emphasizing experimentation through movement rather than simply following instructions.
- Children were encouraged to explore and analyze space, their bodies, and various uses for pieces of equipment, with a focus on self-directed or individualized learning.

- Problem solving through guided discovery emphasized learning and fun using open-ended challenges and goals.
- The teacher guided students through movement experiences by imaginatively and creatively involving their minds and bodies.
- Independently and at their own rates of development, children were given time to think about the challenges and then move in response.
- Each child was evaluated on an individual basis.
- Informality in class structure allowed children to create freely and learn at their own levels of achievement.

Today, in addition to selecting elementary physical education curricula that match their personal philosophies, teachers must be aware of state standards and district curricular requirements. Each elementary school child should develop competency in several movement forms, learn to express and communicate through movement, and be able to demonstrate movement principles while learning motor skills. In addition, children can begin to achieve a high level of health-related physical fitness, gain greater self-understanding and acceptance of themselves and others, and learn how to handle winning and losing appropriately.

Each elementary physical education program should be centered on the concept that movement is a child's first expressive opportunity. Since it is through movement experiences and challenges that the world is discovered, these must be developmentally appropriate for the age, size, and maturational level of each child. For example, parallel and cooperative activities are developmentally appropriate for 5- to 7-year-olds, whereas team sports are not. Dodgeball, relays, and musical

Elementary school students enjoy exploring various movement experiences.
© image 100 Ltd RF

chairs are contraindicated games for this age group because they emphasize hitting classmates with balls, stress speed over technique, involve too little activity, and eliminate rather than include student participation.

MIDDLE SCHOOL PROGRAMS

Middle schools emerged in response to the unique developmental needs of students during this transitional period of physical, social, emotional, and intellectual growth. Students between ages 10 and 14 should have already been taught fundamental movement skills and basic fitness concepts. If they have, they are ready to learn lead-up games, specific sport skills, and cooperative and competitive games and sports. Interest and ability grouping, rather than gender-role stereotyping, are essential during these years.

At the middle school level, time should be spent on developing responsible personal and social behavior, respecting differences among people, and using physical activity for enjoyment, challenge, self-expression, and social interaction. Although seasonal team sports such as volleyball, basketball, and softball may form a portion of the curriculum, these young people need instruction in the skills of throwing, catching, striking, and running independently and through lead-up games. Inclusion of various dance forms, tumbling, outdoor adventure activities, and games

Middle school students can develop physically through participation in developmentally appropriate activities.

© McGraw-Hill Education. Lars A. Niki, photographer

chosen by students will enrich the curriculum. Despite limited facilities and equipment, skill heterogeneity, and large class sizes, physical educators need to creatively design and implement broad curricula that meet the interests and needs of students.

Vital components of middle school curricula are health-related and skill-related physical fitness. Students in this age group are capable of taking greater responsibility for establishing personal goals to enhance their cardiorespiratory endurance, muscular strength and endurance, and flexibility. School programs should creatively reinforce the achievement of these goals using honor rolls on bulletin boards, schoolwide announcements, newsletter features, assembly recognitions, "I'm Fit" T-shirts, or opportunities to lead or select class fitness activities.

Psychomotor, affective, and cognitive standards should guide the development of sequential and progressive instruction. Periodic assessments should be made to ensure the attainment of these standards. Whenever possible, the physical education specialist, who is a certified physical education teacher, should integrate instructional material with other subjects. With these standards in place, middle school students, their parents, and school administrators will value and support physical education programs for every student.

SECONDARY SCHOOL PROGRAMS

In the high school grades, students often prefer to work at achieving and maintaining a health-enhancing level of physical fitness rather than being placed in classes where they again just play volleyball, basketball, and softball. Most students want

In secondary school physical education, students can be introduced to activities in which they may participate during their leisure hours and later in life.
© Erik Isakson/Blend Images RF

to receive instruction in lifetime sports such as bowling, golf, and tennis and in fitness activities such as aerobics or weight training. Facility and equipment limitations can be overcome by using community lanes, courses, and courts and getting students to use personal sport equipment. School gymnasiums can be used for a variety of activities, including aerobics, badminton, rock climbing and rappelling, dance, one-wall racquetball, martial arts, and target archery. Community recreation centers with weight-training equipment and aerobics machines, such as stationary bicycles and treadmills, may be made available to students during the school day. Schools might be more likely to offer a wider range of elective courses to secondary school students if these broadened curricula were available. Learning skills in sports students can enjoyably participate throughout their lives should be a primary focus of secondary physical education programs.

Another area of emphasis should be to create opportunities to develop and implement individualized physical fitness programs. While these may be incorporated into aerobic or weight-training classes, students should be encouraged to establish fitness goals using activities they find personally satisfying. Secondary school students are capable of learning how to initiate and sustain fitness programs they enjoy and will be more likely to continue as adults.

At all levels of education, it is essential that teachers help their students achieve high standards. If the programmatic characteristics just described are implemented, children and adolescents will be able to demonstrate proficiency in various movement and motor skills, maintain physically active lifestyles, and interact positively with others in physical activity settings.

CHALLENGES FACING PHYSICAL EDUCATORS

Instructional

School teachers, including those in physical education, face many challenges. Among these are apathetic students, violence, drug abuse, lack of family support, heterogeneous students in large classes, and discipline and behavioral problems. Despite these factors negatively affecting the instructional environment, teachers are held accountable for student learning.

Apathetic students who do not want to dress out, participate, or behave present a challenge to teachers. Replacing dodgeball or unpopular activities with weight training or non-traditional sports or activities may be an effective starting point. Rewarding appropriate behavior rather than simply punishing misbehavior encourages positive change. Teaching relevant content, ensuring equal opportunity for all students, and making classes enjoyable may not engage every student, but the number of apathetic ones will diminish. Keeping students busy is not education. Teaching must result in learning that engages and interests students.

Sadly, violence in schools is becoming an endemic problem, apparent in increased bullying, fights among students, weapon confiscations, shootings, and gang-related violence. Many schools today hire security officers to patrol the halls, install metal detectors at the doors, and enforce lockdowns to ensure potentially violent situations do not erupt into harmful or deadly occurrences. While abuse of drugs and alcohol is related to some violence in schools, other issues such as

Bullying among students, including physical, behavioral, and emotional, is one of the many instructional challenges facing teachers in schools.
© Ocean/Corbis RF

poverty, lack of parental guidance (possibly associated with single-parent homes), physical deprivations, emotional disturbances, and mental illnesses are contributing factors as well. Too many middle and secondary students, often influenced by peers, choose to engage in petty violations of the law that often lead to serious criminal acts. When these young people learn that the use of force helps them get what they want and they enjoy this domination, they increasingly lash out against whoever interferes with their wishes. If adolescents develop a blatant disregard for authority, they also may attack teachers and administrators in violent ways. Physical education teachers must be vigilant in understanding the potentially volatile situations that may occur in competitive sport situations so they can defuse them. They must be sensitive to the needs of students and work with them individually and collectively to use physical activity to work off pent-up frustrations and channel their energies in positive ways.

When students attend school under the influence of alcohol or purchase and use drugs on school grounds, the learning process is severely hampered. Drug education classes and enforcement of school policies for drug-free campuses are two ways to help reduce the incidence of these problems. Physical educators should use every opportunity to discourage drug use by showing how it adversely affects physical performance and personal well-being.

Dramatic demographic and socioeconomic changes are partly to blame for the lack of parental and family support for education in this country. Approximately half of all children will live in a single-parent household before they reach the age of 18, while over one-fourth will live with only a mother or father at any one time. Often due to a lack of supervision, these children are at greater risk for school dropout, academic under-achievement, living in poverty, and participation in violent crime. Given these circumstances, teachers may have to overcome a lack of parental support to help students learn the value of education. Physical educators can create after-school fitness clubs that could help instill self-worth, confidence, discipline, and responsibility in students.

Many states dictate maximum class sizes, but too often these maximums are ignored for physical education. When school administrators believe that physical education is only play, physical educators may have 50 to 60 students in each class. This is problematic because of the increased chance of injuries with inadequate supervision and crowded instructional and activity spaces. Even with a normal-size class, physical educators face students with heterogeneous abilities. Skill grouping, use of lead-up or progressive games, and curricula that include both cooperative and competitive activities contribute to meeting students' diverse needs.

Disciplinary and behavioral problems may be the most recurring issue facing teachers. Rather than dissipating in an activity setting, these problems are often exacerbated. Some students with histories of misbehavior may seek to use physical education classes as opportunities to dominate others or show off. Physical educators must establish fair and impartial class policies regarding these behaviors and then enforce them consistently. Using timeouts as punishment, rather than exercises or laps, teaches respect for the rules. Rewarding appropriate behaviors with the opportunity to participate in favorite activities is more effective than punishments for most students.

In overcoming these challenges, physical educators must be prepared to do a lot more than just teach their favorite sports and games. Each challenge can become an opportunity to positively affect the lives of students.

Role Conflicts between Teaching and Coaching

Many physical educators in schools and small colleges also coach. In fact, some obtain degrees in physical education to increase the likelihood of obtaining coaching positions. Because of the overlap in instructional knowledge and skill content, this joint career has served many professionals well. When these individuals commit equally to teaching students of heterogeneous ability levels and to coaching the highly skilled, all students benefit.

Conflicts occur, however, because of time and energy constraints, unequal rewards, self-imposed and external pressures, and personal preferences. Most

The teacher-coach spends long hours helping students learn and helping athletes achieve their potential.
© Royalty-Free/Corbis

physical educators in schools are expected to teach a full class load and then coach after school. This schedule results in long days. For those coaching multiple sports, these long days continue season after season. One of four patterns then usually develops:

- A tenured teacher-coach decides that the small coaching supplement is not worth the time demands, so she resigns from coaching but continues teaching.

- A teacher-coach concentrates on coaching, putting little effort into teaching because he views it as repetitive and unrewarding.

- A teacher-coach becomes apathetic about both jobs and just goes through the motions instead of being committed.

- A teacher-coach changes careers.

Pressures to win, whether self-imposed or from external sources, accompany sport competitions. Although some parents have little interest in the quality of classroom instruction provided by the teacher-coach, hundreds or even thousands may pass judgment on a coach's ability to develop a successful team. Accompanying these pressures, which may lead to getting fired for not winning enough games, are the public prestige and status of being a coach.

Resolution of this role conflict is difficult because the conflict usually develops gradually. The teacher-coach needs to continually assess the commitment given each responsibility to ensure it is equitable. Regardless of the pressures, rewards, constraints, and preferences, the teacher-coach as a professional is ethically expected to serve competently in both roles. Suggested strategies to ameliorate some of the teacher-coach conflict might include:

- Encouraging school administrators to define, evaluate, and reward teaching and coaching roles separately

- Allowing the athletic director to specify team responsibilities and lines of authority to preclude potential conflicts between teaching and coaching duties

- Urging school administrators and athletic directors to work together to relieve the excessive pressures placed on coaches by athletes, parents, and team supporters

- Helping coaches balance the time and energy spent in meeting the responsibilities of both teaching and coaching

CHANGES IN LICENSURE REQUIREMENTS

State control of education has resulted in the establishment of licensure standards for public school teachers. Most state departments of education (or the equivalent) specify the standards or competencies that must be met before a person can teach. Many states have developed tests for teacher certification or licensing, while other states use assessments developed by commercial companies such as Pearson and the Educational Testing Service with its Praxis Series. The Praxis Series: Professional

Assessments for Beginning Teachers measures whether candidates possess both the general and specialized knowledge necessary to teach. Praxis includes assessments of academic skills (general for all teachers) and subject matter. Physical education programs include disciplinary content, a specialized methodology of teaching, and the application of knowledge to student learning. Often states have reciprocity agreements with other states so certification or licensure in one is equivalent to licensure in the other. Licensure in a nonreciprocating state requires a teacher to complete one or more courses.

ACCOUNTABILITY

Accountability demands that an individual or institution be held responsible for achieving a specified action. For example, schools and teachers are held accountable for increasing students' test scores because these scores are believed to be indicators of student learning and, hence, inextricably linked with America's economic competitiveness. Accountability matters significantly when incentives and punishments await those who do or do not achieve the performance levels expected by legislators or special-interest groups. While accountability sounds good, this term may gloss over the political agendas of those who believe public schools are failing to meet national academic standards. Some argue that reliance on high-stakes testing fails to address serious fallacies in psychometrics, especially when many of the tests violate construct validity and fairness. That is, many tests distort or misrepresent what students have actually learned because they do not accurately reflect the content of the curriculum or the typical context in which the curriculum is taught. Huge pressures to raise test scores, however, have led to inordinate amounts of time devoted to test preparation, teaching to the test, and cheating when teachers change students' answers or scores.

A **standard** is a uniform criterion or foundational guide used to measure quality. Educational standards determine what children at each grade level should know and be able to do. Schools are increasingly expected to ensure every child can achieve required standards of performance. Most states have adopted national tests and/or developed statewide tests to measure student progress and achievement. State appropriations often depend on the test scores achieved, regardless of the socioeconomic context, the racial and ethnic composition of the student body, or the transient nature of the population. Sometimes the tests used to measure educational achievement bear little relationship to the state or local mandates regarding curricula.

An **assessment** is a measure of knowledge, skills, and abilities. Assessments are tools used by those considered competent to judge student achievement, such as school teachers and administrators. Educators should incorporate a wide range of authentic assessments throughout their programs to deflect an overemphasis on high-stakes test scores. That is, a variety of evaluative measures reflecting the curriculum should be implemented to determine student progress as well as those areas needing more work. Formative assessments are particularly useful for giving students constructive feedback and for determining how to provide individualized remediation.

Just as accountability is important as a member of a smoothly functioning rowing team, it is also essential in instructional programs and the fulfillment of professional responsibilities.

© Karl Weatherly/Getty Images RF

Every physical education class should be designed and taught by a competent and certified physical education teacher. Like every other school subject, physical education should include sequential learning activities characterized by objectives, instructional strategies, developmental levels, content standards, and assessments. Learning outcomes should be identified by grade level, and specified objectives should be assessed at each level by valid and reliable measurements. Validity describes the strength or accuracy of conclusions, while reliability describes the consistency in or repeatability of what is measured. High-quality physical education programs will help students of all abilities develop physical fitness and motor skills, gain a thorough understanding of fitness, nutritional, and health concepts, enact appropriate social behavior, and value healthy lifestyles.

Educators cannot achieve these objectives if children and adolescents take part in physical education only 1 or 2 days per week. Children in elementary grades should have instructional periods totaling 150 minutes of physical education per week; students in middle and secondary school should have instructional periods of 225 minutes per week.

Assessments of program quality in all physical activity settings may include monitoring heart rates to ensure aerobic activities increase heart rates and maintain these rates within the target heart rate zone.

© Duncan Smith/Getty Images RF

Experiences in sport and physical activity programs for individuals of all ages are important for overall intellectual, social, emotional, and physical development. Whether a recreational sport league, individual sport lessons, or a commercial fitness program, appropriate objectives, standards, and assessments will help ensure fun, program adherence, and maintenance of healthy lifestyles.

CAREER BURNOUT

All individuals may experience burnout in their careers if they are faced with unresolved problems or stressful challenges. **Burnout** is a psychological state of apathy about the responsibilities of one's career. This may result in exhibiting the signs and symptoms in Box 10.4. Even people in physical activity-related careers may find their jobs unrewarding or frustrating due to a lack of change or too much change too fast, unchallenging routines, work overload, lack of advancement potential, or threat of job elimination.

Combating burnout has become essential to career survival. Job satisfaction necessitates taking a positive approach toward work responsibilities, with financial rewards, job challenges, recognition, promotion, variety in responsibilities, and professional development contributing to job satisfaction. Receiving positive feedback is particularly helpful in feeling good about one's work. If people are constantly bombarded by negative comments, they will not continue to function effectively. Instead, recognition and praise for completing responsibilities lead to enhanced self-motivation and performance.

While work-related stress probably cannot be avoided, each person should understand what causes stress and how to eliminate or cope with it. Physical educators and exercise and sport scientists have a definite advantage in the

Participation in physical activities, such as golf, can help relieve stress and, therefore, lessen the possibility of career burnout.

© Royalty-Free/Corbis

BOX 10.4   SIGNS AND SYMPTOMS OF BURNOUT

- Physiological changes associated with stress, including digestive problems, fatigue, insomnia, headaches, high blood pressure, increased heart rate, heart attacks, and strokes.
- Feelings of emotional exhaustion, powerlessness, hopelessness, detachment, resentment, cynicism, irritability, insecurity, anxiety, or depression.
- At work, frustration with job-related factors such as task repetitiveness, lack of recognition, and impossibility of advancement or being overworked, underappreciated, confusion about expectations and priorities, concern about job security, or resentment about duties that are not commensurate with pay.
- Less enjoyment of work and personal life.
- Overeating or undereating.
- Excessive drinking or abuse of drugs.

BOX 10.5   DEALING WITH POTENTIAL BURNOUT

Physical

- Get a complete physical exam.
- Get adequate sleep.
- Eat nutritious and timely meals.
- Exercise regularly.

Mental

- Develop coping skills for dealing with stress.
- Understand yourself and how you deal with stress.
- Set realistic goals.
- Learn to manage your time more effectively.
- Take time for relaxation.

Social

- Nurture personal relationships.
- Engage in meaningful service to others.
- Practice healthy communication.
- Express your feelings to someone you trust.
- Keep your sense of humor.

---

latter case because they know exercise reduces or helps manage stress. Everyone needs to attain and maintain a personal level of fitness that not only positively affects productivity and quality of life but also allows opportunities to serve as a role model for others (see Box 10.5 for other ways for dealing with potential burnout).

SUMMARY

Physical activity programs are for everyone. They help people learn fitness and sport skills and incorporate them into their daily lives. It is hoped students and exercise participants of all ages will increasingly enjoy physical fitness activities, reach personal goals, and adhere to appropriately designed programs. Increasingly, public and private health and sport clubs, work site programs, rehabilitation clinics, and retirement homes will be charged with meeting the fitness and activity needs of adults. There will be a growing need for specialists to work in these settings. Advances in technology as well as the proliferation of research will continue to impact and advance knowledge of physical education and exercise science in the future. School physical education programs will continue to evolve, with an emphasis on fitness activities and the development of the whole person. Educational reforms of standards, accountability, and assessments will significantly affect funding for school programs and lead to important outcomes. Although instructional and financial constraints threaten the teaching/learning process, competent teachers will creatively find ways to meet these challenges while being held accountable for helping each student achieve higher standards. Professional involvement and maintaining a physically active lifestyle are two ways to combat job stress and career burnout.

CAREER PERSPECTIVE

Courtesy Andrea Hudy

ANDREA HUDY

Assistant Athletics Director for Sports Performance
Kansas Athletics Incorporated
University of Kansas
Lawrence, Kansas

EDUCATION

B.S., kinesiology, University of Maryland
M.A., sports biomechanics, University of Connecticut

JOB RESPONSIBILITIES AND HOURS

Andrea is committed to maintaining a top quality, comprehensive strength and conditioning program for the men's and women's basketball teams that compete in Division I and
managing the daily operations, maintenance, and functionality of the varsity weight room.
This assists with establishing and ensuring compliance with all weight training, conditioning, and flexibility and plyometrics programs. She ensures effective communication with
the Director of Athletics, coaches, sports medicine staff, and other administrators regarding athletes' nutrition, training programs, and injuries. She models respect and concern
for athletes as a professional example to them as well as other staff members. She demonstrates motivational skills and strategies and effective communication that helps all athletes
maximize their efforts and achieve individual and team goals for fitness and performance.
Andrea typically works between 6 A.M. and 6 P.M. Monday through Friday as well as some
weekend hours associated with travel, competitions, and recruiting.

SPECIALIZED COURSE WORK, DEGREES, AND WORK EXPERIENCES
NEEDED FOR THIS CAREER

Andrea's position requires extensive knowledge, experience, and expertise in strength
and conditioning as well as excellent organizational skills. She believes that intercollegiate
strength and conditioning coaches should have been college athletes, have earned exercise
science degrees, possess certification from the National Strength and Conditioning Association as a Certified Strength and Conditioning Specialist, have earned a USA Weightlifting
certification, and demonstrate effective instructional and motivational strategies. While no
academic degrees are required for her job, Andrea advocates that individuals seeking positions like she holds have the two certifications just named. She has found that coursework
she completed in statistics, English, exercise science, biomechanics, sport psychology, sport
sociology, and clinical kinesiology have positively affected how well she can complete her
responsibilities.

SATISFYING ASPECTS

Andrea really enjoys having the ability to teach and motivate athletes and watch them
grow. She enjoys developing relationships with athletes and constantly being surrounded
by competition. These positive experiences offset the hours she spends with completing
administrative work, budgeting, and evaluating staff.

JOB POTENTIAL

Students usually gain access into and advance in this field beginning with an internship and then may become a graduate assistant, assistant coordinator, coordinator, associate director, and director. When strength and conditioning coaches successfully train athletes, opportunities for their career advancement increase. This process is enhanced through learning continuously, earning advanced degrees, and obtaining higher levels of certification.

SUGGESTIONS FOR STUDENTS

Andrea's advice to students is to be competitive, work hard, keep learning, demonstrate loyalty to your staff, and be willing to do anything that you are asked to do. Professionals in this field must be self-starters.

KEY POINTS

Adherence to exercise	One of the most important factors associated with exercise programs is to get participants, through personal commitment, to persist in engaging in regular physical activity.
Challenges facing recreation and leisure programs	These include demographic changes, altered family and work patterns including latch-key kids, budget reductions, environmental concerns, socioeconomic circumstances of participants, and unique programmatic needs of individuals of all ages and ability levels.
Challenges facing the exercise sciences	These include public health issues, such as obesity and cardiovascular diseases; rising health care costs; lack of adherence to activity programs; inadequately educated individuals conducting fitness classes, prescribing exercises, or serving as personal trainers; and lack of access to fitness programs by many ethnic minorities, females, senior citizens, and individuals with special needs.
Research in the exercise and sport sciences	Much of the research in the exercise and sport sciences is interdisciplinary as expertise from related disciplines can enhance the knowledge discovered or created.
Research-based inquiry	Indexes and databases are rich resources for information in the exercise and sport sciences.
Elementary school programs	The curriculum should focus on fundamental movement skills and progress from simple to complex movements.
Movement education	This approach to learning begins where each child is, proceeds from known activities into new movement patterns, continues within the personal and unique limitations of each child, develops confidence for each

	child since each learns at his or her own ability level, and encourages the freedom to explore more difficult, yet basic, movements.
Middle school physical education	The curriculum should focus on developing responsible personal and social behaviors through team sports, games, dance, and adventure activities.
Secondary school physical education	The curriculum should focus on developing and maintaining a health-enhancing level of physical fitness, including aerobics, muscular strength and endurance, and lifetime sports and activities.
Instructional challenges facing physical education teachers	These include apathetic students, violence and bullying, the use and abuse of alcohol and other drugs, socioeconomic hardships, lack of parental and family support for education, heterogeneous students in large classes (along with inclusion), and disciplinary and behavioral problems.
Accountability	The expectation is that professionals should be held responsible for achieving a specified level of performance.
Standard	Students and professionals can rightfully be expected to conform to a uniform criterion or minimum essential performance as a measurement of quality.
Assessment	The importance of measuring knowledge, skills, and abilities is applicable to many fields.
Career burnout	Decreased performance can result from stress, job-related problems such as lack of support or reward, and overwork.
Coping with career burnout	Physical, mental, and social approaches can help deal effectively or cope with stressors to prevent career burnout.

REVIEW QUESTIONS

1. Describe several benefits or values of participating in regular physical activity.
2. What are several strategies for ensuring adherence to a physical activity program?
3. How do changing demographics affect recreation and leisure services programs?
4. Describe the characteristics of movement education in an elementary physical education program.
5. How should middle school and secondary school physical education curricula differ?
6. What are several instructional challenges facing physical educators in schools?
7. What is accountability, and how does it relate to standards and assessment?

STUDENT ACTIVITIES

1. Talk with five friends about any individual exercise program in which they are (or were) involved. Summarize the factors that led to their quitting or adhering to their programs.

2. Write a one-page paper about your personal accountability in a job you have held in a field related to your major, such as lifeguard, sport official, camp counselor, or sporting goods salesperson. (If you have not had any of these experiences, talk with one person who has and report his or her experiences.)

3. Secure a copy of the state or local elementary, middle school, and secondary school standards and curricula for physical education. Analyze them to determine if the standards are being achieved through a progressive and sequential program.

4. Read two articles in any professional journals that describe how an expanded knowledge base and technology in physical education and exercise science have positively affected noneducational programs. Summarize in two or three sentences the impact each has made.

5. Describe two actual examples of people who have suffered from career burnout. What changes would you have recommended that might have prevented their career burnout?

WEB CONNECTIONS

1. www.ncbi.nlm.nih.gov/pubmed
   This PubMed site of the National Library of Medicine and National Institutes of Health provides access to over 24 million citations in MEDLINE and other related databases with links to full-text articles.

2. www.welcoa.org/
   This Wellness Council of America site helps organizations develop and sustain successful wellness programs.

3. www.cdc.gov/nccdphp/dnpao/hwi/downloads/
   Steps2Wellness_BROCH14_508_Tag508.pdf
   Download a comprehensive guide for the steps for implementing the 2008 Physical Activity Guidelines in the workplace.

4. www.nps.gov/index.htm
   Discover a nation-wide treasure trove of places to visit and things to do at our national parks as you discover history, explore nature, and learn while being active.

5. http://www.acsm.org/public-information/position-stands

    This site provides full-text position stands of the American College of Sports Medicine such as "Nutrition and Athletic Performance," "Quantity and Quality of Exercise for Developing and Maintaining Cardiorespiratory, Musculoskeletal, and Neuromotor Fitness in Apparently Health Adults: Guidance for Prescribing Exercise," and "The Female Athlete Triad."

6. www.helpguide.org/mental/burnout_signs_symptoms.htm

    This site provides information about the signs, symptoms, and causes of burnout and recommends coping strategies.

7. www.ets.org/praxis

    Most states required the completion of assessments, such as the Praxis Series assessments that measure basic academic knowledge, and general and subject-specific knowledge.

8. www.publicschoolreview.com/blog/10-major-challenges-facing-public-schools

    Read about the 10 major challenges facing public schools including class size, poverty, family factors, technology, bullying, student attitudes and behaviors, national legislation, parental involvement, student health, and funding.

11

ISSUES IN SPORTS

LEARNING OUTCOMES

- Students will be able to describe several threats to the integrity of sports.
- Students will be able to explain how and why increased competitive sport opportunities are being provided to females, ethnic minorities, senior citizens, and individuals with special needs.
- Students will be able to articulate the justifications for providing competitive sport programs for youth, adolescents, college students, and adults.
- Students will be able to describe problems facing youth sports, interscholastic sports, intercollegiate athletics, and Olympic sports and point out possible strategies to address each of these.

Sports are fun. Sports provide a setting for people to develop their identities and learn their capabilities and limitations. Genuine satisfaction comes from making your best effort regardless of the outcome. A revitalization of body, mind, and spirit through sports can renew your perspective on life. Cooperation, discipline, emotional control, fair play, self-esteem, character development, and teamwork are the desired outcomes of playing sports. Athletes can learn these values as well as to respect opponents on and off the field. Athletes should accept officials' decisions without dispute. Even spectators can be encouraged to display these values. Models of ethical behavior are especially important for young people, who typically imitate the attitudes and behaviors of school, collegiate, professional, and Olympic athletes.

Sport participants seek to win. "We're number one" has seemingly become the United States' sports motto from youth leagues to professional teams. To produce the best teams, athletes are often expected to specialize in one sport, accept coaches' dictates without question, practice and train with deferred gratification, excel or face elimination, and circumvent the rules when necessary to increase the likelihood of winning. Ethical behavior is often disdained or negatively regarded by coaches, teammates, and spectators, as winning surpasses everything else in importance.

Girls and women, ethnic minorities, senior citizens, and individuals with special needs are being treated more equitably in sports today, but they still face discriminatory practices and biases. Public and private youth sport organizations, interscholastic programs, and elite competitions at the collegiate and international levels share some of these common problems and conflicts. This chapter discusses several of these controversial issues (see Box 11.1).

BOX 11.1   THREATS TO THE INTEGRITY OF SPORT

Academic problems, circumvention of rules to gain competitive advantages, pressures to win, violence, the arms race, and excessive commercialization are major threats to the integrity of sports. Because of the pervasiveness of these negative factors, many of the lofty ideals associated with sport, like fair play and sportsmanship, have eroded to the extent that many people question whether sports can any longer realistically claim to develop character.

Academic Issues

Sports in educational institutions have been associated with a plethora of problems—highlighted by grade changes and athletes receiving unearned grades to maintain eligibility. Whenever athletes realize that they do not have to attend class, study, complete assignments, or even take tests, they quickly devalue education and begin to overemphasize the importance of sports or their achievements in sports. Some high school students, through their own initiative or with the advice of their parents or coaches, seek to meet the requirements to play in NCAA institutions by receiving unearned credits or by getting others to take the SAT and ACT for them, often after they have not scored high enough to be eligible for collegiate grants-in-aid. Despite more rigorous standards for collegiate athletes that require declaring majors and making progress toward their degrees, graduation rates in several institutions remain quite low. Balancing the time demands of being high school or collegiate athletes with those of being successful in the classroom too often leads to cheating, dishonesty, deception, and failure. It also should be noted that failure to take advantage of educational opportunities is a disadvantage to athletes, who are unlikely to have careers in professional sports and find themselves ill-prepared for life outside of sports.

Breaking the Rules

Many coaches instruct their athletes how to circumvent game rules without getting penalized. At early ages, athletes learn that faking an injury to get the clock stopped, refusing to admit touching a ball that goes out-of-bounds because this helps in gaining an advantage, and lying about their legal guardians to play on geographically defined teams are acceptable, and even praised, behaviors. Sports rules also can be broken by violating the spirit of the rules, through, for instance, psychological intimidation, such as trash talking and taunting, or unsportsmanlike behaviors, such as running up the score or refusing to shake the hands of opponents before or after games. Breaking the rules also includes athletes taking anabolic steroids or other drugs they believe will help them gain competitive advantages, accepting money or other benefits for attending certain universities, and refusing to report to training camp because they believe they are underpaid under their existing professional contracts. It sometimes seems as if breaking the rules has become the expectation or normative behavior rather than being classified as what it is—unethical, immoral, unsportsmanlike, and wrong.

Pressure to Win

Pressure to win is exerted on athletes of all ages by coaches, parents, and fans. With an overzealousness for victory, some coaches excessively stress youngsters' arms and bodies, verbally and physically abuse children and adolescents, and teach and model unethical behaviors. Coaches and

(continued)

BOX 11.1   THREATS TO THE INTEGRITY OF SPORT (continued)

parents emphasize winning so much that by age 12 over half of all youth sport participants drop out because they are no longer having fun. Some parents define their status and let their lives be consumed by their children's sport achievements. Others may even withhold love from children who do not perform up to parental expectations. Families have moved or separated and other children have been neglected in the pursuit of potential lucrative professional sport careers for adolescents who show promise of future stardom. Pressure to win at all levels of sports often leads athletes to break the rules as well as to seemingly be willing to do anything to win. This winning-at-all-costs mentality leads directly to an erosion of the values once believed inherent in sports. For example, because winners are so lavishly rewarded, athletes will put their physical well-being at risk through overtraining, drug abuse, and specialization in one sport. Athletes often push themselves too hard and choose to use psychological ploys to gain advantages. The singular focus on winning has become so pervasive that the culture in many sports readily accepts intimidation and gamesmanship as "how the game is played," even though honesty, justice, responsibility, beneficence, and overall integrity are lost in the process. Is seeking to win acceptable only if an athlete honors the letter and spirit of the rules?

Violence

Moral callousness develops when people no longer feel immoral actions are morally wrong. Such may be the case with the increasing prevalence of violence in sports. When coaches teach or condone "taking out opponents," with the intent to injure, athletes quickly realize that intentionally harming another athlete has become the norm for playing the game. Even when rules expressly forbid specific actions, athletes learn that using force to intimidate and even hurt an opponent may lead to a better chance of winning and so is worth the risk of penalty. There seems to be a growing disregard for sportsmanship because violent behaviors are antithetical to it. Is intimidation an inherent part of football, ice hockey, lacrosse, and basketball? Has winning become a cultural imperative, with the benefits and rewards received by the winners so important that fair play is no longer important? In many instances, violent actions in sports have been taught, condoned, and even rewarded because the results of such behaviors benefit the perpetrator of the violence, usually in gaining an advantage that contributes to winning.

The Arms Race

Many who direct youth, school, and college programs and coach the teams believe that to remain competitive they must have the finest facilities, equipment, and uniforms, highly paid coaches, and luxurious travel accommodations. This "keeping up with the Joneses" mentality has thrust these programs into a race to get ahead and stay ahead of others for bragging rights and especially to help in recruiting the best athletes. The millions of dollars representing an ever-escalating arms race, result in selling marketing rights to clothing, scoreboards, stadiums, and naming rights to corporations.

Excessive Commercialization

Commercialization in sport is a reality and, many would argue, a necessity for programs to survive. Corporate funding, fans' financial support, and the media are not inherently bad, but they can become excessive and lead to an erosion of educational values. Local businesses support age-group teams, but it is questionable whether 10-year-olds winning national championships or state titles should serve as a basis for Chamber of Commerce bragging rights. Corporate sponsorships can help youth, school, and collegiate sport teams pay their expenses, but some governing groups have ruled that unhealthy products should not be advertised by public schools and colleges. Television dictates which teams are featured and when and where competitions are held, even though

(continued)

BOX 11.1 THREATS TO THE INTEGRITY OF SPORT (continued)

accommodating this medium often adversely affects athletes' class attendance and academic performances. Unless athletic administrators are willing to set limits on the influence of commercial interests, values such as honor, commitment, cooperation, and sportsmanship may be lost.

Each of these issues threatens the integrity of sports. Unless coaches, sport administrators, and parents choose to model ethical behaviors and educate athletes about moral values and how these should be incorporated into their lives, sports will lose their educational values. Adults should set and maintain standards that will mandate athletes meet academic requirements, abide by the letter and spirit of the rules, and keep winning in proper perspective. Adults should refuse to allow commercial, entertainment, and recruiting interests to supplant fair play and other values.

GIRLS AND WOMEN IN SPORTS

Although the Greeks excluded women from the ancient Olympic Games, and the founder of the modern Olympic Games viewed women's role as cheering spectators, there has been a gradual acceptance of girls and women as sport participants. Traditionally beliefs about physiological differences contributed to the virtual exclusion of girls and women from sports. Research demonstrates that the physical abilities of males and females exist on a continuum. Overall, females are not as strong as men; are shorter and lighter; and, due to total body size, have smaller lungs and lower cardiac output. However, some females possess physical abilities exceeding those of some males. Some female athletes have surpassed the limitations placed on them by running and swimming faster and longer than males. Some females compete professionally against and with males, achieving high levels of muscular strength and endurance, and are proficient in sport skills once the domain of males only. The physical potential of girls and women is not yet known, since they must first have equal opportunities in sports to achieve their maximum potential. Contrary to the writings of the early 1900s, women do not risk sterility when they train strenuously and compete aggressively. Like males, females benefit in multiple ways when they achieve their physical potential.

One reason girls and women have enjoyed expanded opportunities to play and compete has been Title IX of the 1972 Education Amendments. (Table 11-1 includes data about changes in competitive, coaching, and administrative opportunities for girls and women.) Aided by this federal legislation, thousands of school and college females have achieved greater equity in sport. In 1992, the Supreme Court ruled in *Franklin v. Gwinnett County Public Schools* that monetary damages were available under Title IX. The fact that victims could be compensated for inequitable treatment provided an incentive needed to force some schools and colleges to eradicate discrimination. (See Chapter 9 for a timeline of the most important events related to the impact of Title IX on girls' and women's sports.) It should be emphasized that Title IX does not require equal funding in athletics for males and females. This federal law does, however, require equal opportunity and equitable treatment.

TABLE 11-1

IMPACT OF CHANGING SOCIETAL ATTITUDES AND INCREASED OPPORTUNITIES FOR FEMALES IN SPORTS

Interscholastic Sports*

Number of Participants

	1972–1973	1981–1982	1991–1992	2001–2002	2006–2007	2010–2011	2014–2015
Girls	817,073	1,810,671	1,940,801	2,806,998	3,021,807	3,173,549	3,287,735
Boys	3,770,621	3,409,081	3,429,853	3,960,517	4,321,103	4,494,406	4,519,312

Intercollegiate Athletics (NCAA)[†]

Average number of sports for women:

    1978: 5.61
    1982: 6.59
    1986: 7.15
    1990: 7.24
    1992: 7.09
    1996: 7.50
    2000: 8.14
    2004: 8.32
    2008: 8.65
    2012: 8.73
    2014: 8.83

Most popular sports:

1. Basketball
2. Volleyball
3. Soccer
4. Cross country
5. Softball
6. Tennis
7. Track and field
8. Golf
9. Swimming/Diving
10. Lacrosse

Female coaches of women's teams

    1972: over 90%
    1978: 58.2%
    1982: 52.4%
    1986: 50.6%
    1990: 47.3%
    1992: 48.3%
    1996: 47.7%
    2000: 45.6%
    2004: 44.1%
    2008: 42.8%
    2012: 42.9%
    2014: 43.4%

Female athletic directors (females hold 35.8% of all athletics administrative jobs in NCAA-member institutions; no females are involved in the administration of 9.2% of intercollegiate athletics in these institutions' programs):

    1990: 15.9%
    1992: 16.8%
    1996: 18.5%
    2000: 17.8%
    2004: 18.5%
    2008: 21.3%
    2012: 20.3%
    2014: 22.3%

*Data from the National Federation of State High School Associations. http://www.nfhs.org/ParticipationStatistics/PDF/2014-15_Participation_Survey_Results.pdf

†Data from a study by Vivian Acosta and Linda Carpenter, "Women in Intercollegiate Sport—A Longitudinal Study—Thirty-seven Year Update 1977–2014" © 2014 Carpenter/Acosta.

Title IX's provisions relative to athletics have not been uniformly implemented because of gender biases, limited budgets and facilities, and resistance to change. Women have benefited, however, by receiving approximately one-third of colleges' athletic budgets for team travel, recruiting, coaches' salaries, medical treatment, publicity, and athletic grants-in-aid. Regarding grants-in-aid, it should be noted that the number of these awarded to football players leaves fewer for men's non-revenue-producing sports when greater equity for female athletes is achieved.

As programs for girls and women have increased, however, control has shifted to men. Today a much smaller percentage of women coach teams for girls and women than before Title IX was enacted, and few women administer athletic programs for females. Among the factors contributing to the increasing number of men coaching girls and women are too few women with interest in coaching given the number of teams, more equitable salaries for coaches of female teams than was the case prior to Title IX, and hiring practices in which many male athletic directors and school principals prefer to hire male coaches. When female and male athletic programs were combined, men were almost always named to the top administrative positions because of seniority or the belief that they were more qualified. Occasionally, though, a female has been hired to administer an athletic program that competes at the highest collegiate level. Thus, a major issue confronting athletic programs remains the need for more qualified female coaches and sport administrators and giving them more opportunities to coach teams and direct athletic programs.

Over 40 years after its passage, Title IX remains highly controversial relative to athletics, even though in other educational areas, such as admissions and academic programs, equal opportunity for both genders has largely been achieved. At issue, especially at the intercollegiate level, are two major questions. First, depending on who served as president of the United States, the Office of Civil Rights either has or has not been effective in enforcing this law. Second, many college administrators claim the federal government has failed to provide clear guidance about how to comply with Title IX and its policy interpretations or has been too prescriptive

In 1960, Wilma Rudolph became the first American woman to win Olympic gold medals in the 100- and 200-meter sprints.
© AP Photo

about proportionality of female students and athletes relative to males. They often claim compliance with Title IX requires the elimination of men's sport teams.

To help address these issues, the U.S. Secretary of Education in 2002 appointed a Commission on Opportunity in Athletics to examine ways to strengthen enforcement and expand opportunities to ensure fairness for all college athletes. Upon receiving a report from this commission, the Department of Education in 2003 issued a letter of clarification that addressed these two key issues. First, this letter emphasized that nothing in Title IX required the elimination or reduction of men's teams to demonstrate compliance. Second, this letter stressed that any one of the criteria of the 3-prong test for compliance, as established in 1979 and clarified in 1996, could be used by educational institutions to show that they were providing equal opportunities to their male and female students to participate in athletics. These are the three alternative ways to demonstrate compliance:

- Participation opportunities are substantially proportionate to the full-time undergraduate enrollment of males and females.

- When members of one sex have historically been underrepresented among intercollegiate athletes, there must have been a history and continuing practice of program expansion in response to developing interests and abilities of the underrepresented sex.

- In the absence of a continuing practice of program expansion, an institution must show that the interests and abilities of members of the underrepresented sex have been fully and effectively accommodated.

The problem this commission and the subsequent letter of clarification attempted to address was that many athletic directors have for years chosen the "safe harbor" of proportionality (the first alternative) because they believed the other two criteria were more difficult to measure or prove. In seeking to achieve this substantially proportionate number of female and male athletes relative to undergraduate enrollment, many institutions increased the number of their women's teams while also establishing quotas for the number of walk-on athletes permitted on their men's teams. That is, some male athletic directors refused to provide parity in intercollegiate athletics and instead manipulated participation numbers by gender. Numerous colleges' attempts still fail to meet the proportionality requirement. Considerable discontent clouds intercollegiate athletics regarding the elimination of men's teams and ways to comply with equitable competitive opportunities for both genders.

SPORT OPPORTUNITIES FOR ETHNIC MINORITIES AND ESPECIALLY AFRICAN AMERICANS

Members of ethnic minority groups, especially African Americans, have found themselves sport outcasts throughout most of this nation's history. Prior to 1950, sports were rarely integrated, with a few notable exceptions such as Jack Johnson (boxing), Joe Louis (boxing), Paul Robeson (football), Jackie Robinson (baseball), and Jesse Owens (track). Following the Supreme Court's *Brown v. Board of Education* decision in 1954, school desegregation slowly began to open more school and college sport programs to historically underrepresented groups.

Throughout the years, African Americans have experienced blatant discrimination in the form of quota systems (only a small number allowed on a team), position stacking (African Americans competed, often against other African Americans, for a limited number of playing positions because others were unavailable to them), social exclusion from clubs and parties, disparity in treatment by coaches, and weak academic support programs, with little tutorial help. Sometimes these athletes, because of their cultural and educational backgrounds, were ill prepared for the academic demands of college; their athletic prowess had gotten them through a vocational or technical rather than college-preparatory, high school curriculum. Many failed to earn college degrees, thus eliminating themselves from possible coaching positions when their dreams of professional stardom failed to materialize or ended abruptly.

Some ethnic minorities have opposed the NCAA's eligibility rules for Division I competition requiring prospective student-athletes to graduate from high school having successfully completed the following 16 core courses:

- 4 years of English
- 3 years of mathematics (Algebra I or higher)
- 2 years of natural or physical science (1 must be a lab science, if offered)
- 1 year of additional English, mathematics, or natural or physical science
- 2 years of social science
- 4 years of additional courses (from any of the above, foreign language, or comparative religion or philosophy)
- 10 core courses must be completed before the seventh semester; 7 of the 10 must be in English, mathematics, or natural or physical science. These courses and grades are locked in at the start of the seventh semester and cannot be repeated for grade point average improvement to meet eligibility requirements for competition.

Carl Lewis, shown here receiving the baton in the gold medal–winning
4 × 100-meter relay in the 1984 Los Angeles Olympic Games.
© AP Photo

In addition, prospective Division I student-athletes must have a combined (reading and math) score on the Scholastic Assessment Test (SAT) or a sum score on the American College Test (ACT) based on a sliding index that ranges from a core course grade point average (GPA) of at least 3.55 with a 400 SAT or a 37 ACT score to a 2.30 GPA with a 900 SAT or 75 ACT score. See fs.ncaa.org/Docs/eligibility_center /Quick_Reference_Sheet.pdf for Division II and Division II requirements. Some argue that the SAT and ACT are culturally or socio-economically biased against ethnic minorities, and, therefore, the test requirements prove that the predominantly white institutions want to limit the domination of ethnic minorities on their sport teams.

Whether discrimination against underrepresented groups in sports is subtle or overt depends on the school or college, the team, and the leadership of both. Many interesting questions persist: Why are the starters on football and basketball teams predominantly African Americans when student bodies are predominantly Caucasian? Why are members of tennis, swimming, golf, and gymnastics teams almost exclusively Caucasian? Why do fewer African Americans team members who are less highly skilled athletes receive athletic scholarships than comparably skilled Caucasians? What is the status of female athletes who are ethnic minorities? Why are almost all head coaches and athletic directors Caucasian, especially when a high percentage of football and basketball players are African American? (See Box 11.2 for information about participation of ethnic minorities in sport as well as how they fare in securing coaching and sport management positions.)

Some claim that African American athletes are bigger, stronger, and generally more highly skilled than Caucasian athletes. Research does not substantiate these claims. However, it is a fact that some athletes' opportunities in elite and expensive sports have traditionally been limited, resulting in their devoting greater amounts of time and energy to the school-sponsored sports of football, basketball, baseball, and track and field. These four sports also offer the remote possibility for professional careers.

High costs and lack of opportunities have traditionally prevented underrepresented groups from pursuing tennis, swimming, golf, and gymnastics. Private

BOX 11.2   RACIAL AND GENDER REPORT CARDS

Racial and Gender Report Cards are published by Richard Lapchick, who is the director of the Institute for Diversity and Ethics in Sport. These reports provide current and historic data on the hiring practices by race and sex in coaching and sport management in collegiate and professional sports. Grades are awarded in collegiate sports based on the race of head coaches, assistant coaches, athletic directors, and student-athletes overall and in basketball, football, and baseball. For example, in the 2014 Racial and Gender Report Card, college sports received C+ for racial hiring practices and a C− for gender hiring practices. Grades are awarded to Major League Baseball, the National Basketball Association, and the National Football League based on the race of head coaches, assistant coaches, general managers and those in other top management positions, and athletes. Data are provided for these and other categories at the collegiate and professional levels. The latest report cards can be obtained at http:// www.tidesport.org/reports.html. Lapchick also serves as the president and chief executive officer of the National Consortium for Academics and Sports. This consortium of colleges and universities helps former student-athletes complete their college degrees while they serve their communities.

When given opportunities, formerly underrepresented groups such as African Americans choose to compete in a variety of sports.
© Digital Vision/PunchStock RF

lessons, expensive equipment, club memberships, and travel requirements for qual-ity competition discourage some individuals from entering these sports; the virtual absence of role models also reinforces the status quo. It should be noted that female athletes who are ethnic minorities must overcome both racial and gender barriers to receive equal opportunities in sports.

The blatantly discriminatory practices of the past against ethnic minorities in the United States are legally prohibited and largely socially unacceptable today. Yet, residual racism is ingrained culturally in the United States, including in sport, as biases and prejudices, even on the part of owners, coaches, and teammates, dis-sipate slowly. Nearly a half century after the passage of the Civil Rights Act, only a limited number of ethnic minorities are coaches and sport managers in colleges and professional leagues. The media's treatment of ethnic minorities perpetuates disparate treatment through how it praises them for their natural abilities when they achieve at outstanding levels, while claiming Caucasians perform well because of hard work. Sometimes comments in the print and electronic media, even though they may be subtle, elusive, and abstract, contain racial overtones and perpetuate stereotypes.

The historic domination of Caucasians has enabled them to use their power and prestige over underrepresented groups. Caucasians enjoy the highest prestige in sports and remain the standard against which ethnic minorities are judged. Exclusive of the superstars, illustrations of this second-class status for many ethnic minorities in sport may include lower signing bonuses, salary discrimination, and fewer endorsement opportunities.

All athletes, regardless of ethnicity, race, gender, sport, or level of competi-tion, deserve to be treated fairly and equitably. All athletes should be expected to complete their academic work in schools and colleges and earn their diplomas and degrees in preparation for later life. Because of past discrimination, individuals in underrepresented groups may deserve to receive counseling to help them derive the most from their educational opportunities and to learn marketable skills. Since prejudicial attitudes change gradually, everyone should work together to eliminate discrimination in athletics. Coaches must prohibit mistreatment of any athlete on their teams, and administrators must ensure equity for all.

SPORT OPPORTUNITIES FOR SENIOR CITIZENS

Senior citizens have had to overcome discriminatory biases to gain sporting opportunities. As the average age of the U.S. population increases, a greater awareness of the needs of seniors to exercise and compete has emerged. People past 60 years of age are walking, cycling, hiking, swimming, lifting weights, and engaging in a large number of sporting activities with the encouragement of their physicians, who view such activities as good preventive medicine. This enthusiasm for exercise and activity has rekindled in many seniors a desire to compete. The National Senior Games and masters events in national, regional, state, and local competitions are providing opportunities for former athletes and newly aspiring older athletes to achieve in sports in unprecedented ways. For example, in the first National Senior Games, which began in 1987, approximately 2,500 men and women competed in sports ranging from archery to volleyball. Held biennially, the National Summer Senior Games now attract over 10,000 competitors 50 and over in 19 sports. A listing of past competitions, the sports in which competitions are held, and affiliated state organizations can be found at www.nsga.com/. Whether competing for recognition or personal satisfaction, these older Americans are beneficiaries of enhanced strength, flexibility, endurance, and balance, factors that directly improve the quality of their lives. Their activity also reduces the stress of lost spouses and friends and replaces loneliness with new friends and social opportunities.

Public and private recreational programs for older Americans are proliferating. For example, commercial health and fitness clubs offer water aerobics, exercise programs for individuals with arthritis, walking clubs, and other types of programs

Senior citizens expect to have opportunities to engage in and benefit from lifelong physical activity.
© Royalty-Free/Corbis

designed specifically for senior citizens. Many programs for seniors include cardiorespiratory, muscular strength and endurance, and flexibility components appropriate for individuals with histories of cardiac problems or chronic conditions requiring adaptations. Senior centers, either publicly funded or associated with residential homes, offer stretching sessions, a variety of recreational activities, aerobic machines, and physical therapy. Senior citizens are encouraged to continue their pursuit of lifelong physical activity through age group participation in tennis, golf, swimming, and other sports. Through their votes and discretionary incomes, they are demanding and receiving more equitable access to recreational and sporting facilities.

SPORT OPPORTUNITIES FOR INDIVIDUALS WITH SPECIAL NEEDS

In recent years, individuals with special needs have increasingly desired equal opportunity to participate and compete in sports. The Amateur Sports Act of 1978 specified that the competitive needs of athletes with special needs must be accommodated. The Education for All Handicapped Children Act of 1975 mandated that athletics be provided to school students with special needs, and the 1990 Americans with Disabilities Act called for access to public recreational facilities for those previously denied it. These factors and an eagerness and determination to treat everyone equitably have led to a proliferation of organizations and competitions.

The Paralympic Games, which began in 1952, offer international competitions for individuals with spinal cord injuries and in any 1 of 10 impairment types. These games, which are now held every 4 years at the site of the Olympic Games, expanded from 130 athletes from 2 nations to 4,237 athletes from 164 countries at the summer 2012 Paralympic Games in London. (See www.paralympic.org/ for more information about the history and activities of the International Paralympic Committee.) In 1976 the Paralympic Winter Games began, and visually impaired athletes were welcomed to its competitions. The following list of sports attests to the abilities of these remarkable athletes: alpine skiing, archery, athletics (track and field), badminton, biathlon, boccia, canoe, cross-country skiing, cycling, equestrian, football (i.e., soccer; 5-side and 7-side), goalball, ice sledge hockey, judo, powerlifting, rowing, sailing, shooting, sitting volleyball, swimming, table tennis, taekwondo, triathlon, wheelchair basketball, wheelchair curling, wheelchair dance sport, wheelchair fencing, wheelchair rugby, and wheelchair tennis.

Since 1968, the Special Olympics has provided competitive opportunities for intellectually challenged individuals. Although experts initially questioned this program, the overwhelming success of personal training and state, national, and international competitions has verified the importance of giving individuals with intellectual challenges the chance to achieve and be recognized as winners. The 37 official Special Olympics sports for athletes 8 years and older include alpine skiing, aquatics, athletics (track and field), badminton, basketball, bocce, bowling, cricket, cross-country skiing, cycling, equestrian, figure skating, floor hockey, floorball, football (soccer), golf, artistic gymnastics, rhythmic gymnastics, handball, judo, kayaking, motor activity training program, netball, open water swimming, PALA: Get Fit for Sport, play activities, powerlifting, roller skating, sailing, snowboarding, snowshoeing, softball, speed skating, table tennis, tennis, unified sports, and volleyball. Over 6,500 athletes from 165 countries competed during the 2015 Special Olympics World Summer Games in Los Angeles; at the 2013 Special Olympics World Winter Games in Pyeong Chang, Republic of South Korea, more than 2,100 athletes from 100 countries demonstrated their skills.

YOUTH SPORTS

About 45 million children and adolescents (ages 4 to 18) participate annually in youth sport competitions sponsored by cities, companies, and local and national organizations. These youthful athletes ride derby cars, horses, and dirt bikes; throw baseballs, softballs, footballs, basketballs, and lacrosse balls; roll bowling balls; hit golf balls, tennis balls, racquetballs, and table tennis balls; kick soccer balls; participate in a variety of martial arts; turn flips; swim; dive; wrestle; run; and compete in triathlons and many more sporting events. This proliferation of youth sports has been fueled by television, money, civic pride, the desire to produce national champions, parental overzealousness, and professional athletes as role models.

The major issues facing youth sport programs are specialization in one sport, which often results in overuse injuries, an overemphasis on winning, winning-obsessed coaches, parental pressures, and eroded ethical values. The rationale for early and continued specialization in one sport is that only focused training can lead to higher skill levels, enhanced chances of winning, and attainment of long-term goals such as Olympic medals, professional contracts, or collegiate grants-in-aid. When children aspire for what over 99% will never achieve, they miss the enjoyment of playing various sports.

When winning becomes the primary objective, other potential outcomes are lost. Coaches are usually the ones initially caught up in this win-at-all-costs attitude. To fulfill personal ego needs, coaches too often pressure young athletes to play while injured, violate the sport and sportsmanship rules to their advantage, and quit if they are not good enough. Also, coaches' lack of preparation may result in poorly taught skills, improper treatment of injuries, and an inability to understand and deal with children's developmental needs. Some coaches are even guilty of physically, mentally, and sexually abusing young athletes.

While usually well intentioned, some parents impose their wishes on children to play a particular sport. This occurs despite most children's preferences to explore a variety of sports. Too often parental aspirations for their children's success in sports stem from their own needs rather than the children's needs. Children may experience considerable guilt because their parents invest huge amounts of time and money in lessons and competitions, which only pushes these young athletes to more desperately seek success. Parents too often reward results rather than effort and improvement. And when coaches and parents reinforce cheating to win, abusing officials and opponents, circumventing the rules, and stressing the outcome (winning) over the process (having fun and developing skills), important values are lost. In addition, adult-dominated sports rob children of opportunities to make decisions and to learn give and take in organizing their own sports.

Soccer is a popular sport for children.
© McGraw-Hill Education/Ken Cavanagh, photographer

With such a long list of problems, why do youth sports remain so popular? First, American children have a genuine interest in and enthusiasm for sports. Second, the positive outcomes in most programs exceed the negative aspects. There are leagues, organizations, coaches, and parents who emphasize fun and participation and ensure positive physiological and psychological benefits for children.

Through orientation programs, parents should learn about program goals and how to help their children benefit most from their experiences. To help achieve these goals, program administrators need to emphasize the following:

- Making sure that children have fun as the most important goal.
- Developing sport skills.
- Educating coaches so they will teach skills, strategies, and rules in developmentally appropriate ways.
- Playing every child in each game and in different positions.
- Keeping games and participants safe.
- Matching young athletes' abilities and maturity levels.
- Emphasizing playing several sports, not specializing in one sport.
- Educating parents so they model proper behaviors.
- Giving each child an equal opportunity to strive for success.
- De-emphasizing winning.
- Awarding certificates of participation, not trophies.

Youth sports can teach a love of competition that for many continues throughout life.
© PhotoLink/Getty Images RF

- Eliminating individual awards and tournaments that reduce playing opportunities.
- Avoiding all-star, traveling and select teams at least for pre-adolescent youth.
- Teaching and modeling values such as cooperation, discipline, fair play, respect, responsibility, sportsmanship, and teamwork.

Learn more about how selected national organizations support youth sports and the development of values and positive outcomes through these programs in Box 11.3.

A controversial aspect of youth sports is whether strength training is beneficial or harmful. Assuming qualified adults supervise, instruct, and spot youth at all times, workouts begin with stretching, proper technique is taught and used, realistic goals are set, resistance (weight) is increased gradually, and strength training is a part of a

BOX 11.3 SELECTED ORGANIZATIONS THAT SUPPORT YOUTH SPORTS

SHAPE America

(www.shapeamerica.org/standards/coaching/)

- Publishes *Quality Coaches, Quality Sports: National Standards for Sport Coaches*
- Cosponsors the National Council for Accreditation of Coaching Education, which supports qualified coaches for sport participants through programs that provide quality coaching education and conducts National Coaching Educators' Conferences
- Publishes position papers, such as on the "Rights and Responsibilities of Interscholastic Athletes," "A Coach's Guide to Parental Roles and Responsibilities in Sport," and "A Coach's Code of Conduct"

National Alliance For Youth Sports

(www.nays.org)

- Goal—make sports and activities safe and positive experiences, provide children quality instruction, build basic motor skills, and provide programs and services that add value to youth sports
- Offers the National Standards for Youth Sports as a guide for operating youth sport programs
- Provides recommendations for communities for conducting youth sport programs
- Provides information, guidelines, and a process for background screening of volunteers to reduce the risks of liability and potential threat of child abuse
- Its Parents Association for Youth Sports educates parents and encourages them to show good sportsmanship, give positive reinforcement to youth, and keep youth sports in proper perspective.
- Its National Youth Sports Administrators Association provides training, information, and resources so volunteer administrators can set and maintain high standards for youth sport programs.

National Council of Youth Sports

(http://www.ncys.org/)

- Goal—promote participation by all youth in fun and healthy physical activities according to their interests and abilities and promote organized youth sports that develop positive attributes, including healthier lifestyles, self-esteem, fair play, and good citizenship
- Provides guidelines for background screening of volunteers
- Its partnership with the National Center for Safety Initiatives helps youth sport organizations better protect children through due diligence and dealing with the challenges of ethical, legal, and financial issues.
- Its Certified Sports Administrator courses, offered in partnership with an institution of higher education, educate youth sport administrators, managers, volunteers, and coaches.
- Its STRIVE (Sports Teach Respect, Initiative, Values and Excellence) award annually recognizes an Organization of the Year that embraces a "kids first" approach as demonstrated by best practices in youth sports and policies that protect and promote the safety of young athletes.

(continued)

BOX 11.3   SELECTED ORGANIZATIONS THAT SUPPORT YOUTH SPORTS (continued)

Amateur Athletic Union

(http://aausports.org/)

- Conducts the AAU Junior Olympic Games
- Offers national, regional, and local competitions in over 30 sports for individuals of all ages

Examples of Coaching Certifications

- The American Coaching Academy (www.americancoachingacademy.com/) offers an online coaching certification program for youth and interscholastic coaches. Based on the National Standards for Sport Coaches, the content for the eight individual courses includes coaching philosophy and ethics, teaching and communication, safety and injury prevention, athlete growth and development, physical conditioning, skills and tactics, program administration, and program evaluation.
- The American Sport Education Program (ASEP) (www.asep.com) works directly with state high school associations to deliver coaching education programs leading to certification. ASEP partners with hundreds of sport organizations and educational institutions to offer its courses to thousands of volunteer coaches annually.
- The National Federation of State High School Associations (NFHS) (http://nfhslearn .com/) offers two core courses: Fundamentals of Coaching and First Aid Health and Safety for Coaches. When completed they qualify the person to become an accredited interscholastic coach. It offers sport-specific courses in baseball, basketball, boys' lacrosse, cheer and dance, field hockey, football, girls' lacrosse, golf, pole vault, soccer, softball, swimming, track and field, unified sports, volleyball, and wrestling. The NFHS also provides elective courses in concussion in sports, coaching sports in middle school, creating a safe and respectful environment, engaging effectively with parents, high school heads up football, NCAA eligibility, positive sport parenting, sportsmanship, sports nutrition, sudden cardiac arrest, strength and conditioning, teaching and modeling behavior, learning pro: homework helper, learning pro: reading and learning strategies; learning pro: research skills, and learning pro: testing tips.
- The National Youth Sport Coaches Association (www.nays.org/Coaches/) offers its members the opportunity to become a Gold Level Certified Coach through an online course. Volunteer coaches learn information in philosophy and ethics, sports safety and injury prevention, physical preparation and conditioning, growth and development, teaching and communication, organization and administration, skills and tactics, and evaluation.

balanced conditioning program, strength training for children and adolescents can be beneficial. For example, strength training benefits coordination and muscle fiber development by improving motor skills and sport performance, increases lean body mass, aids in the development of cardiorespiratory fitness, enhances self-image and self-esteem, and lowers the incidence of sport-related injuries. There is no scientific evidence that strength training by youth can retard growth.

Many states also have coaches' associations that either are specific to one sport or have coaches from all sports in their memberships. These groups usually sponsor statewide or regional workshops or clinics on specific coaching techniques or strategies, rule changes, and ethics in school athletics, and sport psychology. Many volunteer coaches join the National Youth Sports Coaches Association.

Each year, millions of girls and boys ages 8 to 18 years compete in the largest amateur sports program in the United States, the Junior Olympics. The Junior Olympics are organized by the Amateur Athletic Union and recognized by the United States Olympic Committee (USOC). These athletes compete in more than 3,000 local meets, state championships, regional events, and national finals in baseball, basketball, baton twirling, beach volleyball, bowling, cheerleading, dance, diving, fastpitch softball, field hockey, football, golf, gymnastics, ice hockey, inline hockey, judo, jump rope, karate, Kung-Fu, lacrosse, powerlifting, soccer, softball, sport stacking, strength sports, swimming, surfing, table tennis, taekwondo, target shooting, track and field, trampoline/tumbling, volleyball, and wrestling. The benefits from being a part of the Junior Olympics include making friends, having opportunities to travel, gaining a sense of achievement, and enjoying the excitement of the competitions. Youth also compete in state games, such as the Empire State Games (New York) and the Keystone State Games (Pennsylvania), which provide a variety of sports opportunities for children of all ages. Most of the athletes in these state games have developed their skills through youth and school sport programs.

INTERSCHOLASTIC SPORTS

The National Federation of State High School Associations (NFHS) promotes interscholastic sports as an integral part of the educational experiences of high school students (see "The Case for High School Activities" at www.nfhs.org/articles/the -case-for-high-school-activities). Most physical educators have traditionally favored and supported interscholastic sports because they believe adolescents are developmentally and emotionally able to compete. School administrators stress the beneficial outcomes of fitness, sportsmanship, cooperation, self-discipline, and character development for participants. From a broader perspective, interscholastic sports enhances school spirit and, in many locales, enlists strong community support for the school. The most popular sports for boys based on number of participants are football, outdoor track and field, basketball, baseball, soccer, wrestling, crosscountry, tennis, golf, and swimming and diving. The most popular sports for girls based on number of participants are outdoor track and field, basketball, volleyball, fast-pitch softball, soccer, cross-country, tennis, swimming and diving, competitive spirit squads, and lacrosse.

Today, though, too many interscholastic sport coaches have not been properly prepared to coach. Several factors have contributed to this problem:

- Elimination of many physical education requirements and teaching positions.
- The addition of more specialized requirements for prospective physical education teachers and a reduction of coaching-related courses in colleges.

- Physical educators choosing not to combine teaching and coaching careers.
- More school sports teams, especially for girls, requiring coaches.
- Teachers of other school subjects seeking coaching positions even though they lack courses in exercise physiology, sport psychology, and motor learning to help prepare them to coach.

The NFHS (founded in 1920) and the 50 state and associated high school athletic and activities associations work to protect the activity and athletic interests of high schools, promote the growth of educational interscholastic sports, and protect high school students from exploitation. *High School Today*, the voice of education-based athletics, is an online publication of the NFHS. The National Interscholastic Athletic Administrators Association publishes *Interscholastic Athletic Administration* for school leaders committed to enhancing the educational values of high school sports. There also are state coaches associations and national sport-specific coaches associations that provide a variety of professional development opportunities.

The major problem in high school sports in the United States is an overemphasis on winning. Indicative of this compulsion are year-round conditioning programs and practices, students specializing in one sport, students playing while hurt, and coaches' jobs depending on winning. Advocates of year-round conditioning programs stress that they are needed to develop advanced skills, stay competitive with other teams' athletes, and increase chances for collegiate grants-in-aid. Arguments against single-sport specialization include athlete burnout and overuse injuries; lack of opportunities to acquire skills in other sports, play with other athletes, and learn from other coaches; and exploitation by coaches concerned only with their teams.

Another controversial issue facing interscholastic sport programs is the "no pass, no play" policy adopted by some states. Generally, this policy requires that student players obtain passing marks in all (or most) courses taken during the previous grading period. Supporters state that the purpose of schools is education. Thus, participation on a team, or in any other extracurricular activity, is a privilege earned by those who achieve in the classroom. Advocates also claim this policy will motivate students to achieve academically on a consistent basis. Policymakers, school administrators, and most parents applaud the effectiveness of this policy because students' performances in their class work have improved overall. Opponents disagree, claiming extracurricular activities, especially sports, encourage some young people to remain in school. Experience, though, has shown that although a few students may continue their education only because of the appeal of sport participation, many students seem to be taking their schoolwork more seriously because of "no pass, no play" policies.

The abuse of drugs is all too pervasive in schools. Most adolescents and children, including athletes, have easy access to tobacco, alcohol, marijuana, amphetamines, cocaine, and other legal and illegal drugs. Unless coaches educate their athletes about the harmful effects of these drugs on their bodies, and hence their performances, many interscholastic athletes may succumb to peer pressure and the desire to gain athletic advantages and use these drugs. Too many high school athletes choose to drink alcohol, smoke cigarettes, and use smokeless tobacco. Some of these athletes also use anabolic steroids, often resulting in irreparable physiological damage. Taken to attempt to increase muscle bulk and size for appearance and performance

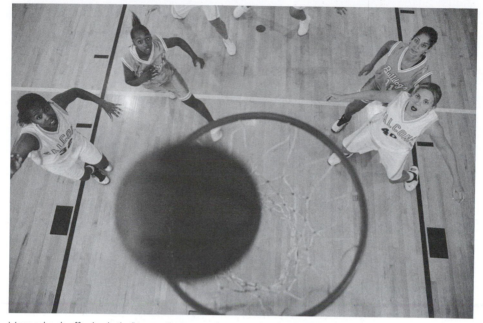

More schools offer basketball teams than any other sport for female athletes.
© Royalty-Free/Corbis

purposes, anabolic steroids interfere with normal growth and development, lead to overly aggressive and irrational behaviors, cause sterility, or even may kill the user.

School sport programs also face other problems such as spectator violence, unsportsmanlike conduct by coaches and athletes, cheating to maintain an athlete's academic eligibility, and program budget cuts. Because of skyrocketing costs, due somewhat to injury and liability insurance and the provision of athletic programs for girls and individuals with special needs, many schools can no longer afford to provide competitive sports as a right. Many high schools are adopting a pay-for-play policy, which means educational allocations will no longer finance sport teams; instead, any student who desires to participate on a team will have to pay for the experience. Although this policy may exclude students who are unable to pay, this trend is becoming increasingly popular, especially in private schools.

INTERCOLLEGIATE ATHLETICS

In intercollegiate athletics, the major regulatory bodies include the National Collegiate Athletic Association (NCAA), National Association of Intercollegiate Athletics (NAIA), and National Junior College Athletic Association (NJCAA). The NCAA, with over 1,200 colleges, conferences, and affiliated organizations, promotes competition through 89 championships in 23 sports for women and men. Athletes in more than 260 small colleges and conferences holding membership in the NAIA compete in 12 sports for men and 11 sports for women in 23 championships. The NJCAA, representing over 500 institutions, conducts championships in 14 sports for men and 12 sports for women. (See Table 11-2 for participation data by gender and competitive level.)

TABLE 11-2

NUMBER OF ATHLETES BY GENDER AND DIVISIONAL LEVEL

	Institutions	Males	Females	Total
National Collegiate Athletic Association IA	128	39,920	36,116	76,036
National Collegiate Athletic Association IAA	121	35,086	28,429	63,515
National Collegiate Athletic Association IAAA (without football)	99	18,049	19,424	37,473
National Collegiate Athletic Association II (with football)	166	45,498	27,264	72,762
National Collegiate Athletic Association II (without football)	145	19,576	18,231	37,807
National Collegiate Athletic Association III (with football)	240	78,877	49,246	128,123
National Collegiate Athletic Association III (without football)	188	26,346	24,963	51,309
National Association of Intercollegiate Athletics I	121	15,516	10,985	26,501
National Association of Intercollegiate Athletics II	136	22,996	15,831	38,827
National Association of Intercollegiate Athletics III	3	497	329	826
National Junior College Athletic Association I	259	17,835	11,637	29,472
National Junior College Athletic Association II	121	8,218	5,195	13,413
National Junior College Athletic Association III	127	8,915	5,068	13,983

Totals	Institutions	Males	Females	Total
National Collegiate Athletic Association	1087	263,352	203,673	467,025
National Association of Intercollegiate Athletics	260	39,009	27,145	66,154
National Junior Collegiate Athletic Association	507	34,968	21,900	56,868

Compiled using the Equity in Athletics Data Analysis Cutting Tool (ope.ed.gov/athletics/) based on institutional self-reported data for 2013 to the United States Office of Postsecondary Education.

Ever since the proliferation of intercollegiate athletic programs for men in the late 1800s, college faculties and administrators have been concerned about the potentially detrimental effects of athletics on academic work. Associated problems then and now include students missing classes because of competing and traveling, receiving unearned grades, and being admitted into colleges even though underqualified. The NCAA, NAIA, and NJCAA have attempted to administer intercollegiate athletics on the basis of educational principles, although regulations concerning these issues rest largely with each institution. The problem each college faces is how to deal effectively with regulations when winning is almost synonymous with survival, especially at large institutions.

Winning teams appeal to spectators and increase interest. When more fans buy tickets, revenues increase. More money contributes to hiring coaches with winning reputations and to recruiting and awarding grants-in-aid to better athletes, who combine to win more games. This cycle (winning = fans = money = winning = fans = money) repeats itself with alarming regularity and tends to spiral into an

RESEARCH VIEW

The Game of Life

The authors of this book examined the precollegiate preparation and subsequent academic performance of athletes and other students in the 1951, 1976, and 1989 entering classes at 30 academically selective institutions. Their analysis of the data led to these and other conclusions:

1. Educational opportunities at the institutions studied have increasingly been rationed in favor of athletes; for example, athletes make up a substantial portion of each entering class.

2. There is a tendency for athletes, regardless of sport, competitive level, and gender, to underperform academically.

3. Sport specialization has resulted in fewer multisport athletes as well as fewer competitive sport opportunities for nonrecruited athletes.

4. Athletes and athletics are less central to the campus culture.

5. Escalating costs for athletic programs threaten other educational uses of limited financial resources.

6. The commercialization of intercollegiate athletics remains largely unchecked.

As the results of this extensive research study indicate, intercollegiate athletics faces significant ethical, educational, societal, and financial issues. Examining the daily newspaper or listening to the evening news often reveals another scandal associated with a fired coach or an athlete arrested for some law-breaking behavior or violation of an athletic association rule. When the graduation rate of African American players on a team is low or athletes submit assignments in their classes that are not their own work, education obviously has been devalued. It is hard to defend how coaches can be paid millions of dollars to change teams regardless of existing contracts, while athletes lose eligibility for transferring institutions. Also, when layers of rhetoric are stripped away, the major controversy surrounding Title IX is not about equal opportunity for females versus sport teams for males; the challenge is how an institution can fund a comprehensive athletic program while enmeshed in a spiraling arms race.

Source: Shulman, J. L., & Bowen, W. G. (2001). *The game of life: College sports and educational values.* Princeton, NJ: Princeton University Press.

ever-widening and more costly circle. The resultant commercialization changes intercollegiate athletics from an extension of an institution's educational mission to a business venture. When winning becomes the most important objective, rules are frequently violated, both during play and in the recruiting of athletes; sportsmanship, character development, and other values are often lost or at least de-emphasized in the process. (See the Research View The Game of Life for what one study of these issues found.)

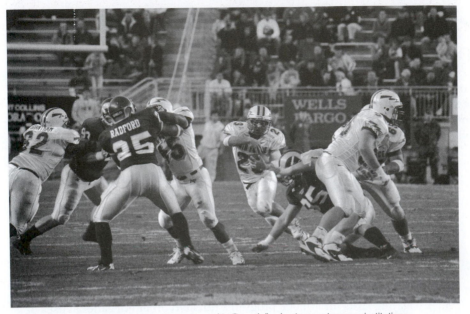

Intercollegiate football teams have become multimillion-dollar businesses in many institutions.
Source: U.S. Air Force photo by John Van Winkle

Why do intercollegiate athletics continue to thrive? There are three major reasons. First, intercollegiate athletics reflect Americans' attitudes, beliefs, and values. Many people believe colleges have the responsibility to offer competitive sport opportunities for students, and they defend the concept that sport participation helps prepare athletes for life by developing physical, intellectual, social, and moral skills and abilities. Second, these benefits exceed the liabilities. Many people think the problems are sporadic rather than pervasive. They add that participants and spectators enjoy being entertained, while college spirit and allegiance are enhanced. Third, athletic teams are effective public relations tools for institutions. College enrollments may temporarily increase as a result of successful athletic programs, especially in football and men's basketball. The provision of entertainment attracts large numbers of spectators to intercollegiate athletic contests, with an accompanying surge in college loyalty that many claim positively affects legislative appropriations and private donations to academic departments, in addition to generous support for athletics.

Realistically, intercollegiate athletics, regardless of the extent of the challenges, will continue to thrive because of its entertainment value and benefits. To accentuate the positive and reduce the negative, the following actions are possible strategies:

Proposed Strategies for Addressing Issues in Intercollegiate Athletics

- Admit only those recruited athletes who meet academic standards of admission to the colleges they attend by eliminating preferred or special admissions.
- Award grants-in-aid for 4 years and increase grants-in-aid to the full cost of education for all athletes.

- Require one-year residency prior to competition for freshmen and transfer students so academic eligibility is based on a student's academic performance in college not on standardized test scores or high school grades.

- Provide academic support services to all students under the auspices of the faculty and academic affairs, not programs solely for athletes administered by departments of athletics.

- Limit sport seasons to one semester and reduce the number of competitions so athletes are allowed to miss no more than 1 day of class per week and no more than 10 days of classes per semester for athletic competition, practice, or travel to competition.

- Require that eligibility for competition requires maintaining a minimum of a cumulative 2.0 GPA.

- Withhold for a period of 5 years one grant-in-aid for every athlete who does not graduate within 6 years.

- Sanction for the first offense any coach and athlete who violates athletic regulations; place violators on a two-year probation from coaching and athletic competition for the second offense; ban violators from college coaching and from competition for life for the third offense.

If some or all of these suggestions are implemented, intercollegiate athletics may become a more positive, educational experience for athletes.

The abuse of drugs by college athletes (see Box 11.4) and the desire by the NCAA to curtail their use have led to drug testing at football bowl games and NCAA championships (see Box 11.5). Although only a few athletes have been barred from competition because of the use of banned drugs, many claim institutional

---

BOX 11.4   NUTRITIONAL SUPPLEMENTS AND SPORT PERFORMANCE

A major controversy ranging through sport at all levels is whether all, none, or selected nutritional supplements and sport enhancement drugs should be banned. Extensive use by athletes of steroids, amphetamines, or other performance-enhancing drugs—which are easily available at health food stores, via the Web, or just across the Mexican border—has led sports fans to question the validity of records and the integrity of sports. The media have repeatedly publicized how athletes have used a variety of nutritional supplements, denied their use of supplements, or tested positive in the use of banned supplements. For example, controversies pervading Major League Baseball, including subpoenas of players and former players to appear before a congressional committee, resulted in more stringent drug policies and the subsequent suspensions of players who violated them.

The most popular nutritional supplements that are presumed to enhance sport performance are briefly described below.

Nutritional Supplement or Drug	Alleged Positive Effects on the Body	Proven Negative Effects on the Body
Protein supplements	• Increased muscle mass	• Excessive amounts converted to fat

(continued)

BOX 11.4   NUTRITIONAL SUPPLEMENTS AND SPORT PERFORMANCE (continued)

Nutritional Supplement or Drug	Alleged Positive Effects on the Body	Proven Negative Effects on the Body
Creatine	• Increased energy in short-duration, high-intensity activities • Enhanced gains in muscle fiber volume • Improved anaerobic performance • Delayed muscle fatigue	• Dehydration of the bloodstream • Potential for renal disease with consumption of excessive amounts • Long-term side effects and dangers are not fully known
Androstenedione	• Increased testosterone levels	• Impairment or shutdown of the body's production of testosterone with excess use • Stunted growth in adolescents
Anabolic steroids	• Increased muscle mass • Enhanced athletic performance • Improved physical appearance	• Mood swings • Elevated cholesterol • Acne • Rapid weight gain • Depression • Out-of-control aggression • Liver damage • Heart attacks and strokes **Specific to males** • Impotence • Development of breasts • Reduced sperm count • Shrinkage of testicles • Difficulty or pain in urination • Baldness **Specific to females** • Facial hair growth • Breast reduction • Menstrual cycle changes • Deepened voice
Human growth hormone	• Maintenance of normal growth • Regulation of energy production and storage	• Side effects that may lead to life-threatening health conditions
Erythropoietin (EPO)	• Increased oxygen absorption • Reduced fatigue • Improved endurance by increasing the rate of red blood cell production	• Increased thickening of the blood (blood viscosity) • Risk for coronary and cerebral artery blockages
Amphetamines	• Increased alertness and concentration • Increased endurance	• Blood flow away from the skin, with increased risk of heat stroke

(continued)

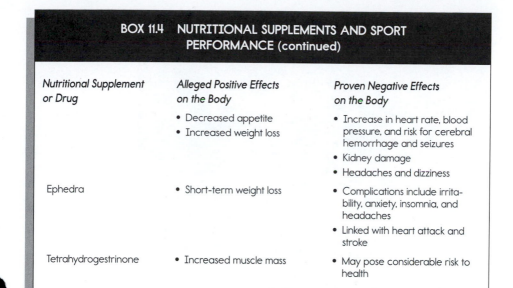

BOX 11.4   NUTRITIONAL SUPPLEMENTS AND SPORT
               PERFORMANCE (continued)

Nutritional Supplement or Drug	Alleged Positive Effects on the Body	Proven Negative Effects on the Body
	• Decreased appetite • Increased weight loss	• Increase in heart rate, blood pressure, and risk for cerebral hemorrhage and seizures • Kidney damage • Headaches and dizziness
Ephedra	• Short-term weight loss	• Complications include irritability, anxiety, insomnia, and headaches • Linked with heart attack and stroke
Tetrahydrogestrinone	• Increased muscle mass	• May pose considerable risk to health

BOX 11.5   DRUG TESTING

Sport governing organizations at the school, college, and professional levels, in an affirmation of their commitment to fair and equitable competition, ban certain performance-enhancing drugs. To prevent athletes from gaining pharmacological advantages through drugs or deter them from the use of drugs that have been proven harmful, participants are required to submit to drug testing on a regular and/or random basis. The National Center for Drug Free Sport, Inc. (www.drugfreesport.com) is the official administrator of the NCAA drug-testing program. See http://www.ncaa.org/sites/default/files/2015–16%20NCAA%20Banned%20Drugs.pdf for a list of the drugs banned by the NCAA. In NCAA-member institutions, athletes are required, in order to be eligible for intercollegiate competitions, to sign a consent form indicating their understanding of the drug-testing program and willingness to participate in it. Member institutions must conduct a drug and alcohol education program once per semester to raise the awareness of athletes about the harmful effects of drug use and to inform them about institutional and NCAA drug policies.

For decades the International Olympic Committee has been concerned about the increasing abuse of drugs to enhance the potential for winning medals in the Olympics—despite the fact that doping contravenes the values and fundamental principles of the Olympics and medical ethics. Because doping threatens the health of the athlete and the integrity of Olympic sport and its ideals, extensive drug testing pervades the Olympic Games and results in the disqualification of gold medalists and public exposure and sanctioning of guilty athletes. Among the prohibited drugs in the Olympics are stimulants, narcotics, anabolic agents, and diuretics. Blood doping and other forms of pharmacological and chemical manipulation also are forbidden.

In 2003 the International Olympic Committee and all Olympic sports joined with delegates representing governments, the International Paralympic Committee and its sport committees, athletes, and national anti-doping organizations in adopting the World Anti-Doping Code as the basis for the fight against doping in sport. The World Anti-Doping Code 2015 can be found at https://wada-main-prod.s3.amazonaws.com/resources/files/wada-2015-world-anti-doping-code.pdf.

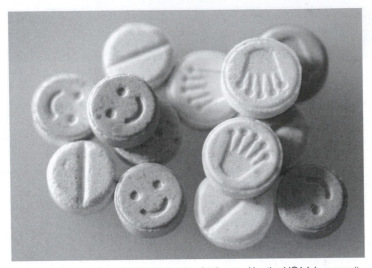

Methylene dioxymethamphetamine (ecstasy) is banned by the NCAA because it is a powerful stimulant that enhances athletic performance.
© Edward J. Westmacott/Alamy RF

drug-testing programs have deterred many athletes from the use of performance-enhancing drugs. Still, many college athletes are guilty of perjury when they sign the pledge required by the NCAA stating they do not use these substances. The drug education programs offered by colleges and universities have failed to eradicate this blemish on the reputation of intercollegiate athletics.

The use of anabolic steroids is especially dangerous. Besides providing unfair physical advantages, anabolic steroids can severely harm those who abuse them. These drugs may cause users to behave violently on and off the field. Their abuse is often linked with an obsession to earn a starting position, become a star player, or get drafted into a professional league. Amphetamine abuse may also occur under the guise of increasing one's aggressiveness and effort. Cocaine, marijuana, tobacco, and alcohol are more likely to be used socially or for relaxation. As with other college students, most athletes' drug of choice is alcohol, even though most are underage drinkers. Coaches, athletic administrators, and professional leagues, therefore, face the challenge of educating athletes about the negative effects of drug abuse as well as about the rules and values violated through their use.

Academic abuses have plagued intercollegiate athletics throughout their existence. To address these, over the years the NCAA has established numerous requirements for high school academic performance as a prerequisite for college eligibility and meeting an institution's academic requirements. Some athletes, often with the assistance of their coaches, have circumvented academic policies—for example, by taking easy courses to maintain eligibility, failing to make progress toward a degree, and not taking advantage of educational opportunities made possible when they receive grants-in-aid. To address these problems, the NCAA has established very specific expectations on athletes that are described in detail in the *NCAA Manual*. For example, the NCAA requires

- Satisfactory progress—Athletes must make progress toward their degrees. After the first year of enrollment, each athlete must successfully have completed at least 24 hours and achieved a 1.8 or higher GPA. After the second year, each athlete must declare a major or degree, have achieved a 1.9 or higher GPA and have successfully completed 40% (at least 48 hours) of the degree requirements. After the third year, each athlete must have achieved a 2.0 or higher GPA and have successfully completed 60% (at least 72 hours) of the degree requirements. After the fourth year, each athlete must have completed 80% of the degree requirements (at least 96 hours) and maintain a 2.0 or higher GPA.

- Degree designation—Athletes must designate a program of study (major) that leads to a bachelor's degree no later than the beginning of the third year of enrollment and thereafter make satisfactory progress toward that degree.

- 5-year rule—Athletes can compete no more than four seasons in intercollegiate competition in any one sport, which must occur within 5 years of initial enrollment (unless granted an exception by the NCAA).

The latest NCAA academic reform package is designed to improve the academic success and graduation of student-athletes. The centerpiece is the Academic Progress Rate, or APR, which assesses a team's academic performance by awarding points each term to athletes on grants-in-aid who meet academic eligibility standards and remain enrolled at that institution. In holding each team accountable for the graduation of athletes, the calculated APR score must reach 930. With failure to achieve this score, which occurs when a student becomes academically ineligible, not only is that player lost to the team but the team also cannot re-award that grant-in-aid to another player for 1 year.

To preserve the integrity of intercollegiate sports, coaches and athletic administrators also must resolve issues of institutional control. Several institutions have failed to keep overeager supporters from giving money, cars, clothes, and other benefits to

Intercollegiate sports have the potential to help athletes develop their physical, mental, and social skills as long as these positive outcomes are taught and reinforced.
© PhotoLink/PhotoDisc/Getty Images RF

athletes. Although not illegal, these actions violate NCAA rules. In the intense recruiting battles for the most highly skilled athletes, many coaches convince admissions committees to lower entrance standards or receive a number of admission exceptions for star athletes. Academically under qualified athletes have led to many institutions being criticized for the low graduation rates of athletes, especially African Americans.

Some athletes' conduct also undermines the values thought to be associated with intercollegiate athletics. For example, actions such as taunting opponents and excessive celebrations run counter to the goals of fair play and respecting opponents. Coaches' physical and emotional abuse of players is another example of destructive behavior. In addition, misdemeanors and felonies, such as driving under the influence of alcohol, using illegal drugs, and sexual assaults and rape, have negatively affected the image of athletes as well as institutions. Another thing threatening espoused values occurs when some athletic foundations willingly pay off the contracts of coaches with whom they have become disillusioned for not winning enough games and then provide millions of dollars to entice a coach with a winning record to break his contract with another institution. Such actions always raise the question of who is in control of athletics. These examples describe a possible lack of institutional control over commercialized intercollegiate athletic programs.

INTERNATIONAL SPORTS

Elite athletes around the world have numerous opportunities to compete in championship events annually, as well as in special events such as the Pan-American Games, the Asian Games, the British Empire and Commonwealth Games, and the World University Games. These events, open to athletes from the countries implicit in the games' titles, are conducted every 4 years except for the World University Games, which are held every 2 years. All of these are important competitions, but the most prestigious internationally are the Olympic Games. Since 1896 (and 1924 for the Winter Games) athletes from around the world have competed every 4 years (except during World Wars I and II) under the direction of the International Olympic Committee (IOC). Since 1994, the Winter Games have been held in even-numbered years alternating with the Summer Games.

The Olympic Games have faced numerous threats to their ideals, with politics being the chief challenge. From the inception of the Games through the attempt by the Nazis to prove Aryan supremacy in 1936 to national boycotts staged in 1976, 1980, and 1984, countries have attempted to use the Olympic Games to advance their political agendas and influence public opinion. The worst political situation occurred during the 1972 Munich Olympic Games when Arab terrorists killed or kidnapped 11 Israelis; all of these athletes, coaches, and officials lost their lives. The banning of some countries and the nonrecognition of others prove the Olympic Games remain political. Athletes competing as representatives of their nations, the playing of national anthems during awards ceremonies, national medal counts, team sports, and national uniforms consistently reinforce nationalism. Governments, financially and ideologically, continue to increase their involvement because international prestige and promotion of their political ideologies are at stake. Judging irregularities often result from political alliances,

Track and field remains the centerpiece of the Olympic Games.
Source: Courtesy of the U.S. Department of Defense

while continued use of performance-enhancing drugs verifies the importance placed on winning.

Commercialism has grown exponentially. For example, the 1968 Mexico City Games cost $250 million to stage, while the 2008 Beijing Olympic Games cost over $40 billion. CBS paid $660,000 to broadcast the 1960 Rome Olympic Games; NBC paid $1.18 billion in rights fees to televise the 2012 London Olympic Games and $4.28 billion for the four Olympic Games in 2014–2020. One blatant example of the commercialism tainting the Olympic Games has been the bribes associated with site selection and privileged treatment of IOC members, most noteworthy the bidding scandal revealed about the 2002 Salt Lake City Winter Olympic Games. The athletes are not immune to commercialism either. Although the Olympic Games were begun for amateur athletes competing for the love of sport, today most athletes are professionals, with each sport's governing federation specifying what competitors are allowed to accept monetarily. Many athletes receive money from their countries based on how many medals and what types (gold, silver, or bronze) they win.

In spite of these problems, the Olympic Games thrive and continue to increase in popularity. The development of friendships and attainment of personal athletic goals are two of the many positive outcomes. Most disdain the boycotts, political maneuvering, unfair judging, and drug abuse, since these incidents detract from the integrity of the Olympic Games and athletes competing in them. Commercialization of the overall staging and athletes themselves is a modern reality associated with the expense of hosting the Games and training costs of athletes, not a reason to end the competitions. Many people advocate either reducing the number of events and entries or lengthening the Games and increasing the number of sites and sports.

As other nations emphasized Olympic sport success in the decades after World War II, the United States found its traditional dominance lessening, often because of other nations' subsidization of elite athletes. To address this, a restructuring of amateur sports in the United States occurred. Following the passage of the Amateur Sports Act of 1978, the USOC established the United States Olympic Training Center in Colorado Springs, Colorado. It offered to National Governing Bodies for each Olympic sport its resources and facilities as training sites for athletes. The USOC has received some federal funding but largely relies on corporate sponsorships and private donations to support its work. Increasingly, athletes in lesser-known sports are receiving funding from the USOC to continue training year-round.

SUMMARY

Sport opportunities for girls and women, ethnic minorities, senior citizens, and individuals with special needs, often limited in the past, are today more equitable, although some barriers persist that only time and an increased commitment to equity will remove. Youth sports too often overemphasize winning, as do some high school sports. Yet most parents support their children's participation in sports because the positive outcomes outweigh any negatives. Balancing educational values with business concerns remains the dilemma facing intercollegiate athletics, interscholastic sports, and youth sports today. Abuses abound, yet the public continues to expect colleges to offer athletic programs as entertainment. Similarly, the Olympic ideals, whether real or imagined, seem to ensure people's support of the Olympic Games as politics, nationalism, and commercialization provide insufficient reasons to cancel the spectacle. The pervasiveness of sports (see Box 11.6) in the United States means people believe sports contribute far more to society than they detract from it. It is the responsibility of those who work in the sport industry to ensure that the potential values to be learned and reinforced through participation in sports are realized by all.

BOX 11.6   SPORTS TIMELINE

Girls and Women in Sports
1971 Association for Intercollegiate Athletics for Women established
1972 Congress passed the Education Amendments that included Title IX

Equality for Minorities
1946 Kenny Washington and Woody Strode (Los Angeles Rams) became the first African Americans in the modern era to play in the National Football League; Bill Willis and Marion Motley (Cleveland Browns) played in the All-American Football Conference

(continued)

BOX 11.6   SPORTS TIMELINE (continued)

1947 Jackie Robinson (Brooklyn Dodgers) became the first African American in the modern era to play Major League Baseball

1950 Chuck Cooper (Boston Celtics) was the first African American to be drafted by a National Basketball Association (NBA) team; Nat Clifton (New York Knicks) was the first African American to sign a contract with an NBA team; Earl Lloyd (Rochester Royals) was the first African American to play in an NBA game

1954 United States Supreme Court passed *Brown v. Board of Education*, which led to school desegregation with subsequently more equality of opportunity for African American students and loss of positions for African American coaches

Equality for Senior Citizens

1987 National Senior Games began

Equality for Individuals with Disabilities

1952 Paralympic Games began to offer competitions for individuals with spinal cord injuries

1968 Special Olympics began to offer competitions for individuals with intellectual disabilities

1978 Amateur Sports Act passed by the U.S. Congress mandated meeting the competitive needs of disabled athletes

Youth Sports

1930 Pop Warner football began

1939 Little League Baseball established

1964 American Youth Soccer Organization established

1967 Amateur Athletic Union's Junior Olympics began

Interscholastic Athletics

1922 National Federation of State High School Associations formed

Intercollegiate Athletics

1852 First intercollegiate sport competition for men held (rowing contest between Harvard and Yale)

1896 First intercollegiate sport competition for women held (basketball game between Stanford and University of California)

1906 National Collegiate Athletic Association established (began women's competitions in 1981)

1938 National Junior College Athletic Association formed (began women's competitions in 1976)

1952 National Association of Intercollegiate Athletics formed (began women's competitions in 1980)

International Sports

1896 Modern Olympic Games began

1924 Winter Olympic Games began

1978 Amateur Sports Act passed by U.S. Congress that revised the organizational structure for competing in international sport competitions

CAREER PERSPECTIVE

BERNADETTE V. MCGLADE

Commissioner of Atlantic 10 Conference
Newport News, Virginia

EDUCATION

B. A., education, University of North Carolina at Chapel Hill
M. A., University of North Carolina at Chapel Hill

Courtesy Bernadette V. McGlade

JOB RESPONSIBILITIES AND HOURS

As Commissioner, Bernadette is responsible for the oversight, development, and administration of a National Collegiate Athletic Association (NCAA) Division I conference, with 14 member institutions and their approximately 10,000 student-athletes. She leads and oversees the conference office and its staff, operation of 21 conference championships, media contracts, multi-media rights agreements, NCAA governance and compliance, internal and external communications, student-athlete honors, awards, sportsmanship, and scholarship programs, financial oversight and revenue generation and distribution, and represents the conference on regional and national boards, committees, and other issues of importance. Working with the presidents or chancellors and athletic directors of member institutions, Bernadette maintains conference members, manages conference finances responsibly, and ensures excellence in conference championships. As the conference leader, she demonstrates integrity, ensures adherence to NCAA, conference, and institutional policies dealing with athletics and academics, and represents the conference nationally. A typical work schedule for Bernadette is 60–75 hours per week beginning at 8 AM and continuing to 7 PM. When traveling to present the conference, especially during sport seasons from August through May, she often works weekends and holidays and from 6 AM to 9 PM as needed. The salary range for the 32 Division I conference commissions is $300,000 to $3 million.

SPECIALIZED COURSE WORK, DEGREES, AND EXPERIENCES
NEEDED FOR THIS CAREER

A minimum of a master's degree and years of experience are prerequisites for becoming a conference commissioner in intercollegiate athletics. A doctoral degree, law degree, or master of business administration, although not required, often is highly sought after and beneficial for career advancement and success. In describing the importance of experience, Bernadette suggests it takes at least 14–16 years working in Division I athletics, including in financial management, event oversight, and other administrative positions to become a conference commissioner. She believed courses in communication, education, finance, and event management were especially helpful to her as were practical experiences gained by volunteering to assist in event management, host operations, and sport facility management. After graduate school and having worked professionally for several years, Bernadette emphasized how beneficial continuing education in leadership development, negotiation skills, and conflict resolution was.

SATISFYING ASPECTS

Bernadette finds working with student-athletes in an educational setting extremely reward-ing. To her, the ability to make a difference in another's person quest to be a champion by setting up and operating top-quality intercollegiate athletic events is satisfying. She gets excited working with outstanding universities to expand their brands, missions, and values. Her commissioner's role is one of constant change thus staying "sharp" by educating her-self about and keeping up-to-date on current trends, technologies, and new ways of meet-ing consumer preferences for sport participation and enjoyment makes for a very satisfying work day and year! Despite all these positives, Bernadette, as a former collegiate athlete and coach, hates to lose a conference member or any competition by a conference member against outside competition. She also remains concerned about student-athlete welfare as intercollegiate athletics becomes more commercialized and potentially threatens integrity and the best interests of student-athletes.

JOB POTENTIAL

Given the limited number of NCAA Division I conferences, career advancement into one of these positions is competitive with only the five "power" conference commissioners higher than Bernadette's current position. However, there are NCAA Division II and Division III conference commissioners as well as similar positions in the National Association of Inter-college Athletics, National Junior College Athletic Association, and other smaller athletic associations.

SUGGESTIONS FOR STUDENTS

Bernadette says that if you are passionate about education, intercollegiate athletics, work-ing with people, and the opportunity to truly help others and make a difference, serving as a conference commissioner is a great career. Being selected for one of these positions is very competitive, so being willing to "pay your dues and work your way up the ladder" by gaining as much experience as you can is very important. She encourages anyone interested in becoming a conference commissioner to be positive, hard-working, and honest while always striving to learn more as education is the key to success! She adds, everyone needs to find the right position so you can be happy, productive, and proud while expressing gratitude every day.

KEY POINTS

Threats to the integrity of sports	These include academic problems, cheating, pres-sures to win, violence, the arms race, and excessive commercialization.
Girls and women in sports	Title IX of the 1972 Education Amendments requires equal opportunity in athletes in financial aid, program areas such as facilities and coaches, and meeting the interests and needs of both genders.
Sport opportunities for ethnic minorities, especially African Americans, in	Historically, with some persisting discrimination today, minorities have been excluded from sport teams, subjected to quota systems and stacking, experienced academic and economic exploitation, been denied

sports	coaching and management opportunities, and been deceived by the myth of upward mobility through sports.
Sport opportunities for senior citizens	While in the past older individuals were not encouraged to participate in sport or other physical activities, because they now are living longer, have more economic resources, and are interested in quality of life issues, they are more active.
Sport opportunities for individuals with special needs	Federal laws such as the Individuals with Disabilities Education Act, Amateur Sports Act, and Americans with Disabilities Act require that individuals with special needs have opportunities to participate in sports as well as have their needs accommodated as spectators.
Youth sports	To eliminate problems such as an overemphasis on winning, burnout, and dropout, youth sports should be focused on every child having fun and learning sports skills in developmentally appropriate ways.
Interscholastic sports	Issues in high school sports, such as too much emphasis on winning, year-round conditioning programs, specializing in one sport, playing while injured, and demonstrating unsportsmanlike conduct, should be replaced by learning sport skills and values such as teamwork and sportsmanship.
Intercollegiate athletics	Academic abuses, recruiting violations, cheating and other unethical behaviors, drug use and abuse, gambling, and sports as commercialized businesses threaten the integrity of college sports.
Nutritional supplements and sport performance	The use of nutritional supplements remains controversial within sports since some athletes will take or use any drug that potentially can help them win; governing organizations have implemented different approaches in dealing with this issue.
International sports	The Olympic Games as well as other elite-level international sport competitions are often plagued with drug abuse, cheating, politics, and commercialization because of the financial benefits that may accrue for those who win.

REVIEW QUESTIONS

1. What have been the positive and negative effects of Title IX on competitive sport opportunities for females?

2. What are the examples of discriminatory practices affecting African Americans in sports?

3. What are three common problems facing youth sport programs, and how would you recommend solving them?

4. What are three issues associated with interscholastic sports, and how would you recommend dealing with each?

5. What do "no pass, no play" and "pay-for-play" policies mean in relation to interscholastic sports?

6. What are three major problems facing intercollegiate athletics today, and how would you recommend resolving them?

7. How has the use of drugs by athletes led to policies governing the use of performance-enhancing drugs by athletes?

8. What are three issues associated with the Olympic Games and how would you recommend dealing with each?

STUDENT ACTIVITIES

1. Interview students about their attitudes toward girls and women in sport. Ask them what financial support women should receive, which sports should be available to them, who should coach them, as well as other related questions. What changes have they observed in society's acceptance or non-acceptance of girls and women in competitive sports?

2. Interview two ethnic minority athletes on your campus. Ask them whether they have experienced discrimination during their sport careers and, if so, have them describe it. Ask them if they have seen or experienced any changes in how they are treated today as opposed to how they were treated when they first began playing sports at the college level?

3. Interview senior citizens who have participated in Senior Games or masters sporting events or who are active sport participants. What are their reasons for competing and for being active? Has their involvement been lifelong, or is it a recent lifestyle change?

4. Based on your attendance at a youth sport event, what were the perceived goals of that program? What should they have been? Was winning emphasized too much? If so, what indicated that winning was overemphasized?

5. Is the intercollegiate athletic program at your institution a business or a component of education? Can it be both? If so, how?

6. List several possible changes that could improve the Olympic Games. Which of these are realistic alternatives?

WEB CONNECTIONS

1. http://ncwge.org/TitleIX40/Athletics.pdf
   At this site you can download the report "Title IX and Athletics: Proven Benefits, Unfounded Objections" published by the National Coalition for Women and Girls in Education.

2. www.womenssportsfoundation.org/

   The Women's Sports Foundation, an advocacy organization, promotes the participation of girls and women in sports and physical activity.

3. www.tidesport.org/

   The Institute for Diversity and Ethics in Sport publishes annual studies on hiring practices in coaching and sport management, athlete graduation rates, and racial attitudes in collegiate and professional sports, including Racial and Gender Report Cards in intercollegiate and professional sports.

4. www.nsga.com

   The National Senior Games Association promotes healthier lifestyles for individuals 50 years and older through education, fitness, and sports competitions.

5. www.paralympic.org/

   The International Paralympic Committee conducts the International Paralympic Games, which are elite sport competitions for athletes with physical disabilities.

6. www.specialolympics.org/

   The Special Olympics is an international program of year-round sports training and athletic competition serving more than 200 million people with intellectual disabilities. Check out this site for a wealth of information about the history, philosophy, and programs of Special Olympics.

7. www.ncys.org

   The National Council of Youth Sports seeks to enhance the experiences of youth participating in sports through educational programs for coaches, parents, and administrators.

8. www.nfhs.org

   The National Federation of State High School Associations serves the state athletic associations that provide playing rules for and oversee 17 sports for over 7.8 million boys and girls.

9. www.knightcommission.org

   The Knight Commission on Intercollegiate Athletics has examined problems facing college sports and published reports with recommendations for reform. This site provides copies of all of its reports.

LEADERSHIP FOR ACTIVE LIVING

LEARNING OUTCOMES

- Students will be able to explain leadership characteristics, theories, styles, and actions, and show how knowledge and application of these can help prepare them for leadership roles in their careers.
- Students will be able to describe numerous names and identities that have been and continue to be associated with physical education, exercise science, and sport programs.
- Students will be able to appraise the consequences of inactivity and articulate promotional strategies for getting those they serve to incorporate physical activity into their daily lives.
- Students will be able to explain how genetics, talent detection, technological advances in clothing and equipment, and medicine and pharmacology are intertwined in the pursuit of winning.

INTRODUCTORY SCENARIO

At 7' 7" and 305 pounds, Jimmy broke every national high school scoring and rebounding record during the 2029–2030 season. A basketball phenomenon, he touched off a recruiting frenzy that quickly exceeded sports fans' wildest imaginations. To get Jimmy, everyone had to go through James Sr., who had genetically engineered his son and then relentlessly conditioned, fed, and trained him physically and mentally using the latest technologies and drugs. James Sr. announced to the world that Jimmy's talents could be obtained, but only for a huge price.

State University offered Jimmy a new car, a condo of his choice, a $100,000-per-year salary, and to rename the basketball arena in his father's honor if Jimmy helped the semipro Golden Knights win the NCAA Championship.

The New York Kings, the leading professional basketball franchise, tried to entice Jimmy to leap to its league from high school. They implored James Sr. to allow Jimmy to sign a $50-million-per-year, 20-year, guaranteed contract. As an incentive, the Kings added a $75-million bonus for each season Jimmy won the league's Most Valuable Player award.

The NRA conglomerate (formerly Nike, Reebok, and Adidas) promised to introduce the Jamming Jimmy autograph shoe within 1 month if Jimmy signed its $1-million-per-week endorsement agreement. If he signed, Jamming Jimmy clothing and sports equipment would be marketed within 2 months.

International Sports Marketing (ISM), however, succeeded in getting James Sr. to grant it monopolistic control over Jimmy's career. Jimmy would play for State University for 1 year before joining the Kings. He would sign with NRA immediately and wear his autograph shoe at the university, but defer the $1 million per week and other endorsements until he joined the Kings. All of the promised payouts were guaranteed; plus, ISM guaranteed it would negotiate for Jimmy an additional $100 million per year in endorsements managed by ISM. Is this scenario too futuristic, or is it a realistic portrayal of where sports are headed? Why or why not?

LEADERSHIP IN PHYSICAL EDUCATION, EXERCISE SCIENCE, AND SPORTS

Leadership is the behavioral process of influencing the behaviors of others in the accomplishment of shared goals. Leadership involves the creation of a vision that empowers others to translate this vision into reality. Empowerment occurs when the leader enhances each individual's feeling of self-worth, unleashes this person's potential, and inspires each individual to accomplish extraordinary results.

Leadership Characteristics

Leadership is vitally important to the operational success of businesses, educational institutions, public agencies, and group endeavors of all kinds. Although numerous characteristics have been identified as important for leaders, these six often have been identified as essential for success:

- Leaders have integrity.
- Leaders are effective communicators.
- Leaders build and nurture strong relationships with people.
- Leaders are visionary and creative.
- Leaders establish, maintain, and model high standards of performance.
- Leaders are intelligent and competent.

Each of these characteristics will be briefly described.

Integrity is the quality of a person's character that fulfills your moral obligations to self and others. Integrity is essential for leaders because without it, people will not believe in the veracity of what is said or done. A leader's integrity is characterized by honesty, sincerity, and candor. Leaders with integrity tell the truth, even when this may be negatively perceived by others or when being less than truthful would be easier or more convenient. Leaders are guided by values that preclude acting based on personal self-interest or winning by harming others in the process. Successful businesses and endeavors are led by individuals who base their decisions on honesty, respect for others, and responsibility in all situations, regardless of the

Leaders use a variety of styles and display leadership characteristics in office, laboratory, and activity settings.
© Image Source/PunchStock RF

pressures they may encounter. Leaders display their character by demonstrating the courage and conviction to live consistently with their values. Leaders make good organizations or companies great by being guided by values as they establish clear performance objectives congruent with these values.

A leader who is an effective communicator, both verbally and in writing, shows respect for others, which includes being a good listener and respectful respondent. Leaders are inspiring when they engage others through their words and actions. A leader understands goals are more likely to be achieved when there is knowledge about these goals, an understanding of their appropriateness, and a commitment to helping to achieve these goals. A leader articulates how individuals will be involved or impacted by the planned action and inspires them through clear communications, so they can grasp why and how to proceed. Good communicators are consistently dependable, decisive, tactful, enthusiastic, knowledgeable, and courageous.

Leaders place a strong emphasis on personal relationships and the quality of their connections with people. Leaders are able to attract and retain the best employees through positive interpersonal relationships. Leaders realize that to mobilize others toward the accomplishment of shared goals, they need to tap into the internal motivations of a diversity of individuals, each of whom is unique. A leader establishes and nurtures a culture (the values, beliefs, traditions, and norms integral to an organization) and climate (perceptions and interactions within an organization) that help each person meet personal needs, pursue interests, and achieve aspirations. The working environment facilitated by the leader ensures flexibility, so all individuals affected can maximize their potential. A few of the keys to nurturing relationships with people include understanding others' perspectives or viewpoints, consulting with and valuing others' opinions, being trustworthy, and dealing compassionately with others. When leaders are focused on valuing people, they tap into their energies, unlock their potential, and increase the potential for extraordinary results. Through the synergistic teamwork of committed people, amazing things can happen.

Leaders are visionaries as they provide clarity and consistency of mission, purpose, and goals. Once leaders have set the direction and desired outcome, they relentlessly facilitate progress toward shared goals. They are able to look broadly and futuristically to determine threats, trends, and opportunities for expanding, refining, or redirecting the work of an organization, educational institution, agency, or program. Leaders are inspiring and optimistic as they view the future from the perspective of possibilities yet to be realized. Leaders are creative as they explore options, innovations, and arenas into which others have not yet moved. Rather than feeling limited by the past, leaders frequently ask how a new market, program, or activity can be pursued. They are risk takers in exploring new opportunities because they envision an unlimited and boundless future. Inevitably, leaders are optimists and inspire others to expand their reach.

A leader establishes, maintains, and models high standards of performance. Leaders set the parameters for the level of performance expected of each person involved and clearly indicate that compromises, shortcuts, or inferior performances will not be accepted. Through modeling high standards, leaders guide others to greater levels of achievement. High standards, when articulated clearly, become realistic stretch goals for intrinsically motivated employees who have committed themselves to achieving them. Leaders incrementally praise and reward those who rise to the challenge and meet, and often exceed, high standards of performance.

Leaders are perceived, at least initially, to be competent because of the positions they hold, but this is not sufficient. Leaders must demonstrate their competence on a regular basis as they interact with others. Through their actions, decisions, and interactions with internal and external stakeholders, they show their knowledge, intelligence, and abilities. Leaders commit to lifelong learning both formally and informally. They are unafraid to admit not knowing, while at the same time dedicate themselves to gaining new knowledge and insights. One illustration of this commitment to learning and lifelong development is through reading. Intelligent leaders realize what is not known, so they are humble about their level of educational attainment and intellectual abilities. Another sign of competence is the ability to ask intelligent questions that can stimulate the thinking of others while verifying the leader's competence. The next section will provide illustrations of each of these leadership characteristics.

Examples of the Application of Leadership Characteristics to Physical Education, Exercise Science, and Sport

Leaders Have Integrity

- Athletic directors show leadership by requiring coaches to consistently follow the letter and spirit of the rules of their sports as well as the policies and procedures of the institution and intercollegiate athletic governing organization.

- Athletic trainers show leadership by ensuring injured athletes are only allowed to return to competition with medical clearance or when there is no risk of additional and related harm to the athlete's former injury.

- Biomechanists show leadership by explaining, fully informing, and documenting through a signed consent form that all participants in the planned research study understand completely the expectations and any risks involved.

Leaders Are Effective Communicators

- Physical education teachers show leadership by explaining how to execute a new movement or sport skill in ways that students can understand fully, practice correctly, and learn properly.

- Personal trainers show leadership by explaining and implementing up-to-date, accurate, and appropriate programs and coaching to clients to help them achieve their goals.

- Youth sport coaches show leadership by conducting a parent orientation session, so parents understand their role is to support and provide positive reinforcement to their children.

Leaders Build and Nurture Strong Relationships with People

- Coaches show leadership by ensuring each player understands his or her role and how each person's contributions can help the team succeed.

- Physical therapists show leadership by gaining the trust of clients by showing empathy for their apprehensions about moving, concerns about discomfort or pain, and struggles with the slow progress to full recovery.

- Exercise specialists in fitness clubs show leadership by providing positive learning, fitness, and socially interactive classes so participants are more likely to persist and develop an affinity for these classes and co-participants.

Leaders Are Visionary and Creative

- Recreational program directors show leadership by envisioning how to expand programs and services for individuals of all ages through partnerships and collaborations despite limited resources.

- Department heads show leadership by transforming a traditional academic unit into a vibrant, energized faculty committed to teaching, research, and service.

- Cardiac rehabilitation specialists show leadership by investigating several alternative and innovative programs to determine the most effective approach to prescribing appropriate exercises for each client.

Leaders Establish, Maintain, and Model High Standards of Performance

- Exercise physiologists show leadership by ensuring the careful and accurate collection of data and reporting of research findings.
- Physical education teachers show leadership by designing their curricula based on state and national standards and helping all students meet these standards.
- Athletic administrators show leadership by setting high expectations for customer service and helping each staff member achieve the desired results.

Leaders Are Intelligent and Competent

- Physical education teachers show leadership by ensuring they are knowledgeable and up-to-date about the movement, fitness, and sport skills they help each student learn.
- Sport administrators and exercise scientists show leadership by collaboratively and tirelessly working to eliminate the use of performance-enhancing drugs in sports at all levels because they know the harmful physical effects and how use of these drugs violates the letter and spirit of the rules.
- Athletic directors in schools and colleges show leadership by ensuring male and female students have equal opportunities in sport because this is the law and morally the right thing to do.

Leadership Theories

To understand leadership more fully, it is helpful to examine some of the historic and current theories about leadership. The great man theory suggests leaders display remarkable abilities or attributes because they are genetically predisposed to become leaders. That is, by accident of birth, these individuals are bestowed with the capacity to become leaders. This theory often is used to explain how the descendants of royal families are destined to lead. The great trait theory suggests leaders inherently possess one distinguishing characteristic that thrusts them into positions of leadership. Charisma most often characterizes these leaders, although this trait also might be military prowess, a vision for the future, or the ability to communicate effectively. John Kennedy was praised as a charismatic leader. The behavioral theory of leadership assumes that leadership capability is learned, so anyone can become a leader. Rather than having an inborn trait or characteristic, leaders are defined by what they do and how they act. Abraham Lincoln, who as president and commander-in-chief during the Civil War saved the union, is an example of this theory.

The situational theory of leadership describes how leaders emerge in specific circumstances. Some leaders come into their leadership roles because the situation calls for their unique abilities. For example, Winston Churchill was praised as an outstanding prime minister of England because he rallied the emotions and actions of his countrymen during World War II. But he was not reelected in the post-war years, since the circumstances called for a different set of abilities. The transactional or management theory of leadership suggests directive leaders take action based on organizational goals, structures, and systems. Transactional leaders are results oriented and tie rewards directly to performance. For example, Franklin Roosevelt brought the United States out of the Depression and prepared the nation for entry into and success in World War II using unprecedented presidential powers. The transformational or relationship theory of leadership is characterized by visionary leaders who set new high goals and create commitment through shared values. These leaders are strategic in that they envision, innovate, build, motivate, and energize organizations, but they also are sensitive to the importance of building relationships with people. Steven Jobs, who created and built Apple, became one of the nation's top businessmen as a transformational leader.

Leadership Styles

In order to be successful, leaders utilize a variety of styles when interacting with people and seeking to achieve their goals as determined by the situation. That is, the most effective leaders are flexible and able to vary their leadership styles as needed. The authoritative or visionary style of leadership focuses on mobilizing people toward a vision. The leader using this approach is self-confident in setting a new direction and serving as a catalyst for change. The participative or democratic style of leadership is used when leaders involve others in the decision-making process of deciding what to do and how to do it. While consensus is sought, the leader retains final authority in making the decision. This leader gets input from as many stakeholders as possible to gain their buy-in and active participation. This leadership style may work best when there is a need for everyone to feel a personal ownership for subsequent actions and a collegial atmosphere is needed. The coaching style of leadership develops people and helps them achieve their potential. Like a coach of a sport team wants to build a cohesive unit, the leader as coach wants those involved to develop their long-term abilities and strengths. Leaders as coaches facilitate learning, productivity, and morale; align individual performance with the team's objectives; and help individuals take ownership and responsibility for their actions.

The delegating or laissez-faire style of leadership assumes colleagues are capable of getting tasks accomplished on their own. Leaders use this style when highly motivated and competent team members have the abilities to control their actions within established parameters. The pacesetting style of leadership can be effective when leaders expect excellence and high standards of performance, as long as these high expectations are not excessive and unending. The coercive or commanding style of leadership is used when immediate compliance is necessary. In a crisis situation, for example, a leader may rightfully demand the execution of directives as the only appropriate course of action.

Another style of leadership is servant leadership, which is built on the belief that leaders are devoted to serving the needs of organizational members by listening and building a sense of community. Abraham Lincoln personified this style of leadership before it was even identified. Servant leaders act on behalf of others, take their responsibilities seriously, treat everyone as equals, and serve an elevating purpose or mission. Servant leaders are patient, kind, humble, respectful, selfless, forgiving, honest, and committed. They dedicate themselves to sacrificing for and serving others above all else. Servant leaders behave in ethical ways based on values, enhance the personal growth of people, and facilitate teamwork for greater success.

When to use each style of leadership depends on what each specific situation requires. It also is determined by each leader's identification and authenticity with the style chosen. Leaders understand the circumstances and people and will utilize a style that matches the situation.

Leadership and Emotional Intelligence

In addition to intelligence, successful leaders have a high quotient of emotional intelligence, which is the ability to effectively manage themselves and their relationships with others. Personal management includes being able to identify and manage individual strengths, such as honesty, intuition, trustworthiness, and resiliency. It includes being self-aware through understanding personal emotions and capabilities, and having a sound sense of self-worth. It includes controlling disruptive emotions, adapting to changing situations, showing the initiative to improve performance, seizing opportunities, and demonstrating optimism.

In addition to personal management, emotional intelligence includes being socially aware and managing relationships. Socially aware leaders show empathy by sensing the emotions of others, understanding their perspectives, and showing interest in their concerns. Leaders are aware of internal and external politics as they recognize and meet the needs of followers, clients, and customers. When managing relationships, leaders guide and motivate through a compelling vision; utilize an influential range of persuasive tactics; bolster the abilities of others through feedback and guidance; resolve disagreements and conflict; build, cultivate, and maintain a web of relationships; and nurture teamwork, cooperation, and collaboration. Emotional intelligence depends on personal and social competence as successful leaders gain mastery over themselves and work effectively with and through others.

What Good Leaders Do

Leadership may be more about what leaders do than their characteristics, styles, or others' labeling them according to some theoretical construct. One way of understanding leadership is to focus on the results they achieve through two dimensions of leadership, namely building relationships with people and tasks and getting the job done (see Figure 12.1). These dimensions can be further divided into quadrants based on the amount of support for relationships or direction in accomplishing tasks that is needed. When leaders perceive that followers are unable to get the job done and unwilling to act, they structure expectations to ensure getting results with less concern for building relationships. Whenever leaders realize that followers are willing to work but lack the knowledge or ability to do the job, they show a high regard for relationships by coaching their followers as they complete the job. When supportive relationships matter the most and followers are able but not yet willing, leaders encourage them until the job gets done. Whenever followers are willing and able, little support or direction is required and leaders are free to delegate. In each of these four scenarios, the specific action taken by the leader associated with supporting relationships or directing tasks determines whether or not success is achieved.

High

Encouraging	Coaching
(use when followers are able and unwilling)	(use when followers are unable and willing)
Delegating	Structuring
(use when followers are able and willing)	(use when followers are unable and unwilling)

1. Supporting Relationships with people

Low ⟶ High

2. Directing Tasks
by getting the job done

FIGURE 12.1

Two Dimensions of Leadership.

Here are few additional examples of what leaders do. They model strong human relations and interpersonal skills while facilitating collaboration among a diversity of people. They demonstrate organizational skills and knowledge. They make timely, informed, and effective decisions. They develop a culture of mutual trust and respect. They learn through the harsh realities of career experiences that leadership is an art, not a science.

Most importantly, though, leaders demonstrate their character and competence on a daily basis for all to observe and follow. Character is at the heart of leadership as values and principled actions shape and give meaning to their lives and those they influence. Character is a true moral compass for leaders who serve as role models living according to timeless values, trust the bond of leadership, display humility, exhibit a caring concern for others, show an attitude of service, demonstrate a fierce resolve to something larger than themselves, and foster an environment of civility. Competence is central to leadership, too. Competence is built upon knowledge, skills, and abilities, which are continuously enhanced through lifelong learning. Competence is enhanced over time through varied experiences, gaining new knowledge, and thoughtful reflection. Competent leaders help others maximize their talents. In combination, character and competence comprise the most important leadership traits and are what great leaders model each day.

POSSIBLE CHANGES IN PHYSICAL EDUCATION, EXERCISE SCIENCE, AND SPORTS

In addition to the importance of leadership and its role, prospects for careers, opportunities to make a difference, and a few challenges await professionals in physical education, the exercise and sport sciences, and various sport-related endeavors. Certainly no one can accurately forecast what the future may hold, but we can draw on the past and look at emerging trends. Several possibilities—in physical education, the exercise and sport sciences, sports, and physical activity for life—exist for young professionals considering careers in these fields to be aware of and consider.

Physical Education

- Physical education teachers will be held more accountable for demonstrating their students are learning.

- In an effort to combat childhood obesity, schools will increasingly meet the national standard of 150 minutes per week of elementary school physical education and 225 minutes per week of middle and secondary school physical education.

- The curriculum in school physical education programs will use technologies such as heart rate monitors, exergames, and non-traditional activities and sports to more actively engage students and enhance their learning.

Exercise and Sport Sciences

- The rapidly expanding knowledge associated with the exercise and sport sciences will require everyone working in athletic training, exercise physiology, motor development, motor learning, sport biomechanics, sport history, sport management, sport philosophy, sport sociology, and sport and exercise psychology to continuously learn to keep abreast with relevant and expanding knowledge.

- Interdisciplinary research will characterize the work of many exercise and sport scientists, because the problems and issues investigated can be more effectively solved and funding more readily available through collaborations that require shared expertise.

- Exercise and sport scientists will be required to enhance their abilities to deliver instruction using a variety of methodologies including online courses and media-enriched lessons in classrooms.

Exercise and sport scientists help elite athletes enhance their performance.
© Karl Weatherly/Getty Images RF

Sports

- Technological advances and pharmacological products will be used by athletes of all ages to enhance their skills and performances.
- Sports as entertainment will grow in popularity at all competitive levels with winning and associated commercialization emphasized even more.
- Sports will continue to be used to teach values to some athletes, while other athletes and coaches will cheat to gain competitive advantages.

Physical Activity for Life

- Quality of life issues, as people live longer, will gain greater importance as individuals realize and seek to gain the health benefits of regularly engaging in physical activity.
- Professionals in fitness-relative careers will be challenged to help those they serve begin and maintain physical activity as an integral part of their lives.

Just as the pole vaulter focuses on the goal ahead, professionals in physical education, exercise science, and sport focus on helping others achieve their goals.

© Digital Vision/Getty Images RF

CHANGING IDENTITY—FROM PHYSICAL EDUCATION TO EXERCISE SCIENCE AND SPORT

When school and college programs involving the development of fundamental movement and sport skills were initially developed in the late 1800s and early 1900s, they were called gymnastics or physical training. Gradually the descriptive term for these programs was changed to physical education as an affirmation that this educational field could uniquely contribute to the psychomotor development of students. The term physical education continues to describe school and college programs that focus on participation in fitness, sports, and other physical activities. State requirements determine the number and length of physical education classes attended by schoolchildren where they learn fundamental movement skills, develop a variety of sport skills, and learn lifetime fitness practices. College elective and required programs in physical education continue to offer young adults opportunities to learn new skills, increase abilities in preferred sport skills, and maintain personal fitness.

The term most often used by nonschool agencies, such as public recreational programs or private sport clubs, has never been physical education. Within the past few years, many of these and similar programs have identified themselves using terms such as fitness, physical activity, and wellness. Since they were not associated with educational institutions, the term physical education never appropriately explained their emphases on fitness and healthy lifestyles.

Following the emergence of the specialty areas such as exercise physiology, sport psychology, motor learning, and sport sociology in the 1970s, many higher education faculty began to question whether the term physical education accurately encompassed the tremendous expansion in knowledge in these new fields. These professors did not want to be saddled with what was perceived as an outdated and constricting name, especially one that was allegedly nonacademic. Years

Children enjoy playing because they have fun.
© Angela Lumpkin

of discussions and national surveys yielded dozens of proposed name changes, but no consensus for a new name for the field emerged. Several advocated for kinesiology; others preferred human movement or human performance as more inclusive of various specialties. On college and university campuses, departmental names continue to vary widely as each seeks to find an identity that describes the scope of what its faculty does and studies.

Most professionals in the fields associated with physical activity will agree their professional history is built on physical education. But they prefer to identify themselves as exercise physiologists, motor development specialists, biomechanists, fitness specialists, or athletic trainers. Like many university departments, this book has used the term exercise science to encompass these and related fields. Individuals in sport history, sport sociology, sport management, and sport philosophy may believe sport sciences more accurately describes what they do. Thus, sport has been included throughout this book as a single vital component in the broad definition of this field. Less important than the preferred name is the commitment to contribute to the knowledge base associated with physical activity and to encourage all people to make physical activity a part of their lives.

PHYSICAL ACTIVITY TRENDS AND THE CONSEQUENCES OF INACTIVITY

One of the goals of *Healthy People 2020* is to promote quality of life, healthy development, and healthy behaviors across all life stages. Despite promotional efforts for physical activity nationwide, trend data indicate that the proportion of adults who do not engage in the recommended amount of physical activity remains over 60%; also, approximately 25% of adults in the United States are not active at all. Yet overwhelming evidence shows that health risks, such as coronary heart disease, increase dramatically in the absence of at least moderate physical activity on a regular basis.

As a result, alarming data show that over the past 20 years there has been a dramatic increase in obesity in the United States. To reemphasize this point, the Centers for Disease Control and Prevention provide historical maps showing state obesity prevalence between 1992 and 2010 at http://www.cdc.gov/obesity/data/prevalence-maps.html and obesity prevalence data through 2014. Eighteen states have a prevalence of 30–35%, while 2 states (Mississippi and West Virginia) have a prevalence of obesity of 35% or greater.

The causal factors for obesity are directly related to the lack of physical activity. Children and adults provide increasing evidence that the energy balance equation is significantly out of balance. Today's fast-paced society is characterized by high-calorie, super-sized fast food or consumption of pre-prepared food, an overdependence on energy-saving devices, such as remote controls and pushbuttons, and technological advancements such as videos, computer games, and television that consume much of people's leisure time. More often than not, individuals of all ages choose to be entertained passively rather than actively engaging themselves. It should come as no surprise, therefore, that extra pounds accumulate when the expenditure of energy is minimal.

Health problems such as diabetes often result. According to the Centers for Disease Control and Prevention, 29.1 million (9.3%) people of all ages in the United States in 2010 had diabetes. Additionally, 86 million 20 years or older, have pre-diabetes caused by their excessive weight. Diabetes, the seventh leading cause of death in the United States, is the leading cause of kidney failure, non-traumatic lower-limb amputations, new cases of blindness, and a major cause of heart disease and stroke.

PROMOTING PHYSICAL ACTIVITY

Heart disease causes approximately 25% of all deaths to men and women in the United States with physical inactivity one of the major risk factors. The American Heart Association (AHA) is a leading advocate for each person engaging in regular, and preferably, daily, moderate physical activity for a minimum of 30 minutes. Since physical activity can prevent coronary artery disease and help manage associated risk factors such as elevated triglyceride levels, hypertension, and obesity, the promotional activities such as those suggested at the URLs listed below should be supported. For example, health care professionals, exercise scientists, sport managers, and others should model active living, ensure schools teach psycho-motor and sport skills, so young people will be more likely to engage in physically active lifestyles, and encourage communities to develop exercise and sport programs for all ages and ability levels. The AHA is a leader in providing informational and promotional resources, such as the following:

- Nutrition (www.heart.org/HEARTORG/GettingHealthy/NutritionCenter /Nutrition-Center_UCM_001188_SubHomePage.jsp)
- Walking program (http://www.heart.org/HEARTORG/GettingHealthy /PhysicalActivity/Walking/Walking_UCM_460870_SubHomePage.jsp)
- Weight management (www.heart.org/HEARTORG/GettingHealthy /WeightManagement/Weight-Management_UCM_001081_SubHomePage.jsp)
- Stress management (www.heart.org/HEARTORG/GettingHealthy /StressManagement/Stress-Management_UCM_001082_SubHomePage.jsp)

Accountability for program content and results is essential and continues to grow in importance. Without quality and benefits accruing to those served, no program merits continuation. If children, club members, athletes, senior citizens, or corporate employees are not being taught the skills and knowledge they seek through activity or sport programs, elimination of the activity, or at least replacement of the teacher or leader, is warranted. Individuals hired to teach programs owe it to their participants to ensure learning. Abdication of this responsibility should lead to others being hired to do these jobs competently.

Linked closely with accountability is the importance of public relations. Traditionally, the perspective taken by individuals in school programs has been a willingness to serve but not a desire to publicize or market programs. Today this attitude is no longer acceptable. Teachers and program leaders, regardless of setting, must publicize the benefits to those who participate in sport and physical activity.

Karate is a demanding, yet enjoyable, recreational and competitive activity.
© PhotoDisc/Getty Images RF

To enlist involvement and financial support, programs must be attractive and successful in meeting perceived needs. An additional outcome of this concerted effort to tell others what physical education, physical activity, and sports can do for them. Here are some examples of ways to promote physical activity, physical education, and sports:

- Get your governor or mayor to proclaim May as Physical Fitness and Sports Month in your state or city.
- Conduct special events such as a family fitness night, a community fun run, or mall exhibitions of physical education during Physical Fitness and Sports Month in May.
- Celebrate National Employee Health and Fitness Day in May.
- Initiate daily fitness programs in schools and businesses to encourage everyone to participate in 10 minutes of stretching and 30 minutes of aerobic activities.
- Develop public service announcements for local radio and television stations that promote physical activity and include fitness tips.

- Write and publish a newsletter or local newspaper articles about popular physical activities, sports, and fitness.
- Involve a local service organization and the community in developing a fitness trail.
- Ask the school and city libraries to display books about physical activity, sports, and fitness.
- Involve senior citizens with school-age children in intergenerational walks or other recreational activities.
- Plan special events in schools, businesses, and public agencies to celebrate Heart Month (February), National Nutrition Month (March), and Family Health Month (October).
- Celebrate National Girls and Women in Sports Day in February.
- Initiate a sports attire day each month to encourage everyone to dress for and participate in physical activity.

Hopefully, these and other promotional initiatives will help people accept responsibility for incorporating physical activity in their lives. The next section describes how important this will be in an increasingly technological world.

PHYSICAL ACTIVITY THROUGHOUT LIFE

Many people, especially in the middle and upper classes, some of whom are responding to health concerns or to manage their weight better, are choosing to become more active physically. Because of social needs and feelings of self-worth, people of all ages are motivated to join exercise and sports programs. Walking, participating at fitness clubs, attending fitness camps, and playing golf are examples of the choices being made.

The sports and fitness movement, recognized now as a part of the American way of life rather than a fad, is initiating dramatic changes in physical activity programs. Consumer demand is readily evident for healthy lifestyles that seek to improve the quality of life through physical activity. Physical educators, exercise scientists, and sport professionals must share their knowledge about physiology, nutrition, psychology, and fitness and skill development. These leaders may conduct programs at a work site as well as in public facilities and private clubs. While helping the corporate executive, they must not neglect lower-income individuals, whose levels of productivity and lifestyles also can be enhanced.

The group whose needs probably have become paramount in the twenty-first century includes individuals 65 years of age and older. Between 1982 and 2050, the percentage of people in this age category will almost double (to over one-fifth of the population). As Americans live longer, they will need lifetime recreational activities, not only to prevent disease and degeneration but also as a way to enjoy happier, healthier lives.

Advances in medicine and technology not only help people live longer but have greatly changed lives in other ways. Cures for some diseases, advances in

Physical activity begins early and spans our lifetimes.

© Ariel Skelley/Getty Images RF

heart surgery to prevent coronaries, and electronically stimulated movement of paralyzed limbs are but a few medical breakthroughs that lengthen and invigorate life. Fewer and fewer household and mundane tasks demand time and energy as machines provide freedom from routine jobs. Technological advances directly influence leisure-time pursuits as well. Better-designed running shoes, exercise machines equipped to monitor fitness levels, biomechanical analyses of tennis strokes or other sport skills, and individualized training paradigms already exist. Undoubtedly advances in sporting equipment, clothing, and facilities will continue to enhance performance as well as pleasure.

Smart phones, texting, and tweeting are only the beginning of technological advances of the twenty-first century. With a service economy based on and mandating communication skills and technology as the norm, people are increasingly turning to sport, fitness, and leisure activities during nonwork hours for rest, stress reduction, and entertainment.

Computer technology already permits exercise scientists to assess fitness levels, design and prescribe exercise programs to meet individualized needs, and monitor the attainment of personal fitness goals. Using database management computer software, corporate fitness leaders can determine the impact of each exercise program offered by using attendance numbers and recording fitness parameters. Sport managers can use computers to generate ticket sales and target

Technology offers all individuals the opportunity to be physically active and compete if they choose to do so.
© Royalty-Free/Corbis

marketing campaigns. Computer graphics, desktop publishing, financial forecasts for athletic programs and clubs, students' fitness report cards for parents, biomechanical analyses of highly skilled athletes' performances, and computer-based play calling are a few examples of technological advances affecting programs. (See the Research View Combining Technology and Health Care for an exciting development in telemedicine and children's health care.)

RESEARCH VIEW

Combining Technology and Health Care

TeleKidcare is a telemedicine project that helps parents obtain health care for their children in Unified School District (USD) 500 in Kansas City, Kansas, which has a student population of approximately 75% ethnic minorities and a similar number on free and reduced lunches. The University of Kansas Medical Center (KUMC) widened the work of its Center for TeleMedicine & TeleHealth (CTT) in 1997 to address the barriers encountered by urban families and schoolchildren when attempting to access health care by "bringing a doctor to the school."

(continued)

School nurses in USD 500 had expressed concern about an emergent alarming trend among schoolchildren who were not receiving care for routine acute conditions, such as strep throat or ear infections, skin irritations, or respiratory ailments. As a result, these children missed several days of school when necessary intervention did not occur in a timely fashion, if at all, due to barriers such as language, inadequate transportation or economic resources, lack of familiarity with the medical community, and citizenship status. When medical treatment was sought, it was often found in the emergency rooms of area hospitals, with their higher costs and adverse impact on scarce medical resources.

TeleKidcare consists of interactive television (ITV) systems placed in a school's health office and in the KUMC Pediatric Clinic that allow the school nurse and child to see, hear, and interact with a physician. In addition, this state-of-the-art telemedicine technology, equipped with a digital otoscope and an electronic stethoscope, allows physicians to diagnose and treat a wide range of ailments, including acute conditions such as ear and strep infections, as well as chronic conditions, such as attention deficit hyperactivity disorder and asthma.

In addition to the nearly 1,900 health care consultations (consults) in USD 500 via ITV over 5 years, TeleKidcare has been instrumental in enhancing the role of the school nurse. No longer simply saddled with various clerical duties, school nurses are enjoying a renewed appreciation from administrators and faculty members alike for their medical assessment skills and ability to inform and educate schoolchildren, parents, and school personnel regarding health and wellness concerns.

Parental survey results indicated that 98% of parents were "satisfied" or "very satisfied" with services offered through TeleKidcare, which provides a safe, nonthreatening environment to facilitate the movement of underserved families into an established health care delivery system at school. By utilizing strategies developed by TeleKidcare, parents can satisfy their children's health care needs without jeopardizing their income, salary, or employment status. By bringing together school nurses, physicians, and parents at the school, this health delivery mechanism provides for a continuum of care unobtainable through traditional school health delivery systems.

SCIENCE AND ATHLETICS

What is the likelihood of becoming an Olympic, professional, intercollegiate, or interscholastic athlete? There are over 306 million people in the United States, with over 7 million high school athletes, less than 500,000 college athletes, approximately 10,000 professional athletes, and less than 800 Olympic athletes. So the answer is that most people will not compete in sports beyond their early years. Yet, even though the odds are stacked against each person, many still pursue an elusive dream of becoming a sport star.

Most elite athletes have genetic advantages, because a person cannot buy what nature did not supply. One strong indicator of future athletic success is who your parents are. The message to unborn children who may aspire to stardom and wealth as professional athletes is "choose your parents wisely."

Genetics

Approximately half of the individuals choosing to use a sperm bank, cryobank, choose athletes as donors because of the potential for inheriting their physical abilities. The process used at a cryobank is to obtain sperm that are active (motile), while slacker sperm are eliminated. This leads to charging around $350 per vial, each with at least 10 million vibrant sperm. One or two vials of sperm are used for each insemination, and it takes six to eight vials for impregnation. Since it takes about 100 million sperm to result in one baby, each child born defies the odds.

The unique genetic make-up of the human genome is comprised of 100,000 genes that instruct the body through a chemical code known as deoxyribonucleic acid, or DNA. While humans share 99.8% of their DNA, the other 0.2% of these genetic building blocks makes a huge difference athletically. For example, one gene, ACTN3, produces a protein that contributes to the ability to generate forceful, repetitive muscular contraction. Genetic Technologies of Melbourne, Australia, offers an ACTN3 Sports Gene Test that identifies whether a person is naturally predisposed toward sprint or power events or has endurance sporting ability. Since the results show the types of sports or events in which a person is most likely to succeed, these results can be used by coaches and athletes to tailor training programs to help athletes realize their potential.

Genetics set biological limits, with physical characteristics largely determined by genetics, such as height, bone structure, the percentage of slow-twitch (endurance) and fast-twitch (power) muscle fiber, body type, ability to pull weights, and vertical jumping ability. Elite athletes are at the extreme end of the curve on physical characteristics. For example, basketball suffers from not having enough tall people, since only 3% of the grown men in the United States are taller than 6'3". The average height of players in the National Basketball Association is 6'7".

Since Michael Phelps's parents were not outstanding athletes, how did he accomplish the remarkable feat of winning eight gold medals and setting seven world records in the 2008 Beijing Olympic Games? The best answer could be, "he won the genetics lottery." Michael Phelps is tall (6'4"), has an extra-long torso and arms (6'7" wingspan), and flexible feet that act almost like flippers. In addition to having an ideal body type, he has swimming talent that enables him to use his body in an optimal aerodynamic way; plus he demonstrated the mental discipline to engage in rigorous physical conditioning. Also, Phelps did not just appear "out of nowhere." He competed in his first Olympic Games at age 15 (having started swimming at age 7). Four years later in the 2004 Athens Olympic Games, he won five gold medals, with record-setting performances and two bronze medals.

How about Dara Torres, who swam in her fifth Olympic Games at age 41? Torres, who won three silver medals and came within one one-hundredth of a second of winning the gold medal in the 50-meter freestyle in the 2008 Beijing Olympic Games, set her first American record in this same event 26 years earlier at age 15. In 2012, Torres missed qualifying for the London Olympic Games by nine-hundredths of a second at age 45. Did she discover the fountain of youth? It is more likely that her secret is associated with a lifelong dedication to fitness, rigorous training, discipline, and ultra-competitiveness. Then there is tennis star Andy Roddick, who recorded a tennis serve of 155 miles per hour (mph). He benefited from the unique ability to arch his back and rotate his right arm 44% farther than the average professional player. The record now is 164.3 mph held by Australia's Samuel Groth. As has often been suggested, you cannot get out (i.e., athletic performances) what was not put in (i.e., genetic or athletic potential).

Talent Detection

Since some individuals seem to have been blessed with potential, how can this be tapped into or realized? In the pyramid approach to talent detection, the millions who are signed up for youth sports comprise the base, with those who perform well moving up and continuing in sports, while the others are eliminated. This is the model used in the United States.

Another approach to talent detection occurs when many parents want to know the sports in which their children are more likely to have advantages. They pay for the Sports Matching and Readiness Tool (SMART), which is a series of physical and cognitive assessments for boys and girls ages 8 to 12. The SMART results for each child's skills and abilities allow for matches of skills with sports and may be used to guide decisions for sport participation and training.

Such identification inevitably leads to specialization in one sport. By age 4 and sometimes even younger, many children in the United States begin playing one sport as they embark on their athletic journey toward superstardom. Parents often sign up young athletes for private lessons or coaching, send them to specialized sport camps, and help them qualify for state, regional, and national championships. Some parents willingly provide technologically advanced equipment, private coaching, and year-round practices and competitions because they are hopeful their investments and sacrifices will give their children the needed advantage to become the perfect athlete. Early maturing youths are initially the most successful in sports, but most youths who peak athletically at early ages drop out when surpassed by later maturing and more physically talented athletes. When children and adolescents begin to compete against more talented opponents, they are forced to reassess their skills and goals. The pyramid structure narrows with fewer and fewer athletes skillful enough to play interscholastic sports and intercollegiate athletics, with only a percentage or two of these playing professionally in their chosen sports.

In the measurement of specific traits or abilities approach to talent detection, a large number of children are screened to identify those with favorable attributes. With the goal of developing the highest number of elite athletes using this approach, the chosen individuals are provided advanced training opportunities dedicated to the development of their skills. This approach has been used in East Germany, the Soviet Union, China, and other nations.

The Australian Institute of Sport (AIS) is an international leader in elite athlete development. Through its talent identification program based on the physical measurements of children, such as vertical jump or 40-meter sprint, AIS matches athletes with the right sports and coaches so nature can take its course. Given the narrow window of opportunity for athletes, the idea is for athletes to specialize in the sports in which they have the greatest potential for success.

Technological Advantages of Athletic Clothing and Equipment

A controversial ethical issue in the 2008 Beijing Olympic Games revolved around the swimming suits worn by some athletes. Similar concerns had been expressed in the past when athletes from wealthier nations and corporate-sponsored athletes had access to athletic clothing and shoes that gave them a better chance of success than athletes without this equipment. Speedo's LZR Pulse swimsuit, made of ultra lightweight, water-repellent material, boasts that it reduces muscle oscillation and skin vibration leading to low skin friction drag. Speedo claims that the LZR Pulse swimsuit shapes the swimmer's body, forcing muscles and skin into a bullet-shape aerodynamic structure that reduces the drag, to allow the swimmer to move faster while expending less energy.

Nike's Swift System of Dress was worn by the U.S. track and field team in the 2008 Beijing Olympic Games. Nike's one-piece, body-fitting track suit is lighter and more breathable, reduces aerodynamic drag across a larger number of surfaces of the body, promotes cooling, minimizes friction, and virtually eliminates seams for a snugger fit and reduced chafing. Nike's uniform provided socks, gloves, and arm coverings to cut wind resistance and drag. This technology also has been applied to athletic clothing worn in cycling, speed skating, rowing, and swimming. No one knows how many of the 43 world records and 132 Olympic records set by athletes at the 2008 Beijing Olympic Games occurred because of technological advances.

Advancements in athletic shoes, clothing, and equipment will help athletes perform at higher levels in the future.

© McGraw-Hill Education/Andrew Resek, photographer

Scientific advancements contribute to faster cars and better conditioned athletes to drive them.
© Royalty-Free/Corbis

Some equipment has helped athletes perform and attain records previously thought impossible. The carbon fiberglass poles used in pole vaulting as they bend and straighten absorb more of athletes' energy and have nearly doubled the heights athletes can vault. Golf balls with special dimple patterns fly farther and straighter, especially when hit by graphite golf clubs with titanium heads. The extra yards these balls travel threaten to make existing golf courses obsolete. Baseballs come off aluminum bats used in intercollegiate athletics and lower levels of competition faster than they do off wooden bats leading to more hits. Major League Baseball players are not permitted to use aluminum bats because the game would cease being the same.

The technology of prosthetic limbs has enabled amputee athletes to record times only about a second slower than the fastest times for Olympic athletes in the 100-meter sprint. The technology of wheelchairs for sports has reached new heights. Carbon fibers and titanium, along with computer-aided design of the suspension, have made possible specially designed chairs for basketball, tennis, and racing. Wheelchairs and prosthetic limbs for sports cost thousands of dollars, thus limiting the number of people who can afford them.

Medicine and Pharmacology

Athletes of all ages use performance-enhancing aids, such as surgeries to repair injured ligaments and tendons. Other athletes use drugs, treatment modalities, and rehabilitative exercises to hasten their recovery so they can return to competition. Some athletes, beginning in youth sport and continuing throughout their competitive years, choose to use performance-enhancing drugs, as they seek to gain competitive advantages. Anabolic steroids in strength sports and erythropoietin (EPO) in endurance sports change the outcome of performances. For example, thousands of East German athletes were given anabolic steroids in the 1970s and 1980s, which helped them achieve at the highest level of sports. EPO, even small doses which may or may not be detectable, increases the oxygen-carrying capacity of the blood. International cyclists have used EPO for years because they found that it yielded prolonged improvements in performance.

Science and athletics are inextricably intertwined today. Whether genetic engineering or talent detection, any early advantage is sought and exploited in order to gain any advantage possible. Technological and pharmacological advances are utilized whenever possible to bolster the chances of winning. There are numerous ethical questions, however, about whether these approaches to athletics detract from dedication, hard work, self-discipline, and other positive values that have historically been associated with participation in athletics.

SUMMARY

Leaders are needed in physical education, exercise science, and sports. Through an understanding of leadership characteristics, theories, styles, and actions, professionals in careers in these areas are better prepared to lead. Future trends include greater accountability for learning, technology-enhanced instruction, an explosion in knowledge, interdisciplinary research, technological and pharmacological effects on sport performances, and the importance of engaging in physical activity throughout life. Numerous names have been and continue to be used to describe the contributions of professionals associated with physical activity, human movement, and sports. Because of the health risks associated with inactivity, professionals must be tireless promoters of the benefits of engaging in physical activity throughout life. The chapter concludes with a look into science and athletics as genetics, talent detection, technological advantages, and pharmacology are intertwined in the pursuit of winning.

CAREER PERSPECTIVE

DANA D. BROOKS

Professor and Dean of the College of Physical Activity
and Sport Science
West Virginia University
Morgantown, West Virginia

EDUCATION

A. A., Hagerstown Junior College, Hagerstown, Maryland
B. S., physical education, Towson State College,
Towson, Maryland
M. S., physical education and sport behavior,
West Virginia University
Ed. D., physical education and sport behavior,
West Virginia University

Courtesy Dana D. Brooks

JOB RESPONSIBILITIES AND HOURS

Dana serves as the chief budgetary and academic officer for the two departments within
the College of Physical Activity and Sport Science. One important feature of these duties is
personnel management, including hiring, supervision, and evaluation of faculty and staff,
and faculty promotion and tenure decisions. He is responsible for all of the facilities used
by individuals in the instructional and activity programs. His duties also include fund raising and alumni development. Given the scope of his responsibilities, Dana typically works
around 60 hours per week and at whatever times these duties demand. The salary range for
individuals in positions similar to his is $160,000 to $200,000.

SPECIALIZED COURSE WORK, DEGREES, AND WORK EXPERIENCES
NEEDED FOR THIS CAREER

Dana identifies courses taken in group dynamics and statistics and workshops completed
in leadership development, strategic planning, and staff development as most beneficial in
helping him fulfill his job responsibilities. In order to qualify for this leadership position, earning a doctoral degree in one of the academic disciplines in the exercise and sport sciences is
required. In addition to his educational preparation, Dana gained experiences in higher education as a graduate coordinator, department chair, associate/assistant dean, faculty member,
and serving on numerous college and university committees (i.e., Social Justice, Search and
Screen, and Athletic Council) as he advanced through the ranks from an assistant professor
to associate professor to full professor.

SATISFYING ASPECTS

Dana is energized by providing a vision resulting in cultural change within his academic
unit. He takes great pleasure in working with a dedicated and professional staff of support
personnel. He really enjoys helping his faculty colleagues reach their professional goals. He
also relishes the ability and opportunity to reward and support faculty, staff, and students
for their many contributions. He is challenged to continue seeking funding to support the
college's mission due to the fact that state appropriations for higher education continue to
decline.

JOB POTENTIAL

While progressing in position and responsibility to dean shows significant career advancement for a leader in higher education, some also may aspire to become a provost or associate provost for academic affairs or a college president. These positions carry with them broader scopes of duties on and off campus.

SUGGESTIONS FOR STUDENTS

Dana offers the following wise counsel to students: (1) do your homework—prepare, prepare, prepare; (2) set long-term and short-term professional goals; (3) develop a strong academic and personal support system; (4) learn to listen and respect your peers; (5) always remember—learning is a lifelong process; (6) have a passion for your job; and (7) leadership is about service to others.

KEY POINTS

Leadership	Leaders have integrity, are effective communicators, build and nurture strong relationships with people, are visionary and creative, establish, maintain, and model high standards of performance, and are intelligent and competent as they influence the behaviors of others in the accomplishment of shared goals.
Leadership theories	A variety of theories, such as great man, great trait, behavioral, situational, transactional, and transformational, seek to describe why some individuals are effective leaders.
Leadership styles	The effective leader successfully uses numerous approaches, such as authoritarian or visionary, participative or democratic, coaching, delegating or laissez-faire, pacesetting, coercive or commanding, and servant, depending on the situation and the individuals involved.
Changes in physical education	Student learning will be enhanced when schools provide daily, quality physical education, offer curricula that use technologies, such as heart rate monitors, exergames, and non-traditional activities and sports, to more actively engage students, and when teachers are held more accountable.
Changes in the exercise and sport sciences	Lifelong learning, interdisciplinary, collaborative, research and technologically enhanced instruction are essential for professionals in the exercise and sport sciences.
Changes in sports	As commercialized, spectator sports continue to grow in popularity, athletes will benefit from technological

advances. They will have to decide whether to engage in unethical actions, such as using performance-enhancing drugs, or learn and demonstrate ethical behaviors.

Changes in physical activity for life

The goal of professionals in fitness-related careers is to help those they serve enjoy the health benefits of regularly engaging in physical activity.

Changing identity

Regardless of the name, such as physical education, exercise science, or sports, it is most important for professionals in these and related fields to emphasize physically active lifestyles.

Physical activity trends

The consequences of inactivity, such as cardiovascular disease, diabetes, and obesity, should be stressed so each person will begin and persist in engaging in regular physical activity and enjoy the associated positive health benefits.

Science and athletics

Genetics, talent detection programs, technological advances in equipment and clothing, and pharmacology will dramatically affect athletes' performances in the future.

REVIEW QUESTIONS

1. Define any two characteristics of leadership, and give an example of how each would be important in your planned career.

2. Compare the transactional and the transformational theories of leadership.

3. Explain any two of the leadership styles and when their use would be most effective.

4. Given the various styles of leadership, what determines what style is most effective for a leader to use?

5. What are three trends of how technology may impact physical education, exercise science, and sport in the future?

6. What are three examples of ways to promote physical activity for all individuals?

7. Describe two ways that science has affected and will continue to affect athletics.

STUDENT ACTIVITIES

1. Interview a leader working in a career similar to your proposed career and ask this individual to respond to these questions: (a) What are the characteristics of a leader? (b) What leadership style or styles are used most often? (c) If this leader uses other leadership styles, in what situations are they used? and (d) What do leaders do?

2. Using at least one written source, other than from the Web, describe how technology will impact your proposed career. Give at least one specific example.

3. Using at least two types of resources (e.g., online, newspapers, magazines, professional journals, and interviews), briefly describe two promotional statements or advertisements about the benefits of physical activity.

4. Describe what you think the changes will be in your career within the next 20 years. Provide at least two specific examples of these changes.

WEB CONNECTIONS

1. www.ccl.org/leadership/index.aspx
    This site for the Center for Creative Leadership, a leading non-profit institution dedicated exclusively to leadership, provides information about research, innovative training, coaching, and assessment to prepare leaders for their careers.

2. www.leadershipdevelopment.com
    One of many sites with information about leadership development, go to this site for free access to *Leader Guide Magazine* and other helpful resources.

3. www.heart.org/HEARTORG/
    This site of the American Heart Association offers extensive information about healthy lifestyles and other resources relative to living a healthy lifestyle.

4. www.seniorfitness.net/
    The American Senior Fitness Association provides professional resources, comprehensive training and certification, and support for fitness specialists who serve older adults.

5. https://bigfuture.collegeboard.org/explore-careers/college-majors
    Use this site to explore majors, careers, and educational opportunities.

6. www.ncppa.org/
    The National Coalition for Promoting Physical Activity is a collaborative effort of public and private organizations working to inspire and empower all Americans to lead more physically active lifestyles.

7. www.worldwidelearn.com

Visit this site to learn more about applying medical and scientific principles to sports, exercise, and the body's ability to perform physically and related career opportunities.

8. www.physicalactivityplan.org/

Learn more about the National Physical Activity Plan, a comprehensive set of policies, programs, and initiatives focusing on increasing physical activity for everyone.

Glossary

Academic discipline   a formal body of knowledge discovered, developed, and disseminated through scholarly research and inquiry

Adapted physical education   a physical activity program for exceptional students who are so different in mental, physical, emotional, or behavioral characteristics that, in the interest of quality of educational opportunity, special provisions must be made for their education

Aesthetics   the philosophical area that focuses on the artistic, sensual, or beautiful aspects of movement

Affective development   an educational outcome that focuses on the formation of attitudes, appreciations, and values and includes both social and emotional dimensions

Agility   ability to change directions rapidly and accurately

Agoge   an educational system for Spartan boys that ensured the singular goal of serving the city-state

Altruism   the selfless giving to other people out of a genuine concern for them without expecting anything in return

Anthropometrics   bodily measurements used to evaluate physical size and capacity during the late 1800s and early 1900s

Arete   all-around mental, moral, and physical excellence valued by the Greeks

Assessment   a measure of knowledge, skills, and abilities that leads to the assignment of a value or score

Athletic training   the study and application of the prevention, diagnosis, treatment, and rehabilitation of sports injuries

Athletics   highly organized and structured competitions among skilled athletes

Balance   ability to maintain equilibrium while stationary or moving

Battle of the Systems   a controversy raging in the late 1800s over which system of gymnastics was most appropriate for individuals in the United States

Body Mass Index   is a measure of a person's weight in kilograms divided by the square of his or her height in meters

Body composition   percentage of body fat or lean body mass

British Amateur Sport Ideal   concept espoused by upper-class males in Great Britain that valued playing sports for fun and competition and not for remuneration

Burnout   decreased performance quality and quantity resulting from stress, job repetitiveness, lack of support and reward, and overwork

Calisthenics   the term used in the 1800s to describe Catharine Beecher's program of exercises designed to promote health, beauty, and strength

Cardiorespiratory endurance   ability of the lungs, heart, and blood vessels to deliver adequate amounts of oxygen to the cells to meet the demands of prolonged physical activity

Categorical imperative   the belief that moral duties are prescriptive and independent of consequences

Chariot race   a three-mile race of seven laps between competitors driving light chariots with four horses; the most popular included gory accidents

Citizen-soldier   the expectation that all Roman males during the Republic must serve the state during war as well as participate in governmental affairs

Cognitive development   an educational outcome that emphasizes the acquisition, comprehension, analysis, synthesis, application, and evaluation of knowledge

Coordination   ability to perform motor tasks smoothly and accurately

Danish gymnastics   program of formalized exercises on command, with no individual expression allowed; based on theme of nationalism

Day's Order   Swedish systemized, daily exercises that progressed through the whole body from head to toe

Deontology   an ethical theory advocating that people have the duty to act in ways that conform to absolute rules of moral behavior; characterized by universality and respect for the individual

Eclecticism   a combination of theories and doctrines from several philosophies into a consistent and compatible set of beliefs

Education of the physical   a belief that physical education's unique contribution within education should be to develop individuals' physical fitness and sport skills

Education through the physical   belief stating that physical education as a field uniquely contributed to the education of the whole person because it included learning through the physical realm

Ethics   the study of moral values; doing good toward others or oneself

Exercise   physical movement that increases the rate of energy use of the body and engaged in for the purpose of getting fit

Exercise adherence   development and maintenance of a physical activity program that results in physical fitness

Exercise physiology   the study of the body's response to physical activity and stress

Exercise science   the scientific analysis of the human body in motion

Existentialism   a twentieth-century philosophy that centers on individual existence and advocates that truth and values are arrived at by each person's choices and experiences

Experiential learning   the knowledge, skills, and abilities developed through involvement in actual work

Field day   opportunities to compete on a one-time basis in sports and activities with the emphasis on fun

Flexibility   ability of a joint to move freely through its full range of motion

Games   may include playful activities, rule-governed contests, and athletic competitions

German (Turner) gymnastics   outdoor exercises that emphasized the development of strong boys who would reestablish and defend the German nation

Gladiatorial contests   competitions of trained gladiators, who used various types of weapons in battling captives, animals, or other gladiators

Grand tourney or melee   combats fought at medieval tournaments under conditions similar to war between two teams of knights

Greek Ideal   unity of the man of action and the man of wisdom

Gymnasium   a site for intellectual and physical activities for Greek citizens

Gymnastics   term used to describe European systems of exercises with or without apparatus; a modern international sport

Halteres   handheld weights used by Greek jumpers to enhance their performances

Health   the absence of illness and disease and a positive state of physiological function that includes physical fitness and the five dimensions of wellness

Health-related fitness   the level of positive well-being associated with enhanced functioning of the heart, muscles, and joints to improve the healthfulness of life

Hygiene   term used in the late 1800s to describe the science of preserving one's health

Hypokinetic diseases   those diseases and health problems associated with physical inactivity and a sedentary lifestyle

Idealism   a philosophical theory advocating that reality depends on the mind for existence and truth is universal and absolute

Inclusion   the placement of students with physical, mental, behavioral, or emotional limitations or special needs into regular classes with their peers

Internship   a supervised period of apprenticeship, related to a student's degree program and career plans, when a student works under supervision to learn practical applications of disciplinary content knowledge

Jousting   a medieval competition in which two mounted knights armed with lances attempted in a head-on charge to unseat each other

Kantian (or non-consequential)   theory stating that actions must conform to absolute rules of moral behavior

Kinesiology   the study of human movement

Knight   warrior during the medieval period

Leadership   a behavioral process of influencing the behaviors of others in the accomplishment of shared goals

Licensure   the credential (or certificate) required for professional employees in public schools that verifies they are competent to fulfill their teaching, administrative, or service responsibilities

Light gymnastics   Dioclesian Lewis's program based on executing Beecher's calisthenics along with handheld apparatus

Massage   the systematic and scientific manipulation, such as through kneading, rubbing, and tapping, of body tissues to therapeutically enhance the functioning of the nervous, muscular, and circulatory systems

Military camps   locations where fathers during the Roman Republic taught their sons the skills needed for military conquests

Motor control   the study of the integration and maturation of muscular, skeletal, and neurological functions in executing movements

Motor development   the maturation and changes in motor behavior throughout life and factors that affect them

Motor learning   the study of the internal processes associated with movement or repetitive actions that result in changes in response or performance

Movement education   a child-centered curriculum that emphasizes presenting movement challenges to students and encouraging them to use problem solving through guided discovery to learn fundamental skills

Muscular Christianity   the philosophy that moral values can be taught through sport

Muscular endurance   ability of a muscle to exert submaximal force repeatedly over a period of time

Muscular strength   ability to exert maximal force against resistance

Nationalism   a pervasive theme stressing promotion and defense of one's country that was the desired outcome of several European systems of gymnastics in the 1800s

Naturalism   a belief that nature governs life and individual goals are more important than societal goals; everything according to nature

Networking   connecting with others on a personal basis in ways to expand professional opportunities

New physical education   a curriculum focused on developing the whole individual through participation in play, sports, games, and natural, outdoor activities

Normal school   a specialized institution for preparing students to become teachers in one or more subjects

Obesity   having a very high amount of body fat in relation to lean body mass, or Body Mass Index of 30 or higher

Page   term used for the boy during the first seven-year training period to become a knight under the guidance of the lady of the castle

Paidotribes   the first physical education teachers, who taught upper-class Greek boys wrestling, boxing, jumping, and dancing at a palaestra

Palaestra   a Greek school where boys learned wrestling, boxing, jumping and dancing

Pancratium   an event in Pan-Hellenic festivals that combined wrestling and boxing skills into an "almost-anything-goes" combat

Pan-Hellenic festivals   festivals open to all Greeks in which athletic contests were a focal point

Pedagogy   the art and science of teaching; the study of theories and application of teaching methods

Pentathlon   a five-event competition that included the stade race, discus throw, javelin throw, long jump, and wrestling

Philosophy   the love, study, or pursuit of wisdom, knowledge, and truth

Physical activity   large muscle movements that may include participation in games, sports, work, daily activities of life, and exercise

Physical education   a process through which an individual obtains optimal physical, mental, and social skills and fitness through physical activity

Physical fitness   the body's capacity to adapt and respond favorably to physical effort

Physical therapy   the treatment of physical injury or dysfunction using therapeutic exercises and modalities with the goal of restoring normal function

Play   amusements engaged in freely, for fun and devoid of constraints

Play day   opportunities for female students to participate on sport teams comprised of students from multiple institutions on a one-time basis with females from other institutions; the emphasis was on social interaction

Playground movement   the opening of supervised play spaces in urban areas so that children could develop physically as well as mentally and morally; used for social control and assimilation of immigrants

Portfolio   a representative collection of a student's work that demonstrates performance, achievements, and experiences

Power   ability to exert force rapidly through a combination of strength and speed

Pragmatism   an American movement in philosophy stating that ultimate reality must be experienced and is ever-changing; as individuals solve the problems of life they become better functioning members of society

Profession   a specialized occupation that requires mastery of knowledge and the meeting of standards demonstrating competence

Psychomotor development   an educational outcome that emphasizes the learning of fundamental movements, motor skills, and sport skills

Purpose   a stated intention, aim, or goal that provides the answer to the question "why"

Reaction time   ability to respond or react quickly to a stimulus

Realism   a philosophical system stressing that the laws and order of the world as revealed by science are independent from human experience

Recreation   refreshing or renewing one's strength and spirit after work; a diversion that occurs during leisure hours

Reliability   describes the consistency in or repeatability of what is measured

Renaissance   a period from the fifteenth to seventeenth centuries marked by a renewed appreciation for classical culture including a sound mind in a sound body

Scientific method   the process of making observations, developing hypotheses, conducting experiments, analyzing data and information, reporting findings, and drawing conclusions

Settlement house   a social reform approach to helping the poor in urban areas deal with issues of poverty, injustice, and acclimatization to a new country; often provided play spaces for immigrant children

Skill-related fitness   achieving levels of ability to perform physical movements that are efficient and effective

Speed   ability to quickly perform a movement

Sports   physical activities governed by formal or informal rules that involve competition against an opponent or oneself and are engaged in for fun or reward

Sport and exercise psychology   the study of human behavior in sports including an understanding of the mental processes that interact with motor skill performance

Sport biomechanics   the study of the anatomical and physiological effects of natural laws and internal and external forces acting on the human body during movement

Sport history   the descriptive and analytical examination of significant people, events, organizations, and trends that shaped the past

Sport management   the study of the theoretical and applied aspects of leading, planning, organizing, staffing, funding, and conducting sporting events

Sport philosophy   the study of the beliefs and values of humans as displayed within sport and an analysis of their meaning and significance

Sport sociology   the study of the social relationships of gender, race, ethnicity, class, and culture in the context of sport and the social behavior of individuals, groups, organizations, institutions, and societies in sporting contexts

Sport studies   a broad term that encompasses the application of components of the social sciences of history, management, philosophy, psychology, and sociology in a sporting context

Sports day   opportunities for female students to participate on sport teams on a one-time basis against females from other institutions with the emphasis on social interaction

Squire   term used for the boy during the second seven-year training period to become a knight under the direction of a knight

Stade race   a footrace in Pan-Hellenic games run the length of the stadium

Standard   a uniform criterion or foundational guide used to measure quality

Swedish gymnastics   movements on command into rigidly held positions that were designed primarily to develop military preparedness for national defense

Telegraphic meet   opportunities for female students to participate in sporting events on a one-time basis and then share scores to compare their performances with females from other institutions

Teleological   refers to theories that focus on the end results or consequences of processes or actions

Thermae   facilities in Rome for contrast baths of varying water temperatures and other leisure activities

Turners   individuals, typically of German heritage, who exercised at a turnplatz

Turnfests   festivals for the exhibiting of German (Turner) gymnastics

Turnplatz   an outdoor exercise area established by Friedrich Jahn

Utilitarianism   a theory that refers to the goal of creating the greatest good for the greatest number of people

Validity   describes the strength or accuracy of conclusions or inferences

Wellness   includes the emotional, mental, physical, social, and spiritual factors that lead to an overall state of well-being, quality of life, and ability to contribute to society

Index

Page numbers followed by f, t, and b, indicate figures, tables, and boxes.